1962

1962

Baseball and America
in the Time of JFK

David Krell

UNIVERSITY OF NEBRASKA PRESS   LINCOLN

Library of Congress Cataloging-in-Publication Data
Names: Krell, David, 1967– author.
Title: 1962: baseball and America in
the time of JFK / David Krell.
Other titles: Nineteen sixty-two
Description: Lincoln: University of Nebraska Press,
[2021] | Includes bibliographical references and index.
Identifiers: LCCN 2020032139
ISBN 9780803290877 (hardback)
ISBN 9781496226563 (epub)
ISBN 9781496226570 (mobi)
ISBN 9781496226587 (pdf)
Subjects: LCSH: Baseball—United States—History—
20th century. | Nineteen sixty-two, A.D.
Classification: LCC GV863.A1 K76 2021 |
DDC 796.357/6409046—dc23
LC record available at https://lccn.loc.gov/2020032139

Set in Minion by Laura Buis.
Designed by N. Putens.

For Mom and Dad

Carl and Sheila Krell began their future together when they got married in 1962.

Contents

Acknowledgments

What began as an idea to write about the two National League teams that debuted in 1962—the New York Mets and the Houston Colt .45s—morphed into an exploration of a pivotal year in America. The change in my plan occurred during the Non-Fiction Book Proposal class at Media Bistro, a continuing-education school in Manhattan with a diverse range of classes for writers. I've had the good fortune to take the class several times under the guidance of Ryan Fischer-Harbage, an outstanding literary agent and mentor. It was Ryan's idea to broaden the subject matter beyond baseball.

The next step was finding a home for the project. Rob Taylor of the University of Nebraska Press gave it one. Courtney Ochsner was the UNP editor assigned to me. All authors should be so lucky to have the confidence, patience, and graciousness of these editors. It was a pleasure and a privilege to work with them. Additionally, Maureen Bemko's copyediting was invaluable. I am deeply grateful to Maureen for her patience, insight, and editing skills.

No self-respecting baseball author can do research without a trip to the Giamatti Research Center at the National Baseball Hall of Fame and Museum in Cooperstown, New York. Five teams are covered in the book—the Giants, Dodgers, Colt .45s, Mets, and Yankees. Cassidy Lent fulfilled my massive request for all player files from these teams for 1962 and suggested additional materials. Jim Gates and Matt Rothenberg were always available for questions. I spent three days in Cooperstown in early November 2015 poring through files of newspaper clippings. But that wasn't enough time. It was clear that another three-day trip would be needed.

After a cousin's wedding in Pittsburgh a couple of weeks later, I drove toward the Pennsylvania–New York state line and then eastward. The trip took eight hours on a beautiful autumn day with the weather somewhere in the high forties, blue skies, and sunshine all the way. Sirius XM's '60s on 6 channel and CDs of *The Jack Benny Program* kept me company. Someone who doesn't appreciate a clear sky with a few hundred miles of driving probably doesn't cry at the end of *It's a Wonderful Life* when the townspeople of Bedford Falls rescue George Bailey from bankruptcy, prison, and shame. That person is to be looked at askance.

I bumped into fellow historian David Bohmer at the Hall of Fame. We shared several conversations over dinners about the joys and challenges of baseball research.

To give context to the events in 1962, it was crucial to get first-person impressions. My deepest appreciation goes to my interviewees for their time: Jo Ann Abajian, Bob Aspromonte, Tanya Bagot, Jayne Barbera, Lucy Billingsley, Nancy Napier Cain, Sherri Chessen, Tyler Corder, Seana Crenna, Gary Davenport, Kelly Drysdale, Mary Early, Kiki Ebsen, Joe Gilford, James Gill, Richard Gordin, Bob Greene, Susan Griffiths, Andrew Guilford, Sandy Hackett, Fred Hofheinz, Jay Hook, Kenneth Jack, Sara Karloff, Kenneth Killiany, Carla Kirkeby, Gavin Koon, Robin Koon, Chris Lemmon, George Maharis, Mike McCormick, Judith Milner, Kim Ogle, Gregory Orr, Brian Parrott, Stefanie Powers, Tina Privitera, Katherine Quinn, Don Richardson, Tommy Schlamme, Martha Rose Shulman, Kris Stoever, George Vecsey, Charlotte Voiklis, Maury Wills, Martha Wiseman, Betsy Wollheim, and Nancy Wyszynski.

The New York Public Library's main branch at Forty-Second Street and Fifth Avenue, guarded by the stone lions Patience and Fortitude, was a crucial place for research. Not all newspapers and magazines have their archives digitized, so the Milstein Microform Reading Room became a haunt. The Rose Reading Room availed me with print copies of *Sport* and other magazines. Appreciation goes to their staffs. Lyndsi Barnes in the Henry W. and Albert A. Berg Collection of English and American Literature helped track down material written by Ken Kesey. Additionally, I estimate that I spent at least 80 percent of my writing time in the Rose Reading Room. It's a great place to let your mind wander around as you contemplate possibilities.

Suzanne Lipkin at the Katharine Cornell–Guthrie McClintic Special Collections Reading Room at the New York Public Library for the Performing Arts at Lincoln Center helped uncover a hard-to-find copy of Milton Berle's 1974 autobiography, a must-read for researchers interested in the early days of television and its ascendance to mass-medium status.

Jeffrey Thomas was the archivist responsible for maintaining the John H. Glenn Archives, part of the Ohio Congressional Archives at The Ohio State University. He was invaluable in helping me narrow my search to materials relevant to Glenn's *Friendship 7* flight and military record. Jeffrey and his team are to be applauded for their insight into the history, biography, and legacy of an American icon. Suzi Urell, a great friend, showed me the sights of the Columbus, Ohio, area, including locations necessary for any culinary fan—dinner at The Top and ice cream at Johnson's.

Ruta Abolins, director of the Brown Media Archives and Peabody Awards Collection at the University of Georgia libraries, ensured that Mary Frances Early's papers were available for research. They revealed untold stories about Dr. Early, the first Black graduate of the university and an unsung civil rights heroine. Ruta's team—Matthew Darby, Adriane Hanson, Jason Hasty, Jan Hebbard, and Jill Severn—was beyond helpful during my visit. I found additional coverage of the University of Georgia's integration from the *Anderson Independent* (South Carolina) and the *Macon Telegraph* (Georgia) with the help of Deborah Ponder in the South Carolina Room of the Anderson County Library and Olivia Bushey in the Genealogical and Historical Room of the Middle Georgia Regional Library.

Tracing the lineage of the Houston Colt .45s ball club—the less explored expansion team in 1962—led me to connect with the Houston Astros; the team's name changed beginning with the 1965 season. With mind-boggling quickness, Mike Acosta, the Astros' team historian, answered questions about Houston's beginnings in the Major Leagues. Steve Grande, senior manager of communications for the Astros, fielded my initial request and pointed me toward Mike. During the Society for American Baseball Research's national convention in Houston in 2014, I took a break from the presentations for a one-day trip to the University of Houston Libraries Special Collections Department. Archivist Vince Lee guided me through the George Kirksey Papers, which are a tremendous fount of information about the creation of the Colt .45s. Jasmine Ali, who in 2020 earned a bachelor of science degree in teaching and learning from the University of Houston, researched 1962 articles in the *Houston Post* and *Houston Chronicle* to uncover stories about the first Major League season for Houston.

The librarians at the John F. Kennedy Presidential Library and Museum educated me on the archives of the thirty-fifth president of the United States, which include the papers of First Lady Jacqueline Bouvier Kennedy. Their assistance included not only fulfilling requests for files but also instructing me on how to best use the library's website for archival searches.

Photographs are essential to complementing the stories of 1962. Credit is due to Maryrose Grossman, who handles audiovisual materials at the JFK Library; Kathy Struss, AV archivist at the Dwight D. Eisenhower Presidential Library and Museum; Michael Pinckney, AV archivist at the Ronald Reagan Presidential Library; John Horne, coordinator of rights and reproductions at the National Baseball Hall of Fame and Museum; Joel Kowsky, photo editor/photographer at NASA headquarters' Office of Communications; Jeff Thomas at the San Francisco History Center in the San Francisco Public Library; Oscar Sosa, photo editor with the U.S. Navy; Julie Grob at the University of Houston Libraries; Sarah Quick, reference archivist, and June Koffi, senior librarian, at the Brooklyn Public Library; Laura Lob, digital archivist, and Lisa Marine, image reproduction and licensing manager, at the Wisconsin Historical Society's Division of Library, Archives, and Museum Collections; and Jeff Stensland and Steve Fink in the Public Relations Department of the University of South Carolina.

In tracking down articles from newspapers across the country, I had the good fortune to be able to rely on outstanding reference staffs. Because of some libraries' policies on not releasing the names of staff, I'll simply thank the entire staffs at the Milwaukee Public Library and the History, Travel, and Maps Department of the Seattle Public Library. Sean Sutcliffe at the Waco Public Library, Lyndsie Robinson at the State University of New York Oneonta's Milne Library, and Molly Donnermeyer at the Cincinnati Public Library accommodated research requests with aplomb, enthusiasm, and unparalleled promptness. Joseph Siegal, an independent researcher, excavated articles from defunct Los Angeles newspapers by consulting microfilm at the Los Angeles Public Library.

The Atomic Energy Museum is a terrific source for information about America's nuclear history. Martha DeMarre, Natalie Luvera, and Michael Hall arranged for a private tour of the museum and its archives. Roberta DeBuff, acting branch manager at the Las Vegas Public Library's main branch, gave me the opportunity to review microfilm of the local newspapers' coverage of President Kennedy's visit to a nuclear testing site.

Martin Grams and Jerry Randolph share my dedication to preserving entertainment history. They were invaluable in my research into production information regarding early 1960s television.

Alexandra Cass compiled a treasure trove of newspaper articles about the films of 1962. Her editorial suggestions were equally beneficial in helping me recount this important annum in cinema.

Finally, praise must be given to those newspaper and magazine scribes, television anchors, and commentators who chronicled the happenings of 1962 in real time. They gave us the first draft of history. We're privileged to enhance their accounts. It's not only our opportunity—it's our responsibility.

1962

Prologue

McCOVEY AT THE BAT

It was a period that threatened to become an exclamation point.

Candlestick Park was for the moment San Francisco's emotional epicenter, radiating nervous energy into every cove, crevice, and cranny of the Bay Area. From the five-star hotels in Nob Hill to the slaughterhouses in Butchertown, from the seafood restaurants in Fisherman's Wharf to the Victorian homes in Haight-Ashbury, San Franciscans felt their heart rates spike with enough adrenaline to power NASA's next Mercury mission.

The World Series. Seventh game. Bottom of the ninth.

Matty Alou stood on third base. Ninety feet away was Willie Mays on second. At home plate Willie McCovey settled into his stance in the batter's box to face Ralph Terry of the New York Yankees. The slugger had shoulders so big he looked like he could carry a cable car on them while walking down Lombard Street.

A single would score Alou and tie the game at 1–1. With Mays's speed, it's quite likely that a second run would score and give the Giants their first World Series championship in San Francisco.

McCovey had a solid batting average—.293 in ninety-one games. It was not a foregone conclusion that he could knock in Alou, but it wouldn't have been wise to bet against him either. When his bat connected with the ball, the sound put Giants fans on that thin line between hope and fear. And so it was on this October day. The crowd watched the ball move through the air like it was shot out of a cannon. What followed was a moment celebrated by some, mourned by others, and remembered by all as a touchstone of an amazing season that changed baseball and an extraordinary year that changed America.

1

"To Walk with the Serpent"

It wasn't exactly the Shot Heard 'Round the World—either the one at Lexington and Concord described by Ralph Waldo Emerson or the one at the Polo Grounds.[1] The former started the American War for Independence. The latter was music to the ears of Brooklynites, for it was the sound of Bobby Thomson ending the 1951 National League's three-game playoff between the Brooklyn Dodgers and the New York Giants with a home run that inspired radio announcer Russ Hodges to scream, "The Giants win the pennant! The Giants win the pennant!"

It could be labeled the Shot Heard 'Round Texas—a group of shots, actually. On January 3, 1962, Houston VIPs brandished Colt .45s, reflecting the moniker of the neophyte Major League team making its debut in the spring. A new bellwether arrived for sports when they shot into the dirt—a symbolic groundbreaking for an architectural phenomenon: a domed stadium. George Kirksey, Earl Allen, Joe Cullinan, Craig Cullinan, Paul Richards, R. E. Smith, and Harris County judge Bill Elliott were the shooters; all except Elliott were members of the Houston Sports Association, the entity elevating Houston to the Major League ranks.[2]

The Harris County Domed Stadium proclaimed an era of technology beating the elements—a steady temperature of 72 degrees would categorize mugginess and mosquitoes as nuisances of the past. Not since the father-son power duo of Vespasian and Titus spearheaded the building of the Flavian Amphitheater—also known as the Colosseum—had the construction of a sports facility been as revolutionary.

Elsewhere during that first month of 1962, four baseball players were recognized with a distinction underscoring their achievements.

At the end of his daily chores as a corporate executive at Chock Full o'Nuts in Manhattan, Jackie Robinson traveled to his home at 95 Cascade Road in Stamford, Connecticut, and enjoyed the nightly quiet of suburbia. But the evening of January 23 was different—he learned from his family that the Baseball Writers Association of America had elected him to the Baseball Hall of Fame: "When I came home from work Rachel was on the phone telling David, our nine-year-old, about it. When she saw me, she dropped the receiver and squealed that I had made it."[3]

There was a sense of closure in the moment. Robinson first met Brooklyn Dodgers general manager Branch Rickey in late August 1945, while playing for the Kansas City Monarchs in the Negro Leagues. He signed with the Dodgers that October; Rickey then sent him to the Montreal Royals of the Triple-A International League, where he led the league in batting average and runs scored; the Royals defeated the Louisville Colonels to win the league's championship, known as the Little World Series.

Before the 1947 season began, Rickey promoted Robinson to the Brooklyn Dodgers.

Bob Feller, Edd Roush, and Bill McKechnie joined Robinson for their induction at Cooperstown in 1962. Roush played most of his career with the Reds in the 1920s; McKechnie is the only manager to capture the pennant on three teams—Pirates, Cardinals, Reds. Feller was the Indians fireballer who had abandoned his baseball career for the navy after the Japanese attack on Pearl Harbor on December 7, 1941; he served with distinction in the

Pacific theater during World War II and threw a four-hitter in his first game after returning from military service in 1945. Sacrificing prime performance years—he was twenty-three when he enlisted—Feller believed that the war effort outweighed personal gains. United we stood. *Divided* wasn't even a word in the lexicon except for textbooks about mathematics and biology lectures about amoebas.

Executives in the triad of CBS, NBC, and ABC rested atop their seemingly impenetrable perch on a twentieth-century Mount Olympus of popular culture. Their broadcasts set a common denominator of entertainment, which spewed through a system of interconnected transmitters, airwaves, and antennae to nicely constructed wooden cabinets housing television screens, tubes, and wires. The products of Emerson, RCA, Motorola, Philips, Olympic, Philco, Sylvania, Westinghouse, and other descendants of Philo Farnsworth's magic box occupied living rooms, dens, and bedrooms from the potato farms of Idaho to the prairies of the Midwest to the penthouses of Manhattan.

Watching television was not a ritual; it was a nationwide habit deeply rooted in our DNA by the early 1960s. Our prehistoric ancestors had gathered around the fire to be entertained, informed, and inspired by their clan's stories; Americans watch television for the same reason. Television's genesis, technologically, dates to the 1840s, when Alexander Bain unveiled his facsimile machine. A century later the medium's Paleolithic era ended in 1948, when Milton Berle became host of *Texaco Star Theater*, an NBC comedy-variety program. A member of the fast-talking, nightclub-trained, anything-for-a-laugh cadre of comedians, Berle was television's first star.

Programming in the broadcast-television paradigm, contrary to popular misconception, is not calculated merely to entertain. Its primary mission—then, now, and always—is keeping the viewer entertained long enough to see the next commercial. This marriage between creativity and commerce is a truly symbiotic relationship; if the conception of a television show happens when a scribe's pen meets paper, its birth occurs during lunchtime deals at 21 in midtown Manhattan or the Polo Lounge at the Beverly Hills Hotel.

Before the 1950s ended, a television set had become a staple in the American home. Americans still gravitated to newspapers for current events, but television had made inroads there too; the first wave of journalists in television news came from radio and newspapers, bringing decades-long pedigrees of working on beats, breaking stories, and developing sources.

A subsidiary of Radio Corporation of America (RCA), NBC gave its parent corporation a double dividend: the opportunity to sell airtime to advertisers and television sets to the public by using NBC programming as the lure. To emphasize RCA's distinction as a leader in color television production, NBC used a peacock logo. Color television was not omnipresent until the late 1960s, so a show broadcast in color was a technological breakthrough—an oddity, even—like high definition at beginning of the twenty-first century.

Tragedy befell show business in 1962's first month when television comedian Ernie Kovacs died after slamming his Corvair into a telephone pole; he was returning to his Beverly Hills home at 2301 Bowmont Road from a party at director Billy Wilder's house celebrating the adoption of a baby by Milton Berle and his wife, Ruth. Kovacs was a television pioneer who tested, bent, and expanded the visual capabilities of television. One episode of his television show featured the entire set built on an angle, filmed to seem level to the viewer. Every time a glass of water was placed on the table, it slid off.

Kovacs's genius would never be fully realized. According to Federal Communications Commission (FCC) chair Newton Minow, television's potential wouldn't either. In the previous year Minow had delivered his "vast wasteland" speech to the National Association of Broadcasters, lamenting the state of the television industry as being propelled by predictability, nonsense, and banality: "You will see a procession of game shows, violence, audience-participation show, formula comedies about totally unbelievable families, blood and thunder, mayhem, violence, sadism, murder, western bad men, western good men, private eyes, gangsters, more violence and cartoons. And, endlessly, commercials—many screaming, cajoling and offending. And most of all, boredom. True, you will see a few things you will enjoy. But they will be very, very few. And if you think I exaggerate, try it."[4]

Television critics too attacked the medium, as is their wont. At the start of the 1961–62 television season, Richard K. Doan of the *New York Herald Tribune*, for example, acknowledged that the new array of prime-time programs offered diverse formats, from action shows to sitcoms to cartoons; quality, however, proved elusive for the viewer. "If he wants television to be three and a half hours nightly, seven evenings a week, of top-grade drama, sparkling comedy, public affairs and educational shows, he is going to be bitterly unhappy," opined Doan. "And if he expects to plop himself in front of the little box every night at 7:30 and find himself charmed until 11, he is in for the same kind of disappointment he has always suffered." Doan concluded, "In short, television in 1961–62 is going to offer something for just about everybody, save possibly the unutterably blas[é], if they are willing to look for it and don't expect to be amused full time."[5]

Indeed, turning the dial to a particular channel in 1962—remote control was not yet commonplace—offered the viewer shows with a tremendous diversity of premises: single fathers, family-based situation comedy, character-based situation comedy, police drama, legal drama, private detective, variety, anthology, medical drama, military, and animation.

But there was potential. Television's decision-makers, ever since Berle, have tried to achieve a balance between what is commercially viable and what will stir excitement. This is the reason why audiences crave innovation but might revert to recognizable genres, tropes, and character types. In a series of *TV Guide* articles about television's "impact on life in the United States," Gilbert Seldes wrote that "the rhythm of broadcasting suggests the same thing at the same time each day, each week, each month. Why gamble?" However, "the same forces operate in the other direction. Above all, sheer commercial competition turns producers toward discovering what new things their medium can do."[6]

87th Precinct star Robert Lansing thought that critics gave short shrift to some shows, particularly to rookie programs looking to get a foothold: "[A] good many TV critics, and I'm generalizing, are prone to do something like that to a new show. I don't know if it's because of time or deadline or what, but a lot of critics don't write criticism. They write uninformed opinion."[7]

Hanna-Barbera (HB), beginning with its launch in the late 1950s, introduced cartoon shows that became as much a part of childhood for baby boomers and Generation Xers as 45 RPM records for the former group and video games for the latter, which saw the old cartoons in syndication. Huckleberry Hound, Yogi Bear, Peter Potamus, Penelope Pitstop, Ricochet Rabbit, and Magilla Gorilla constitute a minor sample of the HB universe. *The Flintstones*, which debuted in the 1960–61 television season on ABC and aired for six years—in addition to *The Man Called Flintstone*, a spy-themed movie in 1966—has the biggest bough in the Hanna-Barbera family tree. In the early 1970s Hanna-Barbera reintroduced Fred Flintstone, Barney Rubble, et al., but the focus was their kids as teenagers. *The Pebbles and Bamm-Bamm Show* was the first of a series of spinoffs, specials, and live-action movies.

Jayne Barbera had the benefit of seeing the magic responsible for *The Flintstones* and dozens of other Hanna-Barbera shows behind the scenes, as she is not only the daughter of one of the founders but was also an HB employee. The partnership between Bill Hanna and Joe Barbera began a little more than twenty years before America first heard Fred shout, "Yabba dabba doo!":

> They were working at MGM Studios making *Tom and Jerry* cartoons, which were used in theaters as an intermission between two movies. In those days using full animation, a seven-minute cartoon took one entire year to make. Because the production costs became so expensive, MGM was forced to close the cartoon department, putting all the employees out of work, including my father and Mr. Hanna. Between those two gentlemen, there were two wives and five children to support. What to do? They decided to venture into the world of Saturday morning television, but they had to develop a new, faster, and less expensive form of animation. Thus, limited animation was born. For *Tom and Jerry* cartoons, every movement of the characters [was] drawn separately: for television, one body was drawn with animation used for the limbs and facial expressions. It was an extraordinarily successful process and became the standard to produce *Huckleberry Hound*, *Pixie and Dixie*, *Yogi Bear*, *The Flintstones*, *The Jetsons*, and all following television series.
>
> I began my career at Hanna-Barbera as a painter during summer vacations from college. Mr. Hanna's daughter, my sister, and I were the first three apprentice painters joining a staff rehired from the MGM department. An animator would draw the characters, then it went to an inker for an outline on a "cel," and then to the painter. We'd turn it over and paint on the back.
>
> Bill Hanna was my boss on the production side, and my father was in charge of the creative side, focusing on story and character development. It was a privilege to be in the room with them and watch their interaction,

how they could feed off each other and end up with this amazing creative entity. To have the experience was to observe pure, unadulterated genius. Because of the MGM closure experience and because they were Depression-era people, they were a bit insecure. I don't think they had a true sense of what they had accomplished, the big picture, if you will, and thus, there was no ego, no arrogance.

When my father and Mr. Hanna ran the studio, there was a schedule from beginning to end. It took twenty-six weeks to do one episode. I made out the schedules—four weeks for a script, one week for revisions; time for the storyboard, layout, animation, xerox, paint, camera, edit, and retakes. It was a very tight and very unforgiving schedule. If a network bought a show in April, that first episode went on the air in September. Without question, time was a very difficult and challenging issue.

Creating a cartoon was done using a production line. The departments were segmented in their responsibilities but worked together—writers, storyboard artists, layout artists, animators, assistant animators, background artists, checkers, inkers/xerox, painters, cameramen, editors—for the final product. It was a privilege to work there. The studio had a very good work ethic, a sense of responsibility, and it could be great fun. One evening when we were really busy and working a great deal of overtime, in order to break the tension, we took our swivel chairs and had chicken races down the hallway! But just for a few minutes!

Mr. Hanna and my father received almost every award in the animation entertainment industry, including Oscars and Emmys. Ultimately, they knew they were interdependent on each other, and most importantly not only did they love what they did, they did what they loved.[8]

While condescension may emerge from quarters of self-important, self-righteous, and self-appointed critics regarding the Hanna-Barbera "limited animation" process, the team's imprint on American entertainment for the last half of the twentieth century is undeniable. Plus, it freed Hanna-Barbera's creative team to focus on aspects just as important to animation but perhaps ignored by the competition. "Limited may have meant fewer drawings per foot of film, but the concept that Joe and I launched was hardly restrictive in either its creative or commercial potential," Hanna wrote in his 1996 autobiography. "As far as Joe and I were concerned, limited animation was the wave of the future. It offered an expansive format that challenged us to make all the right moves in the selection of key images, timing, and the development of clever dialogue and creative voice characterizations."[9]

Condemnations of cartoons and other offerings that Minow, Doan, et al. saw as banal recall similar diatribes hurled toward television's ancestors—burlesque, vaudeville, film. But their negativity mattered not to tens of millions of Americans craving benign amusement after plowing through another day of quotidian tasks of Sisyphean proportions. Prime-time television in turn received welcome, not criticism, across different socioeconomic strata.

One can imagine in the setting of 1962 Connecticut a middle-class insurance executive—an archetype of the mid-twentieth-century male professional—spending the first Sunday of the year dreading his return to work on Monday morning, when he begins his weekly chore of navigating the swells, riptides, and rogue waves in the monotony, bureaucracy, and office politics of corporate America. He calls the end of his day "bringing the ship in to port," a nautical metaphor for getting through the day with his job, sanity, and financial solvency intact. Ignorant, perhaps, of the sacrifice of one's ego demanded by compromise in corporate clashes, his family focuses on the perceived need for material goods in an increasingly status-conscious post–World War II era.

A likely scenario involves a complaint: for example, "Dad, we need a new car. Ours is prehistoric." Sometimes, the matriarch of this suburban clan joins the chorus: "Honey, the kids are right. We need a new car."

He carries out the nightly custom of parking his Buick, Chrysler, or other American-made automobile in the driveway of his two-story, middle-class, colonial-style home in the Constitution State's suburbia; of loosening his tie from the collar of his Van Heusen shirt; of shedding the jacket of his Brooks Brothers suit; of hearing the cacophony of observations from his children at the dinner table about teachers and homework; of settling into his easy chair after dinner; of inhaling the after-dinner aroma of roast chicken, meatloaf, or other nightly entrée cooked in the kitchen's Martha Washington oven; of getting the word from the real boss of the family on the week's social calendar that she created—excepting those involving in-laws, which might arouse a minimal, though ultimately unsuccessful argument on his part; of hearing the clatter of plates as his wife and kids clear the table; and of lamenting the consequences of middle age as his hairline recedes faster than Maury Wills on the base paths.

His brunette-haired teenage daughter might be swooning over her latest crush as an aqua-colored Emerson record player emits "Stranger on the Shore," Acker Bilk's clarinet instrumental backed by the Leon Young String Chorale. Initially created for a British television show, Bilk's slow-paced melody tapped a chord in anyone who ever dreamed of romance underscored by handholding, kissing, and taking long walks on a moonlit beach with a wafting breeze as light as a Fred Astaire soft-shoe routine.

Or she could be in her bedroom practicing the Twist, her ponytail swinging in synchronicity with her hip swivels as the eponymous song by Chubby Checker blasts through her transistor radio; a proper execution of the dance is pretending you are squashing a bug with your feet while toweling your backside. In the January 17 edition of *The Sporting News*, Bill "Moose" Skowron, the Yankees first baseman, declares his affinity for the dance. "The whole family does the Twist, and that includes me," affirms the slugger. "How many guys with sore backs can do the Twist?"[10] Later that year, Checker extends the song's popularity to movie theaters with *Don't Knock the Twist*.

For the literary minded, a novel that became a scandal mentioned the Twist. Set in the fictional village of Ridgefield Corners, New York—a substitute for Cooperstown—*The Sex Cure* is part of the lust-fueled paperback genre popular in the 1950s and 1960s: "The twist might be finished in larger cities but it still had a hold in Ridgefield Corners the way sex had. By ten o'clock tonight, every hotel and summer resort in the area would have a little bit of dance space blocked off and middle-aged women would be on the floor in their bare feet, twisting and dipping and rotating everything that would rotate, giving the men they were dancing with ideas that they hoped would last until they got home."[11]

Aficionados of the hip-swiveling dance found counterparts on *77 Sunset Strip* in January 1962: the episode "Penthouse on Skid Row" features a scene with actors Edd Byrnes and Grace Lee Whitney at the Cloud Nine Dance Hall along with a group of fellow twisters.[12]

Premiering in 1958 and airing for six seasons, *77 Sunset Strip* revolves around Jeff Spencer and Stu Bailey, both former secret agents for the government; the fictional Los Angeles address of the title represented the location of their private-investigation agency. Byrnes plays Kookie, a parking-lot attendant at Dino's, a restaurant owned, in part, by singer and actor Dean Martin; a neon depiction of Martin's face adorns the façade. By the time that "Penthouse on Skid Row" aired, Kookie had been hired by Bailey and Spencer as an investigator.

Byrnes's teen-idol status was iconic. With phrases like "a dark seven" representing a bad week, his vernacular appealed to the younger viewer. He almost had the role in a biographical film about President Kennedy's naval days during World War II. "I lost out on *PT-109*, because with the role of Kookie, I soon found out that I was typecast," explained Byrnes.

> I studied long and hard trying to perfect Jack Kennedy's Boston accent. I thought I gave a very good test. I really looked and sounded the part of a young JFK. I heard through the grapevine that President Kennedy personally called from Washington to Jack Warner's office, stating, "I don't want Kookie to play me." He obviously knew me from the series, but he didn't want to be associated with my character. I really had that accent down cold. In the end, after Warren Beatty turned it down (he was John F. Kennedy's personal choice), Cliff Robertson played the president, but he did it without an accent. Go figure![13]

A fictional version of the Twist appears on *The Dick Van Dyke Show*. In an episode guest starring Jerry Lanning, a teenager named Randy Twizzle invents a new dance named after himself—a combination of the Twist and the Sizzle.[14] It was not an unusual circumstance for 1960s pop culture to become fodder for the situation comedy based on the work and home life of fictional television comedy writer Rob Petrie, inspired by the experiences of the show's creator, Carl Reiner. The episode "The Redcoats Are Coming" features the duo Chad & Jeremy as fictional singers representing music's "British Invasion," led by the Beatles.[15] "It May Look Like a Walnut" pays homage to *The Twilight Zone*, and "The Man from My Uncle" winks and nods at the audience by parodying *The Man from U.N.C.L.E.* and other shows with a spy theme influenced by the James Bond films starring Sean Connery.[16]

In "One Angry Man," Rob serves as a jury foreman. The popularity of *Perry Mason* inspired a laugh from *The Dick Van Dyke Show*'s studio audience—the writers gave the attorneys the same last names as the title character and Hamilton Burger, the weekly foil from the prosecutor's office. Here, the lawyers' duties are reversed from those of their counterparts: Mason is the prosecutor while Burger (spelled Berger in the IMDb.com credits) is the defense attorney.[17]

Elsewhere in 1962, a scene in the surfing-themed episode "Ever Ride the Waves in Oklahoma?" of *Route 66* shows surfers doing the Twist in their hangout.[18] In *Saints and Sinners* Barbara Eden has a guest-starring role as gorgeous, Oscar-winning movie star Nora Love. Suffering mental exhaustion—from being emotionally manipulated by her manager—Nora carries the burden of a mentor's suicide. At the suggestion of the manager, an impromptu get-together for the press is held. Nora ably does the Twist with her guests.[19]

Elvis Presley shows his Twist chops to the song "I Got Lucky" in *Kid Galahad*.[20] In the world of comic books, Dell produced a one-shot comic titled *The Twist*, highlighting a competition for "twisters" involving the fictional Marshmallow Club and Tony's Pizzeria, both located on West Fifty-Sixth Street, between Fifth Avenue and Sixth Avenue, in Manhattan. The story includes a tutorial on different versions of twisting on the dance floor:

Whip—making believe you're cracking a whip
Oversway—one partner leans forward and the other leans backward
Back Scratcher—dancing back to back
Choo Choo—one partner in back of the other[21]

Meanwhile, our archetypal Connecticut insurance executive's ten-year-old son might be found in the classic children's reading position of lying on his stomach, propped up by his arms, as he pores through a new addition to the superhero lineup—*Calling John Force . . . Magic Agent*, a comic-book series lasting three issues in 1962. Debuting with the January–February issue, the title character works for "the most powerful secret organization America has ever known! Not G-Men, not T-men, but a brotherhood of far greater authority—the American Security Group!"[22]

Force, a top ASG operative, derives powers from a medallion featuring Greek columns, each holding a different power—telepathy, illusion, hypnosis, extrasensory perception. Pressing the corresponding column releases the power for Force. In the first issue, President Kennedy gives Force an assignment. Foreign agents working for the Iron Curtain have stolen a device that renders things weightless. Force must recover it before an enemy government uses it to win the Cold War. He accomplishes his mission, but the device is destroyed in the process.[23]

Perhaps the boy indulges in the "space craze," a common pastime for Americans after the Soviets launched the Sputnik satellite in 1957. The United States responded by forming NASA in 1958, selecting seven test pilots as astronauts for the Mercury program, and fostering a patriotic energy for the "space race" against the Soviet cosmonauts. Reading the January issue of *Space World* yields insights into NASA's five-year plan, General Electric's idea for a lunar colony (Project Pilgrim), and a first-person narrative by Soviet cosmonaut Gherman Titov about his seventeen and a half orbital voyages around the earth.[24] It's likely that this boy's reading list includes 1961's *Moon of Mutiny*, the third and final novel in Lester del Rey's Jim Stanley trilogy about space exploration. Robert Irving's book *Electronics*, also published in 1961, would be a useful book if the space race inspired him to pursue learning about science, math, and physics.

Space themes pervade comic books in the early 1960s, so it would be unsurprising to find *Space Man* as part of this youth's reading material. This comic features the adventures of Ian Stannard and Johnny Mack, and it perhaps stretched the imaginations of children envisioning astronauts going into deep space to explore the galaxy.

Throughout the year *The Twilight Zone* offers darker stories related to space. "To Serve Man" embraces hope for humanity when aliens visit our planet, offer technology that solves ills—hunger, for example—and give the humans a book in the aliens' language.[25] A visit to the aliens' planet is the next step. All seems hunky-dory for the humans preparing to depart, until a government cryptographer figures out that the book's title—*To Serve Man*—is literal; it is a cookbook. He is too late to save his fellow humans from boarding the spaceship.

An opposite viewpoint is seen in another episode, "The Gift."[26] An alien accidentally shoots a police officer, so the townspeople believe that he's dangerous. He had offered a gift, but their fear leads them to kill him because they believe that he will injure a young boy who seems to have a connection to the alien. They also burn the gift, only to find that the note accompanying it was mostly destroyed except for the greeting, which explains that the rest of the note had a formula for a vaccine against cancer—all cancers.

Or maybe our archetypal ten-year-old was getting ready for a friend to visit after dinner and play the Milton Bradley board game Supercar to the Rescue—based on the "supermarionation" television show of the same name. Mike Mercury is the test pilot of Supercar, a futuristic vehicle that can also fly. *Supercar* was produced in Britain and ran in first-run syndication in the United States. The board game has a spinner dictating the number of spaces that a player moves on the board with the objective of beating the other players to different disaster scenes—a flood, elephant attack, avalanche, trapped miners, a fire, trapped mountain climber, a hurricane, an airplane crash, a collapsed bridge, a boat about to go over a waterfall.

Also in the boy's collection would likely be the board game merchandised in connection with the CBS television show *The Aquanauts*, focusing on salvage divers in Southern California. Manufactured by Transogram, it has two spinners indicating the status of dive equipment and the longitude and latitude of the divers' locations. The object is to find treasure while battling obstacles—a shark, eel sting, giant clam, octopus, and coral reefs.

While looking through the latest edition of *TV Guide*—a magazine appearing as often in post–World War II homes as the Gideon Bible in hotel rooms—the patriarch of this 1962 suburban Connecticut clan, assisted by bifocals, glances at concise descriptions of that week's broadcast schedule for the television networks and the local independent stations. To take his mind off his imminent return to work, he settles on the nonsensical comings and goings of the New York Police Department's Fifty-Third Precinct police officers on the CBS sitcom *Car 54, Where Are You?*

Set in the Bronx, *Car 54* boasts a theme song explaining the problems of any given day in New York City—a Harlem traffic jam backing cars up to Jackson Heights, a child missing from a scout troop, fights in Brooklyn, a robbery in the Bronx, and Russian premier Nikita Khrushchev arriving at Idlewild International Airport—and a dispatcher calling for Car 54 to protect, serve, and keep the peace in America's largest city.

Car 54 employs the classic comedy dynamic of a slender man paired with a rotund man. It is a familiar model to anyone who ever saw films starring Laurel and Hardy or Abbott and Costello. Fred Gwynne and Joe E. Ross play, respectively, NYPD officers Francis Muldoon and Gunther Toody, the officers patrolling the precinct in Car 54. Muldoon has calm, common sense, and patience. Toody, though good-natured, has none of these qualities; rather, he is inclined toward cluelessness. Muldoon lives with his mother and two younger sisters. Toody lives with Lucille, his overbearing wife with the personality of a dragon when Gunther's actions frustrate her, which is often.

An exchange between Muldoon and Toody in the first *Car 54* episode broadcast in 1962—"The Sacrifice"—honors the prime-time schedule:

"Francis, if you'd really want to study police methods, do what I do. Watch television."

"Gunther, how can you, yourself a policeman, still believe in those cops and robbers on television?"

"Oh, I don't believe in the cops. Just the robbers. Boy, what robbers they got on television."

"All right, Gunther. You just keep on watching television."

"Oh boy! What a night they got on tonight! A big crime night! What a lineup! Listen to this. From six to seven, *Seaside 776*. From seven to eight, *R Squad*. From eight to nine, *The Unmentionables*. From nine to ten, *The American Album of Famous Gang Murders*. From ten to eleven, *The Assassins*. And then they sign off the air with a prayer from the chaplain of Sing Sing."

"Gunther, what would you do in the evenings if it wasn't for television?"

"Francis, I don't even want to think of it!"[27]

Viewers needed to be television literate to get the joke—Toody's litany of titles parodies *77 Sunset Strip*, *Surfside Six*, *M Squad*, *The Untouchables*, *Gang Busters*, and *The Defenders*.

"I didn't always have such a bond with the cops," said Ross in 1962. "Far from it. When I was a kid on New York's lower east side [*sic*], I was afraid of them like most of the other guys. The less we saw of them, the better. I wasn't in trouble that much, but I avoided the cops, anyway. They made everybody uneasy."[28]

The show aired on NBC but got a boost from ABC's *The Flintstones* in a 1962 episode. When a cop is summoned by a dispatcher, the voice mimics the one heard in the *Car 54, Where Are You?* theme song. But the number of the car is different: "Car 34, where are you?"[29]

One can imagine a blonde-haired, green-eyed legal secretary in her late twenties, fingers aching from typing letters, memoranda, and motions at a prestigious Chicago law firm for the previous eight hours. She might window-shop at Marshall Field's for clothes that she cannot afford—even at post-Christmas bargain prices—as the January wind off Lake Michigan delivers a vicious chill that would make Jack Frost shiver. After depleting her Christmas Club account, an innovation designed to help a bank's customers set aside a weekly amount of money throughout the year, she jaunted to Miami Beach for a long weekend in December with three girlfriends. And now, as 1962 begins, Chicago's trademark weather has her pining for Florida's sunshine.

Her calendar overflows with social commitments. She often joins friends for potluck dinners, Cubs games, and Second City—an improvisational comedy troupe that debuted in 1959. She has no shortage of gentleman callers, certainly, thanks to a lithe shape toned by daily two-mile walks, a hairstyle inspired by Jackie Kennedy's bob, and a plain-speaking personality that is neither sycophantic nor dominant. Family is nearby; the member living farthest from Chicago is the oldest of her three brothers, who makes his home in Milwaukee, only about ninety miles away. But once a week she leaves the demanding though enjoyable social life in favor of a prime-time escape to an exotic land more than 4,200 miles from Chicago.

Hawaii.

A republic annexed as a U.S. territory under the McKinley administration in 1898, Hawaii has strategic military value as the headquarters for the U.S. Pacific Fleet—this factoid dominated news stories when the Japanese attacked Pearl Harbor. Trailing Alaska in statehood status by about seven months, Hawaii became the fiftieth state on August 21, 1959, and reached a new awareness in American culture that year, when James Michener chronicled the islands' origins, history, and culture in his novel *Hawaii*. Michener's historical fiction about this archipelago, especially the eight main islands—Niihau, Kauai, Oahu, Molokai, Lanai, Kahoolawe, Maui, and the "Big Island" of Hawaii—takes the reader on a journey through Hawaii's evolution from volcanic explosions forming the islands to the development of a thriving economy in the mid-twentieth century.

As she plops her five-foot, eight-inch frame on her couch after a hastily constructed dinner consisting of salad and leftover lasagna, the secretary turns to ABC's Chicago station, WLS. The show coming on stars Robert Conrad, Connie Stevens, and Anthony Eisley, and *Hawaiian Eye* adds excitement to the image of Hawaii, showcasing the eponymously named private-detective and security firm working from a private compound at the Hawaiian Village Hotel, a benefit accorded because of the firm's services for the hotel.

Hawaiian Eye is part of a television revolution led by ABC. In the early 1950s ABC was a third-rate operation lacking the power of its network competitors, which consisted only of NBC and CBS. Leonard Goldenson, an attorney with the United Paramount Theatres chain, spearheaded the merger of UPT with ABC in 1953; Goldenson became chairman after arranging for a $25 million cash injection. Desperate for programming, he struck a deal with Walt Disney for the programs *Disneyland* and *The Mickey Mouse Club* in exchange for a loan that Disney could use to construct his vision of a theme park in Anaheim, California: Disneyland. Goldenson negotiated a share of the theme park concessions as part of the deal.

A production deal with Warner Bros., the first alignment between a movie studio and a television network for original programming, gave ABC more content. Reflexively, the movie industry looked at television as a threat because of its vise-like grip on Americans' entertainment. Goldenson convinced the Warner Bros. hierarchy otherwise by arguing that the medium provided another revenue stream for the studios, which could use television productions to further amortize the costs of maintaining the Warner soundstages.

And thus *77 Sunset Strip* was born. Warner Bros. expanded its universe by offering other shows with a similar premise: youthful, handsome private detectives with a beautiful woman in their circle. *Hawaiian Eye* came a year later and aired for four seasons, from 1959 to 1963.

Bourbon Street Beat aired only in the 1960–61 season, but one of its characters, Kenny Madison, became a regular on *Surfside Six*, a show set in Miami Beach, which aired for two seasons, from 1960 to 1962. Rex Randolph went from *Bourbon Street Beat* to *77 Sunset Strip* for a season.

Characters crossing over to other shows for guest appearances was a regular gimmick, perhaps even the first instance of it, as *Hawaiian Eye*'s pilot episode begins with *77 Sunset Strip*'s Stu Bailey calling Tracy Steele, played by Anthony Eisley. A meta moment occurs when Steele talks with his partner, Tom Lopaka, played by Robert Conrad, in front of the hotel's gift shop, where sheet music for *77 Sunset Strip*, with the conspicuous Warner Bros. logo, is in the window.[30]

William T. Orr, son-in-law of movie mogul Jack Warner, oversaw Warner Bros. television productions in the 1950s and the 1960s. Orr's son, Gregory, explains:

Girl on the Run was a television film based on stories that Roy Huggins wrote. Edd Byrnes played a killer. But the film was so popular, it became the basis for *77 Sunset Strip* and Byrnes became a teen idol, portraying the fun-loving Kookie, who talked heavily in slang.

ABC desperately needed shows because it was a new network. My father said that my grandfather saw dailies of all the movies, and he certainly saw every movie before it was released. He kept meaning to see pilots and episodes of television shows, but he also kept putting it off until it was too late. They had to ship the shows to New York City for broadcast.

There was a shift in the 1960s regarding content. The networks got more control. Warner Bros. produced *Lawman*, which cast well-known African American actor Sammy Davis Jr. in a guest appearance. In those days, shows had a primary sponsor. For the Davis episode the sponsor was R. J. Reynolds Tobacco, a company with long southern ties, including its attitudes about race. My father was shocked when Reynolds said they wouldn't sponsor the episode unless Davis was removed. Sammy Davis Jr. was a big star, but Reynolds saw only a Black man in a guest-starring role, which they found objectionable. My father refused the directive and switched to another sponsor, Kaiser Aluminum, who was happy to associate itself with the actor.

77 Sunset Strip and the other private detective shows appealed to a generation coming into their own after World War II. They were travelogues showing adventure, exotic locations, and good-looking people in contemporary stories. It was aspirational, in a way. The male characters were cool and worldly. The female characters were sophisticated and sexy without being over the top.[31]

The worldliness of the characters is almost immediately apparent in the series in the second episode of *77 Sunset Strip*, when Spencer dictates the curriculum vitae of his partner, who is accused of murder: "Phi Beta Kappa, PhD in languages, six years with the OSS, punctures a man with a paper knife in his own office after a public quarrel. No, Stu. I don't say you couldn't have done it. But you'd have done it neater."[32]

Toody's devotion to television for entertainment and information in *Car 54* has a counterpart in this *77 Sunset Strip* episode. When Spencer approaches the manager of the Hillside Lanai—a motel where Bailey's new paramour, a married woman, has a room—he says that he's investigating a murder. The manager assumes him to be a police officer. "Just routine. You understand," says Spencer in justifying his interviewing people in the area. The manager responds, "Oh sure, I watch TV."[33]

Route 66, airing from 1960 to 1964 on CBS, offered dramas that were sometimes topical.

Two men in their early thirties—Tod Stiles and Buz Murdock—travel the continental United States in a Corvette while getting involved in the personal lives of people whom they encounter by chance. Martin Milner plays Tod and George Maharis plays Buz; Glenn Corbett, playing Linc Chase, replaced Maharis in the third season. Corbett's character is first seen returning from military service in Vietnam, which was an unusual descriptor for a character in the early 1960s—American involvement didn't ramp up until the middle part of the decade.

Filmed on location, *Route 66* depicts the United States before homogenization charged through the lower forty-eight like a bull at a rodeo, resulting in chain restaurants, superstores, and superregional banks.

"To Walk with the Serpent," the series' first episode of 1962, depicts the evil of white supremacy. Tod and Buz visit the Bunker Hill Monument in Boston, where they meet John Westerbrook, a man with five degrees, including a PhD in philosophy and another in mathematics. Federal agents later tell them that Westerbrook leads the Patriot Sons of Hamilton, a hate group targeting those he deems unworthy of American citizenship. "The history and purity of America must be restored," declares Westerbrook, who has adopted the nickname Monitor. A Nazi-like salute accompanies a catchphrase that his followers embrace with mania—Awake America.[34]

The agents show a film of Westerbrook's presentation, titled "The Face of the Enemy," to Tod and Buz. It includes a Q&A with his followers—one asks about setting up concentration camps. "It's a happy thought, I'm sure. But I'm afraid it's a little premature," says Westerbrook, who plans a domestic terror attack in Paul Revere Mall. To incite chaos, he arranges for a sniper to detonate plastic explosives on top of the Paul Revere statue. After Tod and Buz help the agents stop the attack, police officers take Westerbrook away in a straitjacket.

"To Walk with the Serpent" endured a delay in its broadcast because of the subject matter. On November 7, 1961, the *Boston Globe* reported, "The film has been reviewed by the sponsors and advertising agencies involved and a dispute has arisen as to whether it is worthy of air time."[35] Percy Shain, the *Globe*'s television critic, condemned the episode in his "Night Watch" column, calling it "a dramatically-pointless, venom-filled, absurdly-plotted hallucination about a clearly insane hate-monger whose efforts to arouse Boston's populace to frenzy against non-Aryans seemed almost a desecration of the hallowed shrines of liberty which formed the background of the action."[36]

Milner had an All-American aura baked in integrity. When he passed away in 2015, the Los Angeles Police Department felt the loss—Milner's portrayal of Officer Pete Malloy on *Adam-12*, which ran on NBC from 1968 to 1975, had inspired young men to join police departments, much like *Star Trek* and *Lost in Space* had sparked curiosity in a generation of youth and led them to become aerospace engineers. Milner's widow, Judith, recalls that

> when Martin died, LAPD officers had tears in their eyes when they offered their condolences to me and my family. During *Route 66*, our major chal-
> lenge was finding a place to live on the road because they filmed the show

on location. We didn't want to live in hotels, so we rented houses. In every city we became a part of it. All the crew brought their families, too. The wives were together. The guys had a baseball team, which played the locals. When the show started, we had my first daughter, Amy. Then I was pregnant with my second daughter, Molly. By the time the show went off the air, I had my two sons, Andrew and Stuart.

One example of Martin's lack of pretentiousness happened when we shot an episode in Pocatello, Idaho. Somebody from the local newspaper called and said he wanted to meet and interview Martin. I started dinner and Martin told the reporter to meet him at the laundromat. This was in the days before disposable diapers. Martin did the wash of our baby daughter Amy's dirty diapers while he did the interview![37]

George Maharis says,

Marty and I had a very good chemistry between us. Nelson Riddle's theme song was fantastic. We represented something that was needed at that point with the younger generation—a quality of being out on the road. There was a certain kind of wanderlust in the 1960s. It was a great adventure. On the show you saw America the way it was. The Corvette was originally a light, powder-blue color. But our cameraman, Jack Marta, said it reflected too much light. So they got a brown one.

Buz and Tod represented segments of America, with Marty representing the upper middle class and Buz representing the poorer class, somebody who comes from nothing and makes it. Buz was unpredictable. He was instinctive, impulsive, dedicated. When he believes strongly in something, he will stand up for it. He was not the kind of guy that panicked.

The show was originally called *The Searchers*, but somebody had that name. Bert Leonard, our producer, got the title *Route 66*, which I thought was more interesting. We'd get a script on Saturday night and talk to Stirling Siliphant, the show's creator, and Bert on Sunday. They spent the money to go on the road and do what we had to do. Sometimes we had to wing it and improvise because we didn't have the facilities to shoot the scenes as written. We had great guest stars. Tuesday Weld. Robert Duvall. Nina Foch. Nehemiah Persoff. Robert Redford. Suzanne Pleshette.

As a young man, I used to hitchhike from New York to Cuba. You could take a ferry from the last key to Miami to Havana and get there in forty-five minutes. I told Stirling about my adventures for the show. He was great. You could cut half of his script and it would be better than most.

You could go to a new town in Tennessee and sixty miles in either direction was a different kind of town. Now, you cross three thousand miles and everything is the same. We've lost that part of Americana.[38]

ABC's *The Rifleman*, starring Chuck Connors as Lucas McCain, a rancher and a widower raising his young son, shows Lucas getting involved—often unintentionally and always successfully—in keeping the peace in 1880s North Fork, a town in the New Mexico Territory. Those who challenged him did so at their peril.

The Rifleman ran for five years, from 1958 to 1963. Johnny Crawford starred alongside Connors as Lucas's son. A 1959 profile of Crawford explains the dynamic between the young actor and Connors:

An avid baseball fan, Johnny doesn't miss a chance to skip dancing, singing and acting lessons to root for the Los Angeles Dodgers, which, he tells you with much gusto, is his favorite team. He particularly relishes working with Chuck Connors, who formerly played with the Brooklyn Dodgers. As Johnny expressed it: "Chuck has taught me lots of special little things about baseball. Like how to hold my bat, and how to field the ball and run the bases. He and I are real close. I go out to his house to play ball with him and his sons and swim in their pool."[39]

"[It] is hard to laugh when Connors describes a Western built around a deadly Winchester .44-40 as 'a love story between a father and his son,'" explains a *TV Guide* cover story from January 1962. "It is corny, and perhaps it is also confused, but many believe it is also Connors-McCain. Up in ratings or down, Connors likes to believe that 'in a small way our series is good for family life in America.'"[40]

Connors had a brief career in Major League Baseball, playing a single game for the Brooklyn Dodgers in 1949 and 66 games for the Chicago Cubs in 1951; he played 952 games in his Minor League career. Both his Major League and

Minor League averages were .238. But Connors's athleticism wasn't limited to baseball. He played 49 games for the 1946–47 Boston Celtics of the Basketball Association of America and 4 games the following season. His scoring average was 4.5 points per game.

A combination of timing and geography spurred the athlete's journey to acting. In Connors's 1992 obituary, Bruce Lambert of the *New York Times* wrote, "Mr. Connors had a lackluster sports career, but his towering height of 6 feet 5 inches and his square-jawed masculinity made him a natural for rugged acting roles. When his struggling athletic career landed him with the Los Angeles Angels, a minor-league baseball team, he began picking up minor movie parts and soon gave up sports."[41]

Connors reunited with his former boss in the Dodgers organization—Branch Rickey—during the September 13, 1959, episode of *What's My Line?*, a game show hosted by John Daly and featuring panelists who tried to deduce a hidden-from-view guest's occupation through a series of yes or no questions.[42] Celebrity guests often used fake voices to disguise their identity, while the panelists wore eye masks to prevent immediate identification.

At the time, Rickey devoted his energy, acumen, and stamina to forming the Continental League. After panelist Arlene Francis correctly guesses Rickey's identity, Connors graciously acknowledges the legendary executive. "I remember Mr. Rickey, who actually gave me my career in baseball," states Connors. "And it's a pleasure to see him again."[43]

"It's a pleasure to see you, too," responds Rickey.[44]

A conversation follows regarding the new league. New York, Houston, Minneapolis–St. Paul, Denver, and Toronto already had Continental League rights. When Daly asks about the remaining three slots and potential contenders, Rickey clarifies, "More than we can fill. The embarrassment is in the field of exclusion rather than inclusion. We shall have a very difficult time in choosing the other three. In fact, we are now laboring hard, at the moment, to choose a sixth one, which will be announced surely in the next few days."[45]

Rickey, the league's president, assures the audience that the enterprise will flourish and that it has a target start date of 1961 and a 154-game schedule. "Inevitable as tomorrow morning," declares Rickey.[46] Not quite—the Continental League never gets off the ground; it folds in 1960. But four franchises emerge from the rubble to join Major League Baseball. The Houston ball club joins the New York Mets in the National League's expansion in 1962. The year before, the American League had added the Los Angeles Angels and the second incarnation of the Washington Senators to its roster.

Americans burying themselves in prime-time sitcoms, specials, sporting events, and dramas might have missed an item of geopolitical concern on the television news. Tensions about Cuba's link to the Soviet Union were in the background of Secretary of State Dean Rusk's January trip to Punta del Este, Uruguay, to address a meeting of the foreign ministers of the American states. Calling for his counterparts to "interrupt the limited but significant flow of trade between Cuba and the rest of the hemisphere, especially the traffic in arms," Rusk warned the world to "recognize that the alignment of the Government of Cuba with the countries of the Sino-Soviet bloc, and its commitment to extend Communist power in this hemisphere, are incompatible with the purposes and principles of the inter-American system and that its current activities are an ever present and common danger to the peace and security of the continent."[47]

By autumn the danger was imminent.

Another concern: NASA suffered a detour toward the end of January when the agency's unmanned Ranger 3 mission, intended to take photographs of the moon and land on it, missed the target by an estimated twenty thousand to thirty thousand miles. It was thought that the setback affected the plans for a human landing. According to the *New York Times*, "The failure of the Ranger 3 meant that the United States could no longer hope to have an astronaut in flight while a spacecraft was on the way to the moon, to scout for landing places by human explorers for later in this decade."[48] Later in the year, Ranger 3 and Ranger 5 were also unsuccessful.

The prediction turned out to be false. And a month later, NASA had plenty to cheer about.

2

"Go, Baby, Go!"

When the newly inaugurated thirty-fifth president of the United States proclaimed on January 20, 1961, that "the torch has been passed to a new generation," the calendar backed him up.[1] John Fitzgerald Kennedy was the first president born in the twentieth century.

Kennedy attempted to fulfill that promise in his first year by executing an operation, conceived by President Eisenhower's inner circle, to invade Cuba and overthrow Fidel Castro. The Bay of Pigs operation fell under the auspices of the CIA, which used a group of Cuban exiles dubbed Brigade 2506 and, as part of its air attack strategy, World War II–era B-26 bombers instead of newer fighter planes. About 1,400 Cuban exiles went against 20,000 Cuban troops. Almost 1,200 exiles surrendered, and more than 100 exiles died.[2]

On February 3, 1962, Kennedy took another shot at Castro by authorizing an embargo projected to cost Cuba approximately $35 million in lost trade income—a highly significant impact on Cuba's overall trade income, which ranked in the $100 million range.[3] It was the latest in a series of American economic actions against Cuba.

Eisenhower's tactics had included the Sugar Act, which he signed on July 6, 1960, six and a half months before handing the presidential-leadership torch to the forty-three-year-old Kennedy. At that time the United States got about a third of its sugar from Cuba, a supply line now threatened by the Soviet-Cuba connection. Eisenhower declared, "The Government of Cuba has committed itself to purchase substantial quantities of goods from the Soviet Union under barter arrangements. It has chosen to undertake to pay for these goods with sugar—traded at prices well below those which it has obtained in the United States. The inescapable conclusion is that Cuba has embarked on a course of action to commit steadily increasing amounts of its sugar crop to trade with the Communist bloc, thus making its future ability to fill the sugar needs of the United States ever more uncertain."[4]

The Sugar Act signing came a day after a diplomatic protest against Cuba's taking over refineries owned by American oil giants Texaco and Esso; a Royal Dutch Shell refinery was also the victim of epic belligerence widening the crater between Cuba and the United States. The protest read, in part, "[We] cannot but feel, with profound regret, that the intervention and seizure of these refineries is further evidence and confirmation of a pattern of relentless economic aggression by the Government of Cuba against the United States and other countries designed to destroy Cuba's traditional investment and trade relations with the free world."[5]

First Lady Jackie Kennedy, while her husband balanced the nuances, impact, and cost of military, economic, and diplomatic tactics involving Cuba, Russia, and communism, prepared for her CBS special, *A Tour of the White House.* Giving an inside view of the First Family's home offered an aura of approach-ability for the Kennedys, an aura that had not existed given the avuncularity of Eisenhower, the plain speaking of Truman, and the patrician pedigree of Franklin D. Roosevelt. American couples marked Valentine's Day with candlelit dinners, gentleman suitors giving roses to their girlfriends, and schoolchildren handing out funny cards with sweet messages in cursive writing for the opposite-sex members of their homeroom. But at night, after the adrenaline of love's holiday had subsided, they got a history lesson; Valentine's Day was an appropriate broadcast date for *A Tour of the White House*, given America's affection for the First Lady of the United States. A symbol of youth, beauty, and refinement in contrast to the dowdiness of her immediate predecessors— Mamie Eisenhower, Bess Truman, and Eleanor Roosevelt—she escorted CBS's Charles Collingwood around 1600 Pennsylvania Avenue to vivify the history of one of the most powerful symbols of freedom in the United States. And the world.

CBS's production staff had learned from the mistakes made during a 1952 televised tour conducted by President Harry S. Truman. In a ten-page letter dated September 29, 1961, to Pamela Turnure—the First Lady's press secretary— CBS News producer Perry Wolff had first proposed the idea of showcasing the Kennedys' transition into a new home.[6] A news veteran, Wolff knew how to frame details for a compelling story. In a seven-page letter to Turnure two months before the broadcast, he emphasized the importance of on-site pre-production to help arrange the best possible lighting, camera angles, and sound. He also clarified the special's purpose—highlighting restoration efforts, with Mrs. Kennedy discussing the methods involved.[7]

Wolff's understanding of television's impact informed his vision of how to begin the broadcast—by leveraging the power of the image dictating the story, which was a possibly counterintuitive approach to producers who want everything onscreen to be aesthetically perfect. Clutter formed by furniture, crates, and objects would offer a human element, identifiable to the millions of viewers who had ever moved to a new home.[8]

Legendary journalist and former CBS News fixture Edward R. Murrow, appointed to the post of director of the U.S. Information Agency by President Kennedy, recommended to White House press secretary Pierre Salinger that Mrs. Kennedy also speak lines in Spanish and French. This would, in Murrow's opinion, "add a special fillip to the version for Latin America and the French-speaking areas of the world."[9] It was an opinion worth reckoning, given Murrow's status as the model for news reporters in broadcasting; the Murrow roster of accomplishments includes radio broadcasts from London during Battle of Britain in World War II, the takedown of Wisconsin's communist-hunting senator, Joseph McCarthy, and the celebrity interview show *Person to Person*.

Mrs. Kennedy took Murrow's advice.

A Tour of the White House with Mrs. John F. Kennedy had bipartisan appeal, evidenced by her fan mail. In the postscript to a letter complimenting the First Lady on her "grace and dignity" while "weaving the interesting details into a tapestry of American traditions," a Chicago banker describes himself as a "so-called" Taft Republican—a label foisted upon conservatives in the political mold of Senator Robert Taft from Ohio, the oldest son of former U.S. president and chief justice William Howard Taft.[10]

A New York publishing executive praised Mrs. Kennedy on the "exacting job you have undertaken in order to restore the White House and make it a testimonial to our often-neglected American heritage."[11]

The First Lady also impressed Jackie Mackie's third-grade class at the Hockaday School, a pre-K through twelfth grade private school for girls in Dallas. Inspired by the broadcast, Mackie tasked each girl with the assignment "When I am First Lady at the White House."[12] Dressed in the Hockaday uniform of green skirts, green suspenders, oxford shoes, and a white blouse with a ruffle, each girl handed in her imagination of being in Jackie Kennedy's shoes:

> Since I have gone to Hockaday, I would name the most important room the green and white room. I would make the upholstery green and the wall paper white.

> I would find George Washington's bedroom furniture and put them in my husband's bedroom. I would find Martha Washington's bedroom furniture and put them in my room.

> When I am First Lady in the White House I will build a stable and a "Twist" patio for parties.

> I want to discover the past and restore the past as Jacqueline Kennedy has done.

> I will be on television a lot.

> I would eat off of Lincoln's dinner plates every night. I would sleep in Lincoln's bed too. I would take walks in the garden every day.

I hope to find George Washington's ax, that he chopped his father's tree down with.

I would put a water vase in Abraham Lincoln's room. And in George Washington's room, I would put a table and a desk.

I will try to make everybody happy in America.

I would go to many foreign places and talk to the people.[13]

A fifth-generation Dallasite and a member of one of America's most prominent real estate families, Lucy Billingsley (née Crow), was in Mackie's class. She wrote, "I would have parties for people who live in Washington D.C. and visitors."[14] A year and a half later she was in the eye of the emotional firestorm that shredded the country's soul:

> My dad, Trammell Crow, built the Dallas Market Center. He started out in real estate by building warehouses and then learned about the concept of market centers. The Furniture Mart was the first building in the Dallas Market Center. The Trade Mart was the second building. When President Kennedy visited Dallas on November 22, 1963, he was scheduled to appear at the Trade Mart. So, my father took me and my little brother to the event.
>
> We were going to be the next people to meet the president. Well, the motorcycles peeled off and my dad sat us down and told us not to move. You could see an energetic change. A crisis in motion. We went through a side entry to the building. He brought us to the atrium, put us on a bench, and told us not to move. Then, an announcement was made about what happened to the president and you could see the hush of the room for a long time. We knew he was critically wounded. They held a prayer and I saw the waiters crying. It was jarring to see an adult cry, especially a man. Governor Connally and his wife were in the car with the president and Mrs. Kennedy. He was wounded, but not fatally. The Connallys were friends of my parents and some of the Connally kids were at our house that afternoon.[15]

Hockaday girls and millions of others could find inspiration beyond fantasizing about being the First Lady. Madeleine L'Engle's 1962 novel *A Wrinkle in Time*, which won the Newbery Medal for children's literature, features the story's heroine, thirteen-year-old Meg Murry, with a steely determination to overcome scientific, physical, and supernatural obstacles. Though a bit boy crazy for high-school junior Calvin O'Keefe, Meg cannot be deterred from her mission to solve a cosmic mystery challenging her curiosity, instinct, and persistence.

Charlotte Jones Voiklis, L'Engle's granddaughter, explains that the story's endurance contrasts the publishing world's initial reaction:

> 1962 was important to the book's success. One of the publishers who rejected it said later that she was afraid to take it in 1959. The publisher told my grandmother that she [L'Engle] wouldn't be where she was if it had been published then. My grandmother agreed. She believed that things happen at the right time. It was legible in a different way than it would have been earlier. The Cold War aspect had an impact. She wrote in her journals that she was terrified of Joseph McCarthy. I think that informed her writing.
>
> She could never explain where it came from. The first inkling of the idea or characters overtly coming to her was when the family drove cross-country on a camping trip. The three characters of Mrs. Which, Mrs. Who, and Mrs. Whatsit came into her head when she was looking at a landscape in Arizona. She said that the story came to her and said, "Enflesh me." And then she started writing. She listened to her inner voices, which was crucial because the biggest job of a writer is to listen.
>
> One of the themes of *A Wrinkle in Time* is that love exists at the center of the universe. Yes, there is evil and there is darkness. But there is also a hopeful nature. There are forces that we don't understand and they're good. I think she would say that love is not easy. It is hard and scary. It is also action. But it is what we have. She is definitely the model for Meg, her feelings as a child and the formative sense of self as awkward, unlovable, and misunderstood. Faults can do you in, but Meg's fault of stubbornness saves the day. Like Meg, my grandmother was full of passion. If she saw an injustice, she couldn't be quiet. The scene with Meg's father is a really big one. Watching her father's long and slow decline was really difficult and painful.

The point of the story, to me, is that darkness can be overcome. It is a big struggle, but we're not alone.[16]

Meg's travels through space and time were perfect outlets for children during the early years of the space age. Space exploration became a particular concern when President Eisenhower authorized the creation of the National Aeronautics and Space Administration in 1958. NASA needed astronauts who could endure the physical rigors and tasks of space flight, though those tasks had yet to be identified. Astronauts were at the time considered more as subjects of the flight than active participants. Scientists, doctors, and engineers examined their performance, endurance, and medical changes in an engineered atmosphere of weightlessness to gauge their worthiness for space flight. In his 1979 tome *The Right Stuff*, Tom Wolfe empathizes, "The poor devil would be a guinea pig."[17]

NASA officials immediately looked to physically superior men for the astronaut corps. In the movie version of Wolfe's book two such officials, played by Jeff Goldblum and Harry Shearer, look at films of prospects, including one of a man being shot out of a cannon.[18] "The announcement calling for volunteers did mention test pilots as being among the types of men who might qualify, but it also mentioned submarine crew members, parachute jumpers, arctic explorers, mountain climbers, deep sea divers, even scuba divers, combat veterans, and, for that matter, mere veterans of combat training, and men who had served as test subjects for acceleration and atmospheric pressure tests, such as the Air Force and Navy had been running," Wolfe wrote. "The astronaut would not be expected to *do* anything, he only had to be able to take it."[19]

This contravened Eisenhower's paradigm. The president was keenly aware that this new venture needed a framework of organization, not chaos. He demanded that test pilots—and only test pilots—be the space pioneers because of their acumen regarding flight, plus their status as federal-government employees, which meant their records were easy to research.

Sixty-three applicants sought to be the first astronauts, a term meaning "star voyagers," on the greatest adventures since Magellan and his fellow explorers confronted the seas. Project Mercury replaced the pre-NASA air force program known as Man in Space Soonest.[20]

Still, when Kennedy took the oath of office in 1961, space flight was not a priority—Kennedy's team had not approached NASA administrator Keith Glennan for a dissection of NASA's challenges, personnel, and budget. "As for myself, I still find the state of suspended animation a little difficult to cope with," Glennan wrote in his diary on December 4, 1960, a month after Kennedy's election victory.[21] By the time Kennedy had urged Americans to ask not what their country could do for them, Glennan was on the road to Cleveland, where he served as president of Case Western Reserve University from 1961 to 1966.

Dr. Hugh Dryden revealed similar sentiments during an oral history interview for the JFK Library in 1964:

> After the Inauguration, January 20th, there was a period, which turns out to have been six days, in which there was absolutely no contact with the new Administration. We made some attempts through our regular line channels, public relations people, without success. It was very important because there was scheduled on January 31st a shot of the chimpanzee "Ham" out into the Atlantic. We couldn't visualize the President reading about this in the newspaper and knowing nothing about it. We tried to get this information to him through the public relations channels but there was no success. Finally, on January 26th, I did manage to get into [President's Science Advisory Committee chair Jerome] Wiesner's office to tell him about this so he could tell the President.[22]

Dryden confirmed that NASA had no involvement in Kennedy's inaugural address or the 1961 State of the Union address. On March 19, 1961, he and other NASA representatives met with the president, who emphasized the importance of progressing against the Soviets' leadership in space exploration.[23]

With Glennan's departure, the Kennedy White House needed to decide on who would be the steward for NASA and its direction, whatever direction that happened to be, as long as it pointed to the heavens. Kennedy tapped James Webb, described by space historian Andrew Chaikin as being a "canny bulldog of a politician."[24]

The space race escalated, becoming a defining element of Kennedy's presidency. On November 21, 1963—a day before his assassination—Kennedy echoed his inauguration speech vision of acknowledging, confronting, and overcoming challenges. But he talked of the specifics of space exploration rather than the abstract notion at San Antonio's Aerospace Medical Health Center:

> Frank O'Connor, the Irish writer, tells in one of his books how, as a boy, he and his friends would make their way across the countryside; and when they came to an orchard wall that seemed too high to climb, too doubtful to try, too difficult to permit their journey to continue, they took off their caps and tossed them over the wall—and then they had no choice but to follow them.
>
> My friends, this nation has tossed its cap over the wall of space—and we have no choice but to follow it. Whatever the difficulties, they must be overcome. Whatever the hazards, they must be guarded against.[25]

The Mercury astronauts became household names—Alan Shepard, Gus Grissom, John Glenn, Scott Carpenter, Deke Slayton, Wally Schirra, Gordon Cooper. NASA grounded Slayton because of a heart murmur; he then headed NASA's Astronaut Office, becoming a crucial part of the process of selecting astronauts, creating flight plans, and liaising between the astronauts and NASA's bureaucracy. In 1975 NASA cleared him to be a part of the Apollo-Soyuz project.

Mercury's six solo missions took place between 1961 and 1963. After Mercury, NASA launched two-man crews in Project Gemini, followed by three-man crews in Project Apollo—the missions focused on the moon landing.

NASA's foothold in the American psyche prompted Hollywood to incorporate the space age into its 1960s offerings. *I Dream of Jeannie* aired on NBC from 1965 to 1970. The first episode shows a final stage rocket misfire that forces Captain Tony Nelson to land his *Stardust One* capsule in the South Pacific. Washed ashore, Tony uses logs to make an SOS signal in the sand. On that beach he discovers a bottle that, when uncorked, allows a beautiful, buxom, blonde-haired genie to come out. Larry Hagman and Barbara Eden play Captain (later Major) Nelson and Jeannie, respectively.[26]

Comedy revolved around Jeannie always trying to help her "master," usually worsening the situation, while he strove to keep her true identity hidden from Dr. Alfred Bellows, NASA's psychiatrist. Later in the series, Tony and Jeannie marry.

My Favorite Martian aired on CBS from 1963 to 1966. Starring Bill Bixby as *Los Angeles Sun* reporter Tim O'Hara, *My Favorite Martian* has a premise similar to that of *Jeannie*. A martian, played by Ray Walston, traveling in a flying saucer at 9,000 miles an hour, crashes after missing an X-15 rocket flying at "barely 4,000 miles an hour." After getting rushed out of Edwards Air Force base, where he went to cover the launch for "The West's Most Influential Newspaper," Tim discovers the spaceship and the martian, who proclaims himself to be a professor of anthropology and the "greatest living authority" on earthlings, thanks to his visits over the past 150 years. To disguise the martian's true identity, Tim dubs him "Uncle Martin."[27]

Gilligan's Island, airing on CBS from 1964 to 1967, used a space theme for three episodes.

"Splashdown" shows the castaways trying to get the attention of two astronauts in orbit—Tobias and Ryan—presumably for Project Gemini. Los Angeles sports announcer Chick Hearn introduces the premise: "It was a perfect launch and *Scorpio 6*, with astronauts Tobias and Ryan aboard, is on its way to make space history. This is the most complex and certainly the most ambitious mission ever to be attempted by man in outer space. Tobias and Ryan will maneuver their spaceship to a rendezvous with the unmanned Scorpio E-X-1 capsule, which was sent into orbit three weeks ago. The orbit of Scorpio E-X-1 was changed one hour ago by Ground Control, changed to match the apogee and the perigee of *Scorpio 6*." Consequently, Tobias would transition to the E-X-1 capsule, and the astronauts would return to earth separately.[28]

When the Professor calculates that Tobias and Ryan will be able to see the island during certain orbits, the castaways spell out SOS with tree trunks and set them on fire. Gilligan accidentally kicks a log when his pants are on fire, so the message reads SOL, which the astronauts believe is meant as a personal greeting for one of them—Sol Tobias.

The E-X-1 lands in the lagoon, thereby aborting the mission. But the castaways are unable to use it for their own rescue because NASA's Mission Control blows it up by remote control to prevent classified instruments and data from being stolen.

The other two episodes used Russia and Mars as story fodder. In "Nyet, Nyet, Not Yet," two Soviet cosmonauts crash their capsule in the island's lagoon.[29] In "Smile, You're on Mars Camera," the castaways find a video probe meant to land on Mars.[30]

The Lucy Show, starring Lucille Ball, used a space theme as the backdrop for the 1962 episode "Lucy Becomes an Astronaut."[31]

The Beverly Hillbillies often inserted 1960s popular culture into its episodes. In "The Folk Singers," Jethro initially wants to become an astronaut but changes his mind and decides to become the next big thing in the folk music genre.[32]

Star Trek ran for three seasons and boldly went where no man had gone before; *Lost in Space* tracked the travails of the Robinson family and stowaway Dr. Smith; and *Santa Claus Goes to Mars*, *Marooned*, and *2001: A Space Odyssey* presented cinematic stories from the bizarre to the futuristic.

The comic book is a portable universe suitable for reading at lunchtime, after school, and under the covers, with the blanket providing insulation from the snooping of parents wondering why bedtimes are being ignored. America's space program gave the comic-book industry fodder to match a classic with the future in 1962: *Space Family Robinson*'s first issue was dated December, but kids were likely reading it by Thanksgiving, because comic books are typically released a month or more in advance of the issue date.

Using the premise of Johann David Wyss's *Swiss Family Robinson*, the story of a stranded family, Gold Key's *Space Family Robinson* captured the imagination of comic-book readers from 1962 to 1978. "Lost in Space" was the title of the first story in issue number 2. Three years later, Gold Key began using the "Lost in Space" subtitle on the cover, with issue number 15 (January 1966). But *Space Family Robinson* has a history bathed in controversy.

Del Connell created *Space Family Robinson* for Gold Key. His version consists of scientists Craig and June Robinson, plus their teenagers Tim and Tam. This first family in space launches circa 2001. Also included are their pets—parrot Yakker and dog Clancy, the latter inspired by Connell's family dog. Basically, the family lives on the first space station to orbit the earth, and they encounter aliens and adventures in the theretofore unknown universe when a cosmic blast rocks their orbiting home.

There have been rumors wafting around comic-book conventions for decades that Disney artist Carl Barks actually created *Space Family Robinson*, but the Holmesian work of popular culture historian Ed Shifres exposed this falsehood. Shifres's 1996 book *Space Family Robinson: The True Story* points to a letter received from Barks underscoring that credit for the series should be given to Del Connell. Barks emphasizes that he had no link to Gold Key, save for a comment to an editor that the company should match the *Swiss Family Robinson* template to space and, in turn, dub it *Space Family Robinson*.[33] Further, Barks notes that the excitement of fans blurred the truth, leading to a snippet of Hollywood lore.

It is safe to conclude that the popularity of the *Lost in Space* television show, which ran from 1965 to 1968 on CBS, propelled the addition of the moniker to the *Space Family Robinson* comic-book series, though there was no nexus between the two offerings.

Shifres adds that another futuristic tale took advantage of Wyss's path-breaking work. Hilda Bohem wrote a script titled "Swiss Family 3000," which was commissioned by CBS's director of business affairs, Bud Groskopf, who wanted to be a producer. His two primary ideas set *Robinson Crusoe* and *Swiss Family Robinson* in the future. To avoid conflict of interest, Groskopf used Bohem as a Trojan horse. When he learned of Western Publishing's *Space Family Robinson* under the Gold Key banner, he engaged Bohem to approach the comic-book company about the dramatic rights. This would be a cushion against potential litigation over his *Swiss Family 3000* feature-film idea. A fraternity brother's family owned Western, so Groskopf used his connection to secure the rights; his dream was set to be a reality until Irwin Allen entered the picture. He wanted to use *Space Family Robinson* for a television show, so he approached Western, and it was a dead end. Instead, Allen used the *Lost in Space* title.

After learning about Allen's television show, Groskopf—with Bohem as his beard—took legal action and reached a settlement with Allen and CBS for $20,000. The fraternity brother requested the live-action rights be returned to Western, a proposition that seemed like a no-brainer, considering Allen's project would block the title from being plastered on another work. But in 1991 Innovation Comics distributed a *Lost in Space* series; Dark Horse Comics followed suit, so that its publication would coincide with the 1998 film based on the television show.

Shifres contends that the real inspiration behind the television show was not Irwin Allen but Ib Melchior, who also wrote the 1964 film *Robinson Crusoe on Mars*. By analyzing a treatment prepared by Melchior circa 1960, Shifres concludes that Allen's *Lost in Space* pilot parallels Melchior's vision but was unrelated to the comic book. Both stories use the well-known Robinson tale as a starting point, so similarities are bound to exist. But Shifres's excavations of the various prongs related to the television show raise questions about its genesis.

In an interview with Shifres, Connell reveals that Western Publishing would not get money promised for the production of a television show, despite a contract: "Our legal department did little in the way of objecting. At the time, Western Publishing was doing many comics on 20th Century Fox's TV shows and movies (where Irwin Allen was headquartered with his shows). I objected strenuously to the legal department to no avail. Letting the basic format (and title) to one of our comics get away was evidently not as important as continuing the association with 20th Century Fox."[34]

Shifres numbers forty-two similarities, such as having the year 1997 as the setting. But Allen made highly significant changes to the unaired pilot that created not only differences but also hallmarks for the show. The episode "Stowaway" introduced Zachary Smith, played by Jonathan Harris, one of the great antagonists on television. The character is an intelligent but nasty man whose greed serves as his raison d'être, and he provides conflict for the Robinsons and their fellow astronaut Don West, in addition to the problems already in place—battling alien cultures and environments.

Contrasting nicely with the squeaky-clean Robinson clan and West, Harris's portrayal made Smith the show's breakout character. Allen also added a robot that provided a human-versus-machine theme and made millions of children want one of their own. Allen's unaired pilot was titled "No Place to Hide." It shows the Robinson family and West launching into space on October 16, 1997, to explore the universe for other habitable planets, as the earth suffers from overpopulation. The story provides more detail on the crew's background.

Dr. John Robinson is a professor of astrophysics at the University of Stellar Dynamics; Dr. Maureen Robinson is a biochemist at the New Mexico College of Space Medicine and the first female astronaut in the International Space Administration; nine-year-old Will Robinson is a graduate of the Camdo Canyon School of Science, with the highest grade point average in school history; nineteen-year-old Judy Robinson is a musical comedy actress; eleven-year-old Penny Robinson has the hobby of zoology and a genius IQ of 147; and Dr. Don West is a graduate student at the Center for Radio Astronomy, where he discovered the plausibility of habitability on other planets. In "Stowaway," Don West is a major in the U.S. Space Corps, the Robinsons' mission has a price tag of $30 billion, and the spaceship's name changes from *Gemini 12* to *Jupiter 2*.

In real life, space launches were perfect moments for television. A televised rocket launch became an event propelling the hopes of beating the Soviets in space. Settling into his spacecraft while the Eastern Seaboard entered the REM stage of sleep on the morning of February 20, 1962, a Marine colonel tackled his checklist—a laborious but necessary task—to assure the successful performance of his craft, instruments, and space suit. Strapped inside a capsule at the top of a ninety-three-foot rocket, John Herschel Glenn Jr. was at that moment the most isolated person in the world—a price that the Mercury astronauts paid as they guided their spacecraft, tethered to the earth only by radio transmissions to and from Mission Control. They perpetuated the American tradition of trailblazing in the face of long odds, hardships, and sacrifice.

Glenn was the third astronaut to venture into space; Alan Shepard and Gus Grissom had made suborbital trips in 1961. Educated by his Marine training to stay poised but ready for the next mission, Glenn remained calm while awaiting the chance to put his ten launch delays behind him. A frustrated nation, eager to surpass the Soviets—who had vaulted forward in the space race with Yuri Gagarin's orbit ten months earlier—took solace in Glenn's words: "Just tell them to relax," Glenn said. "They should stay relaxed. I've been at this thing for three years now. I feel fine. Sure, we regret the delays. But as [Mercury astronaut] Scott Carpenter said, it gives us a chance to hone our capabilities."[35]

NASA honored the original seven astronauts by ascribing the number 7 to each Mercury flight. Glenn's capsule, ultimately bestowed with the name *Friendship 7*, had undergone scrutiny from Glenn's children, who considered a list of possible names for the spaceship: Liberty, Union, Independence, Brother,

Advocate, Companion, Partner, Defender, Resolute, Harmony, Republic, Freedom, Voyager, Faith, Faithful, Peace, Hope.[36]

Glenn was a red-white-and-blue icon with a "gee whiz" persona fit for the benign plots of the sitcoms dominating television during the late 1950s and early 1960s. With an inner toughness hardened, heightened, and honed by discipline in the U.S. Marine Corps, Glenn had excelled as a pilot, flying fifty-nine combat missions in the Pacific theater during World War II and sixty-three during the Korean War. Piloting the first supersonic, transcontinental flight crowned his military career. His gung-ho attitude underlined a life propelled by duty—to family, to country, and of course to the Marines.

With a stellar aviation record, Glenn applied to NASA, entering a selection process involving medical tests at the Lovelace Clinic in Albuquerque and Wright-Patterson Air Force Base in Dayton, Ohio; the latter was familiar to Glenn, a born-and-bred Buckeye. "They drew blood, took urine, and stool samples, scraped our throats, measured the contents of our stomachs, gave us barium enemas, and submerged us in water tanks to record our total body volume," recalled Glenn in his 1999 memoir. "They shone lights into our eyes, ears, noses, and everywhere else. They measured our heart and pulse rates, blood pressure, brain waves, and muscular reactions to electric current. Their examination of the lower bowel was the most uncomfortable procedure I had ever experienced, a sigmoidal probe with a device those of us who were tested nicknamed the 'Steel Eel.'"[37]

As Glenn sat in his *Friendship 7* capsule, excitement rumbled down the Florida coastline near Cape Canaveral with shouts filling the air. In the *New York Times*, Gay Talese described the reaction of a man "clenching his fist" while summing his feelings in three words: "Go, baby, go!" Contrasting the cheers, Talese noticed, silence pervaded some quarters: "Perhaps the crowd was quieter because it had been let down by the postponements, or maybe it thought there was no cause for cheering until Colonel Glenn had safely returned."[38]

During the flight, America's latest hero reported to NASA's medical staff that he had "no sensations at all from weightlessness except very pleasant."[39] His blood pressure was 126 over 90, an amazing example of calm in humankind's greatest challenge.[40] Humor suffered no consequence either; he told Mission Control, "I want you to send a message to the Director, er, to the

41

Commandant, U.S. Marine Corps, Washington. Tell him I have my 4 hours required flight time in for the month and request flight chit be established for me. Over."[41]

Glenn had completed three orbits when NASA questioned whether the capsule's landing bag had prematurely deployed, thereby detaching the heat shields. Although scheduled for seven orbits, *Friendship 7* got an order to return. "The package of retro-rockets that would slow the capsule for reentry was strapped over the heat shield," wrote Glenn. "But it would jettison, and what then? If the heat shield dropped out of place, I could be incinerated on reentry, and this was the first confirmation of that possibility."[42] Mission Control calculated that the pressure of the air would force the shields to stay in place. Flight operations director Walter Williams said, "I think it was only a false indication, but we weren't taking any chances."[43]

Weather offered a bright spot for Glenn's splashdown: visibility of ten miles, three-foot waves, minimal clouds.[44] America's first orbital mission ended with the capsule gliding to the Pacific Ocean "within one mile" of the recovery ship, the USS *Noa*, with Glenn describing the spacecraft's reentry as a "real fireball." There was relief from Houston to Honolulu. On board the *Noa*, Glenn underwent debriefing. As an honorary member of the crew, he received a $15 bonus, which he donated to the ship's welfare fund.[45]

NASA, of course, had planned for every contingency. Five weeks before the launch of *Friendship 7*, an internal memorandum outlined strategies to mitigate damage to the Mercury program if Glenn died: "Death of the pilot would likely provoke an enormous public reaction critical of the entire United States manned space effort—particularly in light of the two Soviet manned orbital successes. Therefore, our national leaders must face the possibility of such an eventuality and deal with it in realistic perspective. We must treat that type of accident in the light of an on-going program."[46]

A list of potential disasters included an explosion on the launching pad with no spacecraft abort, a malfunction in the retrorockets or attitude control system (which would cause Glenn to be stranded in orbit), failure of parachutes during splashdown, and search planes being unable to locate the capsule in the ocean. The memorandum incorporated probable text for a statement from President Kennedy in the event of Glenn's death: "To Mrs.

Glenn and members of the Glenn family go my deepest sympathy. It was my pleasure to have known John Glenn. This nation and the entire world share his loss with the Glenn family. Space scientists will revere his pioneering spirit forever."[47]

Vice President Johnson's statement would have pivoted toward the next generation despite the tragedy: "The death of John Glenn in performance of the scientific space-flight experiment to which he had dedicated his talents is a profound and personal loss to me. I propose that the Government establish in his name a permanent scholarship for promising space science students to advance the vital effort in space exploration in which he was engaged."[48] Likewise, a statement by NASA's administrator would have highlighted the space agency's "heartfelt dedication and renewed vigor" to pursue "experiments to extend man's capacity to fly and acquire scientific data for the benefit of all mankind."[49]

Astronauts were already heroes in the public eye, but the *Friendship 7* flight made Glenn a legend for being the first American to orbit the earth. Glenn's duty now revolved around ambassadorial tasks for NASA, including a ticker-tape parade in Manhattan and a worldwide tour. He was the hero of the moment, but it was a fête least expected by the honoree. In the 1962 book *We Seven*, authored by the seven Mercury astronauts, Glenn revealed, "I had known all along, of course, that the pilot of a successful orbital mission was going to get quite a bit of attention. But I could not possibly have been prepared for the tremendous reception which we received when we arrived back in the U.S. It seemed as if this national accomplishment had stirred the nation's pride. As the focus of that pride, I felt overwhelmed."[50]

Opportunities to honor—and profit from—Glenn's flight overflowed.

An unemployed man from Oil City, Pennsylvania, designed a cup and saucer to mark the flight's importance.[51] Glenn, always cordial, thanked the man but declined to participate in any promotion for the design.[52]

Robert Hall Clothes produced a booklet titled "What to Wear in Outer Space" and sent it to Glenn, and America's newest hero responded with gratitude in a letter.[53] There was then a follow-up request regarding a Robert Hall book project to benefit UNICEF and a request to use an excerpt from Glenn's letter. There's no indication that Glenn allowed it.[54]

Approximately ten minutes after *Friendship 7* launched, the Board of Education of the North St. Paul–Maplewood Schools sent a telegram to Glenn announcing that a new junior high school would be named after him.[55]

In Arlington County, Virginia, Special Justice "U. R. Topps" signed a "Warrant of Arrest" for Glenn alleging that Glenn did "take, steal, and carry away certain property, consisting of: the admiration and hearts of his fellow countrymen, and of a value of an indeterminate sum."[56]

A graduate student at Pennsylvania State University authored a paper titled "The Image of John H. Glenn, Jr." to fulfill an academic requirement in her pursuit of a PhD.

Letters from schoolchildren numbered in the thousands.

Some came from PS 71 in the Bronx. Principal Rose E. Skala, a tall woman who signaled her approach in the halls by the loud clicking of her heels on the floor, ruled this institution on Roberts Avenue with the stern governance required to maintain discipline of children on the cusp of adolescence, when rebellion, hormones, and know-it-all attitudes dominate (the school is now named for her). In the Westchester Avenue apartment belonging to the family of PS 71 sixth-grader Tina Privitera, conversation about astronauts was as much a fixture at the dinner table as their traditional meals of manicotti, lasagna, leg of lamb with onions and homemade gravy, chicken cutlets, and a Christmas tradition of pizza with prosciutto and black olives, baked by Tina's Sicily-born mother. Her father had a fascination with space:

> My father, Paul, was a tech sergeant in the air force and a tail gunner in World War II. He used to talk about the universe and how mysterious and big it was. There were so many things we didn't know about it. He was fascinated, and that's what I was feeling with John Glenn's flight. It was just unbelievable that we could go into space. . . .
>
> I had four aunts and uncles. They all lived in the area, and we were always together on holidays and special occasions at my paternal grandparents' house. I sat there and absorbed their conversation about space. On the day of the [*Friendship 7*] flight, I was one of the students chosen to go downstairs in the auditorium to watch the liftoff. It was beautiful and astounding. I think I had a crush on John Glenn because of his bravery.

Space is still very important to me. Secretly, I had a fleeting fantasy to be a spacewoman because it represented breaking out and exploring the unknown.[57]

A special edition of the school's yearbook, *Spirit of '71*, published students' stories about Glenn's heroics. Tina penned a tale framing her as a grandmother telling her grandchildren about the historic flight; she used her siblings' names for the children.

Laura Napier, a friend of the Glenns, authored a personal note of congratulations. "I grew up in New Concord, Ohio, where John is from. The town was ecstatic," explains Napier's daughter, Nancy Napier Cain. "We felt like we could share the spotlight with him and have the town recognized. When John was in the Korean War, Annie and her kids stayed at her parents', who lived across the street from me. When John came home, he'd buzz the neighborhood with his plane, so Annie would know it was time to pick him up at the airport. My family knew him from the time he was a young man and always thought highly of him as an ethical, honest man. They were proud of his accomplishments as an ace, an astronaut, and an upstanding senator. But it was special to be able to say that I knew him personally."[58]

Another Napier daughter is Marj Bryan. She recalls that

our maternal grandmother lived with us, and she was good friends with Annie's mom. We played with the Glenn kids, David and Caroline. Their grandmother's house was fantastic for hide-and-seek; the attic rooms were all interconnected.

We weren't used to having excitement in our small town. The news people were exciting to us because we looked at them as stars. My mother was in a bridge club, and they heard one of the news anchors was in town for several days. They invited him to the club and he came. We just thought it was really cool to get a glimpse of him.

And then of course it was exciting for us when John and Annie came to town for the parade. Probably as exciting as the flight itself. I played the flute in the marching band, so I got to be in the parade. For a number of years afterward, I used to think that this is my ten minutes of fame because I made up part of the crowd for this celebration.

> I think the space program was so important for our country because it was a moment in time where the country really pulled together. It was a point of pride for everybody that we could do this. Everybody was on the same page. It was very uplifting. Something to be proud of.[59]

Richard Gordin, a native of Washington DC, idolized Glenn and the rest of the Mercury astronauts. His fascination began when the Soviet Union launched Sputnik—the first artificial satellite—in 1957:

> I was in fourth grade. You could see Sputnik going overhead. It was a very clear night. Alan Shepard's launch was broadcast over the loudspeaker in my school. There was nothing bigger than space travel to kids my age. The seven Mercury astronauts were American heroes. I was always a little bit science oriented, but everyone followed the space program. The astronauts were always in the newspapers.
>
> We contacted John Glenn through a guy named Nathan Schwartz, whom my family knew. He had clothing store on the north side of F Street, between Thirteenth and Fourteenth Streets. Even though a space launch hadn't happened, the astronauts were celebrities. I didn't fully understand the space race with Russia, but we heard about the capability of rockets delivering an atom bomb. In elementary school we had drills where we practiced hiding under our desks.
>
> America was doing this incredible thing. You didn't have a lot of cynicism, so you could buy into what was going on. You believed we were going to win the space race. Nobody prepared us for the possibility of Russia landing on the moon first. Glenn was, to me, the number-one hero of the space program. I can tell you the other names, but Glenn was the guy who orbited first. He stood out.[60]

As astronauts personally gained tremendous status, so did Houston, long considered a sleepy city on a bayou. It gained a reputation as a metropolis of importance thanks in part to Glenn's successful mission. Synonymous with progress, Houston became a part of the American lexicon because it had the headquarters of NASA. It became an urban hub with worldwide recognition. New York had finance. Los Angeles had entertainment. But the country's attention was focused on the astronauts, which meant Houston being mentioned in every story—print, radio, or television—about space. Glenn's orbit was a shot of adrenaline for Americans looking to gallop past—or at least pace—the Soviets in their space achievements.

It was a great time to be a Houstonian. For baseball fans, it was about to be greater.

3

Shooting 'Em Down

On any given day in March 1962, Roy Hofheinz awoke with a sense of fulfillment as the sun crept into the sky over southeastern Texas. Each dawn meant
that Houston was one day closer to shedding its status as a Minor League city.
Anticipation reigned in the stately homes in River Oaks, the neighborhood
where business executives drank freshly squeezed orange juice as they glanced
at the latest musings of Mickey Herskowitz in the *Houston Post* and of Dick
Peebles and Clark Nealon in the *Houston Chronicle*; in the dormitories at the
University of Houston and Rice University, where baseball talk among the male
student body equaled in excitement the discussions about spring break; in the
morning *minyan* at the Meyerland neighborhood's Congregation Beth Israel,
where Jews recited their morning prayers in Houston's oldest congregation;
in the middle-class, suburban homes of Westbury, named by the real-estate
developer after the town in New York where he had previously been located;
in Sharpstown Mall, opened the previous September as the latest marketplace

for Houston shoppers; in the Joske's, Foley's, and Sakowitz department stores as shoppers looked for bargains, gifts, and the latest offerings; in the River Oaks Theatre, designed in the art deco style; and in Eastwood, where the aroma of coffee from the Maxwell House plant triggered a Pavlovian reflex for a cup of joe.

The city's Minor League team, the Buffaloes, had given Houstonians great baseball enjoyment for the past thirty years. But the new Major League team—the Colt .45s—meant that Major League players would visit Houston. That meant the likes of Willie Mays, Don Drysdale, Ernie Banks. And the new expansion team even had a fight song reflecting the team moniker: "Shoot 'Em Down."

Hofheinz tasked the Houston Sports Association with the responsibility of bringing a Major League Baseball team to the city named for General Sam Houston, whose Texian army had defeated General Santa Anna, Mexico's president, in the eighteen-minute Battle of San Jacinto. An independent country, the Republic of Texas, had resulted from the defeat of Mexico; it lasted about ten years. To be a Texan is to be proud of a heritage steeped in independence.

Later a judge and a mayor of Houston, Hofheinz not only recognized every political, business, and social button that needed to be pushed in Harris County, he also knew every button's size, shape, and the exact amount of pressure required. His résumé boasted influence: elected to the Texas legislature at twenty-three, elected county judge, elected Houston's mayor, and tapped as adviser to Lyndon B. Johnson during the future president's ascent in Congress to the all-powerful position of Senate majority leader. Roy Hofheinz's son Fred, who continued his father's civic legacy by serving a term as Houston's mayor in the 1970s, recalls,

My dad started his career by being a concert promoter to support his mother. . . . He was a consummate public speaker. He often told me that it's more important how you say something than what you say. His political experience made him a great salesman.

He bought the Houston Buffaloes of the American Association because the National League wouldn't grant the Houston territory. That's when the HSA [Houston Sports Association] formed. Then, they disbanded the

Buffaloes to get the franchise rights. Weather problems made it an awful environment to have a Major League team. They built Colt Stadium quickly. I worked on the radio and television side. Most of the Major League teams sold their broadcasting rights to producers. My dad put together his own network and sold the rights. We had fifteen to twenty radio stations in the region, but we had to be careful not to step on other teams' territories, for example, the St. Louis Cardinals. We produced our own show and sold the advertising. He hired two account executives from New York City to manage the network. When the Colt .45s became the Astros in 1965, we had an Astro beauty queen contest, with an entry from each station in our network.

Houston has great natural resources that have provided wealth, which has been plowed back into the city. It was a major civic effort to bring a Major League Baseball team to Houston, headed by my dad's leadership.[1]

The city's professional baseball lineage began in 1888, when Houston played in the Texas League. The Houston Buffaloes were a Minor League icon for decades; they won the Texas League championship in 1931. Managed by Joe Schultz, a former National League journeyman with a career batting average of .285, the "Buffs" compiled a dominant 108-51 record. Its schedule was algebraic.

For the first half of the 1931 season, the Buffaloes tied the Beaumont Exporters with 50-30 records. According to the league's constitution, five games in the second half held the distinction of being playoff games, while still getting credited for the regular standings. By the end of the season Houston had a cushion of fourteen games distancing it from second-place Beaumont.

Two future Hall of Famers played for the 1931 Buffaloes—Joe Medwick and Dizzy Dean. Indefatigable, Dean plowed through Houston's 1931 Texas League competition, compiling a 26-10 record and 1.57 earned run average. Nineteen-year-old Medwick, nicknamed "Ducky" for his gait, hit .305, impressing the Cardinals' front office enough to call him up to the Majors; he joined the team in the middle of the 1932 season, played in twenty-six games, and ended his rookie tenure with a .349 batting average. It was the beginning of an amazing career that ended with a .324 batting average, nearly 2,500 hits, and an MVP Award. The Baseball Hall of Fame website states, "Though Medwick could hit for power, it didn't come at the expense of his ability to put the bat to the ball, as he never struck out more than one hundred times in a season. He was a well-rounded hitter, capable of going outside of the strike zone to drive in runs when needed."[2]

In the 1931 Dixie Series, the Buffaloes faced the Birmingham Barons, champions of the Southern Association. With the series tied at three games apiece, Dizzy Dean started game seven. But his prowess on the mound was not sufficient—Birmingham won 6–3 to capture the Dixie Series crown.

Buff Stadium, a cutting-edge facility, was the home field for the Buffaloes. In their 2013 book *The Houston Astros: Deep in the Heart—Blazing a Trail from Expansion to World Series*, Bill Brown and Mike Acosta write that the venue "was considered a state-of-the-art ballpark by minor league standards and it featured a Spanish-style tiled roof entryway. Buff Stadium became known as a pitcher's park, measuring 344 feet to the left field line, 434 to center and 323 to right with 12-foot walls."[3]

With an innate sense of salesmanship, Hofheinz resolved to break the structure of an eight-team National League. Initially, Houston had a toehold in the Continental League, created to compete with the AL and the NL for fans in a 154-game season. Branch Rickey's involvement as the CL president brought credibility; he had four World Series titles as the Cardinals' general manager, and, in that role for the Dodgers, he helped break baseball's racial divide by signing Jackie Robinson. Behind the scenes, William Shea, a lawyer with political ties to the Democratic Party in New York City, had a fiat from Mayor Robert Wagner to bring the National League back after the Dodgers and the Giants departed for Los Angeles and San Francisco, respectively, in the wake of the 1957 season. The Continental League would be the next best thing. Although the plans for the CL evaporated, Shea saw his efforts rewarded when the National League agreed to give Houston and New York expansion teams— the Colt .45s and the Mets. The American League expanded as well, with the Los Angeles Angels and the second incarnation of the Washington Senators.

To George Kirksey, a newspaper journalist turned publicist, Texas appeared ripe for an ascent to the Major Leagues, with Houston as the launching pad. With his public-relations expertise, Kirksey had to "convince the rest of America that the capital of everything fine and grand lay in a steamy city on the banks of Buffalo Bayou not far from the Gulf of Mexico."[4] But first he needed to get Houston's power base on board. The inaugural step into the city's baseball future happened during a meeting at a Houston bank on January 4, 1957, when thirty-five business leaders listened to Kirksey describe his vision.[5] As a result, the Houston Sports Association (HSA) was created and an executive committee named. Craig Cullinan Jr., whose grandfather had built Texaco, served as the first president of the HSA. Its mission was twofold: promote the idea of a Major League team in Houston while navigating the minefield of city politics that controlled how, when, and where money would be spent. Cullinan attributed the forming of the HSA and his involvement to Kirksey's "considerable powers of persuasion."[6]

The publicity-savvy Kirksey was a master at putting the pieces together, which was no small task considering that he had to balance his spin with the sense of practicality that permeated the city's power base in politics, finance, and real estate. "Kirksey liked best the clandestine meetings, set up through whispered phone calls, conducted on lonely highways near airports in limousines with darkened windows," wrote biographer Campbell Titchener. "There Kirksey would prod old friends and associates to tell him what was going on with the major league owners, what they were thinking, who might be willing to move, how much money they were talking about."[7]

Making Houston a Major League city was not impossible, but it appeared at the beginning of the effort to be an unlikely scenario. "HSA had no money to speak of, no major league stadium, and, most important of all, no franchise," said Cullinan. "The routine became tediously familiar: get a stadium and we will talk to you about a team, Kirksey and I were told on trips to major league cities. Returning to Houston, we were told to find a team and the city might talk about building a stadium."[8]

When the Continental League seemed viable, Kirksey et al. pored through research, projections, and proposals to bolster their argument for inclusion. A 1958 Houston Sports Association press release underscores the importance of baseball to the burgeoning metropolis of 1,195,000; projections indicated a doubling of the population by 1975. On July 26, 1958, Harris County voters overwhelmingly okayed the building of a "new multi-purpose stadium and indoor coliseum" by issuing $20 million in revenue bonds. According to an

HSA press release, "It was one of the largest margins any bond issue ever carried in Harris County history."[9]

A team-naming contest for the Houston ball club garnered approximately ten thousand entries from around the world, with the winner being "Colt .45s," to represent the lore of the West. The name lasted for three seasons. Thereafter it was the Astros. "We had to get rid of the Colt .45s name because of the Colt .45 liquor trademark," explains Fred Hofheinz. "The Harris County commissioners that voted to fund the dome wanted to name it Harris County Domed Stadium. My dad couldn't sell that. He needed a catchy name. Stardome was going to be the name of the park and the Houston Stars would be the name of the team. It was floating for a couple of weeks."[10]

Dinn Mann, a grandson of Judge Roy Hofheinz, sheds further light on the team-naming process:

> The name Astros was the brainchild of my grandfather. He came up with Astros after saying the team would be as connected to NASA and the boldness of the space program as the astronauts themselves. He assembled the entire family, giddy at the originality and forward-thinking message of the franchise's re-branding, the uniqueness in what it conveyed and the place it represented. And he proclaimed the Colt .45s would become the Astros.
>
> Those on hand for dinner that early evening said he stood there, cigar in hand, smiling from ear to ear like the father of a new prince. He repeated the name: Astros, the Houston Astros. We had our identity. New York had the Yankees. This was the answer. We had our frontier and the Astrodome was mission control. The Astros, our flag in the planet. Bob Smith [a local civic leader] was, of course, involved, facilitating the wheels in motion. But the name itself was invented, perfectly pitched to the public and launched by Judge Roy Hofheinz.[11]

CEOs, particularly those in the Lone Star State, envisioned their corporate monikers being attached to the ballpark. It would be a coup of epic proportions to be the leader who obtained the naming rights for the ballpark. But neither money nor influence swayed the judge. "My dad had many opportunities to sell naming rights," says Fred Hofheinz. "The answer was always no. He sold naming rights for the scoreboard but never the stadium. About halfway through the construction, he wanted to sell seats to corporations and upper-income people. He had to alter the western façade to accommodate fifty-two skyboxes. We were the first to do that anywhere in the world. They had twenty seats apiece. He sold them out. The county didn't pay for their construction. That all came out of the Houston Sports Association. We were also the first to have an electronic scoreboard."[12]

Houston ignited its Major League status with victory. On April 10, 1962, the Colt .45s overtook the Cubs 11–2 at Colt Stadium; Houston's infant team swept the Cubs in the series. Bob Aspromonte, Al Spangler, and Román Mejías each scored three runs in the Opening Day bout while Norm Larker and Hal Smith scored one apiece. Mejías smacked the first home run for Houston.

Although off to a prodigious start for their inaugural season, the Colt .45s finished 1962 at 64-96. The lineup consisted of a ladies' man; a Latino ballplayer symbolizing the increasing contributions of Latino ballplayers in the Major Leagues; two players with tempers that could rival TNT for explosiveness; a pitcher who faced tragedy with courage and grace; a rabble-rouser with a new perspective on his career; a twenty-year-old with a bonus that would make Messrs. Wells and Fargo blush; a future Astros manager; and a teenage prospect.

The Bachelor

Houston selected third baseman Bob Aspromonte in the National League expansion draft for 1962. "My favorite memory of 1962 is Opening Day at Colt Stadium," says Aspromonte, who had three hits that day. The Brooklyn native has made a home in Houston since that inaugural year—he retired after the '71 season. He recalls,

> It was exciting to be a part of a new franchise. I think it was a combination of very young ballplayers getting an opportunity and then being surrounded by veterans on those early Houston teams, including [J. Nelson] Nellie Fox and Pete Runnels.
>
> Dick Farrell had a really great impact on the ball club. Bob Bruce was fantastic. Hal Woodeshick was another one. You looked at how they handled themselves. They were very influential in making us work hard but also telling us to enjoy the game. Norm Larker and Hal Smith were older but

played regularly. They dedicated themselves on a 100 percent basis. It's so important to see older players have that influence. Paul Richardson, the general manager, was great in how he selected and handled these players. He took myself and younger players when there were other options.[13]

Aspromonte fit nicely into the cultural template built upon a "boys will be boys" philosophy in the 1960s, the decade when Joe Namath swaggered while Dean Martin swigged, offering touchstones for male fantasies of being successful, famous, and adored by women.[14]

A lifetime .252 hitter, Aspromonte spent most of his thirteen-year career with the Houston Astros, né Colt .45s. A couple of months before the Colt .45s inaugurated Major League Baseball in Houston, sportswriter Mickey Herskowitz heralded the Brooklyn native: "The Brooklyn bachelor is so handsome that you hate him instantly . . . except that Bob won't let you. He never loses his sunny humor, no matter how much kidding he gets about being a ladykiller."[15]

In a 1969 profile, *Sporting News* scribe Al Thomy wrote, "Interviewing Bob Aspromonte in a posh restaurant staffed by micro-mini clad young ladies, is not unlike trying to carry on a conversation with a harried sultan in a chattering harem. It is most difficult to keep his attention."[16]

Attention from females, though an ego boost, boomeranged at times. "All this talk about being a bachelor and the Valentino of baseball doesn't help a bit when I make an error," explained Aspromonte in the Thomy piece. "It comes back at you from the stands pretty often. Once in Houston, after a bonehead play of mine, a fan yelled out, 'Hey, Hollywood boy, what are you doing out there on a baseball field? You ought to be in pictures!'"[17]

Aspromonte started his career in 1956 with the Brooklyn Dodgers, playing in only one game before being sent down. After spending three seasons in the Minors, he rejoined the Dodgers, in Los Angeles by this time. A two-year tenure in Tinseltown gave Aspromonte a gateway to starlets, though discretion was the better part of valor for the baseball bachelor. "I don't like to throw names around," Aspromonte said. "Frankly, I am not interested in having people know my private business. But I will say I have met actresses who are delightful companions, intellectually stimulating and have intense interests in their careers."[18]

During his tenure in Houston, Aspromonte entered Texas baseball lore when he knocked three home runs to fulfill promises to Bill Bradley, a twelve-year-old who suffered blindness and later enjoyed the restoration of eyesight; it is a feat particularly noteworthy because Aspromonte, though a reliable hitter, hit only sixty home runs in his Major League career.[19]

Aspromonte played seven seasons in Houston, two in Atlanta, and one in New York with the Mets. After his playing days, he beat out three thousand applicants for a Coors distributorship.

Roman Mejías's Big Break

Román Mejías also vaulted into the hearts of Houstonians, playing in 146 games, swatting 162 hits, and finishing the 1962 season with a .286 batting average.

Initially a product of the Pittsburgh Pirates organization, Mejías played with the Batavia Clippers in the Pennsylvania-Ontario–New York ("Pony") League in 1953 and the Waco Pirates in the Big State League in 1954. Batting .322 with Batavia and .354 with Waco—where he also notched a fifty-five-game hitting streak—Mejías caught the attention of the Pittsburgh club's brass. Waco sportswriter Oscar Larnce quoted Pirates business manager C. L. "Buster" Chatham on the slugger's prowess: "I don't see how Mejías can miss. He can do everything and is improving every day. He was in Class D last year, then jumped into a tough Class B league and still gets better."[20] Branch Rickey, then the Pirates' general manager, concurred: "Mejías is sure to go all the way. He defends well, runs well, has a good arm and good power."[21]

After six seasons in Pittsburgh, Mejías left. It was a dearth of opportunities that propelled the outfielder toward Houston; Mejías never played in more than ninety-six games with the Pirates—in 1960 and 1961 he played a total of seven games. Plus, the language barrier dampened Mejías's prospects. The Cuban native told a reporter how difficult it was for him to manage without being able to speak English. He reported being lonely and unable to order meals. "I thought I would have to go back to Cuba for food," he said. Someone finally taught him how to order ham and eggs and fried chicken, so he ate that for a long time.[22]

Two home runs and six RBIs on Opening Day reinforced his confidence, which had weakened because of Pittsburgh's treatment of him. Mejías said his successes on that first day made him a "new man." He had been disgusted when the Pirates sent him down to Columbus, because he felt like he was ready to play in the Majors. He thought he was finished until he got the opportunity with the new Houston team.[23]

Mejías had racked up eleven home runs by the end of May. In Houston he had the opportunities that Pittsburgh couldn't offer because of the lineup's strength, a factor that Mejías understood but suffered. "Playing every day is my big break," acknowledged Mejías. "At Pittsburgh I had little chance to break into the line-up [sic] with Skinner, Virdon and Clemente. What hurts is when you know you can help the team but they won't give you a chance. I have been given my chance."[24]

Because of political strife in Cuba during the early years of Fidel Castro's regime, Mejías endured a separation from his wife, son, daughter, and two sisters for fourteen months. After the '62 season, the Colt .45s traded Mejías to the Red Sox for Pete Runnels, and Fenway Park's brain trust strategized to bring the Mejías clan to the United States. It was a stealth operation: "The Red Sox very quietly went about assisting Mejías in his plight. There was no publicity on the Mejías predicament by request of certain officials who felt that any publicity might endanger the family's chance for release from the Castro-dominated island," the *Boston Globe* reported. "Exactly how much the Red Sox and owner Tom Yawkey did for this 31-year-old man will never be told. Yawkey won't let it be told."[25] However it was accomplished, the Red Sox organization did its legacy proud in securing safe transport for Mejías's family in March 1963.

Mejías ended his career in a Red Sox uniform after the 1964 season.

A Temper Grows in Houston

A native of western Pennsylvania, Norm Larker spent nine years in the Minor Leagues before joining the Dodgers in 1958. Nicknamed "Dumbo" because of his ears, Larker anticipated larger exposure in Houston, admitting, "I'm not knocking the Dodger organization. They treated me just fine. But I've finally gotten out from behind the shadow of Gil Hodges."[26]

Larker had a temper and an ulcer—the latter undoubtedly caused by the former—which defined Larker in the press: he was "trigger-tempered," "terrible-tempered," and a "terrible tempered first baseman."[27] Another article reported that "when his temper boils over almost anything is apt to happen."[28]

Houston Chronicle executive sports editor Dick Peebles defended Larker when the Dodgers sold his contract to the nascent Colt .45s after the 1961 season. In his "Voice of the Peebles" column he noted that Larker had one kidney, an ulcer, a deceased father whose demise had happened in "a mine accident," and a deceased brother who had died during surgery. Larker was "an affectionate and congenial man," in Peebles's analysis, which also highlights eight years in the Minor Leagues, waiting for Hodges to retire, and placing second in National League batting averages by just a couple of points. In addition, Larker did not get tabbed as a starter the following season. "After all those things happen to one man, it's a wonder he doesn't have a slit throat. Self-inflicted," Peebles wrote.[29]

Peebles's mention of the batting average referred to 1960, when Dick Groat of the Pirates eclipsed Larker by a couple of points—.325 to .323. It was not a contest governed by purity. In a Cardinals-Dodgers game a couple of days before the 1960 regular season ended, left fielder Bob Nieman trapped a Larker fly ball; the umpires ruled it an out. "Sure, I trapped the ball. It hit right down the line, about six inches from my glove. The umpire was looking at it straight-on. If he had been at an angle, he would have seen it," Nieman said. "The writers asked me about it after the game. What could I say? If I said I trapped the ball I'd have four National League umpires on my neck. I admitted it to Larker, and told him I was sorry, and that just made him madder."[30]

Larker's temper manifested in a Colt .45s game against the Braves on August 1, 1962. When umpire Augie Donatelli sent the first baseman to the egress for arguing a called strike, it was a decision met with as much acquiescence as the Jets showed the Sharks in *West Side Story*.

Larker threw eighteen bats out of the dugout in defiance of Donatelli, who also ejected Al Spangler for trekking from first base to join the battle with his teammate. Spangler's appellate skills marked a deeper severity toward Donatelli, who benefited from Milwaukee backstop Del Crandall stepping into the heat to cool things off or at least prevent an escalation in the violence. Crandall "helped restrain Spangler when his former teammate became even more aggressive than Larker in his attitude toward the umpire."[31]

Teammates were not immune from Larker's temper either. Dodgers skipper Walter Alston tamped down the rage emerging from a brawl between Larker and Maury Wills in 1961, one that began during infield practice at the Los Angeles Memorial Coliseum before a game against the Cubs. Bob Hunter's exclusive story in the *Los Angeles Examiner* cited an anonymous source in the Cubs organization for the chain of events: Wills reacted to Larker's batting of fungoes—that he "figured were too close to his head"—by throwing a ball and hitting Larker in the knee. Verbal insults led to a physical clash during the Dodgers' pregame meeting in the clubhouse. Alston disclosed that he accepted their apologies, fined neither player, and reconciled the issue because he believed Larker and Wills were "regretting their spur of the moment anger."[32]

Of Tantrums and Temple

John Ellis "Johnny" Temple was Larker's temper twin. He began his Major League career in Cincinnati in 1952 and stayed there through the 1961 season. "I'm a holler guy and a take-charge guy," declared the second baseman in a 1957 interview by the Associated Press. "I have the spirit, hustle and aggressiveness. I get on base. I field my position well. I can make the double play. What else can they ask of a second baseman[?] They can't say I'm not colorful."[33] Temple further explained that in 1956, when he received a selection to the National League All-Star team, baseball enthusiasts on the East Coast "moaned" to show their opposition. "Why? Because I don't play in New York City."[34]

Temple began as a "darkhorse candidate for the regular keystone assignment with the Redlegs," according to a 1952 press release in his Baseball Hall of Fame file.[35] Although he saw some playing time in 1952 (thirty games) and 1953 (sixty-three games), he did not became a regular player until 1954. During spring training, Reds skipper Birdie Tebbets beamed, "He's the toughest little monkey I've come across in a long time. Up to now he's called every man on the team a dirty name except me, and I expect to be next. He's a real throwback to the old days."[36]

If there were an All-Star team for pugnacity, Temple would have joined the likes of Ty Cobb, Leo Durocher, and John McGraw.

Temple's outbursts traveled into the fourth estate after a Reds-Pirates game on June 21, 1957, when *Cincinnati Times-Star* sportswriter Earl Lawson, the game's official scorer, marked an error for Temple because a ball, hit by Pirates backstop Hank Foiles, "went through the second baseman." National League president Warren Giles issued a $100 fine. Reportedly, Temple apologized the following day "to Lawson and Redleg players in a closed clubhouse meeting." Many players have been frustrated at a journalist's words or a scorer's decision, but a rise to violence is as rare as an Ohio State Buckeye rooting for the Michigan Wolverines. "It was just a flare-up of temper on my part," stated Temple. "I was mad, wouldn't you be? I'm sorry it happened. Earl's been real good to me. We've been good friends and will be good friends again." Lawson, however, was more descriptive about the source of Temple's fury: "Johnny Temple took a swing at me because I said, 'Why don't you grow up?' That was Friday night. This is Saturday morning. I still feel that Johnny Temple 'should grow up.' In fact, I feel he will grow up."[37]

Five years after that 1957 interview with AP, Temple revised his verbal preferences regarding leadership. "That isn't the right phrase to begin with. You don't take charge of a team. They give you the charge. Some clubs aren't capable of having a leader," said Temple toward the end of the 1962 season, his first of two in a Colt .45s uniform. He further explained that "it's a situation that creates itself. Pee Wee Reese at Brooklyn was the best I ever saw at it. If that surprises you, it's because he wasn't a holler guy. But taking charge doesn't mean you have to be a loudmouth. It's a matter of calling plays, giving the club a spark, chewing each other out when it's necessary, talking to the pitchers . . . lots of things."[38]

With emotions erupting like a west Texas oil well, Temple also had vulnerability, which ignited tears instead of temper when the Reds traded him to the Indians after the 1959 season. While worshippers celebrating Christmas and Chanukah—which began on Christmas Eve in 1959—shopped for presents, Temple "was crying like a baby," revealed Dick Forbes of the *Cincinnati Enquirer*. "For two minutes the telephone line was dead. Johnny couldn't talk."[39]

Trading Temple set off a seismic variance in his emotional baseline—all that he thought and in some way took for granted got yanked away. The fans. Crosley Field. Teammates. "I may sound corny[,] but it just seems like something is missing now. I don't know if I'll ever feel toward a ball club like I feel about the Redlegs," Temple revealed to Forbes.[40]

In a piece authored for the *Cincinnati Post and Times Star*, Temple points out his affection for the fans: "No matter where I go, I know the fans will never be nicer than you Red fans have been to me and my family. It seems to be there's a closeness between ballplayers and fans in Cincinnati that you never find any place else."[41]

In exchange for Temple, the Reds got pitcher Cal McLish and infielders Billy Martin and Gordon Coleman. Temple spent 1960 and 1961 with Cleveland and then joined the boys in Baltimore for 1962. He played in seventy-eight games for the Orioles before being sent to Houston, where he saw action in thirty-one games for the Colt .45s. But he brought more than baseball skills to the team; Temple had a spirit that infected the infant club on the field, in the dugout, and in the clubhouse. The '62 squad had a 19-14 record in its last thirty-three games. "The club was in a rut when I joined it," said Temple during 1963 spring training. "It needed perking up. It could have been anyone else as well as me. We need to change our thinking and we did. We could have won five of those six that last week. We weren't satisfied with our showing."[42]

Temple's career ended in Cincinnati during the 1964 season, unsurprisingly as a result of an uncapped temper. Back in the city whose affection he craved, Temple brawled with Reds coach Reggie Otero in the clubhouse before an August game against the Colt .45s; the game was postponed because of rain. Otero was the most convenient target for Temple's anger but not a justifiable one—when Otero offered a friendly greeting in the clubhouse, Temple pounced like a puma on its prey.[43] Reds management concluded that Temple had neither the ability nor the time to get into shape, and, with no coaching positions available, his only options were to leave the Reds or become a scout for the rest of the season. Temple later explained, "They wanted me to go to Houston. They wanted me to scout clubs coming into Houston. What they meant was that they were exiling me to Houston. They didn't say I was being fired, but that's what it amounts to."[44]

After his career, Temple's poor business decisions, bad investments, and drinking were precursors to a 1977 arrest for larceny as part of a ring. Temple testified for the prosecution to avoid prison.

To a Ballplayer Dying Young

When a ballplayer dies at the pinnacle of physical fitness, it's a reminder that those who perform the Herculean task of pitching a horsehide-covered sphere at 90 miles per hour or smacking that sphere four hundred feet are not gods. Lou Gehrig's "Luckiest Man" speech at Yankee Stadium three years before he died of amyotrophic lateral sclerosis, which chipped away at his body's ability to function in basic ways, stands as the hallmark of sadness in the national pastime. With his words echoing through the loudspeakers in the House That Ruth Built, on July 4, 1939, Gehrig was accepting of the disease that ultimately took his life at the age of thirty-seven. Courage, thy name is Henry Louis Gehrig.

Houston had its own reminder of courage in the face of illness—Jim Umbricht. Cancer won the battle against Umbricht, who died in 1964 at age thirty-three. A Chicago native, he broke into professional baseball with the Waycross Bears of the Georgia-Florida League in 1953, compiling a 4-3 record, 60 strikeouts, and a 2.87 ERA in ten games; he served in the U.S. Army for the next two years and returned to the mound in 1956, with the Baton Rouge Rebels of the Evangeline League. He spent three more seasons in the Minors before moving up to the Majors as a relief pitcher with the Pittsburgh Pirates in 1959. For 1960 and 1961 he played for the Pirates and their Triple-A club in Columbus and then pitched for Houston in 1962. Umbricht ended the season with a 4-0 record in thirty-four appearances. After surgery in 1963, he went 4-3 in thirty-five games.

The Night Owl

If Saint Paul the apostle were a baseball fan in the mid-twentieth century, his letter warning the Corinthians about debauchery might have targeted six-foot, four-inch, 220-pound Dick "Turk" Farrell, a polio survivor who went 10-20 in 1962, a record belying a formidable strikeout total of 203. He had six years of Major League pitching before becoming a Colt .45.

Farrell's physique, energy, and devil-may-care attitude created a tangible presence in and out of the clubhouse. He led a high life as a member of the "Dalton Gang," a group of four players on the Philadelphia Phillies in the late 1950s, including Jack Meyer, Seth Morehead, and Jim Owens. Barreling through life like a bull, Farrell lived with abandon, with no repercussions—or no regard for them. He pushed Larker into a pool in 1961 when they were teammates on the Dodgers.[45] After a loss to the Braves in 1959, he got the boot from a bar in Milwaukee when, with his pitching hand, he "broke a couple of mirrors" and "ripped off some coat hooks."[46] After the mirror incident, Grace Farrell stood up for her husband. "That morning I wasn't even out of bed, and my father came in waving the paper and yelling, 'Well, he did it again. He did it again,'" she related. "I told my father that if you don't like Dick the way he is, you just don't have to like him. That's just the way he is. Dick never makes excuses to anybody. He loves to have fun, and I would never try to change him."[47]

To Farrell, nighttime was an opportunity for joy, not rest. "Dick is a guy who doesn't care if the sun doesn't come up," declared Milwaukee Braves manager Bobby Bragan.[48] But Farrell's nocturnal outlook changed when he realized the financial consequences. "I discovered that I had a chance to make some money out of this game," revealed Farrell. "I'm 30 now, and I figure I've got four, maybe five good years left, and I don't want to waste them. So I grew up," he said. "After a while a guy has got to grow up, get serious, and baseball has treated me good. My father is the superintendent of a cemetery in Brookline, and if it wasn't for baseball, I'd probably be back there right now, digging graves for my old man."[49]

Still, it was his playboy image that endured. After Farrell got sent back to Philadelphia in 1967, *Houston Chronicle* sports columnist Wells Twombly combined wistfulness and sarcasm in a farewell: "A great personality is passing from our midst and henceforth the eyes of Texas will always be a trifle moist. So, let's show some respect. Let's leave our scotch and water glasses at half mast. Let's drape the Playmate of the Month in a black bikini. Let's burn all our private club cards in protest[;] Turk Farrell is gone."[50]

The Bonus Baby

Ernie Fazio notched a dozen games; the chances of playing rather than sitting on the bench provided an irresistible lure for the shortstop to sign with Houston, complemented by a reported $75,000 bonus. "I think the opportunities are greater with a new team," stated Fazio. "Then I met all the top men for the Colts, and I decided I couldn't play for a finer organization."[51]

Fazio signed with Houston on June 23, played an entire exhibition game on June 28 against a team consisting of players from the Texas League's Tulsa Oilers and Austin Senators, and played in his first Colt .45s game on July 3. Only twenty years old, Fazio showed some kinks in the beginning, but team manager Harry Craft remarked, "I'll tell you one thing I liked about him. When he'd boot the ball, he pounced right on it still trying to make the play. He never gave up."[52]

Fazio's playing opportunities jumped; he played in 102 games in 1963. He did not play in the Majors in 1964 or 1965—he was on the Oklahoma City 89ers' roster in the Minors' Pacific Coast League—but returned in 1966 to play 27 games with the Kansas City A's.

A Calm Presence

Robert Perry Lillis, a journeyman Minor Leaguer who later spent three seasons with the Dodgers and one season in which he played for both the Dodgers and the Cardinals, became a Houston icon beginning in 1962. His lack of hitting ability did not affect his fellow Colt .45s. *Houston Chronicle* baseball writer Zarko Franks queried, "Who's the most aggressive player? Who'll apparently risk personal injury to make a play?" The reply was, "Nine out of 10 times you'll get the name of Bob Lillis. Such is the regard of his teammates for this serious-faced athlete with disarming mild blue eyes."[53] Regarding his batting production, Lillis said, "I'm not as bad a hitter as people think I am."[54]

Lillis batted .249 in his first year with Houston, crediting an explosion at the plate to pitching coach Ellis Ferguson "Cot" Deal; in the last forty-eight games of the season Lillis whacked the ball to the tune of a .314 batting average. Unlike Larker, Lillis had a calmness about him. It was disturbed only once, to his teammates' recollection—by Larker. When the fiery first baseman kicked an electric fan in the dugout after grounding out, Lillis and the other Colt .45s sat in Houston's heat that got so bad, you needed a steak knife to cut it. With the team's source of coolness inoperable, Lillis said, "But we needed that fan . . . it's hot." Larker remained uncaring. "Aw, I'll buy you a new one."[55]

Lillis became a Houston fixture, retiring after the 1967 season with a .236 batting average, 817 games, and 549 hits. Staying with the team's Minor League operations as a scout and special instructor, Lillis jumped to the coaching level with the Astros in 1973. After nearly ten years, Lillis became the team's interim manager in August 1982, when the Astros dismissed Bill Virdon. Under Lillis, the team turned around, achieving a 28-23 record in contrast to the 49-62 record during Virdon's 1982 term.

Dr. John J. McMullen, who served as chairman of the board for the Astros organization, was convinced of Lillis's leadership value and rewarded him with the manager position. It was a natural fit for a team in crisis. "This conviction is based not only on Bob Lillis' baseball talent, but, even more importantly, on his character, integrity and loyalty to the organization," stated McMullen. "He has handled himself in extraordinary fashion under difficult circumstances and his personal desire to remain with the Houston Astros in any capacity is the best evidence of his loyalty."[56]

Lillis managed for three more seasons: 1983–85, with a 276-261 record. After 1985 he joined the coaching ranks of the Dodgers.

Rusty

When Daniel Joseph Staub, all of seventeen years old, signed with the Houston Colt .45s in 1961 as an amateur free agent while the team prepared for its 1962 debut, he was subject to the "bonus baby" nomenclature. Nicknamed "Rusty" by a nurse upon his birth on April 1, 1944, Staub became so known. In a 1967 article for *Sports Illustrated*, Gary Ronberg cited Staub's mother in revealing the story behind the dubbing: "'I wanted to name him Daniel so I could call him Danny for short,' said Mrs. Staub, who is, of course, Irish. 'But one of the nurses nicknamed him Rusty for the red fuzz he had all over his head, and it stuck.'"[57]

Playing with the Durham Bulls in '62, Staub hit 23 home runs, compiled a .293 batting average, and won the Carolina League's Most Valuable Player Award. In 1963 he voyaged to Houston for his first Major League season—150 games, .224 batting average, 6 home runs. A stay with the Oklahoma City 89ers in 1964 seasoned the red-haired bonus baby—Staub tore apart the Pacific Coast League with a .334 batting average after 60 games.

In a September 19, 1964, *Sporting News* article, "Return of Rusty: Staub Rides Hot Bat Back to .45s," sportswriter Bob Dellinger reasoned, "Staub, perhaps the No. 1 boy in Houston's renowned youth movement[,] was farmed to the Class Triple-A club in mid-July with a double-dip objective. First, he could play every day and perhaps build up his confidence at the plate; second, he could gain valuable defensive training in the outfield."[58] Further, Dellinger exposed Staub's perception of the demotion to the Minor Leagues: "Sometimes it seems like the world is coming to an end, but maybe it just starts over. I believe I will be back—better prepared physically and mentally."[59]

Staub played in a little more than half of Houston's games in 1964, garnering a .216 batting average. His performance at the plate improved for the remainder of his Houston tenure—batting averages of .256, .280, .333, and .291. Staub also played for the Expos, the Mets, the Tigers, and the Rangers in his Major League career, which ended after the 1985 season.

His time in an Expos uniform began with the team's inaugural season—1969—and lasted three years; he also played part of the 1979 season in Montreal and enjoyed a new nickname—"Le Grand Orange," courtesy his French-speaking fans.

A New Orleans native, Staub was inducted into the Louisiana Sports Hall of Fame in 1989.

The Skipper

Managing the Colt .45s was Harry Craft, a .253 hitter with the Reds from 1937 to 1942, a tenure including two National League pennants and one World Series championship.

Craft joined Cincinnati for ten games at the end of the '37 season. He led the National League outfielders in put-outs in 1938. Honing his managerial skills a decade later with the Independence team in the Kansas-Oklahoma-Missouri League, Craft became a compass for a rookie with talent but lacking in maturity: Mickey Charles Mantle.

During his first two years in professional baseball, Mantle, a kid from Commerce, Oklahoma, played for Craft, first in Independence in 1949 and then with Joplin in 1950. When Craft departed to take the reins at Beaumont for the '51 season, the Yankees had already proclaimed Mantle as the heir to Joe DiMaggio in center field at Yankee Stadium. "Of course, I was happy when Casey Stengel kept me on the Yanks most of the season," Mantle stated, "but at the beginning I wanted to join Craft in Beaumont. I liked the way he managed and I wanted to keep playing for him."[60]

It was not merely Craft's baseball acumen that Mantle prized: "Craft was like my father who also wanted me to play the outfield. Craft later met my father and they became good friends. In fact, Craft was more like a father to me than a manager. I guess I was lucky to have him as skipper my first two years. He started me out right."[61]

When Craft managed the Kansas City A's, he mentored Roger Maris after bringing the slugger from Cleveland. The laconic Maris also praised the skipper: "It was a fine thing for me to play under Harry Craft," said the North Dakota native. "He helped me regain my confidence after my slow start at Cleveland—as a handler of men Harry is among the top managers in my book."[62]

What would the home run race of 1961 have been like if Harry Craft hadn't guided Mantle and Maris?

Memories

Colt Stadium, Houston's Major League ballpark until the Astrodome eclipsed it, remains a fond memory for those who were there in '62 and fodder for Houston scholars. Acosta explains, "Seating colors at Colt Stadium ranged from flamingo red, to burnt orange, chartreuse, and turquoise. Female ushers, called "Triggerettes," wore uniforms made of the same flannel material used for the players, and parking attendants wore orange Stetson hats as they directed cars into sections named 'Wyatt Earp Territory' and 'Matt Dillon Territory.'"[63]

Dinn Mann recalls the bond between the city and Roy Hofheinz:

My grandfather had a love for Houston that was unmistakable. He had the drive and appetite to not only make a splash but to do so in his underrated hometown. Thanks to the confidence he inspired among business power brokers in town, my granddad positioned Houston, the place he adored unconditionally, as damn well prepared to support Major League attractions. He recognized the wave of opportunity as it was happening and rode it. But the difference between recognizing it and having the vision, the instinct, and the wherewithal to get on that wave is the difference between crashing and surfing.

There was a sense of "Why not me?" and "Why not us?" in Houston at that time. If Elvis could come from Mississippi and Tennessee and Frank

Sinatra could come out of Hoboken to achieve household fame, why couldn't Houston compete with the other so-called big cities and have a Major League team? There was a matter-of-fact boldness in his actions, knowing, not just believing, that you could do anything if you put your mind to it.

There's also something profoundly significant about becoming a Major League city.

Houston had a chip on its shoulder. It wanted to become relevant. So the Colt .45s spoke to the ambition and drive of people from that part of Texas, which was starting to get a little more swagger and footing in terms of influence. This was partly because of LBJ, who was vice president.

The Astrodome counted Walt Disney among its admirers. My grandfather spent some time with him. They shared a vision of aspiration, and Disney borrowed from some of my grandfather's ingenuity for Walt Disney World in Orlando. Houston had a solutions-oriented trajectory. One example is the Galleria, a breakthrough, air-conditioned indoor mall concept. My grandfather was a groundbreaker in far-reaching ways. He identified strategic territorial rights for sports teams, media, and sponsors. The Astros' reach extended through Louisiana and all over Texas, and that previously hadn't been practically defined. Also, remember, the South at that time was segregated in many places. My grandfather changed that in Houston and in the face of divisive, racist opposition. Anecdotally, at a moment in that march toward progress and enlightenment, he was taken aback by a citizen at a public meeting who complained about sharing a water fountain with minorities and wondered what she would catch. My grandfather replied as only he could: "Maybe you'll catch tolerance."[64]

Watching this all play out was a twelve-year-old Houston youngster, Thomas Schlamme, who, like millions of his peers, idolized baseball players. Schlamme became a key player in elevating television as an art form, with producing credits including *Sports Night*, *The West Wing*, *Studio 60 on the Sunset Strip*, *Manhattan*, and *Jack and Bobby*. In a 2017 interview he recalled,

I loved the Colt .45s. Colt Stadium wasn't far from my house in southwest Houston. A friend and I went to a doubleheader that was fairly crowded for the first game, but people left by the second game. So we kept moving down until we got behind home plate. If there was a passed ball, you could pick it up.

At first it was disappointing that the team was in the National League because I couldn't see the Yankees play. But later I took pride in the team. When the Oilers came two years before in the NFL, it made me feel like Houston was an important city. Plus, you had the beginning of NASA, so you felt like Houston was substantial. It just felt more like a city with the growth that was going on. If you saw an astronaut, it would be like if you saw Marilyn Monroe. They were mythical figures. So were the Houston ballplayers in the Minor Leagues and the Major Leagues. When you're a kid, the idea of going to baseball games seems remote. You have television and baseball cards as your connections to the game.

My favorite player was Ramón Mejías because he had a big game in the first game. Before we had the Colt .45s, my first baseball game was a Buffaloes game. Pidge Browne hit a home run and he was my favorite player on the Buffs, so I was so excited that he would play for the Colt .45s. You get locked into something when you root for a team. If I take someone who doesn't know the sport, they think the best player in that game is the best player on the team. Baseball was a passion.

Houston had oil and old money, but it was beginning to expand. At that time it felt like capitalism on steroids. In the most general terms, Houston felt eclectic and interesting and diverse. You could go into places that felt different than where you were. The Montrose area was a safe place for alternative lifestyles. But in Dallas I'd feel like a revolutionary. There's something about living in a city that's below sea level. You also felt a type of freedom because you were near a port. Being landlocked wasn't a problem. And it was unbelievably hot. When I made a movie in Mississippi, everyone complained about the heat but me because I was used to it growing up in Houston.

When the Astrodome opened in 1965, everyone wanted to go to Astros games. It gave Houston a stronger identity and national attention. We felt like we were the city of the future. The Mets seemed like the stepchildren of the Yankees. They sort of consumed a loser identity with a 40-120 record in their first season. The Oilers won in their first four seasons, so Houston was a pro football city. Billy Cannon and George Blanda were heroes. In some ways the Oilers swallowed up the attention of sports fans. I followed the team when it went to Tennessee and became the Titans. When I was doing *The West Wing*, we were shooting in Washington DC outside the Daughters of the American Revolution building because the façade looked like the White House portico. We had just finished lunch at the beginning of the fourth quarter. If I ever listed a million places that I never thought I'd be watching the Super Bowl, the DAR would be at the top.

I'm first-generation Houston. My father, Otto, fled Nazi Germany and wound up there. He loved it and felt incredibly fortunate. I loved hearing him laugh. One of the shows that he thought was hysterical was *Hogan's Heroes*, which is set in a POW camp run by Germans in World War II. He worked in the office supply [business] and became stunningly Texan. He wasn't a sports fan, but he wore the Texan-style thin tie and went to livestock shows and the opera. There was a certain pride to being from Houston. When the Colt .45s came, that gave us another reason to be proud of our city.[65]

Houstonians embraced their new Major League status, while Cincinnatians closed a chapter in theirs. Nearly a year to the day after Reds owner Powell Crosley Jr. died, the Reds ball club was sold for $4,625,000. Crosley, the owner since 1934, had directed that the nonprofit Crosley Foundation—created by his will—take the team after his death. Holding 90 percent of the stock and no interest in running the team, the foundation sold the team to William DeWitt, a former owner, together with his brothers, of the St. Louis Browns. To ensure that the team stayed in Cincinnati, the foundation's trustees "searched for possible purchasers of the club and have determined that Bill DeWitt met these qualifications more closely than any other person with whom discussions were had," said Crosley's daughter, Mrs. Stanley Kress.[66]

Cincinnati's National League rivals in Southern California remained in the hands of Walter O'Malley, who was ready to unveil a stadium primed for a fan base that was about to experience an unforgettable season.

4

Chavez Ravine

It was an act of disloyalty ranking with Benedict Arnold and the Continental Army, King David and Uriah, and the 1919 Chicago White Sox. Or so the people of Brooklyn believed when Walter O'Malley packed up seventy-four years of baseball history, adjusted his compass, and moved the Dodgers to Los Angeles after the 1957 season.

Rivers can change course, governments can be overthrown, and legislatures can amend constitutions. But spiriting the Dodgers from Brooklyn was unthinkable. Criminal, even. Devastating. Surreal. Dishonorable. Ebbets Field, after all, was more than a place where baseball was played. It was an emotional touchstone for Brooklynites who incorporated the Dodgers into their daily routine. And that was pretty much everyone from Bushwick to Bay Ridge. Finding fans of the Yankees or Giants in the borough was about as rare as an Inverted Jenny.

To Brooklyn, O'Malley was, as Ajax called Achilles, "a paltry, insolent fellow."[1] But to Los Angeles he was a symbol, maybe even a savior, of Major League Baseball's manifest destiny. Propelled by advances in air travel, a trip to the West Coast, once thought possible only by a train ride lasting several days, was viable by the late 1950s.

O'Malley blamed the team's uprooting on Ebbets Field's obsolescence, lack of parking, decreasing attendance, and New York City's 5 percent amusement tax on tickets.[2] To penetrate the Los Angeles market, he cut a deal with the Chicago Cubs by buying the Cubs' Pacific Coast League team—the Los Angeles Angels—plus territorial rights and the team's home park, Wrigley Field, named after the brick-faced landmark on the north side of Chicago. In return the Cubs got the Dodgers' Texas League team—the Fort Worth Cats. The *Los Angeles Times* estimated the entire deal on the Dodgers' end cost $3 million.[3]

Cultivating a foothold in the Inland Northwest's pride, O'Malley moved the Angels to Spokane. In 1970 the Spokane Indians won the Pacific Coast League championship.

O'Malley's battle with New York public official Robert Moses precipitated the Dodgers' move to Southern California. Moses was a walking, talking powerhouse controlling the Triborough Bridge Authority, which gave him a tremendous amount of influence because of the money generated by tolls for using the city's bridges and tunnels. With the authority to condemn land in New York City for public purposes, his imprints were all over Greater New York, including the Long Island Expressway, which runs about 120 miles through the middle of the island, extending from Manhattan to Montauk.

Moses had refused to condemn land that O'Malley coveted for a new ballpark. Building a new stadium on O'Malley's desired site would contradict the language and spirit of the law because a stadium was not, in Moses's view, a project that served a public purpose. O'Malley dismissed an alternative offered by Moses—the land in Queens that later became the Shea Stadium site. While Dodgers fans might not have believed that the team could leave the borough, there was ample evidence to suggest that O'Malley was not bluffing Moses, Mayor Robert Wagner, or the press. "If it becomes necessary for us to play any place other than Brooklyn, I think the final location is obvious," said O'Malley. "Then it would become a matter of picking the place with the greatest future."[4]

In 1956 and 1957 the Dodgers totaled fifteen regular-season games in Jersey City's Roosevelt Stadium, but Garden Staters' hopes of them moving to New Jersey were short-lived.

For his team's new Southern California home, O'Malley wanted a stadium commensurate with the post–World War II car culture fueled by suburbia's popularity. Rose Bowl? Los Angeles Memorial Coliseum? Wrigley Field? The Coliseum won out, at least until O'Malley could build Dodger Stadium in Chavez Ravine, which would be a real-estate deal that put the team's owner in the company of Burbank, Knott, Disney, Huntington, and other pioneers who changed the landscape of Southern California.

Los Angeles business icon Harold "Chad" McClellan, the president and principal owner of Old Colony Paint Company, represented the city in key negotiations with the man bringing Major League Baseball to Los Angeles. "My first meeting with Walter O'Malley lasted all day," said McClellan. "It was evident at once that even though he knew all about the generous arrangements between other ball clubs and the cities where they were located, he wanted a completely different arrangement if he moved here. O'Malley affirmed our understanding that he wanted to build his own stadium with Dodger financing. He was determined to make his club's stadium the most modern, the most imaginative ever built, even though he had not yet decided where to build it, or when."[5]

The site selected was Chavez Ravine, about a twenty-minute drive from downtown Los Angeles. Oil proved to be a negotiating point, even after O'Malley relinquished mineral rights, because the city wanted space at the ravine for oil exploration. "Politically, the city council could not afford to give up on the possibility of oil, so it required the Dodgers to set aside a site in Chavez Ravine for a rig should experts decide it was worth drilling," explains O'Malley biographer Andy McCue. "Oil revenues would come to the city. O'Malley won the concession that half of those earnings would be charged against the Dodgers' obligation to fund youth sports programs. O'Malley won the same half-and-half division for any oil found under Wrigley Field after it was handed over to the city. These were bargaining victories that would come back to haunt him. Theoretically, the Dodgers could have received $1.7 million in oil revenues. In reality, as the experts were predicting, they received nothing."[6]

But this was more than a real-estate acquisition. O'Malley faced thorny political and legal issues that could affect the Dodgers' goodwill, an intangible but vulnerable asset depending on publicity. To effect the construction of Dodger Stadium, the city evicted families. On Malvina Street in the Chavez Ravine area, all hell broke loose. The Arechiga family was living there, on property owned by the city, and by 1959 they had not paid rent for six years, either to the city or to the previous owner, Los Angeles's housing authority. The *Los Angeles Times* described "children of the family wailing hysterically" and the family matriarch "hurling stones at deputies as movers hustled away her belongings."[7]

O'Malley and the city weren't done yet. They faced the task of securing twelve additional parcels in Chavez Ravine. Had O'Malley been left to his own devices of negotiating with each owner, his charm would have lubricated the process. Alas, the owners were unified. Turning to the city politicos was not an option. "After the controversy surrounding the Arechiga removals, the city did not dare use eminent domain to gain title to these outlier properties," writes historian Jerald Podair.[8]

Fans had other issues on their minds besides lawsuits and allegations that the evictions were racially motivated. There was the matter of transportation to this new mecca of California baseball. After the stadium's completion in 1962, fans who headed to the park by car needed to consult maps, news reports, and word-of-mouth instructions to navigate the ingress and egress points, because the new stadium had meant a reworking of the freeway in the immediate area. While drivers did not need a sextant or a compass to find Dodger Stadium, they might have felt like they did. One newspaper report warned that drivers taking the Golden State Freeway to the ballpark needed to be aware of their surroundings: "Be careful to watch for the Stadium Way off-ramp. It sneaks up on you."[9]

Memories of the Pacific Coast League's Hollywood Stars and Los Angeles Angels were fresh in the minds of Southern California's baseball fans as they inched their Pontiacs and Plymouths toward the national pastime's latest show-place. Their pulses must have raced with anticipation upon entering this new edifice for the historic ball club that originated in Brooklyn. The new home for the Dodgers entered the pantheon of iconic Los Angeles locations—Grauman's

Chinese Theatre, Malibu beaches, and the Hollywood sign. It was a contrast to the grand old dames of baseball built a half century earlier, when Henry Ford began to master the art of the assembly line. Shibe Park, Wrigley Field in Chicago, the Polo Grounds, and Ebbets Field were your grandfather's stadiums. This was a new age, a space age, where California sunshine became God's spotlight on the future, not only for baseball but for America.

Attending a Dodgers game meant being a part of a community, which was especially important for transplants escaping the harsh winters of the Midwest and Northeast for a new start. They joined their neighbors in shouting, "Go! Go! Go!" every time Maury Wills was on base and breathed easier when Don Drysdale took the hill. The fearsome hurler compiled an MLB-leading 232 strikeouts and 25-9 record on his way to the Cy Young Award. Although there's no such thing as a sure thing, it was a good bet that the Dodgers would win if Drysdale had the ball.

But Dodger Stadium's debut was not smooth. Not by a long shot. The infield was a major obstacle for the groundskeepers to get in shape for the two Southern California teams—O'Malley rented out Dodger Stadium to the Angels operation for the next four seasons, until Angel Stadium opened in 1966. Two days before Opening Day, the *Los Angeles Times* reported, "before a single game has been played, it already looks as though it had borne the brunt of the 162 games the Dodgers and Angels will play on it this season. A mower Saturday raised more dust than grass cuttings." Field conditions could affect play: "Plugs from two growing areas are being transplanted to the bare spots, but chances are that bad hops and skids may mar play until the turf takes hold—if ever, what with the constant traffic ahead."[10]

Former Los Angeles mayor Norris Poulson threw out the first ball, an honor bestowed on the politico because of his efforts—self-sabotaging, according to some pundits—in finalizing the deal for a Major League team. Fans leafed through the sports pages to track the developments and found *Times* columnist Jim Murray's verbiage acknowledging Poulson's slightly exaggerated view of events, which included a proclamation that O'Malley was reluctant at best to construct a stadium for the Dodgers. Poulson didn't need to enhance his credentials: "But if you see a jaunty little fellow with a Homburg tilted at a rakish angle pointing to the stadium Tuesday and saying in a laryngitic whisper, 'If it weren't for me, that damned thing would never have been built,' you better believe it."[11]

Fifty-six thousand fans crowded the ballpark for the inaugural game on April 10, a 6–3 loss to the Reds.

For Brian Sidney Parrott—the son of Dodgers ticket manager Harold Parrott—it was the start of a new era for the team that he had accompanied from Brooklyn with his family after the 1957 season. After four years at the Los Angeles Memorial Coliseum, the Dodgers had a permanent home ballpark. But the Parrott clan still kept the team's Brooklyn roots close to their hearts. "I was born at Midwood Hospital on October 3, 1947, when Bill Bevens had a no-hitter going in the World Series," explains Parrott. "[Announcer] Red Barber congratulated my parents twice during the World Series broadcast. Dad was at the game. After my parents died, I went through their papers and found telegrams and letters from thirty-one countries and all forty-eight states [congratulating them on their new baby]. There was actually speculation about naming me Cookie Lavagetto Parrott!"[12]

At ten years old, Brian's world of neighborhoods, candy shops, and Ebbets Field evaporated, leaving him to find new friends in a template of tolerance bordering on disorder. That's how it seemed when he matriculated at Our Lady of Malibu:

> I had culture shock because the kids were so different. When I was at St. Francis de Sales in Rockaway, the final thing I did was sing a song to each class a cappella. On my first day at Our Lady of Malibu, my mother wanted me to wear a tie. I tried to explain that nobody wears a tie. In California kids wore jeans. I looked like Little Lord Fauntleroy. Back home, when a nun called your name, you stood up and said, "Yes, Sister." When I did that in Malibu, the kids looked at me like I was from outer space. Unfortunately, I didn't have close friends like the ones I had in New York. We rented the house [at 75 Malibu Colony] for one year and then my dad bought 89 Malibu Colony for $47,000 in 1959 and sold it for $99,000 in 1965. He thought he was getting away with murder.[13]

What Brian Parrott endured during lunch and recess, longtime Dodgers executive Fresco Thompson faced in the front office. Thompson's jacket-and-tie uniform contrasted—if not conflicted with—Southern California's laissez-faire lifestyle. "One of Walter O'Malley's worries—besides raising money—when the Dodgers made their westward move was what he called the 'Hollywood influence,'" wrote Thompson in his 1964 autobiography, *Every Diamond Doesn't Sparkle*. "He spoke of the Dodger executives being a 'happy family,' and that while the phrase 'going Hollywood' was vaporously defined, it did imply certain changes that he hoped wouldn't happen to any of us." The team owner needn't have worried: "Buzzie Bavasi and I and others from the front office have never been caught in the vortex of so-called Hollywood life: the parties, the pursuit of cinema stars, the name droppings, or socializing with new friends from the movie colony. We still go to work in business suits and not sport shirts. We keep our distance from the 'Dahling, you look terrific' set. Our wives walk into a room filled with people and leave without spectacular entrances and exitings."[14]

Parrott knew the Hollywood folks because they were part of his background. To the extent that glamour consisted of knowing famous people, he lived a glamorous childhood:

> Nelson Riddle's son Skip was a classmate. So were Doug Dragon and Dennis Dragon, the sons of Carmen Dragon. Aly Khan and Rita Hayworth's son went to my school. Lana Turner lived two doors away. Lawrence Welk visited sometimes. James Mason also stopped by on occasion. Our best friend was Jack Warden.
>
> At that time Los Angeles was sprawling, so my dad worked with ticket brokers to sell the tickets. The Coliseum was okay, but the seats were not comfortable at all. Ebbets Field had an odor—it stunk. Dodger Stadium, on the other hand, had a new and clean smell when it debuted in 1962. It was a luxury with vibrant colors. It was like Disneyland for baseball. Parking was on the same level.[15]

It Takes a Thief

In six straight seasons Maury Wills led the National League in steals; for three of those seasons he led the Major Leagues. Attributing his success to Pete Reiser, a former Dodger who led the National League in stolen bases twice and the Major Leagues once, Wills honored him in the dedication of his 1963 autobiography, *It Pays to Steal*: "Pete Reiser has taught me to think positive. Stealing is a matter of confidence, even conceit. It's more than getting a good jump, a big lead. It's being in the right frame of mind."[16]

A slump in Wills's sophomore Major League season—1960—was a turning point. "I was hitting .208," said Wills. "[Reiser'd] take me out for early batting practice in the Coliseum every evening before the game. It wasn't only the instruction he gave me. It was the talking to he'd give me afterwards. We'd sit and talk for an hour and a half. Just sit and talk. It was more than swinging a bat, the talking."[17]

In 1962 Maury Wills became the first Black captain for the Dodgers. There was no color distinction at the Dodgers' new home, 1000 Elysian Park Avenue, just as there had been none at Ebbets Field back in Brooklyn, at 55 Sullivan Place. From a childhood at 3297 Fifteenth Place Southeast in Washington DC, with a minister father and twelve brothers and sisters, Wills became as much a Los Angeles icon as the Hollywood Bowl.

The first 1962 All-Star Game took place in Wills's hometown. Although he did not start the game, it held a special significance:

> My family and friends who I grew up with in the projects were there. Dick Groat was the starting shortstop and he apologized. Stan Musial also did not start. The following year would be his last. During the middle of the game, I turned to Stan and said, "Look at those guys striking out. Why don't you pinch-hit and I'll go in and run for you?" Would you believe that happened? Cardinals manager Johnny Keane was the National League's manager. Musial singled and Keane put me into run for him. Up to that point, it was a 0–0 game. I took it over and changed the game.
>
> Then Clay Dalrymple of the Phillies and Randy Hundley for the Cubs were brought in because I dominated catchers before them. Catchers were there to hit, not just have a good arm. Jerry Grote from the Mets was good. I remember word got around the National League about how it was impossible to steal off Johnny Bench, who had a rifle arm. My ego couldn't wait to play Cincinnati. I got a good lead just in case and I got back each time. Then I got a great jump. When I was a little over halfway to second base, I turned to home plate to laugh at Johnny Bench. To my surprise, here comes the ball. He threw me out by a foot or two. I tipped my cap.[18]

The National League won the game 8–4.[19]

In 1962 Wills won *The Sporting News* Major League Player of the Year and the National League Most Valuable Player Award.

The Slugger

Herman Thomas Davis Jr. had the Dodgers in his blood. A product of Boys High in the Bedford-Stuyvesant neighborhood of Brooklyn, Davis, known as "Tommy," was eighteen when Jackie Robinson broke baseball's color line in 1947. It was Robinson who pointed Davis in the direction of Ebbets Field in 1956. "In fact, I signed with the Dodgers at Jackie's request. I could have signed with the Yankees," said Davis, who vaulted into the Dodgers organization immediately after graduating high school.[20]

Davis played forty-three games for the Hornell Dodgers of the Class D Pony League in 1956, compiling a .325 batting average. In 1957 Davis unveiled his potential with the Dodgers' Kokomo club in the Midwest League. He led the league in at bats (518), runs (115), hits (185), total bases (271), singles (139), stolen bases (68), and batting average (.357).

Reiser also mentored Davis at Kokomo. As Davis racked up hits with the regularity of an assembly line, Reiser said in late August, "You are seeing only about 80% of what he is capable of. Wait until he acquires more polish. He is getting by now on raw skills plus instinct. He reacts well to competition. Give him an objective far out of the ordinary player's reach and he will shoot at the stars for you. He likes competition. He likes to be kept on his toes."[21]

The Dodgers sent Davis to the Victoria Rosebuds of the Double-A Texas League in 1958; he notched a .304 batting average over 122 games before vaulting to the Triple-A Montreal Royals of the International League, where he played 14 games to finish the year. Manager Clay Bryant said, "His potential is practically unlimited. Tom has power, he can throw, and he may be the fastest man in the organization."[22]

Davis's last season in the Minors was 1959. The slugger played under Bobby Bragan for the Triple-A Spokane Indians of the Pacific Coast League. It was another banner year for the Bed-Stuy native. Davis led the PCL in games played (153), at bats (612), hits (211), total bases (315), singles (152), and batting average (.345). In August, Bragan said of the parent ball club, "And I don't see how they can fail to grab him. He has just started to hit his stride."[23] Davis played one game for Los Angeles in 1959.

His eighteen-year career included stints with ten teams—the Dodgers, Mets, White Sox, Astros, Athletics, Cubs, Orioles, Angels, Royals, and Pilots. He had his best season in 1962; he led the Major Leagues in hits (230), RBIs (153), and batting average (.346). In the voting for the National League's Most Valuable Player Award, Davis placed third behind teammate Maury Wills and San Francisco slugger Willie Mays.

Davis's was a plight of simplicity—get in the batter's box, swing the bat, connect with the ball. A cartoon in the August 24, 1962, edition of the *Daily News* in New York accompanying Jimmy Powers's "Powerhouse" column portrays O'Malley puffing smoke in the form of dollar signs spelling "Bargain" in conjunction with Davis getting a $12,000 a year salary. "Tommy is never mentioned in the Hollywood gossip columns. He is no crusader. He has not become embroiled in any residential feuds. He just goes quietly about the business of knocking in runs," Powers wrote.[24]

Perhaps overshadowed by his teammates, Davis did not receive an outpouring of appreciation from the fans. "The fans just don't recognize all of Tommy's talents. He's one real fine base-runner, although he has been a little timid about stealing. He knows he can't steal with Maury Wills, so he didn't try too often," Reiser said.[25]

Los Angles sportswriter Sid Ziff concurred. During Davis's banner year of 1962, Ziff wrote, "If [Frank] Howard had Davis' record today, Cadillac dealers would be discounting his automobiles and gossip columnists would be trying to haul him around the Hollywood night spots."[26]

Dodgers skipper Walter Alston noted, "It's a funny thing, but here was a kid leading the majors in two of the biggest offensive departments, yet, when he came up with men on base, the fans didn't make much noise. But when Howard strode to the plate, they yelled their heads off."[27]

Power on the Mound

The Dodgers' pitching was also formidable. Don Drysdale rammed through National League teams on his way to leading the Major Leagues in wins (25), games started (41), innings pitched (314.1), strikeouts (232), and batters faced (1,289) in 1962. His achievements garnered him the 1962 Cy Young Award.

The fearsome hurler began his journey to the Majors under the watchful eye of his father, Scott Drysdale, a 1930s Minor League pitcher; the elder Drysdale pitched for Los Angeles, Tulsa, and Ponca City (Oklahoma). "His back was hurting, wind in the Dust Bowl was stinging his eyes and he came down with the measles," said Myrtle Drysdale, Scott's mother and Don's grandmother. "I told him to come on home, and he did. He would have been a great player in the majors."[28]

Father detoured son from the pitcher's mound. "Dad started teaching me when I was nine years old," said Drysdale. "But he wouldn't let me try pitching until I had matured a little. Until the day I tried pitching I played second base."[29] Once he became a pitcher, Drysdale and the baseball acted as a single unit of ferocity—he was the cannon launching a spheroid of devastation to the hearts, minds, and souls of National League ball clubs. This six-foot, five-inch Adonis patrolled the pitching mound, with fierceness in his eyes telegraphing fury at a batter even thinking of encroaching on home plate. "He's the hardest loser in the business," said Dodgers executive Fresco Thompson. "The trouble is, he doesn't believe *anyone* should get a hit off him. When he gets knocked around, everything goes black. He says and does things he regrets an hour later, but can't very well take back. He's just too much of a competitor for his own good."[30]

Drysdale had the ability to compartmentalize, a necessary but elusive asset for any professional. In his 1990 autobiography, *Once a Bum, Always a Dodger*, he explains:

I wasn't one of those guys who woke up mad on the day I pitched. I wasn't a bear around the house or anything like that. I didn't wake up in a bad mood, growling at my wife. I think if you dwell on a game all day, you can become mentally whipped. I might have started thinking about it when I drove to the ballpark for a home game, and relaxed in the hotel on the road. But when I got to the ballpark, which was my office, and put that uniform on, I guess I worked myself into a frenzy. I had a pretty good temper—and still do on occasion—but I basically kept my red-ass personality at the ballpark. It all locked in when you saw that first batter staring out at you from the plate. Then, after the game, it was over. That's how I developed that "Jekyll-Hyde" label as a guy who was an SOB on the mound, but a pretty decent drinking companion afterward. As the old saw goes, I was the same guy who would "brush back his grandmother" to win a game one minute, and then sing songs at a baseball writers' banquet the next—as I did at the 1963 affair in Hollywood. My assignment was, "One Love," "Give Her Love," and "Secret Love." See that? All love and kisses.[31]

The future Hall of Famer from Van Nuys, California, held neither fear nor favor regarding critics. "Nothing makes me madder than to have someone say that my getting mad hurts my pitching," Drysdale said. He admitted to having a rotten temper. "So what's wrong with that? Bob Friend of the Pirates and Mike McCormick of the Giants are placid guys, and they lost 35 games last year. I hate all hitters. I start a game mad and I stay that way until it's over. I guess I'm a perfectionist. When I throw a curve that hangs, and it goes for a hit, I want to chew up my glove. I want to bite nails in half. I want to stop time and take the pitch over, but I can't—and that makes me madder than ever."[32]

Drysdale's passion for excellence was not limited in any way to the baseball diamond. *Los Angeles Examiner* sportswriter Vincent X. Flaherty revealed an experience he had had during the Dodgers' 1957 spring training at Dodgertown, a facility in Vero Beach, Florida, once used as a naval base:

In the middle of this lay-out is a large recreation room. Among other amusement gadgets there is a "Ski-Ball" [*sic*] chute—the kind of contraption you see at amusement parks. You roll a ball up the chute and it leaps toward a series of circles within circles. The bull's eye is a small cup not much larger than the ball itself. Drysdale didn't do very well the first couple of nights. But by the third night the writer stood by and watched as Don sped one ball after another into the center cup. He must have dropped in a hundred straight before quitting.

Drysdale seems obsessed with the conviction he must master everything he attempts.[33]

In between his stints on the mound intimidating National League lineups, Drysdale showed hints of his future as a broadcast announcer. Kelly Drysdale remembers her father's penchant for storytelling during his playing career:

He would sit in the dugout and give play-by-play. There would be occasions that guys would kid him about it by saying things like, "There's Drysdale announcing the game again." I think it was an extension of his career later on. If he couldn't play anymore, he could be part of it by being an announcer. He learned from Vin Scully how to paint a picture of the game with words. People told me that they could see the game through my father's announcing. Plus, it was a means of income. Since he had already been in the arena, it wasn't difficult for him to stay there with broadcasting.

His acting was mostly cameos or being a guest star. He was good, but he wasn't going to get an Emmy for his performances! He also cut a record. My dad was a good friend of Frank Sinatra. One day he went down to the Capitol Records building, which also had offices for Reprise, which was Sinatra's label. He cut a record there. My dad would sing in the car like he was on stage. When I hear "A Summer Place," it reminds me of the music my dad used to listen to.

If I had to describe my dad in three words, they would be integrity, devotion, and talent. He had a good upbringing in his childhood, and the Dodgers organization was a good place for him. He was a true competitor. He always strived for the best no matter what he was doing. My dad knew he wasn't perfect, but he strived for perfection because he wanted to be top notch.

He contrived his intimidation on the pitching mound by getting pissed off. But when he came home, he was a great dad. The golden rule was his benchmark. He didn't care if you were a guy selling peanuts at Dodger Stadium or the president of the United States. Everybody got equal treatment from my dad. I think that's a great life lesson. Treat people how you want to be treated.[34]

The California Kid

Willie Davis was a hometown kid, from Boyle Heights. He went from Theodore Roosevelt High School to the Dodgers' Illinois-Indiana-Iowa League team, the Green Bay Bluejays, in 1959, a year after graduating from Roosevelt with the distinction of being the national high-school broad jump champion. Davis got seven games under his belt in the Triple-I League before the Dodgers sent him to the Reno Silver Sox in the California League, where he flourished like a rose blooming in springtime, winning the batting title with a .365 average and leading the league in runs (135), hits (187), batting average (.365), doubles (40), and triples (16).[35]

In 1960 Davis destroyed Pacific Coast League pitching during his sole season with the Spokane Indians—he led the PCL in runs (126), batting average (.346), triples (26), stolen bases (30), and total bases (347).[36] Davis played twenty-two games for Los Angeles in 1960 and began an eighteen-year Major League career; he spent fourteen years in a Dodgers uniform. Davis also played for the Expos, Rangers, Cardinals, and Padres. In 1962 Davis led the National League in triples, knocked 171 hits, scored 103 runs, and batted .285.

The Reliever

When the Dodgers' pitching arms tired, Alston called on Ron Perranoski, who led the Major Leagues with seventy games played and saved twenty games for the Chavez Ravine denizens in 1962. The following year, he led the National League with sixty-nine games played, tallied twenty-one saves, and ended the season with a 16-3 record.

Perranoski had the calmness of a surgeon when he went to the mound. "I know he's got the right temperament for a relief pitcher," explained Alston. "It's like ice-water."[37] Dedicating himself to the relief-pitching role, Perranoski revealed in a 1963 *Sport* magazine interview the importance of being a fireman in the bullpen. "I don't care if I ever start another game. The thing was I wanted to establish myself as a relief pitcher if that was what I had to be. You want to make the majors. With me I wanted to make it even if I had to be the ballboy. When I knew I was going up as a relief pitcher, I was still delighted for the chance," Perranoski stated. "The thing is when you're there, I didn't want to be just a relief pitcher. I wanted to excel in it."[38]

Power at the Plate

Frank Howard was a Goliath with a bat. Playing with the Bluejays in 1958, his first professional baseball season, Howard batted .333; he played eight games for the Dodgers that season. A professional contract made him ineligible at Ohio

State, where he had starred in baseball and basketball. Howard took the field in nine games for the Dodgers in 1959, when he also won the Minor League Player of the Year Award and played for the Victoria Rosebuds of the Texas League and the Spokane Indians of the Pacific Coast League. In addition to the Dodgers, Howard played in the Majors for the Senators, Rangers, and Tigers.

Howard, the National League Rookie of the Year, prompted comparisons to George Herman "Babe" Ruth after crashing an estimated 562-foot home run during a 1960 road trip to Pittsburgh's Forbes Field. Joe Tucker, the Steelers' play-by-play man for more than thirty years—from FDR's promise of happy days to the Age of Aquarius—recounted, "I had the game on the radio and was just parking my car behind the left-field fence when I heard that Howard had hit a home run. I noted where the ball landed, so I paced off the distance from the fence at the 400-ft. mark to the spot where it came down. It was 54 paces, or about 162 ft., so I'd say it had to travel at least 550 ft."[39]

Adding to the moment was a spooky coincidence—on the same date twenty-five years prior, Ruth had hit the last three home runs of his career; he hit six in the entire 1935 season, which he played in a Boston Braves uniform. Ruth's accomplishment belied an otherwise anemic final season—.181 batting average, six home runs, twenty-eight games.

Howard did not compile Ruthian statistics in his sixteen-year Major League career, but they were substantial nonetheless: .499 career slugging percentage, 1968 MLB home-run leader, 1970 NL RBI and home-run leader, and 382 home runs.

A Beloved Dodger

Jim Gilliam was the National League Rookie of the Year in 1953. His path to the Majors took him through the Baltimore Elite Giants of the Negro National League, Montreal Royals of the International League, Nashville Black Volunteers of the Southern Negro League, and Santurce of the Puerto Rican Winter League. Gilliam's rise to the Dodgers forced a round of musical bases for the infielders; Jackie Robinson, a fixture at Ebbets Field's second base position, shifted to third base. It was neither a surprise nor an insult to Robinson, who reminded reporters of his prediction after seeing Gilliam play a game in Puerto Rico: "I told you then that Gilliam might push me off second base, but if he did I'd be playing some place on the team. I didn't say so at the time but third base was what I had in mind."[40]

Billy Cox, he of the glove that fielded dribblers, snared line drives, and grabbed Baltimore chops that would have been base hits under the watch of any other hot-corner monitor, became a utility infielder to make room for Robinson and, in turn, Gilliam. "As for me playing third base, I can't carry Cox'[s] glove—nor can anybody else—but Charley's [sic] the manager and anything he wants me to do that he thinks will help the club I'll be glad to do," said Robinson.[41]

Like Robinson, Gilliam won the International League's Most Valuable Player Award in the year before joining the Dodgers. His 1952 IL stats were 109 RBIs, 169 hits, 39 doubles, 8 triples, 9 homers, 18 stolen bases, and .303 batting average. Glory, for Gilliam, was in the final score of the game. If he contributed, that was satisfactory. Anything more was about as valuable as bringing a cupful of sand to Zuma Beach. "There's no use to look for any individualism in my story," stated Gilliam. "There's no use to look, because it isn't there. I don't get paid to hit home runs or that sort of stuff. I get paid to score a lot of runs, knock in some and move the runner into scoring position." Gilliam added, "I would not rate myself a great ball player, but I think I do a lot of things well—things which beat the other team."[42]

Front office figure Buzzie Bavasi said, "He's like seven men to me. He's an excellent leadoff man. He's an accomplished second-place hitter. He's a lefthanded and a righthanded hitter. He can play second or third."[43] Gilliam, a lifelong Dodger, ended his career after the 1966 season with a body of work resulting in three World Series championships, five National League pennants, and the beginning of a full-time coaching career; he served as a player-coach for his last three seasons. Later in his career Gilliam was on the coaching staff for three pennant-winning Dodgers squads—1974, 1977, and 1978.

Pee Wee Reese, the Dodgers' shortstop from 1940 to 1958, except for his three years of military service during World War II, applauded Gilliam's philosophy of sacrifice. "When he hit behind Maury Wills he was never hesitant to take a pitch and Maury would be the first to acknowledge that he couldn't have stolen all those bases without a lot of help from Jim," said Reese.[44] "I still say don't give me any credit," explained Gilliam in 1963. "If you had seen Maury's legs and the beating he took to steal those bases you'd have to give him all the credit. That was a once in a lifetime year. You can never expect him to do it again."[45]

Gilliam played in nearly every regular-season game in 1962, finishing with a .270 batting average and 159 hits after 160 games.

When Gilliam died just before the 1978 World Series at the age of forty-nine from a cerebral hemorrhage, the tears shed by Dodgers Nation could have filled Chavez Ravine. The Dodgers mourned, wept, and readied to do battle against the Yankees, who sent Reggie Jackson to the funeral as their representative. Jackson, who embodied the brashness of late 1970s New York City, revealed his philosophical side as he explained how he asked Jesus Christ why this gentle man had to leave. "You decided that now was the best time to take him, with the World Series and everyone watching and listening, so all God's children could take a look at Jim and see what his life meant to us all," eulogized Jackson.[46] More than three thousand people showed up at Trinity Baptist Church to pay respects, and the Dodgers retired Gilliam's number, 17. Universally liked, Gilliam was more than a ballplayer—he was that rare combination of selflessness, dedication, and perseverance.

Sandy

Sandy Koufax began his career in 1955—when the Dodgers won their only World Series in Brooklyn, Marilyn Monroe's skirt blew out as she stood on top of a subway grate, Ray Kroc opened his first McDonald's, Rosa Parks refused to move to the back of the bus, and Elvis Presley made his first television appearance. Lured from the University of Cincinnati, where he had a basketball scholarship, the eighteen-year-old alumnus of Brooklyn's Lafayette High School stood out on the university's baseball squad as well—51 strikeouts, 2.81 ERA, 3-1 win-loss record.[47]

He spent twelve seasons with the "Dodgers" label scripted across his jersey above the number 32 emblazoned in lipstick red. With a pitch speed rivaling the Super Chief, Koufax dominated the strike zone. He was a four-time MLB strikeout leader, three-time winner of the Cy Young Award, and three-time MLB win leader. He threw four no-hitters, including a perfect game.

Humility emerged from the southpaw after an outstanding season in 1963, when he led the Majors in victories, shutouts, strikeouts, and ERA, in addition to winning two of the four games in the Dodgers' sweep of the Yankees in the World Series and becoming the first unanimous choice for the Cy Young Award. "However, when people say that I've become the best left-handed pitcher ever to step on a mound, it's embarrassing because it isn't true," wrote Koufax in a piece for *Look* magazine. "I still make mistakes, lots of them. Maybe the worst is getting mad at myself when I walk anybody or make a bad pitch. People say I look poker-faced and don't show emotion. But sometimes things bubble up inside of me and burst out."[48]

Striving to improve upon excellence, Koufax admitted, "Then there are more technical shortcomings. My move to first base isn't as good as it should be. At times, I don't worry enough about the runner, or, at least, I forget about him. I don't think I'm always ready to field the ball. If I've got a lot of time to make a play at a base, I don't like it. I'm likely to throw the ball away. I'd rather be hurried, but sometimes I hurry so much I don't give the fielder enough opportunity."[49]

Koufax's climb to dominance was not a clear one—he was 36-40 after his first six seasons. "I seriously entertained thoughts of retiring at the end of 1960," said Koufax after being elected to the Baseball Hall of Fame in 1972. "I didn't think I was going anywhere and I was ready to look for something else, although I didn't know what."[50]

Enter Norm Sherry.

The backstop advised the southpaw to focus on control rather than speed: "Norm and I decided to try a few new things," Koufax said. "We decided to throw the changeup rather than go so often to the fastball. I decided I wasn't going to worry about how many men I walked[;] I was just going to go out and pitch."[51]

His 1961 results speak for themselves: 269 strikeouts to lead the Majors and an 18-13 win-loss record. In 1962 Koufax went 14-7. Sidelined for two months by what was termed a circulatory ailment in his finger, the southpaw went to the bench after a July 17 loss against the Reds. When he resumed pitching on September 21, he lost four straight, to end the season.

Koufax retired in 1966 after 397 games, 2,396 strikeouts, and a 165-87 win-loss record. He was thirty years old, with an arthritic arm.

Duke

One of the few links in 1962 to the Dodgers' days in Brooklyn was Edwin Donald "Duke" Snider.

Brooklyn kids would wait on Bedford Avenue and try to chase after Snider's home-run balls if they cleared Ebbets Field's stands. Snider went yard 407 times in his career; his batting average was .295. When Brooklyn lost the Dodgers, disbelief followed by mourning reigned across the borough. But the fans were not the only ones hurting when the team moved to Los Angeles. "The thought of leaving these people made us heartsick," wrote Snider in his 1988 autobiography. "No more Bay Ridge? No more McKinneys or Steiners or Barwoods or Baumans for neighbors? No more living close to the Erskines, Reeses, and Walkers? No more taking the subway into New York on Saturday night? No cop telling me he hates baseball while he gives me a speeding ticket? No more Vinnie's Meat Market for club steak when I'm in a slump? And no more 'Duke of Flatbush'?"[52]

By 1962 Snider had become a fixture with the Dodgers organization. At eighteen years old, he played in his first professional season (1944)—2 games with the Montreal Royals and then 131 games with the Newport News Dodgers, where he pounded Piedmont League pitching for a .294 average. Snider followed a stint in the navy in 1945 with a return to baseball; the Dodgers sent him to the Fort Worth Cats for 1946. The next two seasons were split—the Dodgers and St. Paul Saints in 1947, then the Dodgers and the Royals in 1948. Branch Rickey brought him to Brooklyn for good in 1949.

The Helmsman

Dodgers skipper Walter Alston held the reins of the Dodgers for twenty-three years—seven World Series appearances, four World Series championships, and a 2,040-1,613 win-loss record. "I've got the best job in the world," said Alston in his 1976 autobiography, *A Year at a Time*. "Mr. O'Malley has never bothered me. I never bother him. If they want me they call me. I never go near the front office unless it is a meeting I'm called to, and seldom do Mr. O'Malley or [his son] Peter come to the clubhouse."[53]

Alston was a company man, rising through the Dodgers organization after a one-game Major League career with the St. Louis Cardinals. He struck out. Alston managed the Nashua Dodgers, St. Paul Saints, and Montreal Royals before helming Los Angeles. Nashua won the New England League championship in 1946, the first of two years that Alston managed the team. His pedigree of excellence continued: one league championship at St. Paul, two league championships at Montreal, and one Little World Series at Montreal.

Alston owed his promotion to the Dodgers in large part to Bavasi, who prized hiring an insider. "Alston is a sound manager who does things our way. There was some question about bringing in an unknown, but we wanted an organization man. Walt is great to work with. He isn't a yes man and he doesn't kowtow, but you can talk to him," Bavasi said. "There have been plenty of times when he's won a game with a smart move. You never hear him mention that. If Durocher or Dressen let somebody hit a three-and-oh pitch and it paid off, you can bet they'd talk about it. Not Walt."[54]

In a city known for glamour, Alston had no airs about his station as one of the most famous people in Los Angeles. His rural upbringing in Darrtown, Ohio, gave him the baseline of humility complemented by work ethic, character, and substance. Located in the western part of the Buckeye State, Darrtown, with a population of a couple of hundred people, makes television's Mayberry look like a thriving metropolis.

Kim Ogle, Alston's granddaughter, says that the Dodgers manager never adopted the hallmarks of stardom often on view from the celebrities lighting up the seats at Dodger Stadium:

My grandfather couldn't wait to come home at the end of the season, put on overalls, go to the gun club, shoot skeet, and play golf. He never liked the limelight, which was a different manner than Tommy Lasorda. I grew up learning that stars were just people. We would see them at the ballpark. One time Frank Sinatra wanted to come in the clubhouse, but my grandfather wouldn't let him. The only time that I was starstruck was when we went to Caesars Palace in Las Vegas. Cary Grant was there and he was a big Dodgers fan. When my grandfather introduced me to him, I couldn't believe it!

We spent every summer vacation visiting my grandparents for two weeks. I was only six years old in 1962, but I definitely remember seeing the stadium site with the bulldozers while Dodger Stadium was being built. To think that there would be a baseball field was the coolest thing to me. When we got there in '62, I remember so well how shiny the cement was and the smell of newness. I had been to Forbes Field and Crosley Field because I grew up in that region of America. Those ballparks were kind of old and dirty. I remember going to the Coliseum, but to walk into Dodger Stadium and see the landscaping and Japanese gardens was like being in a fairy world. It was just unheard of.[55]

While Southern Californians celebrated baseball's new showplace, Pacific Northwesterners flocked to the Century 21 Exposition world's fair to see the displays predicting American life in the twenty-first century. Washington State had been flooded with news reports about the world's fair since 1955, when Seattle business leader and city council member Al Rochester had an idea to mark the fiftieth anniversary of the Alaska-Yukon-Pacific Exposition in 1909. Resolutions, negotiations, and legislation followed at the highest levels of local, state, and federal government. In an example of private-public cooperation, hotelier Eddie Carlson answered the request of Washington governor Arthur B. Langlie to put his business skills, civic passion, and political savvy to work: "If we can't turn to you in the private sector and have you help us with those things that we in government are supposed to do, how can we in government go ahead?"[56]

It was the biggest thing to hit Seattle since the Klondike gold rush.

President Kennedy kicked off the Century 21 Exposition—America's first world's fair in more than twenty years—by "pressing a telegraph key" and offering a speech by telephone from Palm Beach, Florida.[57] Mouths agape and eyes wide, visitors from around the world joined Americans in roaming the seventy-four acres of the fairgrounds and satisfying their curiosity about scientific visions of the future.[58]

Seattle's KING-TV broadcast of the fair's opening was one of the first—if not the first—examples of television's ability to cover breaking news. Anchored by Charles Herring at the Washington State Coliseum, the special programming had reporters strategically placed throughout the fair for Herring to call upon for interviews with fairgoers, exhibit hosts, and politicians who had shepherded the event from conception to execution. KING's broadcast went to Spokane, Portland, San Francisco, and Los Angeles.[59]

Representatives from around the globe highlighted their countries' contributions to culture, progress, and science. While the fairgoers waited for the president to officially open the Century 21 Exposition, splashes of glamour complemented the speeches by government notables and the fair's executives. Broadway star John Raitt belted out "Come to the Fair" and "Meet Me in St. Louis," while Danny Kaye honored the visionaries who drafted, planned, and built this extraordinary event that broke down boundaries and biases: "People who sought with a fury their place in the Sun. And they sought it with a dedication usually reserved for those who build nations, and discover lands and oceans. Or reach for new thoroughfares in the sky."[60]

The Space Needle was the fair's centerpiece, jutting upward with a Jetsons-like saucer at the top. Travelers sprang to the city's new monorail system—an aboveground mass-transit infrastructure with sleek trains. Teenage couples at the exhibits imagined life in their—gasp!—fifties as they held hands and glimpsed engineers' ideas of future travel, including passengers transiting at 200 miles per hour in a tube and trains operating on air like hovercraft. Ford, General Electric, NCR, Bell Telephone, NASA, and General Motors had exhibits showing the inventions that would change everyday life in the future, including call forwarding and touch-tone phones. The exhibitors were as excited about shaping future lifestyles as Americans were in learning about them. Kitchens. Fashion. Travel. Food. The forecasts didn't always come true, but they seemed possible, if not likely, in a country just two months after Glenn's historic flight. NASA showed a "gripping picture" of the mundane aspects of space flight—monitoring an astronaut's health, pulse, and respiration during a mission—and spacecraft models.[61]

And then there were the more basic needs and desires addressed in the fair's exhibits. In the section dubbed "Show Street, U.S.A.," businessmen enjoying a day off to celebrate the city's historic event visited a theater-restaurant depicting a fantasy skit—astronauts landing on a planet and finding a male-oriented paradise "inhabited by sensuous young ladies wearing little more than out-of-this-world headgear." The orb was called Planet Eve.[62]

But it was not just technology that awed visitors; newcomers to the art world found an outstanding array of pieces. In the text of the fair's official souvenir program, actor and noted art collector Vincent Price praised the world's fair and opined that art fit into the theme: "Museums are the public homes of art. They belong to all of us and are meant to be used by us to enable us to learn to see. They should function for us as visual libraries where we can read the past, the present and—since art is almost always prophetic—the future. The great collections at the Seattle World's Fair afford a magnificent opportunity for us to see a broad cross-section of art."[63]

Seattle's majestic geography formed the backdrop for romance, and *Seattle Post-Intelligencer* columnist Emmett Watson offered interesting early-sixties advice to his male readers. Warning males not to seek out women affected by status symbols, Watson instead suggested looking for female mates with a "fine wide-eyed curiosity about everything." Physical activity was mandated: "She should love to walk. She should have read Proust and she should enjoy poetry and love to search for driftwood on beaches. She should look good in stretch pants, know how to ski, not mind at all if her nose gets red with cold and she should enjoy Sunday concerts in the park and be willing to take ferry rides with you."[64]

There was a tragic story that visitors learned either by word of mouth or later that night on television. An air force fighter plane designated to be part of a flyover for the fair had crashed. The pilot ejected after "difficulty with the plane," which destroyed two houses and killed the couple inside one of them. The husband and wife were in their sixties; the pilot was rescued from Lake Washington with "minor facial scratches." The Associated Press reported that he had tried to put the plane in the water and got a thousand feet above the lake when he ejected. But the plane "began a sudden climb" and then crashed into the houses.[65]

The world's fair gave NASA the opportunity to do some public-relations work. The White House, meanwhile, boosted the space program when national security adviser McGeorge Bundy issued National Security Action Memorandum No. 144, which affirmed the Kennedy administration's dedication to exploring the heavens. With three Mercury missions—and only one orbital mission—Bundy cited the Defense Production Act of 1950, stating that the president had earmarked "the highest national priority category for research and development and for achieving operational capability: APOLLO (manned lunar landing program, including essential spacecraft, launch vehicles, and facilities)."[66]

Viewers couldn't change the channel in 1962 without finding a news report or a television show mentioning the space program. In the *Perry Mason* episode "The Case of the Angry Astronaut," the legendary lawyer, who began life as a creation of lawyer-novelist Erle Stanley Gardner and became a popular-culture fixture with Raymond Burr's portrayal, defends a space hero accused of murdering a general in charge of Project Moonstone, consisting of an earth orbital flight, circumlunar flight, and astronaut landing on the moon. While undergoing physical-stress tests, he suffered emotional issues; the general had fired the astronaut from Project Mercury, the sister project to Moonstone. Grissom, Shepard, and Glenn are referenced in dialogue.[67]

The next real-life Mercury launch was the *Aurora 7* spacecraft. For the second time, America confronted the possibility that it could lose an astronaut in space.

5

Aurora 7, Where Are You?

Scott Carpenter had to move quickly.

Mindful of the dangers that can occur during splashdown, the thirty-seven-year-old astronaut watched through the window of his *Aurora 7* space capsule—steadied by drogue chutes—as it floated toward the Atlantic Ocean after the five-hour flight. Astronauts were not mere passengers in this phase; there was some piloting, too.

Carpenter did not want a repeat of Gus Grissom's splashdown. Grissom, the second American astronaut in space, nearly drowned when *Liberty Bell 7*'s escape hatch blew open before he could secure the craft and recovery crews could get to him. Water began filling the capsule and Grissom's suit; he scrambled out of it and into the ocean, but he did not have a life raft. The recovery team got him out of the ocean, but the incident left a permanent reminder of the risks of spaceflight, from launch to return. *Liberty Bell 7* sank into the sea.

Carpenter was inside *Aurora 7*, and it appeared to be seaworthy. He needed it to stay afloat so he could get out, with his camera, and head up through the bulkhead, because the safety equipment, including an inflatable life raft, was stored in the capsule's nose. With great care, he made his move. If the capsule tipped over and took on seawater, gravity would intervene and send the capsule down like a stone. Carpenter went through his safety checklist, crawled into the nose, tossed the raft into the ocean, and tethered it to the capsule.

"When he failed to raise a response on his radio, he decided to get out of the cramped capsule," states NASA's account of *Aurora 7*'s flight. "Then he saw that the capsule was floating rather deeply, which meant that it might be dangerous to remove the hatch. Sweating profusely in the 101-degree temperature of the cabin, he pulled off his helmet and began the job of egress as it had been originally planned. Carpenter wormed his way upward through the throat of the spacecraft, a hard, hot job made bearable by his leaving the suit circuit hose attached and not unrolling the neck dam. He struggled with the camera, packaged life raft, survival kit, and kinky hose before he finally got his head outside."[1]

The survival kit's search and rescue homing (SARAH) beacon had begun signaling. It was designed to do so automatically in case an unconscious astronaut splashed down; the signals from *Aurora 7* during Carpenter's reentry also gave search and recovery crews a good idea of his location. Plus, there was fluorescent dye surrounding him. America's fourth astronaut looked for patrol planes. He was ready to be spotted, recovered, and debriefed.

But there was a problem with the splashdown of this latest mission in NASA's Project Mercury on May 24, 1962—NASA didn't know where its latest hero and his raft were bobbing like a bar of Ivory soap in the bathtub.

Safely aboard the raft, Carpenter had as much worry as the Harlem Globetrotters have about beating the Washington Generals, thanks to his confidence in the flight plan's contingencies. While news anchors broadcast the possibility that America, for the first time, might have lost an astronaut in space, searchers found Carpenter 250 miles from his planned landing site near the recovery ship, the USS *Intrepid*. A malfunctioning autopilot had caused the gap that was roughly the distance between Los Angeles and Las Vegas.

"I darned near cried when I spotted him," said Lieutenant Robert Goldner, co-pilot of a P2V Neptune, the same model that Carpenter flew during the Korean War.[2] With a crew of six, Goldner and his co-pilot, Jim Hickman, were in a patrol squadron of three Neptunes searching for the latest circumnavigator of the globe. All three received the signals, but Goldner worked out the math quicker. "Are you the ones who said he missed?" inquired *What's My Line?* panelist Johnny Carson three days later, when Goldner and Hickman appeared on the game show with their crew in the audience.[3] Carson's remark prompted laughter from the pilots, the studio audience, and most certainly the millions watching at home. Through a series of questions, the four-person panel deduced that the duo were involved in Carpenter's recovery, but they failed to determine how.

NASA lore portrays Lieutenant Commander Carpenter (U.S. Navy) ignoring systems checks in favor of savoring his flight experience, which nearly depleted his fuel reserves; the NASA version is that he screwed up, almost lost his life, and embarrassed the agency by landing in the Atlantic Ocean 250 miles away from the target.

The truth is more complex and less daunting, for two important reasons.

First, Carpenter proved the importance of a pilot in spaceflight. A pilot can, when required, override automatic systems in a malfunctioning spacecraft. In the 1983 film *The Right Stuff*, which portrays the Mercury astronauts, Carpenter and his space-bound colleagues emphasize the issue to engineers who would rather rely on mechanical processes than human contingencies. It's a face-off between the engineers and the astronauts—the engineers don't see the need for a capsule window, while the astronauts argue for one because they're pilots, and therefore they need to see where they're going and how the capsule reacts. If there's a glitch, the astronaut would need to fly the capsule, which would be impossible without a window.

U.S. Navy psychologist Bob Voas was part of the NASA staff responsible for screening and training astronauts. He pointed out that Shepard's *Freedom 7* and Grissom's *Liberty Bell 7* had "fixed" suborbital flight paths, each lasting fifteen minutes; NASA truncated Glenn's *Friendship 7* flight because Mission Control believed there may have been glitches with the space capsule, glitches ultimately found not to exist. "But with *Aurora 7*, the gyro problem went undetected on the ground and the attitude control system was malfunctioning," said Voas. "The astronaut's eye on the horizon was the only adequate check of the automated gyro system. With its malfunctioning gyros, the space-craft could not have maintained adequate control during retrofire. Mercury Control may have viewed the manually controlled reentry as sloppy, but the spacecraft came back in one piece and the world accepted the flight for what it was: another success."[4]

Second, a space flight is a marriage of execution between an astronaut and ground control. There is a shared responsibility that, in the aftermath of the *Aurora 7* splashdown, got overshadowed in the analysis. Assistant flight director Gene Kranz said, "A major component of the ground team's respon-sibility is to provide a check on the crew. The ground had waited too long in addressing the fuel status and should have been more forceful in getting on with the checklists."[5]

Contemporaneous accounts supported Carpenter's report of mechanical mal-functions causing the 250-mile gulf between the life raft and the recovery ship.

According to Marvin Miles, space-aviation editor for the *Los Angeles Times*, "Project Mercury operations director Walter Williams said the overshoot was caused by a failure in the automatic system which controls the spacecraft's position in space. He said Carpenter had to control the capsule manually, even during the tricky retro rocket firing sequence for re-entry."[6]

Carpenter talked about the mission's specifics when asked, but he did not seek the opportunity to spotlight his achievement. "I had a flight plan that was devoted to science where the other flight plans were more devoted to engineering, looking at the spacecraft itself instead of where the spacecraft got us," said Carpenter in the twelve-episode 2002–3 documentary *Rocket Science*.[7] For reasons that have been ascribed to NASA politics in several accounts decades after the flight, Carpenter never flew in space again. But there's another layer to his being grounded—a motorbike injury, suffered in Bermuda, caused compound fractures to his left forearm that never healed properly. He couldn't rotate his left wrist enough to reach the toggle switches in a Gemini or Apollo capsule.

But before his experience in space, Carpenter was serving on the USS *Hornet* for required "sea duty" as an intelligence officer. It was then that he got the missive that changed his fate. Part of his responsibility was supervising other pilots; his outstanding career as a naval aviator had brought him to the attention of NASA. According to an account Carpenter penned for *We Seven*, an anthology authored by the Mercury astronauts,

> I was already at sea when a letter arrived from the Navy Bureau of Personnel in Washington. The letter went something like this: "You will soon receive orders to O-05 in Washington in connection with a special project. Please do not discuss the matter with anyone or speculate on the purpose of the orders, as any prior identification of yourself with the project might prejudice that project." That was all I knew. I was intrigued, but I spoke to no one about it. The next day, when the mail plane came in, the orders were on it. Since I was now in the intelligence game, everyone guessed that I had been called to Washington for some kind of intelligence briefing. I thought so myself.[8]

On the way to Los Angeles International Airport for a civilian flight to Washington, Carpenter and his wife speculated whether he was being summoned for Project Mercury, because it had been mentioned in that week's issue of *Time*.[9]

NASA administered a battery of tests to determine coordination, stamina, and mental endurance for America's first star voyagers, and Carpenter excelled at those challenges. He lasted longer than his peers on a treadmill test that required the astronauts to perform under increasing inclines and speeds; in a cardiac and lung-capacity test, he pedaled a bicycle with increasing resistance while exhaling. "The purpose of the test was to trap the air we exhaled in order to determine how efficiently our lungs worked," explained Carpenter. "The doctors had seventeen rubber bags standing by for me to fill. But I fooled them. I kept going so long that they ran out of bags. The doctors said this was the first time that had ever happened, so I think I broke that record, too."[10]

The 1983 film *The Right Stuff*, based on the 1979 book of the same name by Tom Wolfe, depicts another lung-capacity test in which the astronauts each breathed into a tube. In the movie they did it as a group; in reality the doctors administered the tests separately. "The record up until then was 94 seconds," Carpenter explains in *We Seven*. "I thought to myself, I'll just count up to one hundred as fast as I think seconds ought to go and I'll try to break this record, too. I counted too slowly, however, and when I finally had to give up I found out I had blown into the tube for 171 seconds without taking a breath. This little victory pleased me very much. The doctors were jumping up and down."[11]

Carpenter had an edge; he drew on his memory of native divers he had met in Hawaii and Guam during his Korean War tour of duty in the Pacific and on his knowledge that a buildup of carbon dioxide in the lungs is what triggered the need to breathe. So he expelled it in small increments.[12]

Carpenter's assignment to the *Aurora 7* had some ironic connections for the new astronaut. He had grown up at the corner of Aurora Street and Seventh Avenue in Boulder, Colorado, where he was fascinated by the night skies. During his Korean War tour of duty in Alaska, Carpenter saw the Aurora Borealis as he patrolled the Arctic Circle; in letters to his wife Rene, he described being awestruck by the cosmic phenomenon.[13]

NASA's work force in Florida had to wait out a series of delays for *Aurora 7*'s launch.[14] To occupy themselves in the meantime there were the Starlite Motel and other nighttime spots around Cape Canaveral frequented by tourists, residents, and NASA staff. To combat boredom, fatigue, and anxiety, the astronauts listened to entertainers like Charlie Manna, Bill Dana, Peggy Lloyd, Oscar Brand, and a cadre of comedians spout space-related jokes. "The work is highly gratifying, the performers say, because everybody is so eager to relax at night away from Cape Canaveral that they will applaud almost anybody who is vaguely humorous," wrote Gay Talese in the *New York Times*.[15]

Aurora 7 launched into the Florida sky on the morning of May 24 with a flight plan doubling down on the three manned Mercury missions under NASA's belt. Carpenter's to-do list included, in addition to piloting the capsule, monitoring a balloon connected to the capsule, taking pictures, and conducting a "food experiment [that] had left crumbs floating in the cabin."[16]

A Mercury astronaut's mission had the support of a team of thousands. While the astronaut traversed space, men and women who would never be known outside their circles of friends, family, and colleagues went unsung. They engineered and built the rockets and spacecrafts, designed and fabricated the spacesuits, and monitored and adjusted the mission from the ground during its execution. They were unsung heroes reducing the challenge of space flight to its basics of mathematical equations factored with velocity, trajectory, and gravity. These slide-rule soldiers knew no glory other than a mission ending with an astronaut returning to *mare oceanum*, then *terra firma*.

For Spacious Skies: The Uncommon Journey of a Mercury Astronaut, written forty years after *Aurora 7* took flight, was the first time that the mission was detailed with specifics from Carpenter's point of view. The memoir fills a void for anyone inspired by *The Right Stuff*—book or movie—or other accounts to learn more about the early days of NASA, the astronauts whose missions led to the two-man Gemini flights and three-man Apollo flights, and the chronicling of an American hero who rejected the lure to cash in on his fame through endorsements and other business opportunities in favor of continuing his work as an explorer.

It's possible that Carpenter turned to the sea with the Sealab project because underwater research gave him the opportunity to submerge himself in unglamorous work. There were no front-page headlines or ticker-tape parades for aquanauts. But Carpenter had already ascended to being a worldwide celebrity and suffered the costs of fame. He neither wanted nor welcomed more public attention.

When he passed away in 2013, Carpenter was honored for his reconnaissance missions during the Korean War; his flights as a navy test pilot; his service on the USS *Hornet*; and for being an aquanaut on the navy's Sealab project, including commanding the Sealab II mission and setting an underwater record for living on the bottom of the Pacific Ocean off California for a month. Obituaries mentioned these achievements, along with personal information—four marriages, childhood in Colorado—but piloting the *Aurora 7* spacecraft would be the landmark achievement that people remembered.

In the same month that Carpenter became the second Mercury astronaut in orbit, his predecessor welcomed his visiting Soviet counterpart Gherman Titov to the United States. Titov's stops included meeting John Glenn and President Kennedy, plus visits to New York and the world's fair in Seattle.

Schoolchildren in the early 1960s may have dreamed of being astronauts, but their fathers dreamed of being Bo Belinsky.

Not a Hall of Fame pitcher by any stretch, Robert "Bo" Belinsky did have a Hall of Fame day: May 5, 1962. He tossed a no-hitter for the Los Angeles

Angels against the Baltimore Orioles. Angels catcher Buck Rodgers, who placed second in the American League Rookie of the Year voting in 1962, proclaimed Belinsky's heater to be the spine of the game. "He could challenge anybody with that fastball. He got the screwball over early, but the fastball set up everything," proclaimed Rodgers, who received accolades from Angels skipper Bill Rigney.[17] Rigney weighed in as well, on Rodgers: "Not to take anything away from Bo, don't overlook the great job Bob Rodgers did behind the plate. He called all the pitches—we made no suggestions from the bench—and Bo shook him off only a few times."[18]

It was the first no-hitter thrown by a rookie southpaw and the first for the Angels, then in their sophomore MLB season. But it had an avenging resonance for Belinsky, who exorcised a ghost of failure in front of 15,886 fans at Dodger Stadium—the Angels' home field from 1961 to 1965—because the Orioles had cut him in 1958. "I don't know about me, but it couldn't happen to a nicer team," said Belinsky after the game.[19] There was also a financial boon: Belinsky sold the game ball to the owner of a car dealership in exchange for ten monthly payments on a Cadillac that he purchased.[20]

Belinsky was a baseball-playing Lothario during the ring-a-ding-ding years of Frank Sinatra's whisky-soaked ballads and Rat Pack swagger and between the television debuts of Elvis Presley on *Stage Show* and the Beatles on *The Ed Sullivan Show*, and he plunged head first into the vortex of fame, where personality trumps—or obscures—talent.[21]

Through 102 games started in eight Major League seasons, Belinsky compiled a 28-51 win-loss record. Performance did not matter to the glitterati, however. Thrust into the spotlight after the no-hitter, Belinsky boozed like he owned stock in a Milwaukee brewery, epitomized a "devil may care but I do not" manner, and rode wave after wave of celebrity female companionship—a perquisite of living, working, and amusing in the metropolitan area known for defining, glorifying, and maximizing sex appeal.

Had Belinsky played thirty years prior, Damon Runyon likely would have created a character based on him.

Belinsky's exploits reached the red zone on the male-fantasy meter when he got engaged to Mamie Van Doren, she of the shapely body that could make a catatonic man jump like a jack-in-the-box. Van Doren rafted on the allure of buxom blondes cultivated by Marilyn Monroe, but Monroe was more than a pretty face and curvy figure offering sex appeal with an undercurrent of innocence backed by a breathy voice. Whispery, almost. Monroe chose to study with the famed Actors Studio in New York to improve her skills after she was already a household name. Van Doren, on the other hand, proclaimed ferocious sexuality, enhanced by her curves. To watch Van Doren sing "Oobala Baby" in the 1957 movie *Untamed Youth* while prancing, shaking, and swiveling is to see Exhibit A of suggestiveness in body, voice, and expression.

Jayne Mansfield, another addition to the lineup of blonde bombshells— which included Sheree North and Kim Novak—had breasts that inspired comedy writer and future talk-show icon Dick Cavett to pen an introduction for his boss Jack Paar, the host of NBC's *The Tonight Show*: "Ladies and gentlemen, what can I say about my next guest, except—Here they are, Jayne Mansfield."[22]

Mansfield died in a car accident in 1967. Monroe, three months to the day after Belinsky's no-hitter, succumbed to a drug overdose. The comparisons weighed on Van Doren. "Hollywood never appreciated my talent," said the South Dakota native in 2000. "I was just another blonde lucky to have a good body. They never looked past that. They never allowed me to be my own woman. So you know what? I said, 'Fuck you, Hollywood.' I just didn't care anymore."[23]

The Belinsky–Van Doren celebrity coupling lasted through the 1963 baseball season. "Our life was a circus," Van Doren said after Belinsky's death in 2001. "We were engaged on April Fools' Day and broke the engagement on Halloween. It was a wild ride, but a lot of fun."[24]

Belinsky claimed the engagement resulted from a newspaper story. When Van Doren asked about a marriage date, Belinsky complied with the tradition of buying an engagement ring. To those in Belinsky's circle, she presented a danger. It was one thing for ballplayers to celebrate with women for short-term, even one-time-only, encounters. Marriage was a different story altogether, particularly when it involved a woman of Van Doren's proportions in body, magnetism, and, most important, fame. Through no fault of her own, she became a source of conflict in Belinsky's baseball circle. "Everybody was ripping me about the engagement," said Belinsky. "They're telling me, 'You're gonna distract yourself. She's no good for the game, Bo.' But every time I would introduce Mamie to them, their goddam tongues would hang out, from [club owner] Gene Autry on down. Everybody wanted to take a nip at her. Oh, it was fast and furious action."[25]

Advocacy was met with silence from Belinsky.

It wasn't too long before he realized that the ones doing the protesting had Van Doren in their sights for selfish reasons. Perhaps thinking her to be a disloyal pushover, which wasn't the case, or believing Belinsky to be an indifferent cad, which also wasn't grounded in reality, his baseball brethren attempted to outflank him when the opportunity arose—or when they created one. The one no-hit wonder revealed some details in 1972:

> For example, when I was going with Mamie, they called me into the office over and over and told me she was no good for me. Finally, when I wouldn't listen, they shipped me to Hawaii. And while I'm there, I get a call from Mamie telling me that the same front-office people who shipped me out were bothering her all the while I was gone. If only I didn't see all that, I would have been all right. But I had this third eye, and when I saw things that I shouldn't have, I overreacted. Usually it was in a way that made no sense, like getting drunk. Maybe I see things out of proportion, or things that aren't even there. Maybe I just don't know how to express what I feel.[26]

Rigney, in contrast, said, "She was the best of his girls. That was one of Bo's bad moves. He should have married the blonde. She would have been good for him."[27] Belinsky blamed the dissolution of the famous and coveted coupling on his smoking—he liked it, she complained.[28]

For the teenager who grew up hustling in the pool halls of Trenton, New Jersey, life wasn't supposed to be segmented into areas of professional responsibilities, familial obligations, and societal norms. "Life is to be lived, man," posited Belinsky. "Some guys play baseball and made a few bucks more than me. What do they have when they quit[?] [A] big mortgage, a wife, a couple of screaming kids and an ulcer. Me? I got memories."[29] Those memories often found their source in the prose of gossip columnist Walter Winchell, who had an exchange system—he found women for the ballplayer and got stories in return.[30] But Belinsky's star power was so strong he could land dates on his own, with liaisons including Tina Louise ("a beautiful broad"), Ann-Margret ("a real pushy broad"), and Paulette Goddard ("probably my favorite class broad").[31] Marriages to *Playboy* Playmate Jo Collins and timber heiress Janine Weyerhauser resulted in divorce; he had a daughter with Collins and twin daughters with Weyerhauser.

Belinsky, who was with the Phillies in 1965, declared that his machismo would have been an asset if he had been on the previous year's squad, which tied with the Cincinnati Reds for second place in the National League; the St. Louis Cardinals won the pennant by one game and beat the New York Yankees in a seven-game World Series. "You know what I hadda done last year if we were that close to the flag and taking a nose dive? I would have gone out and got some big blonde and punched her right out, at Broad and Market. I would have knocked her right on her can and made the headlines in World War II print. Take the pressure off everybody, you know?" he mused. "In those last days, those ballplayers just didn't know what was happening. They needed a fall guy to take the heat off them."[32]

With the adrenaline pumping before and after a game, it was easy to let off steam by finding women all too eager to bed a ballplayer. By the time he left the diamond, though, Belinsky had an emotional tiredness preventing him from enjoying the benefits of women seeking sexual companionship with a ballplayer whose stardom exceeded his skill. In a Talmudic dissection of his process, Belinsky charted his course for sportswriter Myron Cope:

> Finally, the afternoon of the day I'm pitching, girls are calling on the phone asking to come over, or a beautiful girl I don't hear from in a month is climbing my roof to get into my place.
>
> I'm keyed up and I'm partially in heat, you know, because I'm strong. I ate all this good food these four days, I'm real tigerish, and here she slides through the door saying, "Maybe I shouldn't have come." And I say, "That's right, now get out." But then I say, "No. Wait." And it always winds up that this great temptation, which I should have after I pitch, is presented to me right here, you know, and it's very funny because it goes against the grain of baseball.[33]

When Belinsky noticed a woman balancing on a ledge outside his apartment, he took the mantle of Good Samaritan: "I look up and see this delicious-looking broad hanging over the edge and peeking into the glass roof. What could I do? I had to invite her in just to save her life."[34]

Sex did not in any tangible way affect Belinsky's ability to throw the no-hitter against the Angels. Belinsky proffered the benefit as a ballplayer's superstition rather than an endorphin-releasing, mind-clearing, and stress-reducing experience. "Since the day I pitched that no-hitter in Los Angeles, I'm still looking for the girl I spent the night before with," revealed Belinsky. "This was some kind of good-luck gal, but she disappeared out of the picture. I'd met her at Ernie's House of Serfas. Here I was with an ordinary secretary, probably no flashy gal in any way, but a lean, beautiful gal. And this is how I trained for my no-hitter and it came off."[35]

Named for boxer Bobo Olson during childhood "because I got knocked down so much," Bo Belinsky compiled a résumé across Major League Baseball from 1962 to 1970—Angels, Phillies, Astros, Pirates, Reds.[36] During part of the 1966 season he played for the San Diego Padres (the Phillies' Triple-A team in the Pacific Coast League); his altercation with a television sportscaster that year made headlines. Al Couppee, KOGO's sports director, claimed that he ran Belinsky "halfway around the ballpark" after the southpaw challenged Couppee's article targeting his unfulfilled promise on the mound; Belinsky started eleven games, ratcheted a 2-4 record, and boasted an ERA of 4.60 with San Diego. Already a controversial figure with the press because of an encounter with *Los Angeles Times* sportswriter Braven Dyer in 1964, Belinsky, according to Couppee, wrote a letter ending with a challenge that Aaron Burr would have applauded: "If you've got any guts, which I doubt, you know where to find me."[37]

Couppee outweighed Belinsky by nearly fifty pounds, but he was also seventeen years older—forty-six to Belinsky's twenty-nine. And he had a heart condition. Belinsky pivoted, claiming the incident to be a setup:

> Then people start stepping in between us and telling me that he has a bad heart and that I shouldn't be getting him excited like that.
>
> Then about five people get hold of him, and that's when he started telling everybody what he was going to do to me. Well, you know, you can be pretty brave when you know five people are holding onto you.

All I know is that he didn't want to take a swing when nobody was holding him.[38]

The clash with Dyer happened in Belinsky's room in the Shoreham Hotel—a Washington landmark that hosted Franklin Roosevelt's first inaugural ball. It led to a suspension by the Angels in 1964; the twenty-seven-year-old hurler allegedly struck Dyer, a year shy of Social Security age. Belinsky said he "warded off" Dyer by using "the heel of my hand and he fell and hurt himself." Dyer's version: Belinsky "punched several times."[39]

Dyer suffered a cut under his left ear, blackened right eye and a laceration above it, bruise on forehead, double vision, and loss of consciousness.[40]

The fight was ignited after the publication of an Associated Press story by Charles Maher quoting Belinsky on his displeasure with baseball, his job stability with the Angels, and his financial status: "I've gotta make a move. This is my third year with this club and I'm going nowhere financially. I don't think I can ever count on getting the money I should."[41] His statement was seen as an expression of intent to exit baseball.

Dyer sought an audience with Belinsky to follow up. And that's when the wheels started to fall off the wagon. Returning to the Shoreham at 1:00 a.m., Belinsky saw Dyer pulling a stakeout in the lobby; the hurler "denied portions" of the AP article and then left the reporter. Dyer phoned in his new story. Whether propelled by doubt, alcohol, or a combination of them, the hard-partying Belinsky called Dyer an hour later to give yet another version. When Dyer refused to listen, it detonated Belinsky, who ignored the reality of a newspaper going to press being like a plane taking off—once it's gone, you cannot catch it. Verbal threats prompted Dyer to go to Belinsky's room, whereupon the relationship between the scribe and the southpaw suffered a blow. Or two. Or three.[42]

Belinsky wanted to change the story back to its original form, but a "stop the presses" moment exists more in the imaginations of playwrights, screenwriters, and novelists than in the newsrooms governed by ink-stained newspaper editors. It could not be done. "As an athletic feat," wrote Dyer peer Jim Murray, the fight "ranks somewhere between tipping over a baby carriage and poisoning a canary." He concluded that "when you have a 37-year pull in the weights, it becomes even less remarkable."[43]

In December 1964 the Angels traded Belinsky to the Phillies for Rudy May and Costen Shockley, two Minor Leaguers. He ended his career in 1970 with a legacy that does not state—or even hint at—greatness: a 28-51 win-loss record, 4.10 ERA, 146 games played, 102 games started, and 4 shutouts.

The Angels had show-business connections besides Belinsky's dalliances with celebrities, thanks to cowboy crooner Gene Autry's ownership. Radio listeners get bombarded every December with Christmas songs, and Autry had recorded the most popular ones—"Rudolph the Red-Nosed Reindeer," "Here Comes Santa Claus," "Frosty the Snowman." Besides his success in music, movies, radio, and television, Autry had keen business instincts that couldn't be taught in an MBA seminar. Investments in rodeo stock and the World Championship Rodeo Company made Autry a 1979 inductee in the Professional Rodeo Cowboys Association's Pro Rodeo Hall of Fame. His ownership in the Melody Ranch, a popular shooting location for producers needing a western setting, received national coverage when it burned down in August 1962. It had included a western-themed street and indoor soundstages. The fire destroyed not only the infrastructure but also "much of Autry's collection of antiques and Americana." Autry and his first wife, Ina, had owned the ranch only a short time. Workers at the ranch and the fourteen horses made it to safety; the damage was estimated at $1 million.[44]

Autry's portfolio had a prized television asset—KTLA. In December 1960, while Autry's holiday songs got people in the spirit of the season, the singing cowboy led a group of investors to buy the rights to the American League's expansion franchise in Los Angeles. The Angels debuted in 1961; Autry bought KTLA in 1963 and aired the Angels games on the station. KTLA was the Angels' broadcaster until 1995.

In 2002 Angels fans added a World Series championship to their reasons for celebrating Orange County's baseball lineage. But for those old enough to remember, Bo Belinsky was one of the first, if not the first, reason to celebrate. Belinsky bathed in the glow of the Angels' fandom, the adoration of women, and the shadows of his conscience. Ignoring the emotional, physical, and financial tolls created by his wildness off the field kept him cool—the more he pushed aside his conscience, the more fun he had. Given Bo's upbringing in Trenton, it is not a surprise. He had had a less than stellar home life, according to people who knew him quite well in his later years. Decades after his adolescence, people remarked at Belinsky's skills at the pool table; he couldn't decipher the mysteries of an isosceles triangle, but he knew exactly how to hit the cue ball so it struck the 15 ball at the right angle to bounce off the felt bumper into the corner pocket.

Belinsky found a bit of stability in Las Vegas, probably the last place that one would think the hard-partying former pitcher should have been. That journey ultimately led him to work at a well-known automobile dealership owned by a former World War II fighter pilot named Clifford O. "Pete" Findlay. After the war, Findlay ran a gas station in that city, and in 1961 he opened his Oldsmobile dealership there. Thirty years later he added a Saturn dealership that for four straight years was Saturn's number-one dealership in the country. Inspired by his Depression-era upbringing, Findlay had an impact on his community that reached to the educational system—there is a middle school named after him in Las Vegas.

Among Findlay's circle of associates and employees was Rich Abajian, a former University of Nevada–Reno defensive back and former UNLV football coach. He ran the Saturn of West Sahara dealership, cultivated his team, and earned the loyalty of his customers from its opening in 1990 until 1998, when he moved to launch Findlay Toyota, where he stayed until his death in 2016. Findlay's one dealership eventually grew to twenty-eight outlets with 1,700 employees, in Nevada, Arizona, Utah, Oregon, and Idaho. One of those many employees was Don Richardson, who was with Findlay Automotive Group in the Las Vegas area for twenty-three years, from 1991 to 2014. He was responsible for bringing Belinsky into the Findlay organization when it had expanded to three dealerships:

> When I first met Bo, he was just coming back from Hawaii. While we were golfing, he had told me that he sold cars at a Ford dealership in Hawaii. I said, "If you ever need a job, come see me." That was in October of 1991. About five months later, in comes Bo to the dealership. "Is that offer still good?" he asked. I told him, "Absolutely." Then I told Rich, my boss, who told me to get Bo a salesman license.
>
> To be honest, Bo wasn't a real good salesman. He wanted to quit, but Rich suggested that he do public relations work for the dealership instead.

Bo had a baseball pension. Rich offered him $1,500 a month and a company car. Bo couldn't have a phone in his apartment because it would have cost too much money. But he was on the phone at the office all the time for the dealership talking to people he knew across the country. He was a very kind and generous person. He didn't really do a lot of the nuts and bolts public relations work, but he got baseball people to the dealerships.

Dean Chance was his closest and best friend. Every opportunity that Dean had, he put Bo ahead of him so he could get some celebrity status. When Dean came to town once, he was on his way to an Old-Timers Game at Angel Stadium. Bo invited me to go as his guest. One time the old Boston pitcher Mickey McDermott came to Las Vegas to live in a condominium. He visited us at the dealership and said, "Bo, let me make a phone call. Do you want to go to Mickey Mantle's golf tournament in Commerce, Oklahoma?"

Bo died too young. It was the toll of an earlier life that started when the no-hitter gave him celebrity status. That night Walter Winchell took Bo and the Angels catcher, Buck Rodgers, out to dinner. They toured the Sunset Strip. And that became Bo's life when he played for the Angels.

One night he took me to the Sunset Strip after he and Dean hosted a dinner at the Palm restaurant in Hollywood. All the former Los Angeles sportswriters were there. Afterwards, there was a gathering of about twenty people. Dean said, "I'm going back to Anaheim." So, I went with Bo. He said, "I've got this friend, do you want to go to the Sunset Strip?" This is twenty years after he played, and it's like he never left. At one stop, he asked where the owner was. We were told he was in the back room. When we got there, there was electricity in the room.

Bo was in AA, but he had a relapse. He tried to take his life by cutting his wrists. A mutual friend told me that Bo had the presence of mind to call 911, which meant he didn't really want to die. It was the guilt over breaking a sobriety of more than twenty-five years. When I went to Bo's apartment, it was pure squalor. Bo went right back to AA.

Bo had his demons, but you would never know it by the way he treated people. He gave everyone respect, whether it was Curt Flood or Mamie

Van Doren or Dick Allen or Bert Campaneris. He treated everyone the same. He worked hard at the office to get ballplayers involved with us for charity work. We had Rod Carew and Bill Madlock giving batting lessons in batting cages on the lot.

When the Angels trained in Palm Desert, a girl trailed Bo there. During Bo's memorial service, a young man showed up. Dean Chance said it was Bo's son by that woman.[45]

Abajian, Bo's advocate at Findlay, personified the friendliness of Dale Carnegie, the energy of Hoover Dam, and the fitness of Jack LaLanne. He led his Findlay Automotive team with the philosophy of paying attention to the play, not the score. When a potential customer walked onto the lot, Abajian created a mental file of that person, enhancing it with each meeting. Fears, successes, concerns, challenges, and even regrets entered the file as information became available. When a Findlay customer walked into a showroom, it was not the embryonic phase of a sale; it was the beginning of a relationship fostered through Abajian's concentration on building a team.

When Abajian passed away suddenly in February 2016, the turnout for his sendoff required a venue that could hold more than 1,500 people because of the bond that Abajian had fostered through his customers, his friends, and his corporate activities, including overseeing the Findlay sponsorship of UNLV sports. South Point Hotel and Casino, run by former UNLV quarterback Steve Stallworth and former Abajian team member Billy Purcell—the general manager and assistant general manager, respectively—made it happen. Michael Gaughan, the casino owner, approved.

During the early 1990s Rich and Jo Ann Abajian lived in a home that the latter dubbed "The House That Saturn Built." Flush with financial stability as they entered a new phase of their lives, the Abajians never forgot what got them there—or who accompanied them along the way. They shared their home during the holidays, with Jo Ann cooking whatever recipe *The Today Show* declared to be the course du jour. Rich, who was movie-star handsome and had a workout regimen that would have tired men decades younger, looked like he could still sling the pigskin fifty yards, until he died suddenly in 2016 at age sixty-two. Jo Ann recalls the special relationship between Rich and Bo:

Bo would come to our house for dinner and sometimes, he'd stay with us in a guest room. Rich and I would sit around after dinner with Bo, and sometimes his baseball career would come up. I had difficulty reconciling the stories I heard about Bo with the well-mannered, gentlemanly, courtly man that I knew. If we were at a restaurant and I went to the ladies room, he stood up. When I came back, he stood up. It was like something from the nineteenth century.

Rich and Bo were very close. People sometimes thought that Bo was Rich's dad. They didn't do too much to dispel that perception, but if people dug any further, they'd've found out that these two friends were not related. Bo looked older because he had lived a rougher life. Bo was amazing and so was Rich. They just clicked. Rich liked using sports figures as a lure to sell cars. He had Macho Camacho come onto the lot. One time he brought the Boston Celtics to the store. Rich liked athletes because he was one himself and he knew that they had a work ethic, especially about teamwork. That was Rich's credo.

Rich adopted my son, Bruce. When Bruce got married, he went off with his wife during Christmas time. I like to fill my home with those who don't have anyplace to go. Rich and I needed them and they needed us. I think it was tremendously important for Bo. Once, I asked him if he had any regrets. He talked about his daughters.

When things got so bad for Bo when he was trying to get sober, he carried a Bible with him. I just visualized him clutching this Bible and pushing it into his chest when he wanted to have a drink.[46]

Unlike those who relive past successes, Bo Belinsky kept his baseball days as a chapter long since closed. Tyler Corder, the chief operating officer of Findlay Automotive, journeyed to Las Vegas after starting his career in Spokane, Washington, as a repo man out of college. He had worked on Indian reservations and in logging camps and spent eight years in the Bay Area with GMAC, the finance division of General Motors. Corder offers his recollections of Belinsky:

He was humble. You wouldn't know that he was famous. I would ask him about parts of his autobiography. He would laugh and say, "That was me before." I remember asking him specifically about Ann-Margret, who was appearing at one of the casinos. When I mentioned the idea of reaching out to her, he flatly said, "That's way in my past."

Bo only talked about alcohol in that it made him wild. He basically grew up on the streets and made his way by himself. By the time he got to Findlay, he was just a guy trying to make his way in the world. Most days, he went to a restaurant across the street and bought breakfast for Rich and me. He was just happy to be around. Rich was almost a father figure to Bo. He gave Bo a chance and was kind of a mentor. Outside work, Bo didn't have much of a social life. He was living in a humble apartment in central Las Vegas.

Rich made Bo an ambassador for Findlay. Bo mingled with customers and helped with promotions. I remember taking him to St. George, Utah. People loved to talk to Bo when they found out who he was. But Rich had a trait of being a good guy, so he didn't just use Bo. Rich really took Bo under his wing. He really liked hiring athletes because they loved to compete. It's probably one of the reasons that Bo felt at home working with us.

The Bo that I remember was an older gentleman with a limp, kind of shuffling along. You would never pick him out of a crowd as a professional baseball player. When people recognized him, he got this slight grin of satisfaction. He never volunteered information about his playing days, but he answered if people asked him about it. The only time I remember him talking freely about it was during a dinner with bankers that we do business with. He let his guard down to answer their questions, especially the ones about showing up in a limousine at training camp. Other than that, he didn't talk in details or stories too much. There was an emptiness about Bo, but he never complained.

The only time Bo really talked about sports was when Dean Chance would see him and reminisce about baseball.[47]

Belinsky's Major League career ended in 1970 with a win-loss tally of 28-51. It had begun with a brief contract dispute that caused a controversy. Any thoughts of an outstanding tenure on the mound because of the no-hitter in his rookie season had long since evaporated; his 1962 record was 10-11. But

Belinsky's career was more than the no-hitter; he fought through a mercurial tenure in the Minor League, including playing for two teams in 1958 and four teams in 1959. During his time in the Majors, Belinsky got sent down to the Minors in 1963, 1966, 1968, and 1969.

When Pittsburgh sent Belinsky to the Indianapolis Indians—the Reds' Triple-A team in the American Association—after the 1969 season, he had tried to put the fun-loving persona behind him. Maturity and stability were elusive, though in his sights. "I thought having fun was all that counted. Maybe it isn't too late," revealed Belinsky during spring training in 1970.[48] Being in the company of beautiful women had made Belinsky a hero to men and an object of desire to women. Now he was dedicated to making his second marriage work. His alcoholism problem, though, was not yet identified as a threat to his mental, emotional, and physical health. It would be a couple of decades before Belinsky realized that he did not have a preference for alcohol—he had an addiction to it.

And he still loved baseball. "You've heard of hungry athletes making good," said Belinsky at the beginning of the 1970 season. "Well, I was hungry, period. Not just hungry for the chance, but hungry for nourishment. I mean it happened this spring. I mean I had to skimp on food in Tampa, living on a minor league expense account. But I'm not complaining. That's how it is."[49]

It seemed that Reds manager Sparky Anderson aimed to use Belinsky in relief. This was the beginning of the Big Red Machine in the 1970s, so a relief position for an aging pitcher would have been a good spot. Belinsky attributed his success to Pete Rose, who said, "I felt he could help us and I wanted to make sure he didn't do anything to mess it up. I wouldn't let him quit or get down."[50]

Belinsky's attempt to play on a Major League squad in 1970, noble as it was, did not end with the glory that fading athletes desire. He played in three games before getting sent to Indianapolis in May. It was a one-way exodus. "They can't recall me from Indianapolis, so if I go down there I'm locked on a minor league roster the rest of the year. I believe I could help this club and I'm disappointed, but I could see which way the wind was blowing," he said. "This is a fine bunch of guys and I'm glad to have at least had an opportunity to make the team."[51]

There would be no more Major League ballparks, no fans curious to see if he could reclaim a sliver of the ability that he showed early in his career. Belinsky started sixteen games for Indianapolis and went 7-6. In August he went to the Asheville Tourists, the Reds' team in the Double-A Southern League.[52] Belinsky started three games, pitched in two others, and notched an 0-2 record to close out his career.

Bo Belinsky's fire burned brightest on a Saturday afternoon in May 1962. "I don't want to sound like a saint. I'll always be Bo, and there will always be something to work on as far as character defects. But I'm sure the hell not what I used to be. I just want to see if I can clean the slate a little," said Belinsky three decades later.[53]

With the determination of a toddler holding a favorite toy, Belinsky clung to his life in Las Vegas, rested in the security it offered, and feared that it could be wiped away. Finally, Bo had the structure that he had lacked as a child, ignored as a ballplayer, and craved as an alcoholic needing stability. Sinners can be rehabilitated of course, but by their own admission they'll never become saints nor will they label themselves as victims.

Alcoholism is a nasty combatant uninterested in class, wealth, or status. And those who suffer emotional devastation from an addict's decorum, or lack thereof, including the addict, may offer redemption. But the specter of heartbreak, even buried, hovers. It's always there, haunting along with the demon of addiction. Belinsky knew this, which made his Las Vegas circle more precious to him than a left arm that could hurl a 95 mph fastball.

Bo Belinsky did that which was familiar to him—celebrating to excess because people cheered him, because it felt good, and because he didn't know any other way. When the crowd applauds your name, the scribes write it, and gorgeous women whisper it in seduction—or exclaim it in ecstasy—the male psyche coasts on waves of fame, sex, and adoration without attending to the emotional rip currents underneath. Attention, in all its forms, sustained Bo's ego. Liquor mollified it when the noise evaporated. That's not to condone actions that are red meat for gossip columnists, clubhouse yentas, and holier-than-thou types. It is, as they say, what it is.

But the kid from Trenton—the one who got a PhD in hustling by hanging around pool halls while other kids were playing in Little League—suffered bucketfuls of shame that he could never dry off. Not completely. Droplets remained in his soul as badges of tenure in the dark side of a ballplayer's paradise, where the drinks never got warm, the women never stopped fawning, and the fans always showered him with adulation enhancing Southern California's sunshine.

Bo Belinsky would have been the first to tell you that he was undeserving of the love that he found with Rich and Jo Ann Abajian, Tyler Corder, Don Richardson, and scores of others at Findlay Automotive Group. He was the last to know how deep that love went—if he ever knew at all.

"I have a necklace made from a diamond of Bo's ring," says Richardson. "Home plate is on one side, crossed bats are on the other side, and the top is a baseball with a diamond chip. Underneath are Bo's birth and death dates. And when you go to his grave, there are always flowers. Somebody always remembers Bo."[54]

6

Meeting the Mets

With the joy of a child on Christmas morning, a woman, rather matronly in appearance but impeccably dressed, with a fashionable hat adorning her grayish hair and framing a cherubic face, approached Box 4A, Section 16, at the Polo Grounds during the 1962 baseball season. Once a minority stockholder in the New York Giants baseball club, she mourned when the great Giants-Dodgers rivalry left New York City behind and shifted three thousand miles westward.

For Joan Whitney Payson and tens of thousands of other baseball fans, 1962 was a clean slate. An heiress in the Whitney family, the fifty-nine-year-old Payson had the comfort of wealth and the status of society; her family was in the New York 400, an indicator of the city's high-society folks, those who make donations that result in hospital wings, arts endowments, and humanitarian of the year awards. But it was not family that made the New York Mets part of her portfolio. To Payson, baseball was not merely an investment to yield profit, dividends, and financial security. It was a passion. She drove a Bentley with the vanity license plate "MET 1" and a Lark with the license plate "MET 2"—symbols of adoration, not proclamations of grandeur, ego, or prosperity. "Self-conscious about her wealth, she simply refuses to talk about it, and is completely at ease with those of lesser means," wrote David Dempsey in a 1968 article for the *New York Times Magazine*.[1]

If the '62 Mets were a quilt, it would be a patchwork of fabric that was frayed, discarded, or worn. In a bit of publicity hokum straight out of the P. T. Barnum playbook, Mets manager Casey Stengel labeled the team "amazing" in his conversations with the press. The name and its derivations stuck. As an alternative to the "Mets" name, the press used "Amazins" in their copy; the moniker has lasted into the twenty-first century. The Mets' record in 1962 was 40-120, hardly living up to the adjective.

Stengel had gone to Glendale, California, to manage his banking affairs when the Yankees fired him after the 1960 World Series loss to the Pirates; his World Series record with the Yankees since becoming manager in 1949 was 7-3. *Sports Illustrated* writer Robert Shaplen highlighted three reasons for Stengel getting hired to manage the Mets. First, he had "loyalty" to the Mets' general manager, George Weiss, who had hired Stengel for the Yankees when he was a pinstriped GM and got fired along with Stengel. Second, Stengel thought that the Mets' owners had "goodwill" for the team, the city, and baseball. Third, he had something to prove to the "cold and unimaginative management of the Yankees that he is not too old to run a ball team and that he and his old friend Weiss can give their vaunted competitors a run for the money, at least at the box office."[2]

Stengel's efforts paid off. By the beginning of March the Mets had set a Polo Grounds record for season tickets purchased before the home-plate umpire commanded, "Play ball!" on Opening Day.[3]

Despite their win-loss record, the '62 Mets hold a place in fans' hearts. So what if their players were aging or failing or not yet ripe for the Majors? They revived National League baseball in a city thirsty for an alternative to the Yankees. Meanwhile, Stengel reportedly moaned, "Can't anybody here play this game?"

Manhattan's Polo Grounds had iconic moments in its history, graced by Willie Mays's over-the-shoulder catch of a Vic Wertz fly ball in the 1954 World

Series, Bobby Thomson's Shot Heard 'Round the World, and Christopher "Christy" Mathewson's first of two no-hitters. But on April 11, 1962, a new dawn rose over Upper Manhattan when the squad named after a nineteenth-century team took the field. The Mets could not quiet the fervor begun by the departure of the metropolis's two National League teams. But to honor the ancestors, the team adopted Dodgers blue and Giants orange as its colors; further homage included the Giants' interlocking NY on the caps.

In some quarters the idea of replacing the Mets was a pipe dream. After the 1957 World Series, sportswriter Dan Daniel wrote,

> Out of here, the National League will remain out. It never will be back to New York.
>
> They say Mayor Bob Wagner is organizing a committee to study the situation.
>
> Certain persons are trying to get some of the baseball writers in this city to set up a movement for purchase of a franchise to shift to New York.
>
> But nothing will work.[4]

While the Colt .45s attained a mediocre 64-96 record for their inaugural season in the Major Leagues, the Mets had an aura of fallibility with a .250 winning percentage. Mack Sennett's Keystone Kops had a better chance of catching Al Capone than the '62 Mets had of being competitive. *New York Times* sportswriter Leonard Koppett called the team "an orgiastic mixture of defiance and futility."[5] For many players, though, it was a matter of unfulfilled promise rather than outright incompetency.

Establishing a Major League Baseball franchise in the nation's biggest city required leadership evoking respect, inspiration, and confidence. William A. Shea was that leader. His efforts inspired officials to name the Mets' new stadium after him, though it was not an honor that he sought. Always a gentleman who wore a suit jacket at his desk, Shea received from Wagner the assignment of day-to-day responsibility for navigating political and business obstacles. Existing teams did not want to move to New York, so the Continental League was born, with Branch Rickey as president to give the CL gravitas while Shea worked behind the scenes with a roll-up-your-sleeves ethic. When it became apparent that the CL would remain an unexecuted idea, the détente influenced

MLB expansion in the early 1960s—two teams in the American League and two teams in the National League.

A Shea protégé who succeeded him as the chairman of Shea Gould from 1991 until the firm dissolved in 1994, Thomas Constance recalls how political ties with Gracie Mansion led to the unpaid job of gaining the Mets franchise for the city. A baseball player in college, Constance in his seventies looks like he could still field some grounders at third base. The Kramer Levin firm chairman remembers that Shea, whom he called "Bill,"

> lived in Sands Point, and across the street was Mayor Robert Wagner. They were very close friends for many years. When the Dodgers and the Giants left, Wagner said, "This is the greatest city in the world. How can we only have one team?" So he asked Bill to figure out a way to bring back baseball to the National League in New York City. Bill went to the drawing board and got involved with forming the Continental League, which got traction.
>
> He frightened the baseball commissioner because it looked like the Continental League would take off. Bill was analyzing how to get players from the Minor Leagues and other teams. He negotiated with the city council to create a stadium and got creative with financing through municipal bonding and the bank lending. When it came time to name the stadium, Staten Island borough president Albert Maniscalco gave his opinion. Albie was chairman of the city council. He said to me that they wanted to invite Bill to appear before the council. At that time Bill was in Queens having lunch. So Maniscalco called the police and sent a car to bring him to city hall. Of course Bill had no idea what was going on. Then Maniscalco moved to name the stadium after him.[6]

There was a legacy of joy enveloping the Mets tracing back to a square block in Brooklyn bordered by Sullivan Place, McKeever Place, Bedford Avenue, and Montgomery Street. "If you are a starting pitcher, you warmed up in front of the dugout before the game, not in the bullpen," said Don Drysdale of Ebbets Field. "You felt as though the fans were right on top of you, because they almost were. It was a carnival atmosphere, small and always jumping."[7]

A Blast from the Past

Another continuum between the Brooklyn Dodgers and the New York Mets existed in the form of a six-foot, four-inch North Carolinian with two World Series rings from his Brooklyn tenure. Roger Craig was the last pitcher to start a game for the Brooklyn Dodgers and the first pitcher to start a game for the Mets. He hurled himself to a 10-24 record in 1962, which included the loss to the Cardinals in the franchise's first game. Rather than go down a road of despondency, Craig exemplified optimism with the aplomb of a skilled sales rep. "Like I was telling my old Dodger buddy, Don Drysdale, just the other day, I won ten games, or 25 percent of the Mets' total victories," Craig said in a 1963 *Sporting News* article.[8] It was a short path from glory to gloom—Craig notched an 11-5 record on the Dodgers' 1959 World Series championship team.

"Our team wasn't supposed to burn up the league in the first place," said Craig of the 1962 Mets. "I got off to a bad start, because I knew that Casey Stengel was counting on me. I was pressing for the first month, but after that I did my share." Ever an even-keeled analyst, Craig surmised, "I wasn't proud of my record, but I wasn't ashamed of it."[9]

In 1963 Craig went 5-24. It was his last year as a Met, followed by three seasons with a different ball club every year—1964 with the Cardinals, 1965 with the Reds, 1966 with the Phillies. Craig finished his career with a 74-98 record, then managed the Padres from 1978 to 1979 and the Giants from 1985 to 1992. When he wasn't managing, he was a pitching coach, a destiny predicted by White Sox owner Bill Veeck. "He was right," Craig said. "I never forgot that. Every time I'd see him after that, I'd thank him. You learn so much from losing. Because you keep thinking, 'How can we fix that?'"[10]

Choo Choo

Crouching behind the plate for Craig and other Mets hurlers was Clarence "Choo Choo" Coleman, who played in fifty-five games. A .250 hitter in 1962, Coleman began his baseball career in his hometown of Orlando, Florida, where he played in the Florida Atlantic League for a team that changed its name on a near-annual basis: C.B.s (1955), Seratomas (1956), Flyers (1957–58), Dodgers (1959).

Orlando released Coleman in May 1956—he had played in only two games so far that season. A stint with the Indianapolis Clowns in the Negro Leagues for the remainder of 1956 continued in 1957. Coleman then returned to Orlando, playing there in 1958 and 1959. Thereafter it was a journeyman's enterprise, with stops in Macon, Montreal, Spokane, and Syracuse. Coleman played thirty-four games for the Phillies in 1961. His debut year with the Mets included seventy-one games with Syracuse, of the International League.

Coleman got the nod for more playing time in 1963, and he had a .178 batting average in 106 games. He played for Buffalo in 1964 and 1965, returned to the Mets for a half dozen games in 1966, and ended his career with tenures in Jacksonville and Tidewater.

Nothing Lovable about Losing

Al Jackson emerged from the haplessness of the Mets on August 14; a 3–1 loss to the Phillies spotlighted Jackson's perseverance in his 8-20 season. Unthinkable by early twenty-first-century standards, Jackson threw 215 pitches in the game and scattered only six hits. His performance received no enhancement from the Mets' hitting; the Phillies turned six double plays. Further, ten Mets got stranded on base between the ninth and fourteenth innings. Jackson reacted calmly: "It just wasn't my day, I guess."[11]

Baseball folks often describe the '62 Mets as lovable. Jackson believed otherwise. "What's a lovable team? There's nothing funny when you win only 40 games. Things didn't go right for me because I had never been on a losing team before," he said in a 2000 interview.[12]

Casey's Boy

Rod Kanehl, on the other hand, defined lovability. What he lacked in talent he made up for in heart. "He can't play but he busts his fanny for you and I'll bet he'll be all right," said manager Casey Stengel.[13] Jack Mann of *Newsday* conceded, "Whatever they let him do, he'll try. He's the tieing [*sic*] run at the plate who never scores. He's the Mets."[14] A product of the Yankees' farm system, Kanehl bounced around the Minors for eight years—all but one of them on a pinstriped team—after being on the track team at Missouri's Drury College.

When the Mets encouraged fans to create banners, Kanehl was the first player to have his name emblazoned on one.

When Stengel praised him, it was a mark of respect Kanehl remembered with clarity years later because of his affection for the Mets' first skipper.

When Stengel, sometimes referred to as the "old perffessor," died in 1975, Kanehl held the distinction of being the only former Mets player in attendance at the funeral.[15] He recalled that Stengel had typically run interference with the press, building a relationship with media by using bon mots tilting toward the complimentary and away from the critical. "If it hadn't been for Casey, we'd have all been buried. What Casey did was keep the writers off our backs individually," explained Kanehl. "They could write all the bad things they wanted collectively, but Casey wouldn't let them pick on individual players. I think he must have made an agreement with them early in the season, or else it just evolved that way."[16]

And when the Mets moved on without Kanehl after three years, 340 games, and a .241 batting average, he had a grain or two of salt in his emotional wounds. Returning to the Show Me State, where he worked in construction, Kanehl—outfielder, second baseman, and third baseman for the Mets—explained his value:

I thought there would be a place for me in this game. I thought there would always be room for a guy who knows the game and has some intelligence. I know the game from underneath. I know what goes on in the mind of a mediocre ballplayer. I know what it's like to be a bad hitter. I know what it's like to have to battle every time you go up to the plate. I think the Mets were stupid for not keeping me. And you know what hurt most? They gave away my uniform number even before spring training started. They couldn't wait.[17]

In 1964 Mets beat writer Stan Isaacs presented the case for Kanehl to be a manager. Seen as Stengel's protégé, Kanehl would have added continuity to a team struggling to find steady footing after a disastrous debut. Likening him to Leo Durocher, Alvin Dark, and Eddie Stanky, Isaacs advocated that Kanehl, despite mediocre ability, did the "little things" that marked creativity belonging to managerial greatness. Pointing to plays indicating Kanehl's watchfulness,

Isaacs declared, "These are heads-up plays, the stuff of endearment to the man in the stands who can identify with dash and daring more easily than he can put himself in the shoes of the super-oaf who hits a ball three miles. It is traditional for the underdog to overcome brawn with brains, so Kanehl is a particular darling of the Mets."[18]

Isaacs had a soft spot for Kanehl's creative thinking on the base paths and praised the utility player—who played every position but catcher and pitcher in his career—in a 1962 article concerning another Giants-Mets contest. After Jack Sanford walked him with the bases empty, Kanehl caught him, the Giants' shortstop, and their second baseman off guard when he sped for second base upon the requisite touching of first base.[19]

The Cincinnati Kid

Like Kanehl, Elio Chacón spent three years in the Majors: 1960 and 1961 with the Reds and 1962 with the Mets. During the 1961 World Series loss against the Yankees, Chacón played in four of the five games, batted .250, and scored two runs.

Chacon began his professional career in 1956 with the Savannah Redlegs, hitting .278 in 120 games. Later in the season he played a single game for the International League's Havana Sugar Kings. By the time the Sugar Kings migrated to Jersey City later that month and became the Jerseys, Chacón was in the uniform of the parent club in Cincinnati; he played 49 games and compiled an anemic .181 batting average. He finished the season in Jersey City, boosting his average to .266, and then joined Cincinnati for the '61 season.

Minor League Player of the Year

Cliff Cook, a third baseman and an outfielder, trekked through the Minor Leagues before breaking into the Majors in 1959 with the Reds. He played in nine Major League games that year and spent most of the season dominating the South Atlantic League with top-level statistics: 32 home runs, 100 RBIs, and 232 total bases.[20]

In addition to playing in the "Sally" League, Cook had stints in the Georgia-Florida League, the Northern League, and the Western League. After winning the 1961 Minor League Player of the Year Award—a distinction possible because the Reds sent him down—a substantive Major League career looked likely. It lasted five seasons and 163 games. After playing in 6 games for Cincinnati, Cook went to the Mets—with pitcher Bob Miller in a trade for third baseman Don Zimmer—and played 40 games in '62 and 50 in '63, and then he hung up his spikes.[21]

The trade offered a homecoming for Zimmer, who had grown up in Cincinnati. He finished his career in 1965, with the Washington Senators.

Cook had a congenital back problem, which required a spinal fusion; he blamed the Reds for "never bother[ing] to find out about my back and do something."[22] Stengel, ever the blunt orator, exclaimed, "Is that what he said? Well, maybe he's right. And maybe the Cincinnati people just figured they could get rid of some crap."[23]

Same Name, Different Pitchers

Robert Gerald Miller, when reminiscing about the '62 Mets and his 3-17 record nearly forty years after playing at the Polo Grounds, recalled, "Jeez, when I was pitching, things got so bad at times that instead of raking the infield after the fifth inning, the groundskeepers would have to rake the outfield warning track."[24]

The other Mets hurler named Bob Miller, Robert Lane Miller, was the first player the Mets picked in the expansion draft—he had been with the Cardinals—and he went 1-12 in '62.

A Bright Light in a Bleak Season

Frank Thomas steadied the infant squad with a steady output of 152 hits, 34 home runs, and 94 RBIs. A former seminary student, Thomas did not play baseball until he pursued the priesthood. He caught the attention of his hometown Pirates while playing sandlot ball, and it only took seven games for the organization to sign him to their "Little Pirates" team. There was a catch, however. "After 34 games with the Little Pirates I was offered a small bonus to sign with another major league club, but I wanted to play with Pittsburgh," Thomas said in 1958. "So I told the Pirates I'd sign with them if they'd pay off the mortgage on dad's home. I've belonged to them ever since."[25]

Thomas voyaged to seven Major League teams—Pirates, Reds, Cubs, Braves, Mets, Phillies, Astros—that saw him play outfield, first base, and third base. He approached baseball as an honor, especially when dealing with children. In

Thomas's world, players ought not refuse requests from their worshipful fans. "This guy answers every piece of fan mail he gets," said Braves teammate Eddie Mathews. "He'll stand and sign autographs for kids until he gets writer's cramps. Make no mistake about it, Frank is one of baseball's better advertisements."[26]

The Veteran

By the time Richie Ashburn got to the Mets, he was in the twilight of a fifteen-year career that had begun with the Nebraska native and Norfolk Junior College basketball player placing third for the 1948 National League Rookie of the Year. Nestled in Philadelphia's Main Line suburbia, Ashburn's parents turned their Bryn Mawr home into an extension of the Phillies clubhouse—Ashburn, Robin Roberts, Curt Simmons, Charley Bicknell, and Jack Mayo bunked in the homestead. It was a home away from home for the players, all of whom were under twenty-one. "The atmosphere is much like that of a fraternity house, complete with housemother and father," wrote Harry T. Paxton in a 1949 article for the *Saturday Evening Post*.[27]

New York was Ashburn's last stop. A future Hall of Famer, Ashburn gave the Mets respectability, having led the Major Leagues in hits twice, in triples twice, and in batting average once. In a '62 season preview piece for *The Sporting News*, Joe King observed, "The stylish veteran can be a vital factor in holding the new franchise together, defensively and offensively, if he retains a fair degree of his former skill and stamina at age 35. Ashburn will reach that birthday on March 19."[28] In an otherwise dismal season for the Mets, Ashburn swatted 119 hits in 135 games, ending the season with a .306 batting average.

A play late in the season manifested Ashburn's style. During the first game of a Labor Day doubleheader against the Pirates, Ashburn charged toward a Bill Mazeroski fly ball setting to land on either side of the right-field foul line. After crashing into the foul territory's outfield wall, he toppled into the Mets bullpen. He had no recollection of the play when the Pirates' doctor examined him.[29]

The Baseball Hall of Fame inducted Richie Ashburn in 1995.

Félix

Félix Mantilla, though not Stengel's preference for shortstop, got the job when Elio Chacón "pulled a muscle between his ribs" during spring training. There were two red flags for the former Braves shortstop—allegations that he didn't charge the ball and a waning enthusiasm or energy. Mantilla, naturally, rebuffed them. "Maybe they say I get tired or bored. I don't believe it. You have to wait and see how I do," declared the Puerto Rico native.[30]

With a pedigree of stints across Triple-I, the Sally, the American Association, and the PCL, Mantilla jumped to the Major Leagues in 1956 with the Milwaukee Braves. With the Braves down one game to none in a best-of-three playoff with the Dodgers in 1959, a Mantilla mishap gave the second game—and the NL flag—to the fellas from Los Angeles. In the twelfth inning of the second game, he snared a difficult ground ball, hit by Carl Furillo, in the middle of the infield and made a low throw to first baseman Frank Torre. It missed Torre, allowing Gil Hodges to scamper home from second base. Mantilla explained, "I was off balance when I grabbed the ball. It was the only play I had. I had to get rid of it."[31] Braves manager Fred Haney gave his infielder a lifeline—"He was lucky to stop the ball at all and he was out of position to throw—and he threw low."[32] The Dodgers beat the Chicago White Sox in six games to win the World Series.

The Future Congressman

Wilmer David Mizell was born in an Alabama town named Vinegar Bend—a moniker sounding like it belonged in a Frank Capra movie—and began playing professional baseball in 1949 with the Cardinals organization, which put him on its Minor League rosters. "Vinegar 'visited' up and down the main drag of any town he happened to be in, trading chitchat with the barber and giving the local pool halls his patronage," wrote sportswriter Tom Meany.[33]

Friendliness suited Mizell; he eventually became a three-term member of Congress representing North Carolina. Nicknamed after his birthplace, "Vinegar" Mizell spent three seasons in the Minors—one each at Albany, Winston-Salem, and Houston. In 1952 he got the call from the St. Louis squad, which traded him to Pittsburgh in 1960. That was the year the Pirates beat the Yankees in an epic World Series concluding with Bill Mazeroski's ninth-inning home run in game seven for a 10–9 victory, a championship for Steel City, and broken hearts in the Bronx.

About a month into the 1962 season, the Pirates traded Mizell to the Mets. He pitched in seventeen games, compiled an 0-2 record, and got released in

August. A sojourn with the Triple-A International League's Columbus Jets resulted in a 2-1 record, which put a period at the end of Mizell's baseball career.

The Thinking Man's Pitcher

Jay Hook received the moniker "the thinking man's pitcher." Hook, a career 29-62 hurler, went 8-19 in the Mets' inaugural season. According to a New York sportswriter, "He is one pitcher who not only can throw a curve ball, but who can draw diagrams to show how and why it curves."[34]

Reasons for Hook's lackluster performance were numerous though inconclusive. It was not, however convenient it might have been to rationalize, a matter of inability. "There are explanations for a lot of Mets—some of them can't run and others can't throw. Some of them can't think too well and others are too old. That's why they're Mets. There is no explanation for Jay Hook."[35] But his optimism didn't waver:

> One of the great things about baseball is a new game every day. We never thought that we didn't have a chance to win the next game. Just because you lost today doesn't mean you're going to lose tomorrow.
>
> The Yankees' fans were white collar. We had the cab drivers and the bartenders. Banner Day was always fun with the fans bringing homemade banners with funny sayings and drawings. I started a Mayor's Trophy Game at Yankee Stadium. The Mets fans brought banners, but Yankee management said no. So our fans had to leave their banners at the gate. Probably three-quarters of the fans were our fans. I was talking to one of the Yankees, probably Whitey Ford, and he said that they never heard noise like that before at Yankee Stadium.[36]

The First

Hobart "Hobie" Landrith was the first New York Met, selected on October 10, 1961, in the expansion draft that was filling the lineups of the Mets and the Colt .45s. His vocal quality was the subject of a 1951 scouting report for the Cincinnati Reds: "'Pepper pot' little backstop who brings to the major leagues a brand of on-the-field chatter comparatively unheard since the days of 'Gabby' Hartnett. Shrill voice behind plate can be heard all over park."[37]

As the pioneering member of the Mets, Landrith holds sacred ground. Fertile, it was not. In early May the Orioles traded Marv Throneberry to the Mets for a player to be named later and cash; a month later, the Mets named Landrith. Financial strength provided the impetus. "One of Throneberry's most compelling charms was his availability for cash, one of the few departments in which the Mets are in strong contention for league leadership," wrote *New York Times* sportswriter Robert Lipsyte, citing team president George Weiss.[38]

Strawberry? Blueberry? Raspberry? Throneberry!

Marv Throneberry's performance was anything but marvelous, the adjective that echoed his name and became synonymous with the first baseman and right fielder. When Throneberry died in 1994, sportswriter George Vecsey recalled, "There was the day that Marv hit a two-out triple with the bases loaded but was called out for missing first. Even though nearly everyone in the Mets' dugout saw Marv miss the base, Casey Stengel, the manager, started arguing with the first-base umpire anyway. During the exchange, another umpire walked over and said, 'Casey, I hate to tell you this, but he also missed second.'"[39]

As a '62 Met, Throneberry played in 116 games, batted .244, and struck out 83 times. His career ended after the 1963 season.

Throneberry became a pop-culture icon through his appearances in the famed Miller Lite television commercials of the 1970s and 1980s featuring, among others, Rodney Dangerfield, Mickey Spillane, Whitey Ford, Mickey Mantle, Billy Martin, and Bob Uecker.

The Self-Proclaimed King

Out of James Monroe High School in the Bronx, the same learning institution that graduated slugger Hank Greenberg, came Edward Emil Kranepool, of the Castle Hill Road Kranepools. Raised by a single mom—Kranepool's father died in World War II three months before the slugger was born—Kranepool was the hometown boy makes good, joining the Mets the day after getting his high-school sheepskin. He was seventeen years old. "The bidding was pretty good and we needed the money. I couldn't wait," said Kranepool, who became a first baseman and an outfielder.[40] For a family that once lived on a government pension, Kranepool's reported salary of $85,000 was a fortune.[41]

Kranepool played in three games for the '62 Mets but got some seasoning at Syracuse, Knoxville, and Auburn.

Audacity, part of a teenager's DNA, presented in Kranepool's declarations of royalty. "Well, Ed likes to call himself 'The King.' He's been doing it for years," said Kranepool's mom, Ethel, in a 1963 interview. "He'll swing open the front door and shout: 'The King's home.' I laugh because he's still a teenager and he's got plenty of growing up to do."[42] It was, according to the Kranepool matriarch, a case of swagger rather than self-importance. "If a boy doesn't have confidence at 18, when will he? One thing sure about Ed. He's got guts. Maybe more guts than brains."[43]

Kranepool was ultimately the longest-serving Met from the original squad; he retired after the 1979 season.

The Old-Time Dodger

Clem Labine played for the legendary Brooklyn Dodgers alongside Jackie Robinson, Duke Snider, Roy Campanella, Pee Wee Reese, and other players dubbed the "boys of summer" by baseball scribe Roger Kahn. Playing for the '62 Mets challenged optimism, despite Stengel's exuberance. "I had never been on a club quite like that ('62 Mets team)—they were horrible," Labine said.[44]

Stengel's instruction in the team's first practice was something you might teach a kindergartner about the game—he walked the team around the bases and stressed the need to get to home plate. "That was our first day—we didn't even work out," said Labine, who played in three games that season.[45] It was his last in the Major Leagues.

The Journeymen

Herb Moford pitched in the Minors for most of his baseball career, beginning in 1947 with Johnson City in the Appalachian League. His foray into the Majors consisted of brief stints with the Cardinals in 1955 (1-1), the Tigers in 1958 (4-9), the Red Sox in 1959 (0-2), and the Mets in 1962 (0-1).

Larry Foss's Major League career was even briefer: 1961 with the Pirates (1-1) and 1962 with the Mets (0-1).

For Sherman Jones, the Mets' first home-game pitcher, playing on a team of subpar talent did not diminish his outlook: "We got ridiculed a lot and they made winners out of losers. I didn't really like it. I never could accept losing as a joke. I was trying to make a career."[46] Like his pitching brethren, Jones had a fling with the Majors: Giants in 1960 (1-1), Reds in 1961 (1-1), and Mets in 1962 (0-4).

For Kenneth Purvis MacKenzie, a relief pitcher, change was neither a burden nor an embarrassment. It was a fact of life. His MLB career lasted six seasons—1960–65—and took him to the Braves, Mets, Cardinals, Giants, and Astros. MacKenzie described his role in a 1965 article for *Sport*: "A certain anxiety is always with a fringe player. In spring training, say, when you are making your first overnight trip there is always the burning curiosity to find out who you are going to room with. Who you room with lets you know who the traveling secretary thinks is going to make the club. Invariably, veteran rooms with veteran, rookie with rookie, maybe with maybe."[47]

Further, MacKenzie emphasized the emotional impact of the game. "The next time we stayed overnight was on the way north. This time I hadn't been forgotten—my name was penciled in at the bottom of the list. This was not important to anyone but me, of course. When you are battling to make a ballclub, details become enormous and the realization that there is even the possibility that you may be an afterthought is discouraging and depressing."[48]

For a few moments, though, MacKenzie stood out among the '62 Mets. At the end of his MLB days he said, "You probably recall when the Braves came in and we beat them four straight. I pitched in three of those games and had a win and two saves."[49]

MacKenzie's Major League career: 129 games, started 1, and ended his career with an 8-10 record and a 4.80 ERA.

Willard Hunter had two Major League seasons: 1962 (Mets and Dodgers) and 1964 (Mets). A relief pitcher in forty-one games, Hunter's career win-loss record was 4-9. Humor availed when Hunter became the third pitcher, along with Craig Anderson and Ken MacKenzie, to win two games in one day—as a relief pitcher in 1964. "You don't get too many chances to win 'em like that on this club. We don't stay tied too long," said Hunter.[50]

Craig Anderson's two-fer came on May 12, 1962, in relief outings against the Braves. It was an outlier—Anderson lost sixteen straight games in 1962 and extended that losing streak to nineteen in the next two seasons. "As I got into the end of the '62 season I was struggling with it, and I have to admit that it was getting very, very difficult for me because I hate to lose," explained Anderson in 1993. "I was losing games all kinds of ways, but it really didn't hit me hard until the end of that '62 season, and I was happy the year ended," he said. "The '63 and '64 seasons I didn't get a chance to pitch for the Mets except for one month each year, and I lost a total of three games in those two years, and when I finished out I really wanted to get away from the Mets."[51]

Described as a "nostalgic guy," Anderson, despite the downturn, said of the '62 Mets, "I wouldn't trade it for anything."[52]

Ray Daviault's sole Major League season was 1962, when he appeared in thirty-six games, racking up a 1-5 record and a 6.22 ERA with no saves. Bob Moorhead had two seasons in the show—both with the Mets: 1962 and 1965. In the former he started seven games and appeared in thirty-eight for a 4.51 ERA. In 1965 he was used solely as a relief pitcher—nine games, 4.40 ERA.

Joe Ginsberg played his last season in '62. Before playing two games and having five at-bats with the boys in blue and orange, he was a veteran catcher with a slew of credits: Tigers, Indians, Athletics, Orioles, White Sox, and Red Sox. Ginsberg finished his 1948–62 MLB career with a .241 batting average. He began playing professional baseball with the Jamestown Falcons in the Class D Pennsylvania-Ontario–New York League in 1944. But there's no indication that he continued in the professional ranks for the next two years.

In 1947 he joined the Williamsport Tigers in the Class A Eastern League and broke into MLB with Detroit in 1948, playing 11 games, though most of his playing time was spent in Williamsport—107 games, with a .326 batting average.

A jump to the Triple-A Toledo Mudhens in the American Association in 1949 revealed a significant drop to .283 against higher-level pitching in 102 games. He played in 36 games for Toledo and 63 games for the parent ball club in 1950. There were a couple of ventures into the Minor Leagues during the rest of his career—59 games for the Double-A Indianapolis Indians in 1954 and the entire 1955 season with the Triple-A Seattle Rainiers in the Pacific Coast League. He inched toward the .300 mark—.291 with Indianapolis, .293 with Seattle.

John DeMerit also retired from MLB ball after the Mets' first season. A product of the University of Wisconsin Badgers, DeMerit signed with the

Milwaukee Braves for a reported $100,000 in 1957.[53] He spent three years in Milwaukee and in his season with the Mets batted .188 in fourteen games. In 1960 DeMerit played for the Louisville Colonels, the International League champion ball club.

Dave Hillman ended his eight-year Major League pitching career after 1962; his career stats were 3.87 ERA, 188 games pitched, and 64 games started.

Bobby Gene Smith, an outfielder and a pinch hitter, played for three teams in 1962—Mets, Cubs, and Cardinals. His stay in New York lasted about as long as a Republican considers advocating for higher taxes. After a 1-11 start, the Mets traded Smith—who played in eight of the twelve games—to the Cubs for catcher Sammy Taylor. In addition, the Mets jettisoned Labine and Ginsberg—who became free agents—to create space for the newly purchased Hillman and Harry Chiti from Boston and Cleveland, respectively. Barney Kremenko of the *New York Journal-American* emphasized Smith's impact during spring training, describing him as "the hottest bat on the Mets."[54] For the season, Smith hit .210.

Harry Chiti has perhaps the most bizarre entry in baseball trivia books. A backstop with the Cubs, Athletics, and Tigers, Chiti came to the Mets after playing only five games with Detroit in 1961. At the beginning of the '62 season the Mets traded him to Cleveland for a player to be named later. Two months later the player was named: Harry Chiti. He played in fifteen games and batted .195.

Except for Rick Herrscher's thirty-five games with the '62 Mets, the utility infielder played in the Minors from 1958 to 1964.

Joe "Piggy" Pignatano's last MLB season was 1962; he played in 27 games with the Mets and 7 with the Giants. Piggy later became a coach with the Mets. Sammy Drake, a second baseman—also a pinch hitter and a pinch runner—appeared in 25 games for the Mets. He played 103 games for Syracuse and 30 games for Columbus in the International League that year. And it was his last MLB season, too.

Ed Bouchee began his professional career in 1952 with the Spokane Indians and ended it ten years later with the Mets' inaugural squad. But his journey ignites a query—and perhaps fury.

Why didn't his career end sooner?

In 1958 Spokane police arrested the twenty-five-year-old Phillies rookie for indecent exposure; the case involved a six-year-old girl. "I knew I'd get caught," said Bouchee, the father of a three-year-old boy. "I'm glad I got caught now."[55] A month after the arrest he pleaded guilty—two counts of indecent exposure for his actions, which police discovered also included a ten-year-old girl. Bouchee went to an amusement park to find his prey, luring the girls to his car.[56]

In addition to exposing himself, he showed the girl "indecent pictures." Bouchee's punishment was three years of probation plus psychiatric treatment at the Institute of Living, in Hartford, Connecticut; the Phillies paid for the treatment.[57] During the investigation Bouchee confessed to four additional cases involving girls ten, eleven, fourteen, and eighteen years old. MLB commissioner Ford Frick okayed Bouchee's return to the Phillies in July, swayed by the doctors' opinion that the actions stemmed from medical issues cured by the treatment.[58]

Gus Bell, a .281 lifetime hitter in his 1950–64 career and a four-time All-Star, played thirty games for the Mets before he got traded to Milwaukee. His .149 batting average with the Mets did not reflect his talent; Bell nearly doubled it to .285 in seventy-nine games with the Braves. He attributed his hitting prowess to Rogers Hornsby, who managed the Reds during Bell's tenure there: "He steadied me. Most of all, he concentrated on my timing, teaching me to forget about pulling the ball and to aim through the box."[59]

After playing seven games for the Cubs, Sammy Taylor found himself headed to New York. It was his decision, born of financial considerations—Taylor found his salary of $12,000 per year to be insufficient to maintain homes in both his hometown of Woodruff, South Carolina, and Chicago. So he quit. But rumors of marital discord fueled speculation that it was his wife propelling the decision, sourced in concern about Taylor's stay on the disabled list in 1960.[60] The Mets traded for him.

With the 1962 Mets, Gene Woodling capped his Major League career, which dated back nearly twenty years. An outfielder with a dependable bat—a .284 lifetime batting average—Woodling played on the legendary Yankees crew that won five consecutive World Series titles from 1949 to 1953. He began his Major League career in 1943 with the Indians, then missed two seasons for military service in World War II.

When he rejoined the Indians in 1946, hope emerged; with Bob Feller and Ken Keitner returning from service, Cleveland seemed poised for the possibility of conquering the American League. In the Minors, Woodling was a batting leader thrice, for the Ohio State League, Michigan State League, and Eastern League.[61]

Woodling played in eighty-one games for the nascent club from Queens and batted .274. He came from the Washington Senators midway through the season. The switch in leagues seemed to have no effect—he had notched forty-four games and a .280 average with Washington. His tenure with the Mets ended because of a clash with executive Johnny Murphy in the clubhouse. When Woodling encouraged Throneberry to talk to George Weiss about a salary bump, Murphy, like any good desk man, endorsed the front office. Woodling responded. Loudly. It was, according to sportswriter Barney Kremenko, "a blistering attack on the part of Woodling, with some select language spicing Gene's tirade."[62] And so ended Woodling's baseball-playing career.

Jim Marshall, first baseman and outfielder, played in seventeen games for the Mets and fifty-five for the Pirates in 1962. His time in New York was more productive—a .344 batting average. He hit .220 with Pittsburgh.

Joe Christopher made his Major League debut with the Pirates in the "perfect game" that pitcher Harvey Haddix threw against the Milwaukee Braves in 1959—twelve innings of perfect pitching in a 0–0 contest destroyed by third baseman Don Hoak committing an error in fielding a Félix Mantilla ground ball. Mantilla scored on a Joe Adcock base hit.

The Mets promoted "Christy" from the Triple-A Syracuse Chiefs after he pounded International League pitching—.301 in 24 games. He played in 119 games for the '62 Mets and finished the season with a .244 batting average.

Galen Cisco started two games, appeared in four, and contributed a 1-1 record.

The 1962 season was Jim Hickman's first in the Majors; his status was a $50,000 draft purchase from the Cardinals. A utility player, Hickman was at any given time an outfielder, a first baseman, or a third baseman. His praise rang out for all the teams he played for, though the Cubs received the highest acclaim. "It was great playing for the Wrigleys," said Hickman. "I was fortunate to be with some other high-class clubs, the Mets, Dodgers, and Cardinals. But the Cubs were the tops." In his view, "a player can't realize how great the Cub organization is unless he has been around other clubs and noticed the little things. Like I've played with other teams where we spent hours waiting. The Cubs always had charters ready, unless it was an off-day. It was a champagne flight whenever we went to the Coast. Everything first cabin."[63]

By 1966 Hickman was the only player remaining from the original '62 squad.[64]

Charlie Neal, a utility infielder, came to New York from the Dodgers. And it cost more than $200,000 to make it happen. The Mets traded outfielder Lee Walls and paid $100,000 to the Dodgers; they ate the cost of the $125,000 that it cost to buy Walls from the Phillies. And, as part of the deal, the Mets needed to send a player in the $50,000 range.[65]

Chris Cannizzaro played in fifty-nine games at catcher for the Mets from 1962 to 1965, and he is one of nine Major League catchers to have two unassisted double plays; they happened with the Mets in '64 and '65.[66] In addition to the Mets, Cannizzaro's MLB career from 1960 to 1974 took him to the Cardinals, Pirates, Padres, Cubs, and Dodgers.

Contrary to lore, the Mets neither enjoyed nor endorsed losing. Branding them as joyful losers past their prime—if some of them ever had a prime—was incorrect at best and ignorant at worst. Professionals aim to win, no matter the circumstances. To think, speak, or write otherwise did not account for the Mets' striving. "Those things hurt, because no matter what else you say[,] the Mets always tried," explained Hickman. "They made a lot of mistakes, but they did the best they could."[67]

George Vecsey was a member of the Mets' press corps cadre, which had been dubbed "chipmunks" for their youth. What they lacked in experience, they made up for in their passion for reporting:

The story of the '62 Mets is really a New York City story. You didn't have to win a hundred games the first year. The most important thing is that we had a baseball team and could see McCovey, Mays, and Musial coming back to play in New York against the Mets. One of the first night games I covered for the Mets was a game against the Cubs in the spring. The Cubs were fighting not to be the ninth-worst team. It was an extra-innings game, and I was right in the stands above the press box. A fan walks up in the deserted upper deck and says, "I hate to go, but I hate to stay."

We watched our sister papers very carefully to see how they covered the Mets. *New York Post. New York Daily News. Philadelphia Daily News.* It would be self-serving to say that sports journalism is the reason for the allure of the '62 Mets. But the writers were perceptive enough to pick up on something that was happening. Whether on the field or off the field, there was a deep desire in New York to have National League baseball back. To have a team again and so colossally bad didn't matter to Mets fans. Writers took the game seriously. The ballplayers did the best they could. They were really good guys, not grouches about the losses. A guy like Hickman came to understand that this was okay. The players deserve a lot of credit for being good sports about it.[68]

Despite their level of play, the Mets garnered affection from the fans. They tuned in to WOR-TV to see the reincarnation of the Polo Grounds as a Major League stadium and found a broadcast team that stayed together for seventeen years—Lindsey Nelson, Bob Murphy, and Ralph Kiner. "The problem seemed more like one of survival," said Nelson about the Mets' early years. "And yet those fans came out and seemed to have a marvelous time. And the radio and television ratings, right from the start, were better than anticipated. It has often been said that everybody loves an underdog. Well, we surely had an underdog here, and the fans of this big city loved 'em."[69]

While the Mets enjoyed attention because of their new-kids-in-town standing, the Yankees were the talk of baseball after an epic game against the Tigers on June 24; the twenty-two-inning affair ended with a 9–7 victory for the Bronx Bombers.

The first half of 1962 ended with Sandy Koufax notching a no-hitter against the Mets. He walked five batters in the 5–0 shutout and began the game by striking out the first three Mets with the minimum number of pitches—three for each batter.[70] It came just four days after Earl Wilson of the Red Sox blanked the Angels in a 2–0 no-hitter. Boston added another no-hitter to its annals when Bill Monboquette kept the White Sox from reaching base on August 1 in a 1–0 victory. Jack Kralick of the Twins got a no-hitter against the Kansas City Athletics on August 26, also a 1–0 score.

Fans embraced the Mets despite the win-loss record. In prime time, another mention of the space race occurred in an episode of *Route 66* concerning a man's insecurity because of his wife's success.[71]

Baseball was changing in 1962. And so were society's mores.

Liberalism found a home in a northern California city that became known as an unofficial headquarters for protest, counterculture, and antiestablishmentism by the end of the decade. But in 1962, attention focused on the city's meaning relative to the national pastime.

1. Secretary of State Dean Rusk shares his insights after returning from the Punta del Este Conference in Uruguay for the Organization of American States. It was held January 22–31, 1962. The main topic of the conference was Cuba's link with the Soviet Union. Rusk was the only secretary of state for the presidential administrations of John F. Kennedy and Lyndon B. Johnson. White House Photographs, John F. Kennedy Presidential Library and Museum, Boston (Photographer: Cecil Stoughton).

2. Left: Before becoming a television star, Chuck Connors was a professional baseball player in 1940, 1942, and 1946–52. Connors's Minor League teams were the Newport (Arkansas) Dodgers, Norfolk Tars, Newport News (Virginia) Dodgers, Mobile Bears, Montreal Royals, and Los Angeles Angels. In the Majors he played in one game for the Brooklyn Dodgers in 1949 and in sixty-six games for the Chicago Cubs in 1951. National Baseball Hall of Fame and Museum, Cooperstown, New York.

3. Above: Jackie Robinson was elected to the Baseball Hall of Fame in 1962 on the first ballot. Here he celebrates with a night on the town after the Brooklyn Dodgers won the 1953 National League pennant. *Left to right*: Mrs. Rube Walker, Carl Erskine, Jackie Robinson, Rachel Robinson, Mrs. Carl Erskine, and Cookie Lavagetto (coach). *Brooklyn Daily Eagle* photographs—Brooklyn Public Library— Brooklyn Collection.

4. Bob Feller gave up prime playing years to join the U.S. Navy after Pearl Harbor was attacked on December 7, 1941. Feller was elected to the Baseball Hall of Fame in 1962 on the first ballot. In 2006 a ceremony at Jacobs Field honored the Cleveland Indians legend: the commanding officer of the amphibious transport dock ship USS *Cleveland*, Captain Frank McCulloch, presented Feller with an Indians flag that had flown aboard the ship for nearly a decade. U.S. Navy (Photographer: Mass Communication Specialist 1st Class Jason J. Perry).

5. On February 20, 1962, John Glenn became the first American to orbit the earth. The *Friendship 7* capsule he was piloting circled the world three times. It was a massive step forward in the space race against the Soviets. Glenn did not fly in space again until a 1998 mission on the space shuttle. The space program was a signature of President Kennedy's administration. On February 23, three days after Glenn's mission, President Kennedy joined the astronaut for a first-hand view of the capsule. John F. Kennedy Presidential Library and Museum, Boston (Photographer: Cecil Stoughton).

6. President Kennedy set a new standard of charisma for the presidency, while Jackie Kennedy introduced glamour, sophistication, and an understated sex appeal as First Lady. Here the couple arrives at the Washington DC Armory for the inaugural ball. White House Photographs, John F. Kennedy Presidential Library and Museum, Boston (Photographer: Abbie Rowe).

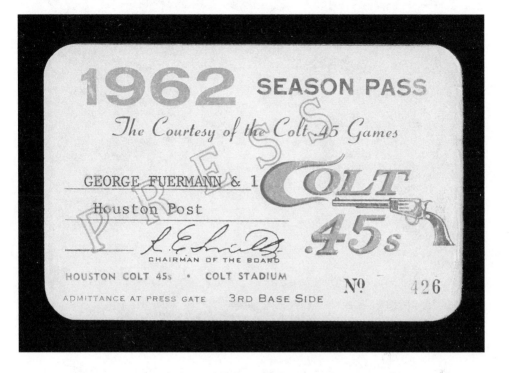

7. Houston became a Major League city in 1962. The Colt .45s built upon the following of the Minor League Houston Buffaloes. This 1962 press pass was issued to longtime *Houston Post* columnist George Fuermann. University of Houston Libraries / Houston Astros.

8. Bob Aspromonte was a favorite for Houston's baseball fans. In addition to crediting the press for building community support for the Astros, he has pointed out the impact of Roy Hofheinz, George Kirksey, and Tal Smith: "They had the foresight and did a lot of work to create an atmosphere of enthusiasm. Houston was football-oriented, so the acceptance of a Major League Baseball team in Houston was incredible." George Kirksey Papers, Special Collections, University of Houston Libraries / Houston Astros.

9. "Go! Go! Go!" The shouts filled the air at Dodger Stadium in 1962 whenever number 30, Maury Wills, took a lead off first base. That year Wills set a new single-season record with 104 stolen bases. His defensive play in the infield often gets overshadowed by his base-stealing acumen. San Francisco History Center, San Francisco Public Library.

10. Don Drysdale (*center*) went 25-9 in 1962 and won the Cy Young Award. Drysdale was dominant, intimidating, and fearless: "My own little rule was two for one. If one of my teammates got knocked down, then I knocked down two on the other team." National Baseball Hall of Fame and Museum, Cooperstown, New York.

11. Scott Carpenter talks with President Kennedy after his *Aurora 7* spacecraft splashdown on May 24, 1962. It was his only voyage in space. During John Glenn's flight in February, Carpenter had served as a capsule communicator at ground control, uttering his famous phrase, "Godspeed, John Glenn." He repeated that famous line when serving as an NBC commentator for Glenn's 1998 flight on the space shuttle. Courtesy NASA.

12. Robert "Bo" Belinsky threw the first no-hitter for the Major League Angels ball club. His romantic life included dating celebrities and an engagement to Mamie Van Doren. Belinsky's career win-loss record was 28-51. He had problems with alcohol and drugs but sobered up in his later years. Belinsky died in 2001, two weeks shy of his sixty-fifth birthday. National Baseball Hall of Fame and Museum, Cooperstown, New York.

13. Manager Casey Stengel's description of the nascent New York Mets as "amazing" stuck with the press and the fans. The team is often called the "Amazins" by commentators. The 1962 Mets went 40-120. National Baseball Hall of Fame and Museum, Cooperstown, New York.

14. Joan Payson sold her ownership stake in the Giants when the team moved to San Francisco after the 1957 season. Payson was then the majority owner of the Mets from the team's inception until her death in 1975. National Baseball Hall of Fame and Museum, Cooperstown, New York.

15. Willie Mays's popularity inspired dialogue in the 1967 movie *Guess Who's Coming to Dinner?* intimating that Mays, the "Say Hey Kid," could be elected mayor of San Francisco if he ran for office. The Giants played in Seals Stadium from 1958 to 1959 before Candlestick Park opened in 1960. San Francisco History Center, San Francisco Public Library.

16. The 1962 All-Star Game was held in Washington DC, which gave President Kennedy an opportunity to meet Stan "The Man" Musial. White House Photographs, John F. Kennedy Presidential Library and Museum, Boston (Photographer: Abbie Rowe).

To my "Do-Bee" friend
From Miss Sherri
KVAR - Ch. 12

17. Sherri Chessen was the beloved host of the children's television show *Romper Room* in Phoenix. The show's format was franchised, so each station airing a local version of the show hired its own host. Chessen was unfairly maligned in 1962 when she sought to have an abortion after learning of the dangers thalidomide posed to the developing fetus. Abortion was not legal in the United States, so she had to go to Sweden for the procedure. Courtesy Sherri Chessen.

18. Left: Marilyn Monroe died in 1962 from an apparent drug overdose at the age of thirty-six. Circumstances around her death have remained murky. The buxom blonde exuded sexuality, but her acting chops in both comedy and drama are underrated. This photograph was taken just after Monroe married former baseball slugger Joe DiMaggio in 1954. The marriage lasted less than a year. San Francisco History Center, San Francisco Public Library.

19. Above: Tom Tresh was American League Rookie of the Year in 1962. He had only played nine games for the New York Yankees in 1961, which was not enough to qualify for voting. In mid-June 1969 the Yankees honored his request for a trade to the Detroit Tigers—his hometown team—to be near his family. During a series against the Washington Senators a month later, Tresh joined two teammates on a visit to the White House. *Left to right*: Tigers teammate Mickey Stanley, Tom Tresh, President Richard M. Nixon, teammate Al Kaline, and Representative Gerald Ford of Michigan. Richard M. Nixon Presidential Library and Museum / NARA.

20. President and Mrs. Kennedy are all smiles as they leave the premiere performance of the musical *Mr. President* at the National Theatre. White House Photographs, John F. Kennedy Presidential Library and Museum, Boston (Photographer: Abbie Rowe).

21. Wally Schirra looks over the flight plan for his mission aboard the *Sigma 7* spacecraft. It was a textbook mission from launch to splashdown. Schirra was the only astronaut to fly in the Mercury, Gemini, and Apollo programs. Courtesy NASA.

22. The last out of the 1962 World Series occurred when Bobby Richardson snared Willie McCovey's line drive with two men on base in the bottom of the ninth of Game Seven. After his playing days, Richardson managed the University of South Carolina Gamecocks. Courtesy University of South Carolina Athletics.

23. Willie McCovey smashed 521 home runs in his career. He was the National League's Rookie of the Year in 1959 and Most Valuable Player in 1969. McCovey led the Major Leagues in on base plus slugging percentage three times. San Francisco History Center, San Francisco Public Library.

24. General Dwight D. Eisenhower talking with paratroopers before D-Day. Eisenhower's leadership was a crucial factor in the Allies winning World War II. His presidency broke the twenty-year grip that Democrats had on the White House. During the Cuban Missile Crisis, President Kennedy called on his predecessor for counsel. U.S. Army photo; courtesy Dwight D. Eisenhower Presidential Library and Museum.

25. Allen Drury, shown here with President Reagan in 1981, was a favorite novelist among politicos in Washington DC. His 1959 novel *Advise and Consent* was the basis for the 1962 movie of the same name. It starred Walter Pidgeon, Charles Laughton, Henry Fonda, Don Murray, Peter Lawford, and Franchot Tone. Ronald Reagan Presidential Library and Museum.

26. Milwaukee Braves owner Lou Perini (*left*) and John Quinn, general manager, take in a game. Perini bought the team in 1945, moved it from Boston to Milwaukee in 1953, and celebrated two pennants and one World Series championship during his ownership. After the 1962 season, Perini sold the team. Wisconsin Historical Society, image WHi-49051.

27. President and Mrs. Kennedy greet members of Brigade 2506 at the Orange Bowl in Miami on December 29, 1962. The brigade members were Cuban exiles involved in the Bay of Pigs invasion, which took place in April 1961. White House Photographs, John F. Kennedy Presidential Library and Museum, Boston (Photographer: Cecil Stoughton).

7

The Best Second-Place
Team in Baseball

The Say-Hey Kid

Tony Bennett may have left his heart in San Francisco, but icons make their home there. Wells Fargo and UnionBanCal set the standard for banking; Levi Strauss for denim; Lucasfilm and Industrial Light & Magic for movies, television, and special effects; Gymboree for children's clothing; the Transamerica pyramid for architecture; Rice-A-Roni for instant sides; Bleacher Report for sports journalism; Old Navy for clothing retail; Electronic Frontier Foundation for freedom of speech; the Golden Gate for suspension bridges; Swensen's for ice cream; Dolby for audio; Digg for news aggregation; Wolfgang's Vault for music archiving; Anchor for alcohol; Fisherman's Wharf for seafood; *Mother Jones* for progressive journalism; Square for mobile payment technology; Orrick, Herrington & Sutcliffe, as well as Weintraub Tobin, for law; *Wired* for technology journalism; Williams-Sonoma for kitchen and home products; Twitter for social media; and Folger's for coffee.

   And Willie Mays for baseball.

Other ballplayers competed; Mays dominated. His prominence is reflected in a line uttered by the Spencer Tracy character in the 1967 film *Guess Who's Coming to Dinner*; he says Mays could become mayor of San Francisco, if he so desired.[1] Whether by design or fluke, it is appropriate that Mays appears more than any other ballplayer in *Centerfield*, the music video for John Fogerty's 1985 baseball homage; it ends with Mays holding a handful of bats, talking to someone off camera, and presumably waiting to take batting practice.

Mays's journey to the Major Leagues was more Archimedean than Odyssean; baseball was in Mays's DNA—his father had been a semipro ballplayer. Like most toddlers, Mays enjoyed playing catch. "But by the time Willie was 6, I'd come home from work and catch him across the street on the diamond all alone, playing by himself," revealed his father and namesake, Willie Mays Sr. "He'd throw the ball up and hit it with the bat and then run and tag all the bases—first, second and third—and then when he got home, he'd slide. He learned that from watching me. I showed him how to slide."[2]

Mays signed with the Negro American League's Birmingham Barons when he was sixteen, though he stayed in high school until graduation; the Barons won the pennant but lost the Negro World Series to the Homestead Grays. Giants scout Ed Montague outbid the Boston Braves to buy Mays's contract from the Barons for $10,000. Mays and his father agreed to a $6,000 contract with the Giants on the day after Willie got his high school diploma in June 1950; that year Mays went on to play eighty-one games for the Class B Trenton Giants in the Interstate League, notching a respectable .274 batting average. Mays's manager at Trenton, Frank "Chick" Genovese, commended the youthful Mays's playing, offering several comments to express his approval: "Junior is the best looking young ballplayer I've seen in many a day," "I believe he has the strongest most accurate arm in baseball," and "He will be an outstanding hitter, I think."[3]

In 1951 Mays went to Minneapolis, played thirty-five games for the Triple-A Millers in the American Association, and racked up a Ruthian .799 slugging percentage. Mays's .356 on-base percentage, .477 batting average, and 10 strikeouts in 164 plate appearances begat an automatic passport to the Polo Grounds. Giants skipper Leo Durocher believed in the prospect and butted heads with owner Horace Stoneham, who resisted until an eleven-game losing streak prompted him to quiet Durocher's bellowing and end the slide.

Stoneham okayed the release of Mays from the Millers and in turn purchased advertising space in Minneapolis newspapers to apologize for spiriting Mays away to the Polo Grounds.

In Durocher, Mays found a father figure, mentor, and soothsayer. The young player's arrival in New York coincided with the Yankees debut of Mickey Mantle. Neither player had immediate success. Mantle got shipped to Kansas City and stood on the brink of quitting until his father challenged him. But Durocher would not let that happen to Mays, whom he considered a protégé, surrogate son, and model ballplayer in one body.

After going 1-for-26, Mays lost confidence. It mattered as much to Durocher as a drop of rain to a lake—he knew Mays's potential the minute he set eyes on the slugger during an intrasquad workout in the morning before an afternoon spring training game between the Senators and the Giants: "Whata show that kid put on! He's just great," Durocher said. "The first time up he struck out and even looked good doing that. What a cut he takes! But the next time he socked the darndest home run you ever did see. I think the ball is still rolling."[4] On Mays's fielding, Durocher boasted, "The kid has a whale of an arm."[5] When challenged by reporters during Mays's rookie season about a drop in his batting average, Durocher responded, "This is the best looking rookie I've seen in 25 years of baseball." He also stated, "In two years Mays is going to be the greatest ever to lace on a pair of spiked shoes."[6]

Mays rose like a phoenix after the rookie slump, batting .274, knocking twenty home runs, and winning Rookie of the Year. Bill Corum of the *New York Journal-American* declared, "I have no hesitancy in saying that he was the greatest prospect of his years and experience that I ever saw come to the majors," going on to say that Mays was "that rare thing in any sport, the seemingly perfect 'Natural' to whom the game he was playing was the biggest, and almost the only, thing in the world."[7]

Mays is the answer to a favorite trivia question: Who was on deck when Bobby Thomson hit the Shot Heard 'Round the World to win the 1951 National League pennant for the Giants over the Brooklyn Dodgers?

The Giants lost to the Yankees in the 1951 World Series; Mays batted .182.

After the 1955 season, the Giants' front office exported Durocher, leaving Mays with a void of stability. "When Leo left, it was like a kid losing his father," revealed the slugger in a 1961 interview. "When [Bill] Rigney came in, it was like the same kid getting a stepfather. I had to get used to Rigney, but Leo knew me inside out. He treated me like I never was treated in my life—on the field and off it."[8]

When Stoneham set up shop in San Francisco after the 1957 season, Mays became an adoptee of the Bay Area, which turned the princes of the Polo Grounds into the counts of Candlestick Park. That November, Mays played in postseason exhibitions at Seals Stadium, but attendance figures did not augur an auspicious beginning for the new addition to the roster of Major League metropolises—a little more than 6,300 people saw his first two games, which pitted Black players from the Major Leagues against an assortment of Minor League players. But, to be fair, the baseball players had competition for attention. San Franciscans were focused on the Oregon-Stanford game, in addition to the 49ers-Lions game, which took place at the same time. Plus, interest in baseball waned after the Pacific Coast League ended its season.[9] While San Francisco achieved Major League status, it ended the life of the Seals, a Pacific Coast League charter member. The last ball in a Seals game sits in the Baseball Hall of Fame as a reminder of a team whose best-known alumnus was Joe DiMaggio.[10]

Taking over Seals Stadium presented a problem for Mays, who pointed out the substandard lights, thick grass, and legendary winds.[11] He then adapted to it, as he did to the cavernous outfield in the Polo Grounds, with its dimension of 480 feet between home plate and the center-field fence; as he did to Candlestick Park, which debuted in 1960 and for decades frustrated players with its unpredictable winds; as he did to ballparks in Boston, Milwaukee, and Atlanta against the Braves; as he did to Ebbets Field and Dodger Stadium; as he did to the two stadia for the Cardinals; as he did to the two stadia for the Reds; and as he did for Shea Stadium, which he would call home at the end of his career.

Hitting a ball anywhere in Mays's vicinity—and even out of it, at times— was an exercise both admirable and futile. It was as if his glove were a magnet and the ball made of metal. Mays's iconic catch in the 1954 World Series—of a Vic Wertz fly ball to deep center field in the Polo Grounds—is perhaps his best-known defensive exploit. But a 1961 catch at Candlestick Park rivals it for being an improbable out. In a game against the Cubs, Mays caught a Dick Bertell fly ball just a few steps from the 410-foot sign. "The circumstances were different, but I think Willie's catch this afternoon was more difficult than the one he made off Wertz," said Giants manager Alvin Dark. "Against Wertz, he had a look over his shoulder before he caught the ball with one hand. This afternoon, it came over his head from behind him."[12]

In a 1964 Dodgers-Giants game, Mays raced from left-center toward right field to snare a Tommy Davis fly ball that surely would have fallen for a double, maybe a triple.[13] Dodgers announcer Vin Scully said that Mays made his two best catches, up to that point in his career, against the Dodgers. Mays did not just perform exploits of speed, agility, and throwing; he commanded the Giants outfield, signaling players to shift according to the batter. "The rule that we had when I played, this one hand, it goes left or right. Anytime that hand moved, you gotta move. The only rule we ever had in the outfield. Now if you didn't see that, you didn't play the next day. Very simple."[14]

Mays's performance on April 30, 1961, exemplifies his power—he went yard four times in one game, leading the Giants to a 14–4 win over the Braves. Only eight players before him and eight since have accomplished it.

Candlestick Park's infield turned into a boxing ring in 1962 when Mays spiked Mets second baseman Elio Chacón in the first game of a doubleheader. Mets hurler Roger Craig, who led the Major Leagues in losses in 1962 and 1963—twenty-four and twenty-two, respectively—allowed Mays to hit a single and earned an HBP when he plunked Orlando Cepeda. With but a moment's hesitation after being hit by that pitch, Cepeda charged toward Craig. Giants manager Alvin Dark tackled his player, relying on football skills honed at LSU. To no avail, Craig tried to pick off Cepeda, who escaped an out because Mets first baseman Ed Bouchee couldn't hold on to the ball.

When Craig tried to pick off Mays, the Say Hey Kid spiked Chacón, who responded with a punch and received several in kind, capped by a body slam. For igniting the brawl, Chacón was ejected. Mays and Cepeda combined for nine hits and one RBI apiece as the Giants took both games.[15]

The Might of McCovey

Willie Lee McCovey, another Alabama son, saw one difference separating him from Mays—their treatment of the press. McCovey acquiesced to the needs of scribes and broadcasters looking for copy. "I always have been that way because Mays was always kind of standoffish," said the slugger.[16]

The seventh of ten children, McCovey played semipro baseball when he was fourteen years old. "My mother had to give permission for me to play because I was so young. They had to promise to look after me, and I was the cleanup hitter," he said.[17] Giants scout Alex Pompez—who had endorsed signing Mays and Monte Irvin—got word on McCovey's potential from Mobile-based scout Jesse Thomas. So McCovey tried out with the Giants at a Florida camp in 1955.

He was seventeen years old.

The Giants' management sent McCovey to the Sandersville Giants in the Class D Georgia State League, where he played in 107 games, knocked 19 home runs, batted .305, and notched 125 hits; nearly 1 out of every 5 hits was a double. In 1956 he hit .310 for the Danville Leafs in the Class B Carolina League. The Giants moved McCovey up to the Dallas Eagles in 1957; his average fell to .281 in the Double-A Texas League, still a solid number. He cracked .300 again the following season in the Triple-A Pacific Coast League, where he played for the Phoenix Giants and hit .319.

McCovey played in ninety-five games for Phoenix in 1959, notching a .372 average; he entered the Major Leagues on July 30, 1959, with a performance justifying the confidence of Pompez and Thomas. In the Phillies-Giants contest, McCovey went 4-for-4 against ace hurler Robin Roberts—two singles and two triples, plus two RBIs—and began a twenty-two-year career earmarked for Cooperstown: Rookie of the Year Award; six All-Star Games; 521 home runs; eighteen grand slams; leading the National League in home runs three times; leading the National League in RBIs twice; leading the Major Leagues in on-base plus slugging percentage three consecutive years; and a National League MVP Award.

Raising standards and lowering despair for the Bay Area's baseball fans, McCovey smashed through National League pitching like a bowling ball through pins, if the ball were made out of grenades and the pins were made out of plywood. His performance on September 22, 1963, is one example— three consecutive home runs in a 13–4 victory against the Mets.

The Keenness of Kuenn

Harvey Kuenn became a Giant before the 1961 season, bringing batting skills that earned him a spot in eight consecutive All-Star Games, the 1953 American

League Rookie of the Year Award, and the 1959 American League batting average crown. Although power was not a trademark for him, as it was for Mays and McCovey, he led the American League in hits three times and the Major Leagues once.

Kuenn's career .303 batting average, though far from the magic number of 3,000 hits (he had 2,092), defined consistency in a fifteen-year career. In 1962 his 68 RBI total was the third highest on the ball club, behind Mays and Cepeda. And Kuenn did it in fewer games—Mays and Cepeda played in all 162 and Kuenn, 130.

Retiring after the 1966 season, Kuenn moved to coaching and managing. There are leaders who approach baseball with a Lombardi-like focus on winning, based on striving to obtain psychological, emotional, and physical fulfillment through 100 percent effort. Their desire to win is pure. Their process, deadening.

Harvey Kuenn was not one of them.

"Look, you guys can flat out hit, so go out there and have fun. Don't be stone-faced on the bench. If a guy breaks a bat, laugh about it and he'll laugh with you. When you laugh and have fun, you get relaxed," said Kuenn before the 1982 American League playoffs—he had ascended from being the Milwaukee Brewers hitting coach to manager in the middle of the season.[18] The Brewers had a 23-34 record when Kuenn took the reins; they finished at 95-67. Nicknamed "Harvey's Wallbangers," the Brewers lost the World Series to the Cardinals in seven games.

Kuenn shot to baseball prominence when he won the Rookie of the Year Award with the Detroit Tigers. "The rookie's success is a rare example of general baseball prophecy coming true," stated the *New York Herald Tribune*. "From the start of spring training last year, a brilliant future was predicted for Kuenn. However, Fred Hutchinson, the Tiger manager, said only that Harvey would start the season at short. Kuenn not only started, but finished there, playing in 155 games."[19]

In his fifteen Major League seasons, Kuenn played for the Tigers, Indians, Giants, Cubs, and Phillies. When the Tigers traded Kuenn to the Indians for Rocky Colavito at the beginning of the 1960 season, team president William DeWitt certified the rationale. "I have a high regard for Kuenn's ability as a player," said DeWitt in an Associated Press article. "But we felt we needed more power at the plate and we're hopeful this move will help us score more runs."[20] Tigers manager Jimmie Dykes revealed, "It was a deal in which we had to trade consistency for power."[21]

Indeed.

In 1959, while Kuenn led the American League in batting average, Colavito led in home runs—forty-two. He hit thirty-five dingers in 1960.

Kuenn only spent one season in an Indians uniform before making the move to San Francisco.

San Francisco's Skipper

Giants manager Alvin Dark was a member of the legendary 1951 Giants, who soared to the National League title on Bobby Thomson's home run off Ralph Branca—and a scheme discovered decades later involving a spy-glass in the center-field offices to learn the opposing catcher's signs. A Louisiana-born, church-going, tithing Baptist, Dark suffered publicity for his biblical dedication, which he hoped to keep secret, especially the financial donations. When he spoke at a Bible class in Yonkers, New York, in the mid-1950s, a reporter slithered unnoticed into the believers' inner sanctum. The ballplayer-turned-manager who earned his first dollar by delivering newspapers and carved out a budget, including church donations, had his personal connection to religion exposed. It was not in Dark's nature to disclose—and certainly not celebrate—his commitment to God. His mother wrote, "I asked Alvin once if he ever prayed for his team to win. He shook his head. 'I don't believe God answers prayers to win. How could He—and be fair to both sides?'"[22]

Mays initially praised Dark during the manager's rookie season at the helm—1961—and compared him to Durocher for knowing how to handle players. "You strike out and he pats you on the back and tells you to forget it," Mays said. "The worst thing a player can do is strike out; I mean he feels worse about it when he walks back to the bench. The other night, I struck out the first time up. Dark was the first one to meet me at the dugout steps, and he slapped me on the back and said, 'That's nothing, you'll get him next time.' It made me feel good, and I had a good night the rest of the game."[23]

It was a contrast to Dark's playing days, when the shortstop exploded upon defeat.[24] Eddie Stanky—Dark's double-play partner—said, "Maybe there's never been anybody who cared so much about winning ball games as Al. For sure, nobody inspires his players more. Ten years ago he played every game a dozen times—once on the field, the rest in his hotel room. And even in his sleep he was bearing down. He'd wake up at 2 in the morning with some idea of how to make a play. But it goes even deeper than winning. He worships baseball itself—as an art—so much that if they banned him from the parks, he'd dry up and blow away."[25]

If Dark felt the player wasn't living up to potential, he laced his tirades accordingly. Giants hurler Jack Sanford went from mediocre to premier when the skipper pried open the blinders keeping Sanford from seeing possibilities. Sanford went 24-7 in 1962, including a streak of sixteen straight victories. "I *knew* I wasn't that good. The 350 games I'd pitched in before I met Alvin proved it. But he made me see how little you really know yourself," Sanford said.[26]

Dark chose a platooning strategy for his catchers—Ed Bailey and Tom Haller.

Bailey at the Bat

Lonas Edgar "Ed" Bailey Jr. hailed from Tennessee's Strawberry Plains, a town that sounded like a place Barney Fife would visit on a weekend trip. Signing with the Cincinnati Reds in 1949 after a disastrous academic performance during his freshman year at the University of Tennessee, Bailey followed the advice of his father, who applied down-home common sense to combat a lure that would have snared many others: "Some folks criticized me for letting him sign with Cincinnati when he had a chance to go with the Yankees, but I figured they would give him a square deal, and I thought they might need young ballplayers more than the Yanks."[27]

Bailey signed for a $13,000 bonus.[28] Cincinnati's front office sent him to the Ogden Reds ball club in the Class C Pioneer League in 1950, racking up a .313 batting average in 124 games, 87 RBIs, 23 doubles, 11 triples, and 7 home runs. A 1951 Reds scouting report stated, "Considered one of top young prospects in Cincinnati organization. Big and strong, fleet afoot, long on aggressiveness and fighting spirit."[29] It also mentions that thirteen Major League teams tried to sign Bailey.

After spending the next two years in the military, Bailey rebounded with the Tulsa Oilers in the Texas League in 1953. Absence did not weaken his skills: 118 hits, 26 doubles, 21 home runs, and 88 RBIs. Bailey joined Cincinnati for 2 games in '53 and stayed there for the '54 season, playing in 73 games, then spent most of '55 with the San Diego Padres in the PCL. He played in 108 games for San Diego and 21 games for Cincinnati in '55.

Bailey credited his defensive success to Reds manager Birdie Tebbetts, affirming, "Birdie taught me how to get the ball away quicker. I used to feel for the seam on the ball first when I put my hand in my glove. Birdie taught me to grab the ball, and then find the seam I wanted to finger while I was drawing my arm back for the throw."[30]

Holler for Haller, Yell for O'Dell

A star at the University of Illinois in football, baseball, and basketball, Tom Haller defected from the Fighting Illini to join the Giants organization after his junior year; the twenty-year-old signed for a bonus reported to be "a little more than $50,000."[31] He played in the Minor Leagues for three seasons before Alvin Dark brought him to the Giants in 1961.

Winners, it is often said, want to play every day. If it's a crucial game, they need to. William Oliver O'Dell defined that paradigm. MVP of the 1958 All-Star Game, when he played for the Baltimore Orioles, O'Dell had a desire that manifested in a "pitch me or trade me" declaration when his innings pitched fell from 202⅔ in 1960 to 130⅓ in 1961. "I can't stand sitting around and watching other guys pitch," said O'Dell. "If I can't contribute, I don't want to wear the uniform."[32]

Dark responded by using O'Dell for 280⅔ innings in 1962. Although he led the Major Leagues in hits allowed, O'Dell compiled a 19-14 record.

Great Expectations

Orlando Cepeda destroyed Minor League pitching before coming to the Giants in 1958:

> 1955: Kokomo Giants, Mississippi–Ohio Valley League, .393, 91 RBIs
> 1956: St. Cloud Rox, Northern League, .355, 112 RBIs
> 1957: Minneapolis Millers, American Association, .309, 108 RBIs[33]

Cepeda's rookie year in the Major Leagues continued that pace: .312, 96 RBIs, and 25 home runs. He led the National League with 38 doubles and won Rookie of the Year honors. In 1962 Cepeda played in his fourth consecutive All-Star Game—he was an All-Star seven times in his seventeen-year career. In 1999 Cepeda was inducted into the Baseball Hall of Fame.

Tagged as temperamental, Cepeda received support from McCovey, who viewed the San Francisco fan base as setting expectations that were impossible to meet. Cepeda joined the Giants ball club during its first season on the West Coast, thereby making him the fans' own, rather than Mays, who enjoyed a mythic status from his New York exploits. But that wasn't altogether a good thing for number 24 either. "The fans and press resented the adulation that New Yorkers had lavished on Willie [Mays] before the Giants moved to the coast in '58," McCovey noted in an article for *Sport*. "They adopted a 'show me' attitude about Mays and then stubbornly refused to believe even when shown."[34]

McCovey also took responsibility, explaining his explosive rookie year in '59 as overshadowing his teammate. "To get my hitting into the lineup, Cepeda was moved off first base," explained McCovey. "He was tried at third base and was eventually sent to the outfield."[35]

Cepeda adapted:

.355 in 1959
.343 in 1960
.311 in 1961
.306 in 1962

In 1961 Cepeda led the Major Leagues in RBIs with 142. Kuenn remarked, "He's built like an oak tree. He can be fooled by a pitch and still hit line drives with only a piece of the bat on the ball. When you watch him gripping the bat at the plate in practice you have the feeling he's going to squeeze sawdust out of the handle."[36]

The Rookie and the Veteran

Bob Garibaldi scored a reported record bonus of $150,000—the largest for the Giants. A phenom from Santa Clara University, Garibaldi chose to make

Candlestick Park his new home. One of a dozen teams vying for Garibaldi's pitching services, the Giants had an appeal "even though one or two offered me more," said Garibaldi. "The Giants are the hardest-hitting team I've ever seen and pitchers like runs. Too, I'll be playing close to home."[37]

Garibaldi pitched in nine games and twelve innings in '62 for an 0-0 record. He bounced between the Giants' farm clubs in Tacoma and Phoenix for most of his career, which ended after the 1972 season with the PCL's Hawaiian Islanders. His Major League tenure consisted of stints with San Francisco in 1962, 1963, 1966, and 1969. Injury cut short his potential. "I hurt my arm in spring training of 1963. I tried to impress somebody, throw too hard, too fast. Also, I tried to change the way I was throwing," said Garibaldi in 1973.[38]

The 1962 season was par for the course for Billy Pierce, a hurler who is primarily identified with the White Sox. Pierce spent two seasons in Detroit and thirteen in Chicago before coming to the Giants in 1962, when he went 16-6. A workhorse, Pierce had mound credentials that were welcome: he led the Major Leagues in ERA in 1955, led the National League in wins in 1957, and led in complete games from 1956 to 1958.

Pierce honed his control ability under the tutelage of Paul Richards, a former Major League catcher, teammate on the 1945 Detroit Tigers, and manager of the Colt .45s. Richards had managed Pierce with the White Sox. "Then the first thing I knew, Paul would catch the ball, examine it carefully, step slowly in front of the plate and then flip it back to me," Pierce recalled. "I'd grab it fast, but Richards would ignore me. He'd study his glove and, not until he got good and ready, would he give me the sign for the next pitch. I soon got the idea. Once I'd controlled my overeagerness and paced myself better, I was able to control the ball."[39]

The Shortstop

Giants shortstop José Pagán was a human vacuum, snaring balls at will during his patrol between second base and third base. Dark called the Puerto Rico native "the silent anchor of a good infield."[40] He was known as a quiet guy who went about his business at shortstop, without the dazzle exhibited by Mays et al. Baseball, to Pagán, was a way of life. Where others sought rest after a baseball season, Pagán kept going. Between the Major Leagues and the Winter League, he hovered around 270 games each year.

Pagán's trek to the Major Leagues began in 1955, with the El Dorado Oilers, the Giants' Cotton States League squad. Playing in about three-quarters of the schedule—97 of 120 games—Pagán batted .273; the Oilers finished in second place with a 70-50 record, behind the Monroe Sports.

With the Danville Leafs in the 1956 Carolina League, Pagán hit .283 and smacked 160 hits, seeing action in 147 of 152 games. The Leafs finished in third place with an 83-69 record.

Spending the next two years with the Springfield Giants in the Eastern League, Pagán was a bright spot on a team that went 55-84 in 1957 and barely played .500 ball in 1958, with a 68-65 record:

1957: .264, 143 hits, 133 games
1958: .298, 153 hits, 126 games

On defense, Pagán was also an asset, leading the Eastern League's second basemen with 332 put-outs and 299 assists in 1957. Another outstanding year followed; in 1958 Pagán was the leading third baseman, with a .965 fielding average, 125 put-outs, and 232 assists.

His 1959 season with the Phoenix Giants in the PCL underscored his talent; he hit .312. And he also got his first taste of Major League pitching that year, batting .174 in 31 games. He refined his skills with the Tacoma Giants—also in the PCL—in 1960. It resulted in a .295 batting average in 128 games and a rebound to the Majors for 18 games and a .286 average in San Francisco. Pagán became an everyday player in 1961—134 games, .253 average—and his fielding was also valuable to the Giants. In 1962 Pagán led the National League's shortstops with a .973 fielding average.

Felipe Alou

Pagán's best friend on the Giants was Felipe Alou—later the first Dominican manager in the Major Leagues when he succeeded Tom Runnells in the middle of the 1992 season as the Montreal Expos' helmsman.[41] Alou managed the team for 125 games and stayed in Montreal till 2001, when he got released after a 21-31 start. Alou also managed the Giants from 2003 to 2006.

During his playing career, Alou was an outspoken sort who fought for Latin American players. His disgust for Major League custom culminated when

Commissioner Ford Frick responded to Alou's playing after the 1962 season for the Dominican Republic team by issuing a $250 fine. While Frick may have seen Alou's actions as mutinous, they came from financial duress. "In my country there is practically no industry, and very little work," explained Alou. "We are ballplayers; it is the only thing we can do. Take away baseball from us in the winter, and you take money away from us."[42] Alou also lamented the impact of the income tax structure, which did not allow him to list his wife and three children as dependents because he was not a citizen.[43]

McCormick and Davenport

In 1962 Mike McCormick was five years away from winning the Cy Young Award and the Giants were at arm's length from being feared contenders. "We had the best second place team in baseball," declared McCormick, who compiled a 5-5 record. "I had a sore shoulder, so I was kind of a second fiddle to the situation that was going on," said the hurler. "I liked the weather in San Francisco, but a lot of guys hated the wind at Candlestick Park. I used it to my advantage. I never got tired because of the cool, fresh air. In other stadiums, like Crosley, you'd be worn out."[44]

Third baseman Jim Davenport pulled off a double play on July 14 that had veteran baseball watchers scratching their heads to remember a similar exhibition of fielding prowess. On a no-out ground ball during a Giants-Phillies game with runners on first and second, Davenport fielded it, touched third base for the force out, and whipped the ball to second base instead of first base. Throwing to McCovey would have been the standard choice for a double-play grounder.

Davenport assessed the situation, and his options, based on the runners— Sammy White on first base, Tony Gonzalez on second base, and Bobby Wine at the plate. "I know Wine is fast and that White isn't," Davenport said. "I lost precious time finding third base to tag it and didn't have anywhere else to go but to second. The long cross-diamond throw to first would have been late."[45]

Davenport won the 1962 Rawlings Gold Glove Award.

If there were a contest for the title of "Mr. Giant," Jim Davenport would be a formidable contender. He spent his career in black and orange, from 1958 to 1970, after three seasons in the Minor Leagues. His tenure as a coach, a scout, and a brief stint as a manager in 1985 added up to fifty-one years with the organization; he also managed the Triple-A Phoenix Giants for three years. An infielder usually found at third base, Davenport had a career .258 batting average. The 1962 season was his best; he batted .297 with a slugging percentage of .457 and 144 hits. "I learned about observing from my dad," said Jim Davenport's son Gary, who had a three-year Minor League career in the 1980s and has coached in the Giants organization since the early 2000s. Like his father, the younger Davenport played the infield:

> I grew up with the coaches. I thought I was preparing to be a player, but I really was becoming a coach. I was twelve years old when dad quit playing, so I got the inside view of the managerial side at a young age. I knew what to expect.
>
> I also learned how to be humble. He was probably the most humble person you could have met. He always deflected success onto other players.
>
> In the early 1960s the Giants had amazing players, but they kept taking second place every year. The Dodgers kept a step ahead. But the fan base was very dedicated. My impression of Candlestick Park when I was growing up is that it was a tough place to watch a game because of the cold. My dad always said that he would have loved to have been a player at AT&T Park because the climate difference was huge. They used to wear rubber because of the cold. Ron Hunt wore a diver's outfit under his uniform. Dad felt that playing at Candlestick was an advantage because other teams wanted to play quickly and get out of there. By the time the game started, winds picked up. The fan base endured the cold. They were dedicated, for sure.
>
> The player that he played with the most was Mays, who was the focal point of the Giants in the 1960s. He was also really close with Bobby Bonds. The Giants could afford to have a third baseman with good defensive skills because they had good hitters at other positions.
>
> I didn't realize what I was actually watching until much later. I appreciate it a lot more now. It was a blessing to grow up and be in the clubhouse with those guys.[46]

The Owner

San Francisco's Major League status came from Horace Stoneham, who inherited the Giants from his father, Charles. Stoneham's decision to move the team from New York to San Francisco proved controversial in some quarters, traitorous in others. The Giants, after all, were a team of New York City baseball icons. John McGraw was a pugnacious strategist responsible for championships early in the twentieth century, Christy Mathewson was an educated ballplayer inspiring through his work ethic on the pitching mound, and Carl Hubbell was an admirable workhorse with an eighteen-inning shutout against the St. Louis Cardinals among his accomplishments. Heritage cannot, however, obscure the bottom line. "The kids? I feel sorry for the kids," said Stoneham. "But I haven't seen many of their fathers lately."[47]

Although baseball lore depicts Dodgers owner Walter O'Malley as the persuader in the duo's move to California, it was Stoneham who first announced the change. San Francisco was not the only suitor for Stoneham—other possibilities were Texas (a location between Dallas and Fort Worth), Oakland, and Minneapolis, where the Giants had the Triple-A Millers.[48] Noting a lack of parking, fan migration to the suburbs, and diminishing attendance—the same challenges suffered by O'Malley—Stoneham appeared committed to moving, no matter what his counterpart in Brooklyn did.[49] Seeing Stoneham linked to San Francisco seemed quite like Guy Lombardo doing his New Year's Eve performances from Fisherman's Wharf instead of the Waldorf Astoria Hotel. "Horace Stoneham was so thoroughly and completely New York that when talk of the transfer of the Giants came up, I doubted that he would go through with any move which meant forsaking Broadway," wrote Dan Daniel. "There never has been a New York club owner who so thoroughly represented the city."[50]

By the 1960s Stoneham had become an anachronism. The Giants ball club was an heirloom, not an engine for profit. That's not to say that Stoneham disregarded the bottom line, but sentiment on a spreadsheet was not a calculable asset beyond perhaps the category of goodwill. His compadres showed strategy, forethought, and discipline in forming their squads, both on the field and in the front offices. But Stoneham had a bond that his competitors lacked. Baseball was in his blood, and therefore the team's operation was a clan, not a corporate beast.

Stoneham's lack of aggressiveness in shaping a team had been a red flag to Leo Durocher, who came to the Giants from the Dodgers in 1948, after Dodgers general manager Branch Rickey showed no urgency in keeping the feisty skipper aboard when a one-year suspension for association with gamblers ended. It struck Durocher as a mess that he had to clean up: "Personal sentiment should never enter into a baseball judgment, but with Horace it almost always does. As soon as I took over the club in 1948, for instance, I knew this was a trouble job because I had no speed. I had no speed. I had to play one-type ball. I took Stoneham aside and pleaded with him to consider some trades and to get some guys with legs."[51] By 1962 Durocher was back with the Dodgers organization as a coach.

Giants fans felt Durocher's agony. They appreciated Stoneham's avuncularity but mourned the loss of potential caused by it. There might have been something deeper at play, though, resulting from a basic emotional need. In 1958 a *Sports Illustrated* story suggested that Stoneham's live-and-let-live philosophy filled a void: "Stoneham runs the Giants as if they were one big family, which, more than most teams, they are. This often resulted in the operation being called 'old-fashioned,' overloyal and dilatory; but, in part at least, this is simply a compensation for his own lack of family ties. He would like to be bound by them, but no longer can be."[52]

The portrayal by Robert Shaplen, titled "The Lonely, Loyal Mr. Stoneham," depicts a man who was "extremely shy" and "frequently found solace in drinking."[53] Stoneham sold the Giants in 1976; he died at the age of eighty-six in 1990.

The Dominican Dandy

Juan Marichal was San Francisco's ace pitcher in the 1960s. He led the National League in wins twice and the Major Leagues once. In 1966 he went 25-6 and led the Majors in win-loss percentage. His stamina was substantial; he led the Majors in complete games twice, pitched twenty-two complete games in 1964, tallied thirty complete games in 1968, and topped MLB pitchers in 1965 with ten shutouts. Like a rocket launch, Marichal powered his left leg toward the sky before hurling the ball. His extended limb was a precursor to devastation for National League hitters. In 1962 he notched an 18-11 win-loss record.

The Announcer

San Francisco fans joining neighbors for Mill Valley barbecues, playing in Walnut Creek schoolyards, and cleaning Redwood City kitchen windowsills listened to Lon Simmons on KSFO 560 AM give the play-by-play broadcast. He ended his first tenure with the Giants after the 1972 season; his second stint was from 1976 to 1979. In 1981 Simmons went across the bay to Oakland, where he announced A's baseball for fifteen years, only to return to the Giants for a third tenure—1996–2002. Simmons's career included being the Golden State Warriors announcer for one season in the mid-1970s and the San Francisco 49ers play-by-play announcer, a job that included Super Bowl XXIII.

In 2004 Simmons received the Ford Frick Award, an honor bestowed by the Baseball Hall of Fame on outstanding broadcasters. He had never been to Cooperstown: "I was supposed to come here with the A's (in 1994), and they had the strike. And when I was with the Giants, Russ (Hodges) and I were supposed to come back here for something. I don't know what got in the way. I can suspect—probably a bar between here and somewhere."[54]

A good radio announcer explains the nuances of the game, describes the physical setting, and gives a reliable sense of the game for the listener. A great announcer makes it seem like the listener is at the game. No matter how many Giants fans expressed their adoration, no matter how many times he exclaimed, "Tell it goodbye!" upon a Giants home run, Simmons maintained decorum free of ego. "I did not before and do not now consider myself the quality of a Hall of Fame announcer. I do say this, the people of San Francisco convinced me you don't have to be a national announcer to make a difference. You can be local. The thing about baseball is it's a national game that's played locally. It's the Pacific Coast League, it's Little League or it's Babe Ruth League. People get ties to that."[55]

On July 10 President Kennedy threw out the first ball to start the first of the two All-Star Games in 1962. San Francisco contributed Felipe Alou, Cepeda, Davenport, Mays, and Marichal to the National League All-Star team. Marichal got credit for the 8–4 National League victory. But there was another landmark event involving baseball that month; it happened nearly two weeks after the All-Star Game, when the Chicago Cubs sprinted onto the turf and dirt at the Friendly Confines—known to trespassers, tourists, and teams as Wrigley Field. Their game against the Philadelphia Phillies was a groundbreaker—it was part of the first telecast courtesy of the Telstar satellite—ninety seconds of play were beamed to European viewers. For Americans abroad, it was like a postcard from home to hear sportscaster Jack Brickhouse in the top of the third inning.[56]

The first transatlantic telephone call via Telstar took place in July, when British scientists communicated with their American counterparts. Technology had turned a corner. And so did the art world, through criticism of consumer culture—or mirroring of it—in the works of Roy Lichtenstein and of Andy Warhol, who debuted his first one-man gallery exhibition on July 6 at the Ferus Gallery in Los Angeles. *Campbell's Soup Cans* was Warhol's signature work for this event, which showed that pop art was manifesting a golden age in consumer culture. Whether Warhol consciously determined to depict, mock, or interpret consumerism is a matter of debate, conjecture, and interpretation of his comments and one's own views. Art, in any case, is in the eye of the beholder. Connoisseurs in galleries, museums, and lecture halls often attach meaning to artistic works that the artist never intended. But the works of Warhol and of Lichtenstein, who placed comic book panels in his paintings, blare a nexus between product and consumer that was indelible by the 1960s. Even without the names on the labels, a supermarket shopper will know the difference between a can of Coca-Cola and a can of Pepsi.

The fact that the soup can painting came in 1962 further evidences the immense power that brands carried in American culture. What sponsors began in the 1930s on radio became a mass medium of communication with consumers, and they continued into the 1950s with television. Brands and slogans became synonymous with one another, as did their television shows. Kraft, Philco, and Westinghouse had their names in the titles of drama anthologies. Celebrities too were aligned with their sponsors—Jack Benny and Jell-O, for example.

America's nuclear defense saw benchmarks in July 1962. An explosion created the Sedan Crater in Nye County, Nevada, as the result of an underground nuclear test. The blast left an impression 320 feet deep and 1,280 feet in diameter. The Starfish Prime test exploded a 1.4 megaton hydrogen bomb about 250 miles above Johnston Island, setting off the first artificial electromagnetic pulse. The bomb's flash could be seen 750 miles away, in Hawaii. Little Feller I ("Small Boy") was the last atmospheric nuclear test by the United States.

And on Kwajalein Island, also in the Central Pacific Ocean, a Zeus missile got within two kilometers of an Atlas missile. That's sufficient for a nuclear warhead to render an incoming missile ineffective.

Operation Sunbeam (also called Operation Dominic II), a series of tests, racked up another loss—a Thor missile exploded on the launch pad at Johnston Island.

NASA saw a good news–bad news month. Major Robert M. White broke a record when he flew an X-15 to nearly sixty miles above the earth; NASA considers the fifty-mile mark to be the beginning of space. The Launch Operations Center in Florida went into service on July 1.[57] But *Mariner 1*, a spacecraft designed to fly by Venus, was destroyed "at the edge of space" because it flew erratically.[58]

The film *Advise and Consent*, based on the book of the same title by veteran Washington journalist Allen Drury, played in theaters, revealing the controversy, scandal, and intrigue caused by a secretary of state nominee with possible communist leanings. Inside-the-Beltway types hurried to buy tickets for more than the entertainment value of a good political yarn; they wanted to identify real-life counterparts, if any, among the characters and see how close the story came to reality. *Washington Post* film critic Richard L. Coe described it as "a crackerjack story" filled with "stellar performances and expert craftsmanship."[59] Peter Lawford plays a handsome senator with an eye for the ladies, a scenario believed to be an homage to his brother-in-law, President Kennedy, during the president's time as an unmarried member of the House and then the Senate. Charles Laughton, Don Murray, Walter Pidgeon, Franchot Tone, and Lew Ayres are also in the ensemble.

Drury's novel formed the basis of a series that peeks inside congressional corridors, dinner parties, and power bases of the nation's political infrastructure. While audiences saw Drury's story at the movie theater, they could read his newly released 1962 sequel, *A Shade of Difference*. This story revolved around America's involvement with the United Nations and a revolutionary from an African country.

Drury's nephews, Kenneth Killiany and Kevin Killiany, have revived the Drury novels, which had been long out of print. Kenneth underscores the importance of the "Druryverse" in political fiction:

When my uncle wrote *Advise and Consent*, there hadn't been a major political book since *Democracy*, by Henry Adams. It opened up the humanity of the process and showed the sausage-making part of it. He was interested in what happens when well-intentioned, serious human beings are called upon for serious challenges. One reader said that he's amazed that Al gave everyone on every side the chance to say what he believes. He knew Joseph McCarthy personally and saw him become unhinged, so he put that in the novel with the Van Ackerman character.

He was covering the Senate for the *New York Times* when he started to write *Advise and Consent*, and he put himself in the book. But his character's name was the name of the newspaper. He did the same with the other reporters. They did not have personal names. He attacked the herd mentality of the press relentlessly. It bothered him because he took his job seriously.

There are some very interesting things in *A Shade of Difference*. The Panamanian has a hatred for the United States, but he cannot explain to himself why he has this all-consuming hatred. That is one of Al's insights. People have beliefs and prejudices but not reasons. He did not accept the idea of a universal desire for freedom. I asked him when I was young why leaders in other countries do things that our leaders don't, and he said that's what they want and what the citizens want. He was always interested in what prompted people.

In *A Shade of Difference* there's an important theme of liberal Americans wanting people to be free in other countries. But an African leader shows that we didn't always practice what we preach, especially when it came to racism. And this is the early 1960s, before the civil rights movement really took hold.

The journalism thing happened early for him. He wanted to be a writer. Through family connections, he got a job on the local paper. He wrote an editorial for FDR to not be vague regarding joining the British in World War II. He ended up going to Washington for sightseeing, walked into the UPI office, and got a job as the Senate correspondent. The quality of his writing led to him being recruited by the *New York Times*. He said that he got tired of going to the same parties with the same people and writing about the same things. Nobody had ever been that big with a political novel, but he worked hard. He was able to sustain the quality with the first three books. So, he left journalism believing that he had given Washington his best. He didn't realize with *Advise and Consent* how his life had changed completely and that he didn't need Washington anymore.

Advise and Consent makes the reader feel in the middle of the Capitol Building with the names flowing by. An editor wanted him to cut part of it. He said that he would cut every senator from the opening chapter not mentioned later in the book. People will find humanity and the genius of the American system in the *Advise and Consent* series. We need to remember that.[60]

8

Miss Sherri, Mary, and Marilyn

Sherri Chessen began a career in television with great promise. An attractive brunette, she had the je ne sais quoi required to be an effective host on *Romper Room*, a children's television show franchised across the country. Station managers who wanted to air *Romper Room* had to license from Claster Television the rights to the show's format—a host chosen by the station, specifics about the show's set, and planned daily instruction for the children about manners, sharing, and teamwork through games, lectures, and kindness.

Chessen's ease, kindness, and charm made parents in Phoenix, Arizona, feel safe to leave their children in her televised custody. To parents, she was a godsend. To children, she was Miss Sherri.

When a private choice to terminate a pregnancy became a public story, Chessen faced an unwarranted media frenzy robbing her of her privacy, ruining her career, and making her a target of scorn for those who wanted to impose their religious, social, and medical interpretations on others—no matter the psychological, reputational, and emotional cost. The Supreme Court ruling in *Roe v. Wade* was still eleven years away.

Her decision became fodder for self-righteous sorts lacking the capacity but not the authority to okay an abortion because legislators and the judiciary had not addressed an issue with fire and brimstone on one side and potential physical, mental, and emotional wreckage on the other. Chessen was wise enough to avoid becoming a symbolic martyr for a cause and strong enough to withstand the psychological fallout that would have felled most women.

What got lost in the bromides of antagonists was the reason behind Chessen's decision: she had taken thalidomide, a popular tranquilizer, during her pregnancy. Its disastrous effects of stillbirths and deformities such as truncated or absent limbs were just beginning to be revealed. What was hardly considered by her detractors, if at all, was the impact if a pregnant woman in their own circle had consumed this drug. They claimed that they would not terminate the pregnancy if they were in the same position. But they weren't—and Chessen prayed they never would be—nor were they volunteering to adopt the affected children, tend to them, or pay the gargantuan medical costs incurred should a thalidomide-affected child survive. And Chessen never asked, either publicly or privately, as those choices were not hers.

Those who proclaimed to speak in the name of God apparently forgot the biblical precept in Matthew 7:1 about not judging unless you want the same measuring stick applied to your actions. Clearly, "Judge not lest ye be judged" was a biblical rule left at church rather than lived in practice.

Ignoring the devastating impact that thalidomide had on fetuses—causing women to give birth to heads and torsos with, in some cases, only one limb— led to knee-jerk reactions steeped in religious platitudes that, if taken literally, make everyone a sinner heading to confession hourly for soul cleansing. Those labeling Chessen the murderer of an unborn child neither knew the details of her pregnancy nor cared to know.

Keeping her maiden name after marrying Robert Finkbine—a rarity of nomenclature bordering on heresy according to social norms of the era— mattered not to the fedora-wearing, male-dominated, and shortsighted press referring to her incorrectly as Sherri Finkbine. Although the press and, in turn, the public, labeled Chessen as the one attempting to terminate, it ignored, or at least sidelined, the saliency of a couple making this decision together. By name, Chessen was an appendage in media coverage; by deed, unfairly, a solo.

It was not a choice of convenience, as critics who launched volleys of verbal abuse would have liked the public to believe. It was to some not even a choice at all. Chessen's decision to terminate came after consultation with her doctor about the impact of thalidomide. Should she deliver, the chances of a normal life for the child would be nil.

To them, Chessen was a two-dimensional figure rather than a human being faced with a fight that she neither sought nor wanted. It was a fight that she lost in the courts, compelling her to go to Sweden for the termination. To supporters, though, she was also two-dimensional, seen as a symbol rather than a woman burdened with unwarranted publicity, judgment, and invasion of privacy for her decision.

Chessen's identity became public after she described her experience to the wife of the publisher of the *Arizona Republic*. She hoped that the newspaper would print a warning about the devastation caused by thalidomide use during pregnancy. "Not even for one second could I bring a child into the world, knowing how it would suffer," she cried.[1] Her initial request that the newspaper keep her name out of the article was downplayed. What made matters worse—and better, in a sadistic way, for biblical guardians using her as an example to promote their own views on termination—was her profession. Had she been a housewife, a bookkeeper, or a real estate agent, Chessen likely would not have been a household name in 1962 beyond the borders of the forty-eighth state.

Her trajectory to television began when she was the age of the children she taught, entertained, and enlightened on *Romper Room*:

> Entertainment has been part of me for my whole life. When I was five years old, our school held a Christmas program where fourteen of us kindergartners were the show's finale. Each of us held a big cardboard square with a single letter that would spell out "Merry Christmas." We were told to walk on stage, look only at the audience, and smile. I, with the first *M*, however, saw fit to check down the row and saw that the little boy third from the end had his *M* in "Christmas" upside down. So, I sighed a huge

sigh and walked all the way across the stage, turned his card upright, and spun around to the clapping audience. I curtsied and grinned and a career was born.

When I entered the University of Wisconsin in the early 1950s, television was new. I became part of a program on Wisconsin Public Television called *The Friendly Giant*. I did the voices of the fence, the chicken, and carried props around.

Before my senior year, I married Bob Finkbine, who was also a student, a year ahead of me. After we graduated, he with his first master's degree, me pregnant with our first baby, Bob taught sixth grade and coached football in his hometown of Lawrenceburg, Indiana. Two more babies later he received a job offer at the ASU child learning, preschool program in Tempe, Arizona. So, three babies in tow, it was off to the Sunbelt, perpetual summer, and wild but wonderful opportunities.

Our children were three, two, and six months old as we settled in Arizona. And I decided that I'd like to go to work. This was in 1958. I knew that I wanted to work in television because it was new and exciting. Channel 3 hired me for its continuity department, where we wrote the commercials and introductions to shows. One of the directors, Phil Rock, approached me one day and said, "Sherri, they're having auditions at Channel 12 next Monday for a children's show. They're looking for women between twenty-one and thirty with a college degree. I think you'd be perfect for it."

They had a big cattle call of women to audition for *Romper Room*. Bert Claster of Baltimore, Maryland, the owner of the franchise, called it a school, not a program and the hostess was the teacher, not star or any other such nomenclature. I got the "job."

I eventually won two Emmys, one for the show and the other for Outstanding Female Personality. It sounds Pollyanna-ish, but I was never invested with a lot of ego and my self esteem is nothing to brag about . . . weird for an actress. One of my shortcomings is that I never liked that much attention. I wanted to stand out, but I didn't like being recognized. On November 22, 1960, Bob and I had our fourth child.

In the summer of 1961 Bob was on a school trip in England and he brought back pills that I was told were tranquilizers. No Google then. I didn't know about the egregious effects until July, when I was two months pregnant. There was a newspaper story about England passing a law allowing euthanasia on babies born of mothers who had taken thalidomide. Horrified beyond words, I asked my doctor to check out the meds I had self-prescribed. He wired Germany, where the pills were produced.

When the telegram came back that these pills were thalidomide (strong), my doctor said simply, "Sherri, my wife and I also have four children, and I'm going to say the same thing to you that I'd say to her. We need to terminate this pregnancy, and if you really want a fifth child you can start again next month under better odds. You need to write a letter to a three-man medical board." "What if they don't agree?" I asked worriedly. My doctor said, "I already spoke to them. Your operation is next Wednesday."

The gravity didn't hit me until I realized that the date was my son Mark's sixth birthday, and I objected. The doctor said, "You'll be here." He told Bob, "If she wavers in her resolve, show her this picture." I wavered. He showed it to me. I wish I hadn't insisted on seeing the picture, as it was six babies propped up on a sofa with only their little heads showing and bodies tightly swaddled where their limbs should be. I had nightmares for years because of that picture. We wrote the letter.

It was the day of my thirtieth birthday. When we came home from his office, we had had plans to get away for the weekend, but there was no way I was going to leave my four children for two days of rest and fun. I told Bob that I had to do something to warn others about thalidomide. I have to call the newspaper. When I did, I learned that Julian DeVries, the medical reporter, was doing an article on thalidomide and asked if he could call me. "He won't use my name, will he?" I asked naïvely. "Of course not, dear" was her reply.

I was shocked on Monday morning to find the article on page 1 that described, but didn't name, us—four children, father a teacher at Scottsdale High, etc. I did *Romper Room* for an hour not having even a remote inkling that it would be the last time I would be allowed to be Miss Sherri.

After the program I was summoned to the production office for a phone call.

It was my doctor calling to tell me that my operation on Wednesday had been canceled. He said that the article's details meant that the county attorney could make a citizen's arrest on that person for violating Arizona law. Abortion was only valid in cases involving the life of the mother. He ended with, "I have a Catholic associate and if this gets out, I might as well have my practice on the moon!"

I hung up the phone, sighed, put my hands on my hips like I was five years old again, and called the county attorney's office. A young attorney named Charlie Stevens answered. I asked what I thought was a generic question: "How can the county attorney interfere with the lives of private citizens by declaring what a mother can and can't do to take care of her family?" There was a slight pause and the attorney said softly, "I know who you are, Miss Sherri. I have a daughter who's four years old. I had the flu last week and we watched you every day on *Romper Room*. I'm a father and strongly believe in what you're trying to do. If you need an attorney, I will represent you pro bono." Charlie Stevens was true to his word. He and his partner eventually went to court to ask for a declaratory judgment on the definition of "life" in the "life of the mother" clause in the abortion statute.

In building their case, they decided to send me to two psychiatrists whom they hoped would say that it would be psychologically impossible to carry a fetus that could be a head and a torso. It's abusive. The first psychiatrist had an ugly disposition, and I can get very sassy with people who are tough with me. He showed me cards and wanted me to do a "first association" test. He obviously was trying to make something sexually illicit out of my wanting an abortion.

One card had a woman on the bed and a man standing over her with his pants unzipped.

He asked me what the man was thinking.

I said, "'Damn, I have to go to work and my wife can lie in bed.'" After a series of these cards and my all too sassy retorts, he sent a report that not only should I have the termination but claimed I was inadequate as a mother. Also, my four kids should be taken away by family services, and furthermore I should be sterilized to prevent any more children.

The next day I saw the other psychiatrist. I walked into his office and he was eating donuts. I was careful to appear prim and proper with him after my ugly experience the night before. He was very avuncular. A nice, gentle soul. He offered me a donut and asked if I wanted to look at the newspaper. I asked if he had any questions. He said, "I believe in what you're doing. My letter is already written."

Then the attorneys passed on a judge that they shouldn't have. He had raised [a sibling with Down syndrome] and was very sympathetic to my case. My lawyers were given the next judge in line, who threw the case out of court. Yale McFate said, "As a man, I would like to rule on this case. As a judge, I cannot." The judge advised me to go to another country.

They put me in Good Samaritan Hospital while this was going on because the hospital's creed declared they would help anyone in medical need. But a radio news program report out of NYC stated that the hospital voted to violate the creed and dismiss me from the hospital. And that they did. Bob said, "We're getting a visa and going to Japan." What we didn't know is that when we got to LA, the Japanese consulate didn't want to have potential anti-Japanese demonstrations. Bob argued, but the Japan trip didn't happen. We had also heard from a reporter in Sweden. I took to the phone again.

My uncle, Jim Chessen, was a doctor and the chief of staff of Denver Presbyterian Hospital. "The news has reached Denver, sweetheart, and I can't help you." He had sent me to college, and I felt I was letting him down.

Then the letters began. I got advice from people telling me to fill a bathtub with gin. I can't remember if I was to drink it or just soak in it. There were magic potions to help grow limbs. Someone wanted to parachute me out of a plane hoping to cause a miscarriage, ad nauseam. The mailman started bringing letters in huge bags. My mom had come down from Minnesota to help with the kids, and my youngest brother was fourteen and declared himself in charge of the mail. I remember him saying that some of the people who agreed with me were as crazy as the ones who didn't. He claimed to know their bias just from their handwriting on the envelopes.

There were people outside our house all the time. My mother baked chocolate chip cookies and brought them out. "Mom," I said, "we're trying to get rid of the press, please don't feed them!"

When we went to get my visa, a man stopped us on a downtown Phoenix corner where I had stopped to cry, saw me, [and] said, "Honey, you're probably really upset, but you do what's best for you and your family and to hell with all those guys." New resolve!

We flew to LA. I wore a blonde wig and walked like a pregnant lady with towels stuffed underneath. We got past all the reporters with no interviews and no pictures. I thought that they would hear my heart beating because it felt so loud. A friend of my mother's met us at the airport concerned because I was "so far along." When I started unloading towels from beneath my blouse we all had a well-needed laugh.

In LA we saw a television show with host Joe Pine interviewing a doctor about my case. "In the light of all you know, do you blame Mrs. Finkbine for doing what she's doing?" Pine asked. "No, I do not," responded the doctor. And the shocker in those days, Pine retorted, "Neither do I!" Unheard of in those days for a reporter to voice an opinion. Just ask Linda Greenhouse, who as a Pulitzer Prize winner did the same decades later and stirred endless controversy.

In Sweden, they hid us away in the newspaper vice president's summer house. I remember thinking that if I felt the fetus move, I didn't know if I could go through with the termination.

I also didn't know that I was fired from *Romper Room* until I was back in Phoenix and went blithely into work. Ray Smucker, the vice president of the NBC station in Phoenix, took me aside and said that I was no longer fit to handle children. Then, this same man had the audacity a few years later to call and ask me if I knew where his daughter could divest herself of an unwanted pregnancy. Now, I was some kind of expert on the subject . . . not!

There was a Gallup poll about my decision and 52 percent of the respondents agreed with me. The TV station gave me a token fifteen minutes of broadcast time to do a magazine type of show. What they hadn't planned on was it attracting a sponsor, which it did. *Here's Sherri* with my co-host Dwayne Brady became one of the first talk shows. Then, I got pregnant again. I remember sitting behind this huge crate which was part of my set and thinking that as soon as the station found out about the new pregnancy, they could easily fire me because the people who agreed with me would say it's wonderful, those who didn't would say the same. So, I was punished when I DIDN'T have a baby and further punished when I DID.[2]

Chessen's prominence made her a symbol for feminists, which was in some sense ignoring the fact that she was a victim of celebrity, not a victor in the situation, having suffered an invasion of privacy by a press craving to put a face on the abortion issue. She was not a symbol of any political, social, or medical movement nor did she want to be. She was a wife, a mother, a daughter, a journalist, a sister—"a mother above everything else." A month after the termination, she told newspaper reporter Dorothy Kilgallen, "I don't intend to become a crusader on the subject."[3]

As often happens with those in the public eye, Chessen received more than approval from her advocates; she also received requests for advice. In 1968 she said, "But, really the most I encounter now is people asking for help. I don't want to give advice—I don't want anyone to think 'I've lost a baby because of her.' I love children and representing something as sad and reprehensible as abortion was abhorrent to me back then, but I've always believed it's a medical necessity and still fight for abortion to stay available."[4]

Intolerance overlapped with viciousness for Chessen because of beliefs about pregnancy, beliefs fostered in homes, associations, or religious institutions. For every advocate of her choice—and her right to make it—there was a detractor without knowledge of the details. She did not want to be a part of the abortion debate, much less the center of it.

But ask her about the aftermath of her abortion and she will tell you, "Bob and I weren't cursed, as so many predicted, but blessed with two more children. I can't imagine my life without them and the grandchildren that followed. Yes, love prevailed."[5]

The battle for civil rights was another topic that generated heated debate in 1962. There are unsung heroes and heroines of the civil rights movement, those who confronted racism with their quiet determination to be judged on merit rather than scorned by prejudice. While advocates organized marches, gave speeches, and advised citizens about voting rights, tens of thousands of Black Americans chose to make their mark in the workplace, which had racism rooted in bedrock that the biblical Samson would have found difficult to move in mid-twentieth-century America. If your name was Doyle, Murphy, or another moniker suggesting origins in the land of leprechauns, you faced rejection from companies embracing the "Irish Need Not Apply" slogan; if you were familiar with a diet of matzoh ball soup, kreplach, and brisket, you might find yourself with a pink slip while the higher-ups said, "He doesn't look Jewish." Being an American citizen did not protect from ugly labels being foisted upon those with origins beyond the country's borders—Italians, Germans, Japanese, Chinese, Jewish, Irish, et al. suffered. It was one big melting pot divided into sections where brick walls of bigotry separated Americans in thought, behavior, and action.

Racism took a hit in the 1954 Supreme Court decision *Brown v. Board of Education of Topeka*, which mandated desegregation in schools. In 1957 Arkansas governor Orval Faubus ignored the case and a subsequent ruling. For backup, he called out the state's National Guard to stop Black students from entering Central High School, theretofore a segregated facility. President Eisenhower responded by federalizing the National Guard and ordering a thousand paratroopers from the army's 101st Airborne Division to keep the peace. It was a crucial part of the country's progress on civil rights, which happened not in large waves but in small ripples.

Although Dr. Mary Frances Early had a dedication to music, a universal language with dialects ranging from soul to country, she focused her energy on teaching schoolchildren. Whereas some people might have expressed anger at the bigotry Black Americans suffered, Early expressed compassion. In 1958 her fifth-grade class in Atlanta's John Hope Elementary School corresponded with a class at another school. The students became pen pals until her counterpart received a class picture and wrote a letter suggesting that Early might have confused the all-white school with a similarly named "colored school." If that's what happened, Early's counterpart suggested that the segregated school would probably like to connect with a correspondence project. Meanwhile, the teacher indicated that the all-white school where she taught would find another correspondence partner.

Although likely authored with good, though ignorant, intentions, the letter drips with condescension and the assumption, common of the era, that people should stick to their own kind, whether the designation is one of race, religion, or heritage. Early wrote a note to herself indicating that she pitied the other teacher.[6]

Seeking to do graduate work at the University of Georgia in Athens, Early followed a path carved by Charlayne Hunter and Hamilton Holmes—the first Black students to enroll at the University of Georgia. At best, they could expect to be ignored and at worst, physically attacked. A court ruled that they had the right to attend the university. A group labeled Students for Passive Resistance issued a proclamation upon the court's ruling:

> We, the student body of the University of Georgia, fully deplore and resent the court-ordered intrusion of two Negroes in this century-old white institution.
>
> It is more than obvious that these people are not here to secure an education as they assert, but to further the social schemes of those who would destroy the most basic of all freedoms—the freedom of association.
>
> The courts have illegally usurped the powers of the State and the school officials to deal with this matter. It is up to us to save the University from destruction.
>
> While we disavow the use of violence in any form, we hereby pledge ourselves to the use of the ultimate weapon so widely and effectively used by these people—the weapon of "passive resistance."
>
> We will NOT welcome these intruders.
>
> We will NOT associate with them.
>
> We will NOT associate with white students who welcome them.
>
> We love our school.
>
> We will save it.[7]

Hunter and Holmes got to Athens because of William A. Bootle, a federal judge who ordered the university to admit them. Georgia governor Ernest Vandiver sought to close the university by cutting off the spigot that sent money to Athens. Bootle's decision came before Vandiver could act, enjoining him and the state auditor from taking action to disrupt, stop, or interfere with the university's operations.[8]

On January 6, 1961, Bootle filed his opinion in *Holmes et al. v. Walter N. Danner, Registrar of the University of Georgia*:

> After a careful consideration of all of the evidence admitted at the trial, the court finds that, had plaintiffs been white applicants for admission to the University of Georgia[,] both plaintiffs would have been admitted

to the University not later than the beginning of the Fall Quarter, 1960. It is the further finding of the court that plaintiffs, citizens of the State of Georgia applying for admission as students to the University of Georgia, a public tax-supported university of the State, are otherwise qualified, but have been denied admission solely because of their race and color. The court further finds that, although there is no written policy or rule excluding Negroes, including plaintiffs, from admission to the University on account of their race or color, there is a tacit policy to that effect, and that defendant Danner has pursued such policy in denying the plaintiffs' applications for admission. The court considers it worthwhile to discuss some of the evidence which leads it to make the findings above stated, although the discussion which follows must, in the interest of brevity, be limited to the most compelling evidence.[9]

Bootle's findings indicated that the University of Georgia had never enrolled "Negro" students, none had applied for admission before 1950, and at the time the case went to trial only two others had previously applied for admission—Horace Ward to the law school in 1950 and Ida Rose McCree to the university in 1960. "Limited facilities" was the reason given for denying Hunter and Holmes the opportunity to enroll. Hunter had tried five times: fall quarter, 1959; winter quarter, 1959; spring quarter, 1960; fall quarter, 1960; and winter quarter, 1961. Holmes had attempted to do so three times: fall quarter, 1959; winter quarter, 1960; and spring quarter, 1960. Bootle's analysis went to the granular level, exploring the processes of the university in determining the number of students to enroll, deadlines for decision-making, arrival dates of prospective student applications, and housing. It was revealed that the university had grilled Holmes, asking, Have you ever been arrested? Have you ever attended interracial parties? What is your opinion concerning the integration crises in New Orleans and in Atlanta? Give some insight into the workings of the student sit-in movement in Atlanta. What are some of the activities of the student sit-in movement, and have you ever participated therein? Do you know of the tea houses (or coffee houses or Beatnik places) in Atlanta, and have you ever attended any of them? Do you know about the red light district in Athens? Have you ever attended houses of prostitution?

Since you are interested in a pre-medical course, why have you not applied to Emory University, since it is in Atlanta?[10]

Bootle ruled, "Apparently the interview was conducted with the purpose in mind of finding a basis for rejecting Holmes."[11]

Bootle noted that white applicants were not subject to the same line of inquiry.[12] Further, he judged that the university's right to set standards for admission was neither absolute nor limitless: "The intent of the injunction herein granted is only to restrict the exercise of that right and duty so as to forbid admission requirements which will deny to Negroes equal protection or due process of law and to forbid denial of admission to Negroes, who are qualified for such admission, solely on the ground of their race or color."[13]

Additionally, he ruled that "had it not been for their race and color," they would have been admitted and, in turn, that they could not be refused admission.[14]

Three days after Bootle's ruling, Chief Judge Elbert P. Tuttle, in the Fifth Circuit of the U.S. Court of Appeals, denied Danner's request for a stay.[15]

A campus riot caused Governor Vandiver to move Holmes and Hunter to Atlanta in the middle of the night because their safety was in jeopardy. He later learned that the students had been suspended. But he blamed Judge Bootle and Athens mayor Ralph Snow:

> By the suspension order the other night, officials of the university recognized the imminent danger presented to the public by the presence of plaintiffs on the campus.
>
> Law enforcement officers of great experience have added their opinion which has been transmitted to me that tinder-box conditions exist.
>
> In spite of this, the federal judge has taken his action of today without regard to the consequences.[16]

To say that the demonstrations were active is like saying Shakespeare dabbled in storytelling. Protesters aimed to get Hamilton and Hunter kicked out, through violence if necessary. They threw rocks at the windows of Hunter's dorm, breaking ten panes. Several police officers were injured and sent to the hospital, and several students and university officials sustained "minor" injuries. To those who saw Hunter and Hamilton as a threat to their exclusive club, violence was their only option.

Speaking about Autherine Lucy, a University of Alabama student suspended for her safety, a Georgia student said, "They're integrated at the University of Alabama, legally. But there are no n——s going to school there." This was not a one-and-done issue. The same student threatened, "The suspension of the two n——s here was caused by the demonstration. If we caused them to leave one time, we can do it again."[17]

It was a matter of racial pride rooted in ignorance, bigotry, and deep hatred: "The students started the demonstrations. Everybody knew we had to do it," the student said. He also claimed, without attribution, that his discussions with "several top state officials" yielded a statement of affirmation: "They said, son, I'd be right in there with you."[18]

When Mary Early saw the images of riots on the Atlanta evening news programs, she was appalled. Then, inspired. She had known Hunter and Holmes from Turner High School in Atlanta. "I was five years ahead of them," Early explained. "I met them when I was sent back to Turner High for student teaching. [Charlayne Hunter] wanted to interview me about my writing the Turner High [School] song."[19]

Early's personal connection to the two students affected her.

"I was particularly peeved because they were Turner students," Early said. "I was chomping at the bit to get involved in the civil rights movement. My father was an entrepreneur, but he was not formally educated. He had a restaurant on Auburn Avenue, and he taught me and my brother that we were as good as anyone else. Nobody had opened the doors of the graduate school after Charlayne and Hamilton, and I was not assured that I would get in," she recalled. "When I went down to the university, they had inaugurated a lot of ploys to keep Blacks out. They probably didn't want a third Black student so soon. Three days after the riot, I applied. When they got my transcript, they realized that I was Black. It took till May to get accepted."[20]

The University of Georgia confronted Early's pursuit of higher education with an investigation scouring the music student's personal life. Georgia's racial attitudes were approaching a change, but that was a slow task in the state that produced the second KKK in 1915. University officials discovered impeccable credentials to their probable surprise and dismay. Early was a candidate for valedictorian at Clark College; taught music at a YWCA in Bear Mountain, New York; was in Who's Who Among Students in American Universities and Colleges; graduated magna cum laude from Clark; played clarinet in the college's marching band and concert band; received no grades lower than a B at the University of Michigan; scored 100 on road signs for her driving test, 100 on road rules, and 83 on the driving test; no marriage license found at the Court of Ordinary, Fulton County; and the Georgia Department of Public Health, Bureau of Vital Statistics checked from "July 1, 1952, through December 1960" and no record "found that a child had been born to Mary Frances Early."[21]

It also detailed her brother's $4 fine in 1954 for speeding, $1 fine for a parking violation in 1954, and a $5 fine for a stop-sign violation.[22]

Early did not seek to be a civil rights pioneer but an advocate for music education. Her reason for selecting UGA was the curriculum.

She underwent an interrogation with a barrage of intrusive questions:

I, too, had an interview with Danner and his assistant—Paul Kea. My interview was not very pleasant. Danner asked me if I had visited a house of prostitution—just as he had asked Hamilton [Holmes]. I responded in the negative[,] saying that I was a professional and had no interest in prostitution. He also told me that UGA was not required to accept my credits from the University of Michigan[,] where I had studied the previous summers—and that I would lose all of that time and money. I told him that what I had learned—I would never lose and that I wanted to attend UGA. I don't remember any other questions that he asked. I was so absorbed in not becoming confrontational that I just don't remember now.[23]

The arrival of Black students ignited curiosity among white students whose exposure to people of color was likely limited to portrayals as servants in movies, to rock-and-roll musicians, and to ballplayers. But curiosity morphed into violence when Early began her studies on June 12, 1961, went to the Snelling Hall cafeteria for lunch, and became a target:

Some students began throwing lemon slices at me as I stood in the line to get food. They didn't stop until one landed in a serving tray. The cafeteria manager came out and told them to stop. I was so upset that I couldn't eat my food. I sat alone. If I sat at a table with other students—they would get up and move. I told Corky King, the minister for the Presbyterian Student Center about the incident. I told him that I didn't intend to return to Snelling—I would just eat in my room. He told me that this was just what the students wanted and that I should return. He told me that he and his wife, Mary Lisle, would accompany me on the following day. They did go with me to Snelling on the next day. No lemon slices from ice tea glasses were thrown. I continued to eat there—albeit alone and the incident did not repeat.

When I returned for the Spring 1962 quarter and roomed with Charlayne—we never ate together at Snelling. We did have a few meals at the Continuing Education restaurant. I continued to eat at Snelling.[24]

The university's administration tried to leverage the new students, whether seeing them as a threat or a nuisance. In a letter dated February 19, 1962, Dorothy D. Elder of Women's Housing and the Office of the Dean wrote Early concerning the spring quarter, suggesting that her status as a graduate student might mean a preference to live in Athens and, if so, there might be an offer of assistance. Early made a handwritten notation: "She assigned me right back to the 'Black Suite' in Center Myers Dorm to room with Charlayne. We were the only graduate and undergraduate students who roomed together at the Univ. of Ga. They even tried to charge us extra for our self-contained kitchen and bathroom. When we refused to pay the additional fee and suggested that we take it to court, they backed off hastily. We heard no more about it."[25]

Another letter, on March 9, indicates that UGA had no dormitory for graduate students. Early's handwriting is in the margin: "All a lie I discovered! Who told them that? I certainly didn't. I did not like a room directly on the street at the ground floor!"[26]

A gathering of the Turner High National Alumni Association in 2004 emphasized the bond that Turner students have, the platform for education that spurred Early, and the teachers who inspired her:

I had been interested in joining the band while at Booker T. Washington High School [in Atlanta], but the band director there wanted me to play the tuba and *I* wanted to play the clarinet. At Turner, I had the opportunity to play the clarinet in that mighty Turner High marching band! We were awesome in our new green and white uniforms and I thought that I was in heaven. Little did I know then that this activity was to shape my future career. Our band director, Dr. B. Wayne Walton, was not only a caring and knowledgeable teacher, he was a marvelous role model. I determined then and there that I wanted to become a band director—a career that was not common at that time for a young lady! That is exactly what I did—despite the naysayers who thought that this was not appropriate.[27]

If a student is lucky, he or she has at least one teacher who made a difference. In 2004 Early received a letter confirming her place in the pantheon of educators for whom time knows no bounds; her lessons about music appreciation had stayed with the letter's author, who had been Early's student nearly forty years back. The former student describes taking her two daughters, ages eight and nine, to see *West Side Story*. As they lost themselves in the adventures of the Jets and the Sharks, the excitement ignited a memory of seeing *The Sound of Music* when Early took her students to the movie theater. Not only did Early open the world of music to children, she also made sure that instruments were available to those who couldn't afford one. The letter reminds Early about buying a clarinet on credit, which happened because of Early's involvement. The decades passed, but the teacher's impact didn't. The letter's author said that at fifty-one years old she had begun studying classical guitar. The "greatest love for music" was because of Mary Early.[28]

Early was not a teacher steeped in ancient lesson plans. Like the groundbreaker she was at the beginning of the 1960s, she stayed current. While others balked at technology, she embraced it. At an education conference in 1988 at Georgia State University, she gave a presentation titled "What's a Computer Doing in My Music Room?" A drawing of an Apple IIGS graces the cover.[29]

Thus, besides being a crusader in civil rights, Early was a leader in music education. In a 1983 letter to Warner Rogers, an associate superintendent of schools, Early stressed the importance of music for elementary schoolchildren and, if possible, of having a music specialist as their teacher. It was a stand against the possible elimination of music programs.[30] As a member of the Music Educators National Conference (MENC), Early served on a MENC advisory panel, answering questions from educators in *Teaching Music* magazine. Issues covered included concert etiquette; transition from teaching at a college to teaching at an elementary school; developing a grading system beyond S for satisfactory and U for unsatisfactory; guiding students with talent; assembling an orchestra with students ranging from grades 6 to 12; suggestions on how teachers can handle their vocal problems and lack of range in a classroom; teaching fourth and fifth graders how to tune a violin; and keeping students' attention as the school year comes to an end.[31]

She contributed biographies of Hall Johnson and Roberta Martin to *American National Biography*, published by Oxford University Press, and to *Notable Black American Men*.

Early's efforts gained national attention when *Newsweek* highlighted an electronic lab that she taught; the lab educated about two thousand underprivileged Black children in the South in a five-week course. Although she is not mentioned by name, the lab is described as a "revolutionary crash course" in which students learn guitar by seeing chord changes on slides.[32]

About a quarter century after receiving her master's degree in music education from the University of Georgia in 1962, Early's undergraduate alma mater, Clark College, gave her an award on Founders Day acknowledging her place in the state's history as the first Black alumna from the University of Georgia graduate school and the first Black president of the Georgia chapter of the Music Educators National Conference. Other educators were also recognized with awards.[33]

If there was any doubt about Early's ability, it was erased with a term paper that she had turned in on May 14, 1962—"Music for the Blind." Her professor gave it an A+ with a handwritten note: "A very interesting paper. I enjoyed reading it [and] learned some details of the Braille music system."[34] Decades before others, Early saw the importance of arts education for children with special needs.

On August 14, 1962, Mary Frances Early got assigned to the John Hope Elementary School, beginning in September.[35] On August 16 she graduated with a master's degree in music education. She later earned a specialist in education degree from UGA, in 1967.

Early's peers recognized her excellence in the early 1980s, when she was elected to the presidency of the Georgia Music Educators Association. As Early has noted, "each state had a similar organization that was under the umbrella of our [national] organization," the National Association for Music Education.[36]

Better late than never, UGA finally recognized Early's importance: "UGA forgot, for 38 years, my role as the third [Black] student to enter and the first to receive a degree. I was discovered in 1997 by Dr. Maurice Daniels when he interviewed Donald Hollowell and [Jesse Hill] for a documentary about Horace Ward. Daniels was teaching at UGA but had never heard my name in connection with UGA's integration. He did research and found that this was true."[37]

Recognition, though belated, underscores Early's importance to Georgia, music, and civil rights. Her plaudits include an honorary doctor of laws degree in 2013, an annual lecture in her name since the year 2000, and a professorship in her name since 2003. In January 2018 she received the President's Medal, an award reserved for the most accomplished people in the University of Georgia's family. In September 2018 the documentary *Mary Frances Early: The Quiet Trailblazer* premiered. On October 10, 2018, she joined a group of University of Georgia giants for the unveiling of her portrait, which is placed just outside the university president's office.[38] It's a testament long overdue, though of course some of the composers whose work Early studied didn't get their just recognition for decades after their deaths. Centuries, in some cases.

For the woman whose body occupied crypt number 33 at the Los Angeles County morgue, recognition was a burden. To the morgue's workers, she was coroner's case number 81128. To the world, she was Marilyn Monroe.

There aren't enough words in *Roget's Thesaurus* to describe her. Monroe leapt off film screens with enough sexual energy to power electric grids from Seattle to Sydney. Luminescent. Gorgeous. Sexy. Alluring. Delightful. Glamorous. Enthralling. Captivating. She could read the dinner menu aloud and make men ravenous for food and lust for her face, body, and voice. Billy Wilder directed her in *Some Like It Hot* and *The Seven-Year Itch*, two comedies showing Monroe's expertise at playing a sexual character made all the more attractive by not understanding, or acknowledging, her physical allure. "Maybe she was tough to work with," said Wilder. "Maybe she wasn't even an actress. But it was worth a week's torment to get those three luminous minutes on the screen." In his view, "they've tried to manufacture other Marilyn Monroes and they will undoubtedly keep trying. But it won't work. She was an original, and there'll never be another."[39]

Laurence Olivier, Monroe's co-star in *The Prince and the Showgirl*, did not, like so many of his brethren, offer cover for the Hollywood machine that can build up and shred egos with aplomb. "I blame Hollywood for making Marilyn Monroe the complete victim of ballyhoo and sensation," said Olivier. "Popular opinion and all that goes to promote it is a horribly unsteady conveyance for life. She was exploited beyond anyone's means."[40]

Her use of sleeping pills and alcohol was not known to the public. But insiders knew. "It was one of the best-kept secrets in the Hollywood world of make believe," wrote show-business columnist Earl Wilson. Wilson claimed that her former husband Joe DiMaggio told Hollywood friends of his concern "as recently as two weeks [before Monroe's death]."[41]

Born Norma Jean Mortenson on June 1, 1926, Marilyn Monroe was transformed by a nose job, a shift to blonde hair, and a sexual thirst running through the country's post–World War II zeitgeist after two decades of brainy, sophisticated, and witty females dominating movie theaters. Barbara Stanwyck, Bette Davis, and Katharine Hepburn played characters that could go toe-to-toe in dialogue with a man. Their strength predated the feminist movement by thirty years.

Monroe represented the ideal for men who wanted a woman to be seen and not heard, unless it was to whisper affection, soothe injury, or adore him with the gentleness of a summer wind that could cut through a blistering heat. Men fantasized about her and wondered why three husbands—James Dougherty, Joe DiMaggio, and Arthur Miller—could not hold on to her. Women fantasized about being her and wondered how, with all her beauty and talent, she could not find love.

It is a burden of celebrity to have one's private life dissected, judged, and sometimes mocked with surgical precision by the press and the public. When she is described in books and portrayed on the screen, she is reborn in a sense, thanks to her biographers and the thespians who play her. They cover the biographical territory familiar by now—mentally ill mother, orphanage, first *Playboy* Playmate of the Month in 1953 (because of the 1940s modeling photos purchased by publisher Hugh Hefner), elevation to stardom, "blonde bimbo" persona, three marriages, and her death, which has ignited conspiracy theories, including murder because of her alleged knowledge of UFOs and sexual relationships with Attorney General Bobby Kennedy and President John F. Kennedy.

The television show *Smash* (aired on NBC, 2011–13) showcases the development of a Broadway musical biography of Monroe called *Bombshell*. In the finale to the first season, naïve Iowan Karen Cartwright, portrayed by Katharine McPhee, reaches her dream, as in the classic going-out-there-an-understudy-and-coming-back-a-star storyline. Deciding on Karen over Ivy Lynn, the daughter of a Broadway legend, director Derek Wills, a classic example of an obnoxious genius, coaxes the unknown Iowan when he realizes that her fiancé, Dev, slept with Ivy, who didn't know his identity. It is Derek who explains, perhaps better and more succinctly than any other Marilyn Monroe aficionado, that Monroe too understood heartbreak.

And so Wills triggers a crescendo to the out-of-town premiere of the show-within-a-show, climaxing with McPhee delivering her performance of a song—"Don't Forget Me"—that begins with a breathy voice issuing the title as a sad plea, then a sincere request, then an authoritative demand. Her voice gets stronger and more resonant, indicating the internal battle that Monroe must have been feeling as she bounced around Hollywood, like a pinball that caromed off bumpers and racked up points only to fall straight down the middle because of the unseen magnet that, sooner or later, pulls the ball out of play.

When McPhee delivers a line insisting that people who are broken need protecting, it rivets the *Bombshell* audience to Monroe's pain—what she endured and what she failed to endure. If eyes don't well and lips don't tremble, then the next action should be checking the carotid artery for a pulse. Ivy, played by Megan Hilty, gets the *Bombshell* lead in the second season, when the show hits Broadway, a result of Karen leaving for another show. Hilty's rendition has such bombast that it makes the audience realize that Monroe was not the fragile creature some deemed her to be, particularly toward the end of her life, when 20th Century Fox fired her from *Something's Got to Give* for consistently skipping work.

From the 1980s to the 2010s Susan Griffiths was the go-to Marilyn Monroe portrayer, racking up a list of credits, including *Growing Pains*, *Marilyn and Me*, *Quantum Leap*, *Pulp Fiction*, *Dark Skies*, *Timecop*, and *Curb Your Enthusiasm*. She observes,

> For Marilyn to get where she got gives an oh-my-God! feeling. But once you get there, it's harder to stay there. If you're already dealing with issues, they become worse. It's incredibly hard for a woman to maintain the image and then do her job. I've had to fight to let the demons come in when I portray Marilyn. When you're climbing, there are a lot of voices that you can't listen to. She became something that I wanted to master. When I was shooting *Pulp Fiction*, I stayed in the lane of studying her to get the nuances down.
>
> Marilyn comes off the page of the script and off the screen. They say that she revved herself up so much that she was electric. Even in the interviews she's amazing. In order to light up a room, you have to have a thousand watts. She lit them up and made you feel something. She was the American Dream—rags to riches. Her sexuality was given and then laughed about. I find that women love her more than men. She just struck a chord that nobody else could and paid the price for it. I get to have some of that understanding when I portray her.
>
> I love her because she was so brave. She took so many chances, put herself out there time and time again. We're all drawn into the beauty, but there was a depth to her. People saw the superficial, but there was a tremendous amount of depth. That's why she had the energy. The ones that do the best bimbos are the best actresses. I really do believe she was brilliant. It's a mistake not to understand the problems, but there were things on her end that were difficult. Success comes with a price. It couldn't light the darkness or fix her or fill her up. I have so much sympathy for her.[42]

James Gill is one of the world's foremost painters of Marilyn Monroe, with work dating back to late 1962. His contributions, along with Andy Warhol's, cemented her place in the art venue of popular culture. "The tryptic that I painted in September [1962] that went to MOMA in November was in MOMA before Andy's," Gill says. "But my painting is three black-and-white images behind three images at different stages of her life. Mine is a comment on her beginning, middle, end. Andy's was a variation on colors."[43]

August had begun with a baseball rarity and ended with the same—a no-hitter. Bill Monboquette gave New Englanders reason to cheer in a season that was as exciting as flat soda; the Red Sox finished in eighth place out of the ten AL teams. Monboquette's feat against the White Sox neared perfect-game status, but a second-inning walk prevented it. The Red Sox won the game 1–0. Likewise, Minnesota Twins hurler Jack Kralick dismissed twenty-five members of the Kansas City A's before pinch hitter George Alusik walked on a 3-2 count. The Twins won their game by the same score.

These were high points in an already exciting baseball season. For the Twins, the no-hitter was an extra shot of adrenaline, as they trailed the Yankees by only three games at the end of August. But the princes in pinstripes marched through September on their way to their thirteenth World Series in sixteen years.

9

Pinstripes

Between 1947 and 1961 the Yankees appeared in twelve World Series and won nine of them. The lineups were by this point as well known to baseball fans across the country as to fans in the Bronx. There was no reason to think that excellence in pinstripes would end in 1962. When the Yankees secured the American League pennant on September 25, it reinforced the declaration of a baseball sage named Berra that an event could be déjà vu all over again.[1] Mickey Mantle was a highly significant factor.

The Marvelous Mr. Mantle

What Mantle's female companions saw in bed and what his teammates saw in the clubhouse was a man who sacrificed his body for the game that he loved. It was not unusual for Mantle to get taped before a game that other players with similar aches and pains would have sat out. Injuries be damned; he determined to play through the pain. There was speculation—both by Mantle during his lifetime and by other prognosticators to this day—about whether he could have done better had he taken care of his body, that is, had he opted out of the postgame partying. But how much better could Mantle have done than 536 home runs, a .298 batting average, sixteen All-Star selections, five times holding the Major League lead in runs scored, a Triple Crown season, five times holding the Major League lead in walks, and an on-base plus slugging percentage of .977?

The 1962 season was pure Mantle: a .486 on-base percentage to lead the Majors and a .605 slugging percentage to lead the American League. The combined 1.091 number led the Majors. But the year's popular culture got contributions from Mantle in two films—*Safe at Home!* and *That Touch of Mink*. The former was a feel-good movie for the kiddie demographic: Little Leaguers who lived vicariously through the main character, who vows that Mantle and Maris will show up at a gathering for his fellow ballplayers. It's a lie that would have fit nicely with any of the standard sitcoms of the day featuring the consequences and a lesson learned about fibbing. Despite his pleas, the sluggers say no. But in early 1960s all's-well-that-ends-well fashion, the kids get to visit spring training and meet the Yankees.

Tom and Tony

Tom Tresh vivified the All-American image, a homogenization of the boy-next-door persona honed through mid-twentieth-century popular culture. Andy Hardy. Archie Andrews. Beaver Cleaver and his brother, Wally. It was more than a façade; Tresh's midwestern humility dictated his career decisions, beginning with his first opportunity in professional baseball in the late 1950s. Besides the parental values instilled in him, Tresh had an insight into the game through his father, Mike, a former Major Leaguer with the Chicago White Sox from 1938 to 1948 and the Cleveland Indians in 1949.

The bonus rule of that era capped a player's signing payment at $4,000 in 1957. "My father and mother pointed out that the bonus wouldn't be worth the loss of a college education," said Tresh. "They'd been very good to me. Dad has never ordered me to do anything; he explains and tries to convince me. He convinced me that I should enter Central Michigan University instead of turning pro."[2]

And so, Thomas Michael Tresh of Allen Park, Michigan—a Detroit suburb—matriculated at CMU. Lucrative offers later ignited another round of balancing between money and education; Tresh signed with the Yankees for a $30,000 contract. Money won out, but not at the expense of a college degree; the Treshes struck a deal allowing the second-generation Major Leaguer to attend college in the off-season. In 1961 Tresh batted .315 for the Richmond Virginians—the latest stop in his Minor League career, which also took him to New Orleans, St. Petersburg, Binghamton, Greensboro, Amarillo, and Binghamton again—and won the International League Rookie of the Year Award.[3] "I promised my parents when I signed that I would finish college," explained Tresh after the 1962 World Series. "They wouldn't hold me to that now, but they made me realize the importance of college," he said. "I've just had a good year; but this is a tough game and every year may not be so good. My education is an insurance policy in case something goes wrong somewhere along the way."[4]

Tresh began the 1962 season as a replacement for Yankees shortstop Tony Kubek, an Army Reserve member who got called up for military service. Kubek, a Yankee fixture since his rookie year of 1957, contrasted the buoyancy enjoyed by other players. Where they were gregarious, Kubek was stoic. In a profile for the *Saturday Evening Post*, Ed Linn wrote, "In the Yankee clubhouse last year, Tony was a natural butt for the goatish kidding that shy rookies are almost always subjected to—especially when it is discovered that the rookie can be made to blush. Tony would stand there until they were finished with him, a half-quizzical, slightly embarrassed smile on his lips. Then he would shrug and walk away."[5]

This approach, relaxed rather than confrontational, raised Kubek's stature and lowered his guard. According to *Newsday* sportswriter Stan Isaacs, "Kubek . . . is one of the most popular Yankees because of his courtesy, his honesty, his lack of pretense." Isaacs suggested that the young man "mocks stuffiness and makes himself the butt of most of his humor." As a result, "he is the leader of the young Yankees, and his easy approach to the world helps to counteract the cold Yankee image as automatons in gray flannel suits."[6]

Kubek's reticence with clubhouse jocularity did not reflect shyness on the field. "I've heard that business about my not being aggressive enough," said Kubek. "But I never could understand what they meant by it. I always ran hard, slid hard and barreled in to break up double plays. If that's what aggressiveness means, then I think I have always been a very aggressive player. If it means making a lot of noise, I guess I'm not."[7]

By 1962 the denizens of Yankee Stadium were viewing Kubek as a reliable contributor to the team's fortunes. A Milwaukeean, Kubek had fantasized about playing for the Yankees when he was a boy; he wore the team pinstripes for his nine-year career. "Even when I was a batboy for my father's industrial league team back in Milwaukee, the Yankees were my goal," he said. "No, it wasn't any hero worship of any particular player. I just felt that this was the greatest team and the team I wanted to play for some day if I was good enough."[8]

The kid from Milwaukee got his wish. He won the Rookie of the Year Award in 1957 with a .297 batting average, 128 hits, and .716 OPS (on-base plus slugging percentage).

Kubek's dominance at the shortstop position presumably precluded Tresh's moving forward in the Yankee organization. It was an embarrassment of riches for the Yankees' front office, which knew Tresh's value but confronted the reality of having too many kings and not enough thrones. "Tresh is a Yankee ballplayer, no doubt of it. He's really hot now," said Yankees general manager Roy Hamey in 1961. "But he faces a tough job next spring. How's he going to push aside the league's best shortstop, Tony Kubek?"[9] Naturally, concerns about Tresh's climb from the Minor Leagues prompted queries about readiness. "Yes. I am not kidding myself or you about being another Tony," explained Tresh. "But I had my best season with Richmond last year and Ralph Houk thought that good enough to merit a shot at the opening."[10]

Tresh comported himself well in the Yankee lineup in 1962, quite a feat considering the pressure of replacing a fan favorite on a squad with nine World Series titles in the previous fifteen years. It was not a new paradigm for the Yankees; Joe DiMaggio's exit, for example, prompted a cloud of concern hovering over Mantle in the early 1950s, who was assigned number 6 to highlight an orderly procession of legends: Ruth with number 3, Gehrig with number 4, and DiMaggio with number 5. It was not a permanent numeral. After a demotion to the team's Minor League ball club in Kansas City, Mantle returned to the South Bronx and got tagged with number 7. A legendary career followed.

Tresh explained that it was rightful for Kubek to reclaim the shortstop position. "How could I be hurt by that? The guy has been here five years and he was the best in the league," declared Tresh. "I'm pleased that I had a chance to show myself to the league. I expected that I'd be a utility infielder if I made the team until Tony was called back [to military duty]. I hated to see it happen to him, but it was a break for me."[11]

It was graciousness in pinstripes.

Whether Kubek's return would nudge Tresh out of the lineup remained a question mark, made even more questionable by Tresh's output. With the diplomacy of Dag Hammarskjöld, Kubek responded to press inquiries during his homecoming in August. "I've only watched [Tresh] for a week," he clarified. "You can't judge a shortstop in that time. I'll tell you one thing, I heard he's made some good throws on relays and now I believe it. He's got a great arm."[12]

A couple of weeks after Kubek returned, Yankees skipper Ralph Houk installed him at his old position and put Tresh in left field. It was a maneuver neither favoring Kubek nor punishing Tresh. Heading toward a Rookie of the Year Award, Tresh created an opportunity for Houk to add value, so it was not a case of keeping the infield area between second base and third base warm for Kubek until he returned from his military service. Joe King of the *New York World-Telegram and Sun* thought the decision was easy. "Of course Kubek should be at shortstop," wrote King. "He is an old, trusted winning clutch-hitting agent at the position, whatever the competence of the worthy Tresh."[13]

Roger

Kubek's absence was not by any means a dominant anxiety at Yankee Stadium. Being a Yankees fan meant being at ease with a lineup as deep as the Harlem River alongside the iconic ball field. The 1961 season was a tough one to follow, though. When Roger Maris knocked a Tracy Stallard fastball into the right-field stands at Yankee Stadium on the last day of the season, it ended a chase of Babe Ruth's single-season home-run record, set in 1927. Maris's sixty-one round-trippers stirred debate about whether it was a bona fide record; Ruth hit sixty home runs in a 154-game season whereas Maris had 162 games because 1961 was an expansion year that added 8 games to the schedule. The Teapot Dome scandal, President Andrew Johnson's impeachment, and King Edward

VIII abdicating the British throne had less controversy combined. At least for baseball fans. In 1991 MLB commissioner Fay Vincent declared Maris to be the holder of the record, which has been surpassed, as of 2019, by three players—Sammy Sosa, Mark McGwire, and Barry Bonds.

Maris, the winner of both the 1960 and 1961 American League Most Valuable Player Award, nearly doubled his salary when he signed with the Yankees at the beginning of the 1962 season. Although the specifics were kept quiet, his salary was believed to be in the $70,000 range.[14]

Maris's 1962 stats were valuable but nowhere near as stratospheric as his output in 1961, when he led the Major Leagues in home runs and the American League in RBIs and runs scored. His home-run tally beat Babe Ruth's single-season record of sixty dingers, once thought to be unbreakable:

1962: 33 home runs, 100 RBIs, 92 runs scored
1961: 61 home runs, 141 RBIs, 132 runs scored

The Southpaw

Whitey Ford, a native of Astoria—a Queens neighborhood named for businessman John Jacob Astor—had a demeanor that shielded him from the perils of either the swollen ego that so readily accompanies success or the deep frustration following failure. There was no bluster. No blarney. No bloviating. Edwin Charles Ford neither believed in egomania nor owed his success to it. "He possesses an innate modesty," wrote Sid Gray in a five-part profile for the *New York Post* in 1961. "He's honest, sincere, unobtrusive, calm. Blessed with a keen sense of humor, he's never malicious. Because he gives respect, the Yankees respect him. He won't make anybody the butt of his jokes just for a laugh. He doesn't take himself too seriously and kids himself over his new role as Yankee players' representatives."[15]

Overshadowed by the slugging exploits of Maris and Mantle, the latter exiting the chase at 54 home runs because of an infected hip, Ford's 1961 stats led him to the Cy Young Award: 25-4 win-loss record (led American League in wins), winning percentage of .862 (led the Major Leagues), 209 strikeouts (career high), two games won in the World Series, and World Series MVP Award.

Ford did not reach these accomplishments alone of course; Elston Howard hit .348, Luis Arroyo saved thirteen games for Ford, and Mantle and Maris combined for 115 home runs. At the beginning of 1962 Ford addressed the sting of critics who were underscoring Arroyo's contributions:

> I hope you will not misunderstand what I am going to tell you. . . . Ever since September, I have been hearing about the many times I was relieved by Arroyo last season. I owe much to him. He is a great pitcher and this coming season much will depend on him and his ability to duplicate his 15 victories in 65 appearances of last year.
>
> Well, I have tired of listening to insinuations that but for Arroyo I would have been of no great consequence.
>
> So, top item on my 1962 agenda is to pitch many more complete games.[16]

It didn't happen. He pitched seven complete games in 1962. There were eleven such tallies in 1961. His 1962 record was 17-8.

The Religious Yankee

The RBI record for a World Series belongs not to Ruth, Mantle, DiMaggio, or Gehrig but to Robert Clinton Richardson, from Sumter, South Carolina. With twelve RBIs in the 1960 World Series, Richardson was a key factor in the Yankees' postseason success that fell short of a championship courtesy of one swing of the bat by Bill Mazeroski, Richardson's second-base counterpart on the Pirates. Maz's bottom-of-the-ninth home run ended an epic game that saw the lead change hands more times than payoffs at Tammany Hall.

Despite being on the losing team, Richardson had an achievement that secured him the prize of a Corvette courtesy of *Sport* magazine.

While some merry men of the Yankees ball club pursued extra innings of enjoyment with liquor and lasses, Bobby Richardson was a human refuge of clean living. He played in the Minors from 1953 to 1955 and got some Major League experience with the Yankees in 1955 (eleven games) and 1956 (five games). In 1957 he left the Minor Leagues behind for good and hit .256 in ninety-seven games.

Richardson's teammates respected and perhaps even envied him for his anchor of faith. And Richardson never stood in judgment of those who gallivanted around New York City as if it were designed for Dionysian pursuits. The Yankees' second baseman was no preacher to those who followed a path paved with joy rather than sacrifice, immediate pleasure rather than delayed gratification. Judgment had no place in the locker room, further underlining Richardson's respect for and from that pinstriped contingent basking in after-hours bliss at bars to cap a game day, which more often than not had resulted in victory.

Richardson ascribed his faith to Reverend J. H. Simpson, who visited the ballplayer's household by invitation, spoke of Jesus Christ, and asked Richardson and his two sisters "whether we each knew that we, too, had sinned."[17] It was a Richardson trademark to be a guidepost offering direction without insistence. "But any time you take a stand there's respect," said Richardson. "I feel I have this respect from the players. As far as profanity goes, I don't have to use it. I wish the others didn't but I believe you lose their respect if you go around preaching."[18]

It was an understanding rooted in affection that gave Richardson the room to say as he pleased, live as he determined, and befriend as he wished. "When I talk to Richie, I talk very slow and careful. I have a habit of using too many bad words I don't like to use around him," revealed Yankees first baseman Moose Skowron.[19]

"I try to be careful what I say when he's around," said Mantle.[20]

"You feel embarrassed if you say some of those things in front of him," said Yankees manager Ralph Houk.[21]

"Now Bobby, I'm going to have a couple of drinks, but I want you to know that it's because I'm flying," said Johnny Blanchard, in explaining that alcohol calmed his nerves.[22]

Richardson, like so many others with devoutness at the core, viewed life as a never-ending attempt to live up to principles while knowing that missteps will happen. Everybody falters in life, just as they do in baseball; nobody has an error-free scorecard over the long run. This fueled Richardson to perform better. "We keep on failing and making errors in life, but as we consistently seek to conform to the image of Christ, and make him our goal and our purpose in life, and give him the honor and the glory, he forgives us, he develops the talents he has given us, and he grants us the conqueror's reward, the incorruptible crown that never fades," wrote Richardson in a 1971 essay.[23]

Even the most zealous can be pushed only too far. When Richardson got plunked by Angels hurler Eli Grba on June 3, he tossed some words toward the mound on his way to first base and doubled down once he got there. Fisticuffs were imminent as Grba took a step in Richardson's direction, only to get intercepted by the umpire, Ed Runge. After the inning Grba expelled his commentary, which prompted the third base umpire, Ed Hurley, to get involved. If words were fireworks, this would be the Fourth of July. "And pretty soon everybody was jawing at everybody else," wrote Leonard Shecter in the *New York Post*.[24]

It was heated. And personal. Richardson made fun of Grba's nose. "Richardson said he'd punch him in the beak," reported Runge.[25] Hurley confirmed the diatribe at the third-base line, which included Grba dismissing Richardson as an offensive threat with a .220 average. "That's when Richardson said, 'He's got enough beak for both of us.'"[26]

Richardson, at five feet, nine inches and 172 pounds, would have looked diminished but no less determined against the six-foot, two-inch Grba, who was 40 pounds heavier.

In 1962 Richardson led the American League with 209 hits. He was the eighth Yankee to pass the 200-hit barrier in a season; Babe Ruth did it three times, Earle Combs did it three times, Lou Gehrig did it eight times, DiMaggio once, Red Rolfe once, George Stirnweiss once, Phil Rizzuto once. It was Richardson's sole season with 200 or more hits.

The Groundbreakers

Elston Howard was the first Black player for the Yankees when he took the field in 1955, eight years after Jackie Robinson broke baseball's color line in Brooklyn. It was a battle to rise in the Yankees hierarchy, according to veteran sportswriter Sam Lacy of the *Baltimore Afro-American*. "The lone colored player in an organization which wants no part of his race, Howard is a pawn in the hands of operators who have no conscience and who refuse to recognize the quality of mercy any time it seems likely to interfere with their plan," wrote Lacy the year before Howard's Major League debut.[27]

In his rookie year Howard pounded American League pitching for a .290 average and ten home runs in ninety-seven games. He entered the 1962 season as the recipient of the St. Louis Baseball Man of the Year Award. A native of the Gateway to the West, Howard batted .348 in 1961.

After his career Howard became the first Black coach in the American League—with the Yankees of course. When Yankees manager Billy Martin and slugger Reggie Jackson clashed egos and traded shouts in the Yankee dugout at Fenway Park after Martin pulled Jackson from the outfield in a 1977 game against the Red Sox—because he thought Jackson didn't run fast enough to field a base hit—it was the six-foot, two-inch Howard who was key in separating the two, who were close to throwing punches.

Héctor López too was a racial trailblazer. He was the first Black manager in organized baseball when he took the reins of the Buffalo Bisons of the International League in 1969. "I heard the things said to other black players when I was playing, but I never heard any of it said to me. In Buffalo people were behind me; they wanted a good ball club. Nowhere I managed on the road did I hear heckling about color. I was treated like any other manager," said López in 1970.[28] The Bisons were the Triple-A team for the Washington Senators. Ted Williams, the Senators' skipper, had chosen López to manage the team.

During a June–July streak in 1962, López played in 19 of 21 games and batted .320; the Yankees won 14 of those games. He ended the season with 106 games and a .275 average, an improvement over his 1961 numbers—93 games and a .222 average. On his thirtieth birthday, July 8, he crushed a two-run home run in the top of the ninth to put the Yanks ahead of the Twins at Metropolitan Stadium in a 9–8 victory. "You can't hit good unless you play," declared López. "Last year Ralph [Houk] told me he knew I could do better. He told me I wasn't getting much of a chance to play. He knew it was hard for me to hit when I did play. It was nice of him to tell me, you know?"[29]

Joe

Joe Pepitone wore pinstripes during the decade that began with the Yankees marking excellence by winning two of five World Series, from 1960 to 1964. Born on October 9, 1940, to Willie and Angelina Pepitone, he had two older brothers, Jimmy and Vincent, and a younger brother, Billy. Jimmy lived with an aunt a block away, beginning when he was four and a half; the living arrangement lasted for eight years. Because the aunt was childless, the Pepitones entrusted Jimmy to her.[30]

Pepitone credits an uncle nicknamed Red with inspiring his interest in baseball, though the lessons could be brutal: "He started catching with me when I was seven or eight. As I got older, nine or ten, he'd throw harder and get angry when I missed one. If I missed easy ones, he'd smack me, and Willie smacked him."[31] A star at Manual Training High School, Pepitone played on the Nathan's Famous Hot Dogs semipro team with players in their early twenties. He kept pace with them, batting .390.[32]

During his senior year at Manual Training, Pepitone got shot in a school hallway in March 1958 when a classmate was fooling around with a .38 revolver near Pepitone's locker. The bullet went through his body after hitting a rib and "missing three vital organs by inches."[33]

Teenagers danced to Bobby Darin's singing about splishing and splashing, women gossiped about Elizabeth Taylor forming an epic Hollywood love triangle by stealing Eddie Fisher from Debbie Reynolds, and the Yankees advanced toward their twenty-fourth American League pennant as Pepitone signed his first professional baseball contract. On August 13 he agreed to play for the Auburn Yankees of the Class D Pennsylvania-Ontario–New York League, seeing action in sixteen games and batting .321 in 1958. His signing bonus was $25,000.[34] The *New York Daily News* praised Auburn's newest outfielder and first baseman as an "outstanding Brooklyn baseball prospect."[35] In the off-season Pepitone played in the Florida Winter Instructional League.

Passion for baseball earned Pepitone respect from his manager, Steve Souchock: "I'm delighted with young Pepitone. He came here with no pro experience. We signed him right out of Brooklyn's Manual High School, but the boy loves to play ball and has shown surprising power."[36]

With the Fargo-Moorhead Twins in the Class C Northern League in 1959, Pepitone played in 123 games; knocked in 87 runs; and hit .283, 35 doubles, 12 triples, and 14 home runs. In 1960 he jumped to Class A ball—the Binghamton Triplets in the Eastern League. Described by Binghamton sportswriter

John Lake as "darkly handsome," Pepitone stood tall, at six feet, two inches, and weighed 178 pounds.[37] Once boasting a head of curly hair, Pepitone had conformed to baseball's shorter—sometimes shorn—style. When he refused a mandate to get a haircut, Souchock took matters—and clippers—into his own hands to assure shorter locks.[38]

By June, Pepitone's destiny to play in Yankee Stadium had gotten another endorsement when veteran scout Bill Skiff said, "Playing center field for Binghamton, this 19-year-old left-hander all the way, has it all." In the scout's opinion, Pepitone "could be the next big Italian player at Yankee Stadium. We've been famous for them, you know—Tony Lazzeri, Joe Di Maggio [sic], Phil Rizzuto and Yogi Berra."[39]

Pepitone batted .260 in Binghamton, then found himself in an Amarillo Gold Sox uniform in 1961. One of seven unanimous selections to the Texas League All-Star team—the league's six managers made the selections—Pepitone tore up the Lone Star state, batting .316 with 87 RBIs, 24 doubles, and 21 home runs.[40]

Next stop: spring training with the 1962 Yankees, who were riding atop the baseball world after their iconic 1961 season, which ended with a defeat of the Cincinnati Reds for the World Series title. "[Pepitone] certainly has come a long way. He can run, throw, hit, play the outfield and also first base. I would say he has an awful lot going for him," said Yankees skipper Ralph Houk.[41]

Pepitone played in sixty-three games for the Yankees in his rookie season, batting .239 and hitting seven home runs.

Yogi

Yogi Berra was in the twilight of his career in 1962. His stats across the board dropped from 1961—batting average nearly 50 points, from .271 to .224, and playing time from 119 games to 86 games. His last year as an All-Star was 1962. In June he marked his two-thousandth game as a Major Leaguer. Although not as powerful as Mantle or Howard, Berra was the compass that pointed the Yankees in the direction of winning. On the occasion of his two-thousandth game, sports journalist Red Smith wrote, "It is not possible to exaggerate his importance. He has been the keystone, the binder, the adhesive element that has held this team together when everything else changed."[42]

A World War II veteran, Berra spearheaded the Yankees dynasty from the late 1940s to the early 1960s. He received three MVP awards, twice placed number two in MVP voting, hit 358 home runs, played in fifteen consecutive All-Star Games, and had five 100-RBI seasons. Berra retired after playing four games with the Mets in 1965.

Although he was known for malapropisms, Berra had a shrewd insight into the game. He had two stints managing the Yankees and a ten-year run with the Mets as a coach and manager, 1965–75. His helming began when Gil Hodges died of a heart attack at the beginning of the 1972 season, and his tenure included the "Ya Gotta Believe!" season of 1973, when they clawed their way to the World Series but lost to the mighty Oakland A's dynasty in seven games. Berra also coached the Astros during their mid-1980s greatness, including the NL West championship.

Yogi's first managerial experience, in 1964, lasted one season. By any other metric, it was successful—World Series appearance, 99-63 regular-season record. After the Yankees lost to the Cardinals in seven games, he was dismissed. When he came back to the Yankees twenty years later, the team notched a respectable 87-75 record. Sixteen games into the 1985 season, with a 6-10 record, owner George Steinbrenner fired him. But he didn't do it in person, which Berra saw as a sign of disrespect. Berra, in turn, refused to come to Yankee Stadium for any events. No Old Timers' Day. No throwing out the first pitch. No days in his honor. Berra, one of the most beloved baseball figures, was no longer in his eyes a Yankee. The rift endured until 1999, when Steinbrenner visited the Yogi Berra Museum and Learning Center in New Jersey and admitted his wrongdoing.

Paul Linke directed the one-man show *Nobody Don't Like Yogi*, an off-Broadway production that *Variety* called "a mournful, if affectionate study of a principled man who is strong enough to stand up for his values, even when it costs him what he loves best."[43] Premiering off-Broadway at Lamb's Theatre, the play starred Ben Gazzara. Tom Lysaght wrote and Paul Linke directed. Linke became a 1970s fixture on television in *CHiPs*, playing Officer Artie Grossman. After his first wife died from cancer in 1986, Linke authored and performed the one-man show *Time Flies When You're Alive*. It premiered in Los Angeles and was filmed for HBO. The play's emotional authenticity made Linke a go-to director for one-person shows:

I grew up in Queens and Long Island in the 1950s as a Yankees fan. Yogi was a core member of those teams. Innately, there was a sweetness and authenticity to him. Even with the trappings, the championships, and the kudos, he stayed true to who he was. He happened to fall into a situation surrounded by some of the greatest players who ever laced them up.

In the play there's the notion of going home. Yogi coming back to Yankee Stadium after being fired by Steinbrenner and what it was like for him that day. It allowed Tom to create this world around that return. Yogi is an interesting character because he's not a leading man or a tragic figure, but there's something about his journey that spoke to me because I was a Yankees fan. I loved that time so much.

I was sitting at a table with Ben early in the rehearsal process. He brought a lifetime of experience and became Yogi Berra right in front of me. We had great designers—Tony Walton for the set and Ken Billington for the lighting. Simple is always better in telling a story.

Yogi appeals to us because he's an everyman. He was a real down-to-earth everyday person.[44]

Moose

Moose Skowron, the Twist aficionado, had been a staple of Yankees lineups since his rookie year of 1954, when he batted .340 in eighty-seven games. A 1951 scouting report from the Yankees Instructional School in Arizona described him as having "Major League Power" and recommended Class A ball. His fielding, noted as "good enough," prompted a suggestion: "This boy has to get a position and stay at one position. Either left field or third base. Has spirit and has the disposition to go all the way. Important thing is to select his right position."[45]

The Yankees installed Skowron at first base. He played in 108 games in 1955: .319 average, 17 doubles, 3 triples, 12 home runs, and 61 RBIs. Batting advice from manager Casey Stengel helped with consistency in 1956 as Skowron played in 134 games, batted .308 with 21 doubles, 6 triples, 23 home runs, and 90 RBIs. "Stengel showed me that the way I was batting I could not pull many balls," Skowron said. "I had been driving homers into right field from my righthanded stance and he said I should be getting a lot of them into left."[46]

As the team readied itself for the 1962 season, Skowron agreed to a $3,000 raise and a salary of $35,000. He wanted to remain in pinstripes. "There is only one place to play ball—New York—and I hope I finish my big league career where I started," said Skowron.[47] Unfortunately for Yankees fans, Skowron's career took a three-thousand-mile detour to Los Angeles, where he joined the Dodgers after 140 games, 80 RBIs, 23 home runs, and a .270 average in 1962. In exchange, the Yankees got pitcher Stan Williams.

There was a point after the trade when Skowron considered leaving the playing field and becoming a coach at his alma mater, Purdue University. "A fellow has to quit baseball some time," said Skowron. "However, I have a couple of months to make up my mind. All I can say at this time is that I'm giving it serious thought."[48]

Skowron made sure that the people around him got acknowledged—and not just the guys in the clubhouse. "I wish you would say something in the paper for me," said Skowron. "Say, first of all, the Yankees treated me wonderful, and say I'm sorry to leave the guys. We had some real class guys on that ball club. We always did the whole nine years I was with them," he added. "Then say something nice about the ground crew, Pete Sheehy and Pete Previte in the club house. Mr. Topping and Mr. Webb were good to me. Don't leave anybody out."[49]

Skowron's playing time took a hit, along with his batting average—eighty-nine games and .203. But when the Dodgers faced the Yankees in the 1963 World Series, they swept in four straight; Skowron played in all four games and hit .385—the second-highest average behind Tommy Davis's .400. He had found a home. After the Dodgers won the World Series, Skowron said, "Now I can stay in Los Angeles this winter." He had thought he was "going some place else, but now I want to stay here this winter and work." Wistfully, he wondered, "Maybe I can even come back next year after all this. I love the Dodgers. I don't want to leave."[50]

It was not to be.

In 1964 the Senators coughed up $42,000 for Skowron, who didn't deserve it based on the numbers. But there was an intangible value to having Skowron. Senators manager Gil Hodges believed that the '63 average was a blip. "Skowron has always been a good hitter, he'll hit well for us and what he did in

1963 doesn't change my mind about him," said Hodges.[51] With more playing time—146 games—Skowron boosted his average nearly 80 points, to .282 in 1964. He blamed eagerness for the slide. "When I was in there, I was trying to make good in too much of a hurry and got myself all fouled up," he said. "The more intense I got about it, the more of my good swing I was sacrificing."[52]

Skowron finished his career with the Chicago White Sox; 1967 was his last season.

Clete, Luis, and the Two Ralphs

There was as much chance of Clete Boyer being in the 1962 Yankees lineup as there was of Perry Mason winning a case. Boyer played in 158 games, with a steady presence at the plate, batting .272 with 68 RBIs and 18 home runs. But it was his glove at third base that was valued by the Yankees. "He is the best I have seen in this league," said left fielder Bob Cerv. "Did you ever see anybody play third base so close in as Boyer does at times? He dares 'em to hit it by him, and they can't. It must be great to be a pitcher with a man like that behind you snapping up two-base hits."[53]

When Boyer competed against his brother, Ken, in the 1964 World Series, the citizens of Alba, Missouri, followed the game with pride. All 336 of them. The Boyers had seven sons and seven daughters; one of the daughters died at eighteen months. Every son signed a professional baseball contract—five with the Cardinals organization. Clete, Cloyd, and Ken went all the way. Ken got the honor of being named *Sporting News* Player of the Year. After the '64 World Series, their mother, Mabel, talked about an even smaller burg where the family had lived before Alba: "Cossville had a population of 12 to 15—and the folks built a makeshift field." It was the boys' second home. "And the boys played ball there all day. They'd go after breakfast in the morning. They'd come home for lunch, then play all afternoon. Not only our boys. Boys came from all around."[54]

Clete Boyer, the pinstriped one, resented Casey Stengel decades after the 1960 World Series, when Stengel pulled him for a pinch hitter in the second inning of first game. "That is still inside me. It was so embarrassing," said Boyer in 1998, nearly forty years later.[55]

Ralph Terry topped the American League with 23 wins in 1962. He also led in games started (39), innings pitched (298⅔), and home runs allowed (40).

He praised catcher Elston Howard for his success, calling him "psychic" for his perceptiveness: "He thinks with the pitcher. He's got that wonderful sense of knowing just what ought to be thrown in any given situation."[56]

Luis Arroyo came into 1962 after an outstanding season backing up Whitey Ford and his brethren. He led the Majors in games played (65), saves (29), and games finished (54). Along the way, he compiled a 15-5 record. You don't need to be Copernicus to figure out that the saves and victories amounted to nearly half of the Yankees' 96 wins in 1962.

Leading the Yankees was Ralph Houk, who filled Casey Stengel's shoes. No easy task, this. Stengel had snared World Series titles in 1947, 1949, 1950, 1952, 1953, 1956, and 1958. He notched AL titles in 1955, 1957, and 1960 but lost the series in seven games each time.

Houk helmed the Yankees from 1961 to 1973, then managed the Detroit Tigers from 1974 to 1978 and the Boston Red Sox from 1981 to 1984. A World War II veteran, Houk played a backup role to Berra after World War II, seeing sporadic action—ninety-one games from 1947 to 1954. He then managed the Denver Bears of the American Association from 1955 to 1957, winning the American Association championship in his last season in Denver. When Houk took over the 1961 Yankees, it was a team for the ages—a 109-53 record. In his autobiography, *Ballplayers Are Human, Too*, Houk describes the awe of Opening Day at Yankee Stadium: "I've read that wearing the Yankee pinstripes gives a player the feeling he's on top of the baseball world. Believe me, it's the Stadium that makes you feel you've got to do your best. The Stadium looks like a historical building from the outside, one that's been standing there a long time and will remain there forever, like the Coliseum [sic] in Rome. Baseball history has been made in the Stadium. A fellow wants to make more baseball history there—that's the way I felt that day."[57]

New York was the center of the universe for baseball and other matters— Wall Street and finance, Broadway and acting, skyscrapers and architecture, Lincoln Center and the arts.

Or so it seemed.

On television screens in the early 1960s, comedies with rural settings began to take hold. The bumpkin was not a new character type for storytellers—the Ma and Pa Kettle movies were quite popular, featuring as they did two characters seeming to lack a modicum of intelligence, common sense, or worldliness but always coming out on top.

On CBS *The Beverly Hillbillies* debuted on September 26, 1962, for a run that lasted nine years. The plot revolved around Jed Clampett, a "mountaineer" from the Ozarks who struck oil when he shot at a creature he hoped to turn into food. Instead, he got $25 million from the O.K. Oil Company, moved to Beverly Hills, and became a neighbor and customer of Milburn Drysdale—president of the Commerce Bank of Beverly Hills. Jed and his clan—daughter Elly May, mother-in-law Daisy Moses, and son Jethro—had no ill will toward anyone, including those filled with condescension (for example, Drysdale's wife), because they thought these kinfolk were akin to invaders of the societal structure in Beverly Hills. And the Clampetts' good nature always came out on top.

The banal exploits of the Beverly Hills bumpkins appealed to an audience because the fish-out-of-water theme never presented the Clampetts as fools to be scorned, mocked, or ridiculed. It was the hoity-toity crowd that got its just deserts when attempting to outsmart the clan.

Buddy Ebsen, who played Jed Clampett, notably had missed out on one of the biggest movie roles in Hollywood history. Originally cast as the Tin Man in *The Wizard of Oz*, Ebsen had to bow out because of a reaction to the aluminum dust. After his run on *The Beverly Hillbillies* he had another hit show, in which he played the title character in the private-detective drama *Barnaby Jones*. He made a cameo in the 1993 movie *The Beverly Hillbillies* as Barnaby Jones in a wink and nod to the audience.

Kiki Ebsen, a singer and one of the actor's seven children, recalls that her father's career spanned seven decades because of his passion for performing:

Dad was used to getting bumped around by Hollywood. He had difficulty finding roles, music or otherwise, and got rejected after World War II. No one knew how big *The Beverly Hillbillies* was going to be. Paul Henning, the show's creator, was such a brilliant writer. He created the role of Jed Clampett with Dad in mind after seeing him on television, possibly in *Northwest Passage*, and convinced Dad's agent to get him a meeting. By that time Dad was semiretired and in his fifties. We had moved to Balboa Island.

The show had an undeniable chemistry. The actors were different enough so that when they got together, it homogenized into a brilliant sitcom. Great casting, brilliant writing. Dad and Irene [Ryan] had a long history in the theater, so they knew how to get into characters and make it work. The sheer amount of experience that my dad had on stage before the show included thirty years of vaudeville, stage acting, singing, and dancing. He was an incredible dancer. Look at *Banjo on My Knee* and *Captain January* with Shirley Temple. *The Beverly Hillbillies* did not define him as an artist, but he enjoyed the fame that it brought him. He truly enjoyed people. It was almost distracting as a family because we couldn't go out. As he got older, it was harder to let go of that fame.

My grandfather was a dance teacher and had a dance studio in Orlando. My dad and his sister were a dance team there. They were competitive dancers and got paid to perform. He found his way to the stage through dance. When he initially set out in his late teens to go to college, he intended to be a doctor. After a couple of years the family ran out of money. So he borrowed $25 from his sister and went to New York City. He got a job in the chorus and was fired immediately because he was too tall. But he saw that he could work as a dancer.

He was extremely proud of *The Beverly Hillbillies*, so I think his legacy is perseverance when people told him to stop and his ability to transition across different stereotypes with a lengthy career. On his ninetieth birthday, he was dancing and performing. He started painting in his eighties. I think he really loved the physicality of performing and making people laugh. That's what he was early on. The goofy guy. He never wanted to call in a performance. He liked being in the moment. He never worried about screwing up. I think that's what really drove him and was a big part of his success.[58]

The mansion used for establishing shots in *The Beverly Hillbillies* belonged to Arnold Kirkeby. Carla Kirkeby grew up in what became one of popular culture's most famous abodes, located at 750 Bel Air Road. It was not unusual to find business leaders, Oscar-winning actors, and socialites visiting the Kirkeby household:

I was only one year old when we moved in. The story that I heard from my father was that Lyn Atkinson had built the house and fashioned it after the Palace of Versailles as a dream home. He was almost finished but ran out of money. My father was doing short-term loans at the time and loaned him $200,000 to finish the house. This was about 1943–44. Atkinson finished it, but he couldn't pay back the loan. My father couldn't eat the loss, so he had to take the house back and we moved from Chicago. Atkinson's daughter told us that her father spent so much money doing the house and he was so upset that he would sit in an apartment on Wilshire Boulevard with binoculars and watch the house.

My father was in the hotel business. He owned the Hampshire House and Sherry Netherland in New York, Drake in Chicago, Kenilworth and Fountainbleu in Miami, Beverly Wilshire in Beverly Hills, and Nacionale in Havana. So, we moved around a lot. Then, he built Westwood Village and the Kirkeby Center. He did a lot of developing in Honolulu. After the situation with Atkinson, my father said that he would never make another loan on a house.

His family didn't have money. They moved from Bergen, Norway, to Chicago when he was fifteen. When he and his brother turned seventeen, my grandfather kicked them out of the house and gave them $25 each. He started his business career being a runner in the stock market and a night manager at a hotel in Chicago. He was a quiet man.

My mother was Carlotta Cuesta de la Madrid. She grew up in Spain and Tampa. Her family was in the cigar business. My father had loaned money to a man to build a shopping center in Tampa. When he was there on business, he met my mother at a party. Her father was very wealthy and did not like my father. She was engaged to marry the richest man in Tampa. But my father followed her to Spain. He always got what he wanted.

My father was killed in the American Airlines crash in March [1962], so he never got to see the house on television. People would come by, and they really thought that the Clampetts lived there. We got about thirty people a day. Some would picnic on the lawn. And then it got on the maps of famous houses. It became a sort of nightmare. We finally put in electric gates. I think it was only used in the show for about one year.

There were six bedrooms upstairs, and they were generously sized. There were also four bedrooms for the household help, plus a guest room. We had a train that went all the way around the property. My uncle built a car that I could drive on the grounds. My friends wanted to come to my house, but I wanted to go where they lived. They had sidewalks where you could ride your bike. We didn't have that.

When I went to Stanford, I would watch the show, but I never told anyone that it was my house. It's amazing how popular the show was. I've been on eleven safaris, and on my first one in the early 1990s there were two girls from New York City who were attorneys on our trip. They were singing the theme from the show. So we're having a drink and my friend told them that the house belonged to my family. Our guide's wife was English, and she couldn't believe it. I was astonished that she knew about it. They played the reruns every day in England.

It's a fabulous house. My friends would come over, and then new kids in school would come over too. They would tell me that I lived in a mansion. I didn't understand because it was just my home. I didn't think of it as this giant mansion because it didn't seem that big to me. One girl asked how much money my father had. It was upsetting. Eventually I told my mother that I didn't want new people coming. It was upsetting when they talked about the house like that.

We had great art because my father wanted it in the house. But he didn't know anything about art, so he got advice from his friend, Colonel Michael Paul. He bought paintings by Van Gogh, Matisse, Monet, and Gauguin.

For forty years we had the house. Jerry Perenchio, an entertainment mogul, bought it after my mom died in 1985 and totally redesigned it. We waited until the right offer, and Jerry was a great fit because he loves the house like we did.[59]

For the New Englander with the toothy smile in the Oval Office, September was a month when two highly significant actions cemented his legacy in civil rights and space. Kennedy stepped in when Mississippi governor Ross Barnett refused to let James Meredith enter the state university and become the first Black student there, despite a ruling by a federal court. Threats of using the

National Guard and other force, if necessary, to protect Meredith's right to become a student at the University of Mississippi prompted Barnett to concede with a streak of defiance that made him look like a hero standing for southern pride: "Surrounded on all sides by the armed forces and oppressive power of the United States of America, my courage and my convictions do not waver. My heart still says 'never,' but my calm judgment abhors the bloodshed that would follow."[60] Two men had already died in a riot. U.S. Marshals, under Kennedy's order, escorted Meredith; in 1966 a sniper shot Meredith during the March Against Fear, a civil rights walk from Memphis to Jackson. Once he had recovered, he got back to the event, which had an estimated fifteen thousand participants.

In a speech delivered on the campus of Rice University in Houston, Kennedy proclaimed that the United States should prioritize a moon landing and make it happen before the end of the 1960s. His speech framed space exploration as the next point on the human continuum, joining the scientific achievements of penicillin, television, and nuclear power. Kennedy's words drip with inspiration, looking ahead to the possibilities of space as a peaceful arena for exploration rather than contemplating the victories already won. But Kennedy did more than inspire—he localized his speech to the crowd, including their community as part of the space effort: "So it is not surprising that some would have us stay where we are a little longer to rest, to wait. But this city of Houston, this State of Texas, this country of the United States was not built by those who waited and rested and wished to look behind them. This country was conquered by those who moved forward—and so will space."[61]

The passage that became a hallmark for NASA tapped an emotional chord for the Rice community, stressing a rivalry ranking with the Hatfields and the McCoys, Harvard and Yale, and Macy's and Gimbel's:

> But why, some say, the moon? Why choose this as our goal? And they may well ask why climb the highest mountain? Why, 35 years ago, fly the Atlantic? Why does Rice play Texas?
>
> We choose to go to the moon. We choose to go to the moon [applause]. We choose to go to the moon in this decade and do the other things, not because they are easy, but because they are hard, because that goal will

serve to organize and measure the best of our energies and skills, because that challenge is one that we are willing to accept, one we are unwilling to postpone, and one we intend to win, and the others, too.

It is for these reasons that I regard the decision last year to shift our efforts in space from low to high gear as among the most important decisions that will be made during my incumbency in the office of the Presidency.[62]

Kennedy's vow to beat the Soviets in space got reinforcement with the next Mercury flight. But the speechmaking skills that were on display at Rice would come into play in another conflict with the Soviet Union, one that became a hallmark of his White House tenure.

10

"Well, Hang on Tight"

Splashdown.

It's the part of NASA's Mercury, Gemini, and Apollo missions signifying the end of a mission. There would a debriefing of course and a medical checkup. But the capsule hitting the ocean meant that the astronaut had arrived home. When Wally Schirra's *Sigma 7* capsule came back to earth after a six-orbit voyage that took nine hours and fourteen minutes, NASA moved another step toward catching the Soviets in the space race.[1] Schirra joined Shepard, Grissom, Glenn, and Carpenter as heroes, with their names cemented in the chronicles of American achievement. "From countdown to splashdown it was the most flawless flight by an American astronaut," reported Howard Simons in the *Washington Post.*[2]

Except it wasn't.

Schirra's flight on October 3 almost got clipped after the first orbit, but not because of Schirra, the only astronaut to fly in the Mercury, Gemini, and Apollo programs. His flight suit was registering a couple of degrees higher than NASA's benchmark of 85 degrees Fahrenheit. Concern about dehydration and its potential effect on Schirra's judgment placed the mission in jeopardy.[3] But if anyone knew how to solve this particular problem, it was this particular astronaut. "The suit had been my special area of responsibility," explained Schirra in his 1988 autobiography, *Schirra's Space*. "I inserted cool water into the system at a very slow rate, advancing the knob a half a mark at a time and then waiting ten minutes. My logic was that if I added water in a hurry, a heat exchanger might freeze, and then I'd be in real trouble. As I was nearing the end of the first orbit, the temperature needle started to drop. It had reached ninety-plus degrees, which was hot but not unbearable. The problem was solved through no great amount of human ingenuity, but the point was it was solved by a human."[4]

Splashdown took place less than five miles from the recovery ship—the USS *Kearsarge*. On the same date a Mars meteorite landed in Africa; 126 meteorites have been classified as coming from Mars.[5]

Baseball fans in San Francisco and Los Angeles had their attention elsewhere on October 3; the last game of a three-game playoff would decide whether the Giants or the Dodgers would face the Yankees in the World Series. But they knew about Schirra's triumph when an announcement appeared on Dodger Stadium's "message board" in the seventh inning.[6]

The rivals had tied for first place; each team tallied a 101-61 record. With Dodger Stadium debuting in 1962, an NL pennant would cap an inaugural year of excellence. The Los Angeles incarnation of the Dodgers had already given their fans a World Series victory in 1959, defeating the Chicago White Sox in six games. But a world championship, or even an NL pennant, would be a glorious prize for the modern structure occupying the massive site named Chavez Ravine. And either possibility seemed likely, until fans learned results of the Giants' games. Willie Mays had an on-base plus slugging percentage of .999, for a third-place finish in the National League, behind only Frank Robinson and Hank Aaron; he led the Major Leagues with forty-nine home runs. San Franciscans counted on Mays to perform with aplomb the same way they counted on fog to obscure the bay.

The 1962 season was typically Maysian for the center fielder: .304 average, 189 hits, and 141 RBIs. He was also responsible for getting the Giants into a playoff scenario—in the last game of the season he bashed a solo home run off Dick Farrell of the Colt .45s to put the Giants ahead 2–1. It was a slim margin, but enough to win the game.[7] The Dodgers' loss to the Cardinals put the rivals in a tie for the pennant.

Mays had complements. Harvey Kuenn swatted 148 hits for a .304 average, nearly 40 points above his 1961 performance; Jim Davenport batted .297; and Orlando Cepeda batted .306.

San Francisco's pitching staff was exemplary; the four leading pitchers combined for a 67-43 record: Billy O'Dell (19-14), Jack Sanford (24-7), Juan Marichal (18-11), and Billy Pierce (16-6).

John Roseboro caught 128 games for the Dodgers in 1962. Most famous for a 1965 brawl capped by Giants hurler Juan Marichal hitting him in the head with a bat, Roseboro revealed the tension between manager Walter Alston and his most famous coach—it enhanced the pressure the Giants felt in their scamper to catch up to the Dodgers later in the season. The lads from Los Angeles got distracted. "Also, Leo Durocher and Alston were feuding," explained Roseboro in his 1978 autobiography, *Glory Days with the Dodgers and Other Days with Others*. According to Roseboro,

> Durocher had been coaching third and taking over, as is his way, and taking chances. Alston called him down for it, took command, and became conservative. We had been an aggressive club, but we went into a shell and started trying to hang on. We spent so much time looking at the scoreboard to see how the Giants were doing, we stopped doing for ourselves. If they won, we were depressed. If they lost, we were elated, but it was as though we didn't have to win then.
>
> I became aware of this and started to get on guys about it, but they had gotten into the habit and couldn't break it.[8]

National League Playoff, Game One—Candlestick Park

The Dodgers got blanked 8–0 in the first game of the NL playoff. Mays again was the hero on offense. He hit two home runs; Pierce threw a three-hitter. "I've never found any club to be a soft touch," said Pierce. "Believe me, it's hard work all the way."[9] But the Giants were quick to warn that resting on laurels is for the foolish and the ignorant. "We could lose the next two easy," said Mays.[10] "We haven't won this thing yet," said Giants manager Alvin Dark.[11]

Alston argued that the Dodgers' past indicated a change for the future. The recent slump for the boys from Los Angeles was at the forefront of his thesis: "This club is due to go on a two game winning streak. [T]he Dodgers have lost 11 of their last 14 and seven of their last eight."[12] What was more frustrating about the slump was the lack of familiarity in riding out a downswing. "A lot of these youngsters haven't been through this kind of pressure before," said Duke Snider, whose rookie season was 1947. Snider and Wally Moon got the only two hits in the season-ending loss to the Cardinals. "As soon as we get a run, we'll be all right. You add pressure on yourself by trying too hard sometimes," reasoned Snider.[13]

Fans who couldn't get enough baseball could tune in to ABC and find Jimmy Stewart starring in "Flashing Spikes," an episode of the drama anthology *Alcoa Premiere*. The story revolves around a former ballplayer who got kicked out of baseball because of bribery accusations and the younger ballplayer whom he befriends.[14]

National League Playoff, Game Two—Dodger Stadium

It seemed that the Dodgers would soon be cleaning out their lockers for the last time in 1962 when the Giants mounted a 5–0 lead before Dark sent Sanford to the showers in the sixth inning. "He was completely worn out and part of the reason was a bad cold," explained Dark. "He had done the best he could and we couldn't hold it for him."[15]

And then the Dodgers awoke from their slump—seven runs and ten batters in one inning—and won the game 8–7. Where once there was frustration, there was now contentment. Optimism invaded the Dodgers' clubhouse. "We'll win it now," said Durocher. "A game like this perks up the whole club. I haven't seen the guys so relaxed in a long time. You know when we really began to relax? When we were behind 5–0 in the sixth inning."[16]

National League Playoff, Game Three—Dodger Stadium

Optimism reigned at Chavez Ravine for the fans anticipating a victory to secure the pennant. It increased as the Dodgers inched toward the final out.

The Dodgers were an inning away from going to the World Series. They led 4–2 on their home turf with one out in the top of the ninth. Then the Giants piled on hits and runs to quash the Dodgers' hopes for vanquishing the ghosts from a 1951 afternoon in a horseshoe-shaped ball field when the sky was gray and a three-game Dodgers-Giants playoff came down to the ninth inning. *Los Angeles Times* sportswriter Frank Finch opened his recap by comparing the Dodgers' loss in 1962 to 1951, "when Bobby Thomson did you-know-what."[17]

The final score was 6–4. Any hopes for a bottom-of-the-ninth rally were unmet.

The Dodgers mourned. But it was more from shock than sadness; they were ahead by four games with eight left in the season when the Giants clawed their way onward to force the playoff. "It happened. But you can't understand how it happened," said Maury Wills. "We have the greatest team in baseball and we just can't understand. Well, maybe we do understand. But some things you can't say. You have to be diplomatic."[18] Dark pointed out the handicap that his counterpart, Walter Alston, suffered when his powerhouse couldn't pitch. "I admire him as a manager and a man on a lot of counts," said Dark. "Don't forget he lost Sandy Koufax for three months; there isn't one of us who could have afforded to lose any starting pitcher for that length of time and Koufax was having one of the greatest years of all time. That he got his team even into a playoff after a loss like that means he did a great job."[19]

When the Giants returned from doing battle at Chavez Ravine later that day, they had no opportunity to rest before playing the Yankees; Game One of the World Series was scheduled for noon at Candlestick Park. But there was a crowd of well-wishers and worshippers awaiting them. "The Giants came home last night and it was the biggest thing since V-J Day," wrote Peter Trimble in a front-page story for the *San Francisco Examiner*.[20]

World Series, Game One—Candlestick Park

In just five years the Giants had given their new metropolis a World Series team. Even the prisoners on Alcatraz focused on the matter at hand—about 80 percent of the inmates stayed in their cells to listen to Game One on the radio.[21] The Giants lost 6–2, but former AL hurler Billy O'Dell got some nice words from Mickey Mantle: "He was always in and out but now he's inside more. He certainly didn't give me anything good to hit."[22]

Maris fared well in Game One with two hits—a double that knocked in two runs and a single. But it was the defensive play of Giants outfielder Felipe Alou that triggered jaws dropping among the 43,852 attendees at the first World Series pitting teams from the West Coast and the East Coast against each other. Maris's double might have been a home run had Felipe Alou not intercepted it. The outfielder snared the Maris blast, but it didn't stick in the glove; Alou said that his elbow hitting the outfield wall prompted the ball to leap out.[23]

Alou, in his 2018 autobiography, recalls that exhaustion had combined with an anticlimactic aura after the playoff against the Dodgers. The first four games of the World Series would take place in four of the next five days, which meant that the Giants would have played ten games in ten days—including a doubleheader against Houston to end the regular season. "Some of the other Latino players and I chatted before the game—in Spanish, of course—and we wondered what could be more exciting, more electric, than what we had just experienced against the Dodgers," said Alou. "I heard some of the other guys saying things like, 'What more can we do?'"[24]

San Franciscans delighted at an old-fashioned squeeze play when José Pagán scored an RBI with a bunt that sent Mays across home plate. It was a noteworthy addition to the tally—Ford had gone scoreless in the World Series for 33⅔ innings—he blanked the Milwaukee Braves in 1958, Pittsburgh Pirates in 1960, and Cincinnati Reds in 1961. Mays was responsible for the Giants' other run, tying the game at 2–2 in the third inning when he singled home Chuck Hiller from third. Clete Boyer knocked a solo home run in the seventh against O'Dell. Two more notches in the eighth inning and another in the ninth secured a victory for the Yanks. Mays's total for the day was three hits.

Houk offered words of praise: "Ford was the difference. When you have a pitcher who looks that good, your club looks good. We had our best shot at him in the third inning but Orlando hit into the double play."[25]

Kuenn pointed out the fatigue factor of playing three playoff games and Game One being the fourth in a row. But he did not use it as an excuse: "No matter how you try, you just can't get up psychologically quickly enough from a hot playoff and come storming into a World Series the next day. You could sense that our bench wasn't as lively as it was in Los Angeles. I'm not alibing [alibi-ing], but I am sure that they will find us a tougher outfit tomorrow."[26]

Boos against Maris didn't faze the soft-spoken guy from North Dakota. A year away from the home-run chase relieved the stress put on him by the fans and the press: "I'm in an altogether different frame of mind than a year ago at this time. Last year, the pressure was unbearable. I was beaten and tired after chasing Babe Ruth's record all year," Maris said. "Now I'm relaxed. Nobody expects me to do much, which is fine with me. I like it better that way."[27]

Giants manager Alvin Dark kept his optimism focused on Game Two. Praising Ford, the skipper said, "They can't throw two guys in a row as good as he is." Any thoughts of the fourth game in four days sapping strength from the San Franciscans were dismissed: "We weren't tired. It was just Ford. He pitched a great game. That's all."[28] Cepeda, however, was benched for the second game after Dark admitted that the slugger's winter ball activities might have caught up. His winter work put Cepeda at more than two hundred games played for a year.[29]

Schirra's space flight mattered little to Giants fans. "No if's, and's, or but's about it, there was more interest in the Giants' game than in Walter M. Schirra Jr.'s orbital flight around the globe," one journalist commented. "You can draw your own conclusions to such evidence as three television sets (out of four) at a downtown department store being tuned in on the Giants' game, or the fact that everywhere you went you heard local folk asking for the latest score of the third and final playoff game."[30]

After the National League playoff, the first World Series game seemed anti-climactic for some, perhaps because it was the Yankees' thirteenth appearance in the Fall Classic in sixteen years. It was an expected autumnal occurrence, like leaves turning in the Mid-Atlantic and northeastern regions, schoolchildren returning to classes after summer vacation, and turning the clocks back an hour. But to say that the Yankees were dominant during this period is to ignore fantastic competition from the senior circuit. Seven of the thirteen appearances went the full seven games. Of those contests, the Yankees were 5-2, losing to the Dodgers in 1957 and the Braves in 1958.

The start of the 1962 World Series provided a glimpse into the tension to follow; the score was tied from the third inning to the eighth inning. Sports journalist Red Smith lamented, "Probably it was the contrast with the wild untidiness of the National League playoff that made this workmanlike production seem dull. With the score tied most of the way, there should have been a mounting sense of drama. It's hard to get worked up watching 'The Little Minister,' however, when you've just been through 'Son of Frankenstein.'"[31]

After the victory, one celebrant showed his dedication to the Yankees by setting off "a lighted firecracker." His choice of location was a doorway. But he got off light because the judge shared his allegiance: "The maximum penalty is $100 or 90 days in jail, but I'm a Yankee fan. The fine is $15."[32]

World Series, Game Two—Candlestick Park

Game Two went to the Giants, thanks to Jack Sanford's splendid performance on the mound. While battling a head cold, Sanford restricted the Yankees to three hits.[33] The 2–0 shutout was the first blanking for the boys from the Bronx in the Fall Classic since Warren Spahn held them scoreless in Game Four of the 1958 World Series; that was seventeen Series games ago. It was almost a two-hitter—Mantle's double was the third hit for the Yankees, but it didn't happen until the ninth. Once a skinny ballplayer, Sanford had been passed over by the Braves in the late 1940s. He found his way to the Majors with the Phillies in 1956, then got traded to San Francisco for righty Rubén Gómez and catcher Valmy Thomas in 1958.

Sanford pitched on two days' rest, having been the starting pitcher for the second game of the playoffs with the Dodgers.[34]

The Giants' first score came in the first inning, when Hiller led off with a double, then moved around the bases thanks to a sacrifice bunt and a ground-out. McCovey added the second run with a smash solo homer in the seventh inning.[35]

It was the fifth game in five days for the Giants. Yankees pitcher Ralph Terry was awed: "I though[t] these guys were supposed to be tired."[36]

World Series, Game Three—Yankee Stadium

The teams headed to the House That Ruth Built for the next three games. More than seventy-one thousand baseball-minded citizens crowded into Yankee Stadium to see the battle for the championship continue. Maris once again came through for the pinstripers in Game Three. He was responsible for all three of the Yankees' tallies in the 3–2 victory; the runs were scored in an error-filled seventh inning for the Giants outfield. The baseball and the Giants' gloves were like two magnets with the same poles opposing each other.

It began with Tom Tresh singling, then moving to third when Felipe Alou couldn't get a handle on a Mantle drive that should have been a single but allowed the Oklahoman to go to second on Alou's error. Maris then singled to right and found himself in a similar situation when McCovey's misjudgment and "fumbling" sent him to second base. "The single, of course, would have scored Tresh and Mantle in any event," wrote John Drebinger in the *New York Times.* "By the time McCovey got through fumbling the ball, however, Maris was on second and McCovey was charged with an error."[37]

Maris fled to third base on an Elston Howard sacrifice fly to Mays. It was a risk, considering Mays's legendary throwing ability. "I saw Howard hit the ball to center and I knew about Mays's throwing ability," Maris said. "I figured it would be close, but I also knew I had a shot and so I took it. Why? Because three runs are better than two."[38]

Dark heaped neither blame nor concern on Mays. "There's a lot of center field in the Stadium," Dark said. "Howard's ball was hit deep and Maris is a good base runner. It would have taken a perfect throw by [Mays] to get Maris and I'm not even sure that he could have done it even with a perfect throw."[39]

Dark yanked Pierce and sent in Don Larsen, a mediocre pitcher who had notched a permanent place in the record books when he pitched a perfect game for the Yankees against the Dodgers in the 1956 World Series. Now Larsen etched frowns on the faces of Giants fans when he hit Moose Skowron. With Maris on third base, he was a threat to score. As long as Larsen could get Clete Boyer to hit the ball on the ground, there was a good chance at a double play. And so it appeared that would happen when Pagán fielded the ball and "quickly flipped" to Hiller, who "failed to handle the ball cleanly." Boyer beat the throw to first, Maris scored, and the Yankees had their third and final run. The Giants fought back in the ninth with Ed Bailey's two-run homer; Mays was the other run scored, having doubled to start the inning. The attendance fell nearly 130 short of setting a World Series record—71,434 versus 71,563 for Game Four of the 1958 World Series.[40]

Things might have turned out differently had Bill Stafford not intercepted an Alou liner with his leg in the eighth inning. Dark surmised, "If Felipe had gotten a hit, as he deserved, we would have had runners on first and third with one out. In that situation, I feel we might have gotten to Stafford. But he pitched a fine game."[41]

Indeed. It was touch-and-go for a moment, though. "After I got hit, I was a little dizzy. But they put some ice on the leg and gave me some smelling salts and I felt better," said Stafford, who pitched the whole game.[42]

World Series, Game Four—Yankee Stadium

In Game Four the Giants retaliated and tied the series at two games for each team with a 7–3 victory. Fortunes turned for Hiller, who smashed the first World Series grand slam for the National League; he had borrowed Pierce's thirty-one-ounce bat.[43]

Houk pulled Ford in the sixth inning for a pinch hitter. The Yankees had men on first and second, two out. "When we started to get men on base that inning, I asked Whitey how he felt. He said he didn't have his best stuff," explained the Yankees skipper. "Now, if his turn to hit hadn't come around, I probably would have let him start the next inning and see if he got into trouble. As it was, though[,] here was my chance to win the game. I had no way of knowing if I'd get another—and as it turned out, we never did get another man on base until two out in the ninth."[44]

Ford confirmed, "I wasn't tired at all, but I wasn't pitching at my best. We talked it over and I agreed it would be best for the club to get some runs while we had the chance. We didn't get any more, but you have to go with your best shot."[45]

The strategy failed; Tony Kubek grounded out to end the threat. Dark and Houk jousted with hitting and pitching replacements in the seventh inning. Jim Coates replaced Ford and let two Giants get on base—walking Jim Davenport and giving up a double to Matty Alou, pinch-hitting for José Pagán. With one out from striking out Tom Haller, Coates had runners at second and third. Dark then called for another pinch hitter to replace Larsen. Ed Bailey grabbed a bat, but Houk countered by sending in Marshall Bridges to the mound. Dark responded by replacing Bailey with Bob Nieman, a right-handed hitter to face lefty Bridges. Houk ordered an intentional walk, and Dark called on Ernie Bowman as a pinch runner.

Harvey Kuenn had topped .300 in the 1962 regular season, so the hopes of Giants fans rose. But the mighty Kuenn popped up for an infield fly. With two outs, Hiller crushed a grand slam.[46] "I thought he might throw a fast ball, in fact I was hoping he would," said Hiller. "The pitch was high and inside. When I hit it, I thought it had a good chance of going out of here, but I hit so few, I didn't know."[47] "I didn't know he had that much power," said Bridges.[48]

World Series, Game Five—Yankee Stadium

After being postponed by a day because of rain, Game Five found a hero in Tresh, who sent a Sanford fastball into the stands for a three-run home run.[49] "I was only looking for a base hit," explained Tresh. "I was choking a bit on the bat to protect the plate. I was really surprised because he hasn't given me a pitch like that in the whole Series."[50] The 5–3 victory saw a rematch of Ralph Terry and Jack Sanford—they had battled in a pitcher's duel tied at 2–2 in the eighth until the rookie's home run. Tresh's dad, himself a Major League player with the Chicago White Sox from 1938 to 1949 with a career .249 average and two home runs, found his eyes moistened when his offspring knocked the home run: "The instant Tom hit the ball, I knew it was going all the way. And the instant he hit it, I cried. I didn't care who saw me, and when I went back to our seats, I guess there were tears in my wife's eyes, too."[51]

Those who thought they knew better than Dark when it came to leaving Sanford in the game had overlooked the analysis preceding a manager's decision. "Jack just pitched too good in the game to come out before he did," explained Dark. "He was going to have to lose his own game in a situation like that. When a guy can pitch as good as he can pitch, I want him on the mound as long as he can be on it. If he'd been getting hit, it would have been different. But to me it was like he'd pitched a shutout until then. The two runs the Yankees had off him were gifts."[52]

World Series, Game Six—Candlestick Park

The teams headed to San Francisco for Game Six and, if necessary, Game Seven, but Mother Nature drenched the Golden Gate's environs. The rains had soaked the field, so some decision-maker employed three helicopters to fan the outfield. It was a two-hour effort, with the choppers "never more than six feet off the ground." Still, the grass remained "soggy." The game was postponed for three days.[53]

The delay was worth the wait for Dark's squad, which gave oxygen to hopes for a World Series title with a 5–2 victory.

In the fourth inning of Game Six Whitey Ford made a rare error during a pick-off play when a delinquent throw to second base caused the runner to scamper home. The Giants added two more runs to the tally. Houk caused debate among armchair managers in the fifth inning; behind 3–1 with two men on base and two out, he sent Ford to the plate instead of a pinch hitter. Ford whiffed and gave up two more runs in the bottom of the inning. He was never in danger of being pulled. Houk said, "We still had four more turns at bat and Whitey's my best pitcher."[54]

The Giants, according to Dark, had information from the AL exports that proved invaluable in breaking down the strengths, weaknesses, and tendencies of the Yankees during the contests. "Basically, what we did was to depend upon what our former American Leaguers like [Billy] Pierce, Don Larsen and Harvey Kuenn were able to tell us about the Yankee hitters," Dark said.[55]

Pierce pitched a masterpiece, but he measured it against Game One of the playoff, when he blanked the Dodgers 8–0. "At his age, I don't think Billy will ever match that one (playoff game) again," said Dark. "He threw much harder against the Dodgers. He pitched well today but I don't think he threw real hard. The only real fast pitches he made were the last two, when he struck out Maris for the final out. I don't think he had as much stuff today as he did in New York, when he lost the third game to Bill Stafford."[56]

New York Mirror scribe Dan Parker, whether due to analysis or emotion, leaned toward the Giants winning:

As a coat of arms for the San Francisco Giants, who are in a fair way to win the world's baseball championship in their first crack at the bonanza, I would suggest an eight-ball couchant, against the background of a wall, with a giant rampant. The eight ball represents what the club has been coming from behind this season as far as memory reacheth [*sic*] not to the contrary.

A wall is what the club has had its back against more often than a cow with the seven-year itch. The giant rampant typifies the National League champions emerging from every crisis they faced in their quest for the grail.[57]

World Series, Game Seven—Candlestick Park

The seventh game of a World Series has no parallel. What begins in February with ballplayers shedding winter fat lasts through the anticipation of Opening Day, the dog days of August, and, if the fans are lucky, a gut-wrenching pennant race. The two best teams square off as autumn begins to send the mercury down a few notches. Whatever happened in the previous 162 games is irrelevant. Nobody cares. Or remembers. As in any profession, you're only as good as your last achievement. For the Yankees it had nearly been a tradition since World War II to appear in the World Series, but the Giants hadn't been there since 1954, when Willie Mays performed what some consider to be the greatest catch of all time when he raced toward the outfield fence and caught a Vic Wertz fly ball with his back to the infield, then whirled around and fired the ball. Giants hurler Don Liddle came in to relieve Sal Maglie after Maglie put runners on first and second with a walk and a single. Liddle's alleged response is part of baseball lore—"Well, I got *my* man."

In 1962's version of World Series Game Seven, the Giants went to the bottom of the ninth trailing the Yankees 1–0.

Willie McCovey held the hopes of San Franciscans in his batting grip when he turned his wrists and connected with the ball. It was a sound that resonated, triggering the fans' delight or dejection, contingent upon your loyalties. In that split second San Franciscans felt hope rush through their veins. But it died as quickly as a lit match in a hurricane. McCovey's line drive went to second baseman Bobby Richardson. "He couldn't have hit it much better. But I don't care how hard they hit them if they hit them at somebody," said Yankees skipper Ralph Houk.[58] Tresh and Maris got some praise when Houk emphasized their fielding. For the former, he stated that Tresh had "saved the game."[59] Tresh stunned Mays with a catch that was improbable to the slugger: "I don't know how he got to it. He musta been playing me wrong. Nobody in the National League plays me that way."[60]

It was a game of redemption for Ralph Terry, who had suffered heartbreak in the bottom of the ninth inning of the 1960 World Series when Bill Mazeroski won it for the Pirates with a home run. This time, "my heart was in my mouth," Terry revealed, as McCovey was at bat and awaiting the pitch.[61]

But an overlooked victor was Mickey Mantle, who batted .120 for the series and got picked off first base in Game Seven. Richardson's grab caused a celebration that made everyone forget about it. Richardson summarized, "It was a sinking line drive, right at me, not a hard chance. One side or the other, though, and I don't think I could have gotten it. It was hit so hard."[62] Only a couple of inches would have done it. Richardson knew it. McCovey knew it. Everyone in Candlestick Park knew it. "I'm the luckiest man in the country. If the ball goes a foot or two higher or to one side, I'm the loser," said Terry.[63]

And Mantle, ever the southern gentleman, showed humility by excluding himself: "It was one of my biggest thrills, them winning it."[64] He explained that being anxious at home plate caused the downfall, which included five strikeouts: "I think I got that home run in mind and I'm overanxious and overswinging."[65]

Another Mays turn at bat got tempered by Maris. Pinch hitter Matty Alou led the Giants' ninth with a bunt single; Terry struck out Felipe Alou and Hiller, then Mays crushed a ball to right field. That hit looked deep enough to score Matty Alou and tie the game, but Maris fired it to Richardson, the cutoff man. "That was the play of the inning," said Richardson. "If he threw it to me on a hop, the ball slows down and Alou scores. But he threw me a strike. I saw the coach half way down the line and I thought it was the runner. I was glad it wasn't."[66] Houk gave Terry the green light to continue. "I asked Ralph if he wanted to pitch to McCovey when I went out to the mound," said the Yankees skipper. "He assured me his control was still good and that he would pitch carefully to McCovey, walking him if need be."[67]

Terry, who had a perfect game in the sixth inning, received accolades from Dan Parker in the *New York Mirror* for his accomplishment:

> Terry's four-hitter has been excelled in some respects and matched in others. But no pitcher in the long and brilliant annals of post-season baseball has matched it for courage. In the clubhouse after his classic, Ralph, who had

lost five World Series games (including the second game this time) before he finally broke through to victory in the fifth game, with a catch in his voice, exclaimed fervently: "I thank God for the second chance." Every Yankee who will cut in on the lion's share of the jackpot with him should drop to his knees and echo Ralph's prayer of thanksgiving. He had saved the day after even the Old Master, Whitey Ford, had failed. And he came up with the finest effort of his career to make up for all the bad breaks Fate had dealt him in previous Series.[68]

Skowron scored the Yankees' sole run during a double play. "This was one helluva ballgame and yet, it is almost ludicrous," wrote Dick Young in the *Daily News*.[69] Young pointed toward the NL playoff, a seven-game World Series, and a one-run decision for the championship.

As San Franciscans mourned and New Yorkers celebrated, the Cuba-U.S. tension began to take hold in a more visible manner. It was not something that happened suddenly. CIA intelligence from the Cuban underground revealed that Fidel Castro had been on track for an alliance with the Soviet Union early in Kennedy's presidency. A memorandum declassified in 1996 explained that Castro was proactive in developing ties with the Soviets and strengthening military capabilities with inhumane tactics:

> You can say that Fidel has Russian tanks of the Stalin model and platforms prepared for the implacement [*sic*] of anti-aircraft cannons of all types on top of hospitals, colleges, public buildings, etc. and that the construction of platforms for rockets are almost ready in the fields in the area of Soroa and of Jaruco, and also all of the bridges, tunnels, and roads are mined. It appears that Russian planes, of the MIG type, are hidden in San Antonio or in San Julian.
>
> The interchange of propaganda and students with Russia is immense. If the Americans do not hurry, by the end of the year already Fidel will mix communism in the rest of the Americas.[70]

In May 1961 a letter to President Kennedy from a Cuban mother illustrated the personal cost that Castro's leadership had exacted. Signing her letter only as "Maria," she explained that her two sons had been part of the Bay of Pigs invasion. One was in a Cuban prison and the other was trying to get back to the United States by asking for asylum in the Havana embassy of a Latin American country. Her passion was evident as she praised Cuba and denigrated Castro for his dictatorial ways.[71] Although Kennedy received criticism for refusing to send enough troops to occupy Havana, a Dominican general—who was a West Point alumnus—stated that Kennedy's decision was the correct one. A White House memorandum for Kenny O'Donnell, a longtime Kennedy adviser dating back to JFK's first run for Congress in 1946, summarized the general's outlook: "An occupation force of great strength composed of American troops would then have been required. Castro and his Communist cohorts would have carried on a guerrilla-type of warfare and although the American occupation troops would control Cuba in the daytime, the Castro Communist-type guerrillas would take over at night. He said that the drain on human life, as a result of ambushes and assassinations of American troops, would be high. In addition, he stated that from the point of view of Latin America, this course of action on our part would be disastrous."[72]

The Soviet Union's nexus with Cuba went beyond ideology; there were missiles in the island country courtesy of Soviet leader Nikita Khrushchev.

Kennedy's confrontation with Castro and, in turn, Khrushchev over the missiles lasted thirteen days. The crisis was depicted in the 1974 TV movie *The Missiles of October* and the 2000 film *Thirteen Days*. All ideas were on the table, including that of U.S. Air Force chief of staff Curtis LeMay, who advocated the bombing of Cuba's missile sites.[73] Kennedy, however, saw the crisis as diplomatic chess, not military checkers. Each action, declaration, and bluff demanded consideration of how it would affect the position of Cuba and the Soviet Union. Placement of the missiles alone certainly amounted to provocation, but Cuba had not taken any further steps. Kennedy wanted his presidential advisers to measure all options and prospective reactions before any missives were sent or meetings with counterparts took place. The next substantive move was a naval blockade of Cuba, which sent a message that the island would be cut off from naval passage. A deal with the communists resulted in the Soviets taking their bomber planes out of Cuba; the blockade ended on November 20, 1962. To complete its part of the deal, the United States took its Jupiter missiles out of Turkey in April.[74]

The Cuban Missile Crisis demanded that the president comport himself with the gravitas necessary to convey assurance to the American people that war was a last resort. Television had reached the critical test that Edward R. Murrow had been concerned about—whether a television was "merely lights and wires in a box" or an invention capable of informing the public.[75] It was without exception the latter. Kennedy's speech to the nation on October 22 was a cease-and-desist oratory demanding that the Soviets pull the missiles from Cuba and announcing the blockade.

Americans tuned in at 7:00 p.m. Eastern on October 22 to find the president—once lauded for his youth, charisma, and confidence—transformed into a sober, solemn leader. That afternoon he called on his predecessor, who had mastered the art of leadership during World War II and extended it into his presidency, though Dwight D. Eisenhower preferred to be called "General" after leaving the White House. In turn, and quite appropriately, Eisenhower referred to his successor not with the informal label of "Jack" but with the respectful title "Mr. President." Kennedy consulted him on his views about the Soviets' next move and warned that an invasion of Cuba was possible but not likely in the immediate future:

> "General, what about if the Soviet Union, Khrushchev, announces tomorrow, which I think he will, that if we attack Cuba, that it's going to be nuclear war. And what's your judgment as to the chances they'll fire these things off if we invade Cuba?"
>
> "Oh, I don't believe that they will."
>
> "You don't think they will."
>
> "No."
>
> "In other words, you would take that risk if the situation seems . . ."
>
> "Well, as a matter of fact what can you do? If this thing is such a serious thing here on our plank, that we're going to be uneasy and we know what things [are] happening now, all right, you've got to do something. Something may make these people shoot 'em off. I just don't believe this will."[76]

At this point in the conversation, there's a pause. It's a half second of silence broken by nervous laughter that continues for the rest of the conversation between the two leaders, who, along with nearly three dozen other presidents, were burdened with being freedom's beacon of leadership. "In any event, I'll say this. I'd want to keep my own people very alert," expressed Eisenhower. "Yeah. Well, hang on tight," Kennedy responded.[77]

Six days later, Kennedy updated Eisenhower, indicating that the United States would take an invasion of Cuba off the table.[78] He also informed former presidents Harry Truman and Herbert Hoover.[79] There was one casualty in the Cuban Missile Crisis—U-2 pilot Rudolf Anderson Jr. was shot down over Cuba. It inspired Kennedy to end the crisis with diplomacy rather than force. Kenneth Jack, former naval photographer and coauthor of *Blue Moon over Cuba: Aerial Reconnaissance during the Cuban Missile Crisis*, explains that obtaining visual evidence of missiles was crucial for the pilots assigned to the task:

> The part that the movie *Thirteen Days* got wrong was that [navy reconnaissance pilot William] Ecker's plane actually got shot. Chris Lawford, who played him, said there were birds in the area. But the ground crew knew what the pilots were flying and that the mission was top secret. They didn't have or need much more information, so there would be no explanation given by the pilots.
>
> The role that Kevin Costner played, Kennedy aide and friend Kenny O'Donnell, lobbied Ecker that he should not tell the Joint Chiefs of Staff that he was shot at. If he did, the chiefs might not get Kennedy's approval for an attack. That also didn't happen. The part they got right was when Ecker goes to Washington and says that the mission was a piece of cake and all their questions will be answered when they see the photos.
>
> The military component was a critical point of the Cuban Missile Crisis. It gave Kennedy the resources to determine the status of Cuba. The U-2 couldn't do that because it was flown at such a high level. They didn't give the real close-up that our aircraft were able to do.
>
> The depiction of the first flights over Cuba [was] mostly accurate. They were approximately five hundred feet over ground. That was one of the

advantages of our aircraft. We could fly low enough to avoid being shot down by missiles, but we were shot at by gunners.

Kennedy's military experience is central to his role. In 1961 the Bay of Pigs debacle happened. He went along with the CIA and the military. It was a total disaster. That gave him insight into what his role as president was. It's not to take advice at face value. He needed to do more research on his own. This approach gave him strength during the crisis to resist attacking immediately. It was critical because errors in the decision-making process can occur. He was patient in determining what advice was the most meaningful and appropriate.[80]

Kennedy's October 22 speech to the nation about the crisis begins with the immediacy of danger—the ballistic missiles can reach Washington DC and "any other city in the southeastern part of the United States, in Central America, or in the Caribbean area."[81] Then the president talks about the development of sites that will have missiles with a possible reach into the Western Hemisphere and part of Canada.

Imminence is emphasized: "But this secret, swift, extraordinary buildup of Communist missiles—in an area well known to have a special and historical relationship to the United States and the nations of the Western Hemisphere, in violation of Soviet assurances, and in defiance of American and hemispheric policy—this sudden, clandestine decision to station strategic weapons for the first time outside of Soviet soil—is a deliberately provocative and unjustified change in the status quo which cannot be accepted by this country, if our courage and our commitments are ever to be trusted again by either friend or foe."[82]

To reinforce the point that Cuba dominated its citizens through the stranglehold of communism, Kennedy connected to them in his speech. His emphasis on freedom owed to an aide who was familiar with the concept prized by Americans and craved by those below the southern border. "References to Latin America and the hemisphere were inserted along with or in place of references to this country alone," recounted Kennedy speechwriter Ted Sorenson. "And a direct appeal to the Cuban people was expanded considerably by one of Kennedy's top appointees in [the Department of] State from Puerto

Rico, Arturo Morales Carrión, who understood the nuances in Spanish of references to 'fatherland,' 'nationalist revolution betrayed' and the day when Cubans 'will be truly free—free from foreign domination, free to choose their own leaders, free to select their own system, free to own their own land, free to speak and write and worship without fear or degradation.'"[83]

As important in the address as the reference to freedom is the omission of any mention of the aims that the hawks advocated in the Executive Committee of the National Security Council. Sorenson remarked, "But Kennedy struck from the speech any hint that the removal of Castro was his true aim. He did not talk of total victory or unconditional surrender, simply of the precisely defined objective of removing a specific provocation."[84]

Americans adjusted the "rabbit ears" antennae on their Zeniths, Philcos, and RCAs to find a prime-time show and take a break from the worry about nuclear missiles smashing into the Eastern Seaboard, if possible, but *The Eleventh Hour* would not assuage concerns about communism. The show about psychology and psychiatry broke new ground on matters of the mind, using scenarios in courtrooms and government agencies or involving private patients to reveal complexities, vulnerabilities, and mysteries in human behavior. In the October 24 episode, "I Don't Belong in a White-Painted House," the FBI engaged the lead characters—a psychologist, Dr. Paul Graham, and a psychiatrist, Dr. Theodore Bassett—to find out why a communist defector wants to return to the Soviet Union after seven years in the land of the free and the home of the brave. He's willing to abandon his wife and young son because the pull of his deeply rooted beliefs in living without free will outweighs the privilege of freedom in America. But when his wife threatens to accompany him with their son, the sacrifice of their freedom becomes too much to bear. The family stays.[85]

Kennedy had proven his leadership with his handling of the greatest crisis since Pearl Harbor. On television, game-show host Johnny Carson got tagged with boiling down the news of the day into humorous bite-sized chunks that could be easily digested by an audience before drifting into slumber. When Carson took over NBC's *The Tonight Show* on October 1, 1962, he began a thirty-year reign on late-night television.

A month that had begun with another successful Mercury mission plus the excitement of a National League playoff and an epic World Series ended with a country that, while basking in peacetime, learned that the threat of nuclear war was no longer theoretical or just something for novelists and producers to write about but quite real. Besides Kennedy's leadership during the Cuban Missile Crisis and his oratory that could be inspiring, humorous, or informative in terms both understandable and revealing, a new presidential symbol emerged in 1962. Raymond Loewy, a designer of such American icons as the Coca-Cola bottle and the logos for oil giants Shell and Exxon, redesigned the emblem of Air Force One. General Godfrey McHugh, the president's air force aide, got an earful from his designer pal about the need to improve the presidential plane's façade. With a new plane on the way, it was the optimum time to redesign.[86]

Presidential lore has it that Kennedy chose the Caslon font to reflect the handwritten title of the Declaration of Independence.[87]

11

Somewhere, Erasmus Is Smiling

Americans would never be the same. Kids who learned "duck and cover" to survive a nuclear attack by hiding under their schoolroom desks in the 1950s were teenagers and young adults during the Cuban Missile Crisis. What was once a drill to be endured had become an exercise to be mastered. With it came an entrenchment of the us-against-them philosophy described by the youthful Kennedy. His smile conveyed warmth, confidence, and a hint of sexuality; the October 22 address to the nation gave him the gravitas that every president needs to rely on—and every American needs to see—in a national crisis. Tens of millions of people watching on television from Burbank to Bangor realized a precept that defined future candidates: he looked like a president.

It was like a global playground fight, with an arrogant bully taunting a target and the target responding with resolve rather than fury. But instead of fists, the threatened conflict would be waged with nuclear weapons that could kill or injure millions. Two weeks after the crisis ended, a story about bullies in a small town named Mayberry and a weak though tough-talking deputy named Fife emphasized the necessity of standing up to those who think that size and strength are assets entitling one to a disregard of the law. Don Knotts won five Emmy Awards for portraying Barney Fife, the anxious but well-meaning sidekick to his cousin, Sheriff Andy Taylor, on *The Andy Griffith Show*. Andy was smooth in handling a crisis, often employing Solomon-like wisdom to end a dispute. Barney was a nervous sort, demanding that laws be followed to the letter, comma, and period. In the episode "Lawman Barney" the deputy marks his territory after a couple of roadside bullies refuse to take their produce wagon out of Mayberry. Selling on the side of the road is illegal in the North Carolina burg.

When Andy tells the duo about his deputy's exploits as "Barney the Beast," along with a couple of other fearsome nicknames, the peddlers adhere to Barney's rule. But the deputy is unaware of the boss's interference when he returns to disperse the men without his boss. After they discover that Barney's reputation is fictional, they remain steadfast in selling their wares. Andy, in turn, heads to their location to get them out of town. Barney insists on tagging along and then demands that Andy get out of the car so he can confront the peddlers, and his fear of them, on his own. When they move toward him and are just a few inches from his face, Barney repeats an earlier mantra of Andy's about the badge. "You're both a lot bigger than I am. But this badge represents a lot of people. And they're a lot bigger than either one of you. Now, are you going to get movin'?"[1] Barney is quietly elated when Andy congratulates him, then slumps with exhaustion at the realization of what he accomplished and how the situation could have gone a different way.

Power, like beauty, is in the eye of the beholder.

"In the opening scene, Knotts shows a completely flawed character that lets the size of the two men intimidate him," explains David Browning, a Barney Fife tribute performer. "His ability to show deep hurt and embarrassment sets the tone for the rest of the episode. The subtlety of his serious segments [was] so polished that it is almost as if he were not acting at all and that is the beauty of what he did. In 'Lawman Barney,' you are able to understand that bullies are bullies if allowed to be that way. Andy was able to indirectly teach Barney that regardless of the size of the adversary, you can still stand your ground if right is on your side."[2]

There was plenty of fodder for political talk as the country absorbed Kennedy's handling of the crisis. Eleanor Roosevelt passed away during the first week of November, and Americans may have been reminded of how Franklin Roosevelt's management during the days after the Pearl Harbor attack and throughout World War II helped defeat the Germans and the Japanese. Former vice president Richard Nixon, a GOP standard-bearer, lost his bid to be governor of California and threatened to leave politics:

> As I leave you, I want you to know, just think how much you're gonna be missing. You don't have Nixon to kick around anymore, because, gentlemen, this is my last press conference . . . and I hope that what I have said today will at least make television, radio, the press . . . first recognize the great responsibility they have to report all the news. And second, recognize that they have a right and a responsibility if they're against a candidate, give him the shaft. But also recognize if they give him the shaft, put one lonely reporter on the campaign who will report what the candidate says now and then.[3]

Nixon's political hiatus was not permanent—he won the 1968 and 1972 presidential elections.

After the election that fall Bostonians toasted with mugs full of Haffenreffer beer in working-class bars while the Beacon Street crowd celebrated with hundred-year-old brandy in a surge of dynastic pride not seen since Babe Ruth pitched for the Red Sox; Edward M. "Ted" Kennedy, the younger brother of the president and the attorney general, had won the U.S. Senate race against George Cabot Lodge, himself part of a dynastic clan.[4] Kennedy's margin of victory was two hundred thousand votes.[5]

On prime-time television an early November episode of *Sam Benedict* had a Jewish theme, which was, and still is, a rarity for broadcast networks. For Jews, it was a reminder in the wake of the missile crisis that customs, rituals, and lore sustain communities through the worst of times. In the episode, a pregnant woman who was married in a civil ceremony wants to persuade her agnostic husband to have an Orthodox Jewish wedding ritual. She enlists the title character, a famed San Francisco lawyer, for his assistance. Although it's not a legal matter, the blunt, gruff barrister agrees to help.

One indicator of the husband's distaste for religion takes place during a long shot of the couple going into temple. The wife goes through the custom of touching the mezuzah and then kissing her fingers. The husband waves his hand dismissively. But by the end of the story he has relented and, surprising the rabbi, recites a prayer: "Sh'ma Yisrael Adonai Eloheinu Adonai Echad" (Hear, O Israel, the Lord Is Our God, the Lord Is One).

The episode also has a baseball connection: the first appearance of the rabbi takes place on a baseball diamond, where he's umpiring a pick-up game for kids who appear to be of junior high school age.[6]

When Sam finds out that a *minyan*—a group of ten men—is required for the nuptials to be certified, he rounds up as many Jews as he can find at the courthouse, claiming that he'll go to Israel if he has to. Like the character he portrayed, Edmond O'Brien did not sugarcoat his feelings: "If the *Sam Benedict* series hits, I don't know if I'll like it. I really don't enjoy crowds. I think the public likes whatever they are told to like. I don't know, perhaps I'll suddenly become an idiot who'll enjoy standing there and signing autographs. I can't think of anything I'd rather do less right now."[7]

Sam Benedict aired for one season.

As Americans trashed their Halloween pumpkins, put away the costumes, and began preparing for the Thanksgiving season, it would be unsurprising to find *Seven Days in May* and *Fail-Safe* on nightstands, coffee tables, and office desks. Released during October, these books offer alternate universes laden with fears generated by the Cold War, and the Cuban Missile Crisis enhanced their relevance with volcanic proportions. They reached the top of the best-seller list.

Seven Days in May gives a scenario that President Eisenhower had warned of in the final address of his presidency before Kennedy took his place in the Oval Office. When World War II ended in 1945, its impact on munitions and weapons manufacturing led to a surge of the defense industry—comprising 3.5 million people—in the country's economic sector.

Eisenhower, who had risen from being a brigadier general noted for administrative skills at the time the Japanese bombed Pearl Harbor on December 7, 1941, to a five-star general overseeing the Allied forces in the European theater during World War II, explained that the military's reach into local, state, and federal governments must be managed. If not, its influence would lead to unnecessary skirmishes in the name of freedom and, in turn, the country would devolve into a political state run by the military, either overtly or covertly. "In the councils of government, we must guard against the acquisition of unwarranted influence, whether sought or unsought, by the military industrial complex," Eisenhower stated. "The potential for the disastrous rise of misplaced power exists and will persist." Furthermore, "we must never let the weight of this combination endanger our liberties or democratic processes. We should take nothing for granted. Only an alert and knowledgeable citizenry can compel the proper meshing of the huge industrial and military machinery of defense with our peaceful methods and goals, so that security and liberty may prosper together."[8]

General James Mattoon Scott was a literary example of Eisenhower's warning. *Seven Days in May*, written by Fletcher Knebel and Charles W. Bailey II, reinforces the notion that a military coup in the White House could happen with a man charming enough, savvy enough, and powerful enough at the helm. The fictional Scott was such a man. Using betting information on the Preakness Stakes as a code for his cohorts, Scott employs his plan to gather powerful military men, plus a right-wing broadcaster, to combat President Jordan Lyman, who pursues a peace treaty with Russia.

Lyman's views are not only abhorrent to Scott, they are disastrous to a country's image of strength. Only a political infrastructure with a greater military influence will prepare America for its future, or so Scott believes. What makes him dangerous is not his belief system but his charisma, which provides a gateway to implementing his plan. A popular figure, Scott had the foundation to make the plan palatable to the electorate. Necessary, even.

Just as Kennedy looked the part of a president, the Scott character looked like he was destined for the disciplined career to be found in the armed forces. "He was by all odds the most popular public figure in uniform and probably in the United States, a fact that was of considerable concern to friends of the President," write Knebel and Bailey. "A brilliant officer, Scott demonstrated perfectly that mixture of good will, force and magnetism that men call leadership. The nickname ["Gentleman Jim"] had been hung on him in high school because of an early eye for meticulous personal appearance and a rare ability to grasp the niceties of adult manners. It had stuck to him at West Point and ever since."[9]

Disagreement on diplomacy with Russia prompts Lyman to confront the general, who comes dangerously close to success with his masterful subterfuge cloaking the conspiracy. At the plan's core is the formalization of a group using military funds to execute its goal of taking over the government under a cloak of secrecy. This contradiction of liberty could not be tolerated. The country's government balances upon a fulcrum of checks and balances; the civilian leadership in the Oval Office manages the military while Capitol Hill's denizens authorize, investigate, and oversee its funding.

Scott's secret unit—Emergency Communications Control—trains at a secret base to create the blueprint giving power to the officers who believe that Lyman's brand of diplomacy weakens not only America's standing in the world but also its security. The president's irrefutable evidence of a coup is a memorandum from a Scott dissenter—an admiral who has detailed Scott's plans, including the Preakness code. In turn, President Lyman checkmates Scott and his band of brothers, who look at democracy as clay that can be reshaped on a pottery wheel rather than bedrock that cannot be moved from its place. Their resignations are submitted and described as voluntary, though by presidential request. Had they not resigned, Lyman could have put them through an embarrassing trial revealing their treasonous behavior. For a military man, sedition is a nasty accusation that will permanently stain an otherwise exemplary legacy in the eyes of the public.

The DNA of Eisenhower's address can be found in Lyman's words during a televised speech at the end of *Seven Days in May*:

I should take a moment here to explain my own concept of the civilian-military relationship under our system of government. I deeply believe, as I know the overwhelming majority of Americans do, that our military leaders—tempered by battle, matured by countless command decisions, dedicating their entire lives to the service of the nation—should always be afforded every opportunity to speak their views. In the case of the treaty, they were of course given that opportunity.

But once the President and the Senate, as the responsible authorities, make a decision, then, my fellow citizens, debate and opposition among the military must come to an end. That is the way in war: the commander solicits every possible view from his staff, but once he decides on his plan of battle, there can be no disputing it. Any other way would mean confusion, chaos and certain defeat. And so it also must be in the councils of government here in Washington.[10]

Knebel and Bailey's scenario offers the country's literary-minded, bookstore-browsing, library-card-carrying populace a chilling depiction of democracy's fragility in the early 1960s. Winding down the day with a chapter or two before bedtime conjured nightmarish images of a military officer able to command respect, project authority, and utilize personality to cultivate power, achieve a dictatorship, and abandon the constitutional framework that the Founding Fathers created to root the government in stability.

There had been stories before *Seven Days in May* with similar warnings. Sinclair Lewis's 1935 novel *It Can't Happen Here* shows the result of a populist candidate defeating Franklin Delano Roosevelt and applying a totalitarian approach to running the country, including weakening the legislative branch, disassembling state governments, and using violence to shut down protests.

Whereas *Seven Days in May* focuses on a military-civilian tug-of-war for the nation's reins of power, *Fail-Safe*, authored by Eugene Burdick and Harvey Wheeler, outlines the impact of nuclear-armed pilots passing the "fail-safe" position—the point where they cannot be recalled. Technology forms the basis for the fail-safe plan; the pilots are operating under the belief that America is at war, so they complete their mission of bombing Moscow. The American president, in hopes of salvaging a workable relationship with Russia, orders the bombing of New York City.

Although the president is unnamed, it is presumed to be Kennedy. There is a premise that technology eliminates the chance of human error because it is a better determinant of practicality, efficiency, and viability. During a conversation with Soviet premier Khrushchev, he laments the inevitability of progress. "In one way, we didn't even make the decision to have the computerized systems in the first place," says the leader of the free world. "These automated systems became technologically possible, so we built them. Then it became possible to turn more and more control decisions over to them, so we did that. And before we knew it, we had gone so far that the systems were able to put us in the situation we are in today."[11]

The Pentagon pushed back on the novel's scenario, stating that the president, not any type of electronic signal, gives the strike command to the bombers. Further, the *New York Times* cited Secretary of Defense Robert McNamara, who expressed confidence in the fail-safe plan but acknowledged the ongoing improvement of systems: "We are alert to the dangers of accidental war. We believe we have adequate safeguards built into our present system to ensure that our massive nuclear strength will remain under control of the properly constituted authorities at all times." He added, "However, we are not compla-cent to the dangers in this area. Hence, we have expanded our research and development efforts to make sure that we will continue to have the necessary safeguards."[12]

Allen Drury, a veteran Washington DC reporter, dissects the political layers of the United Nations in his 1962 novel *A Shade of Difference*, the second of six books in the *Advise and Consent* series. This path-breaking work revealed the inner workings of Washington DC. Drury's opus hit bookshelves in 1959, and the film version debuted in 1962.

Descriptions place the stories in the late 1960s or early 1970s; the fictional Harley Hudson, a vice president who ascends to the presidency at the end of *Advise and Consent* when the unnamed president dies, is mentioned along with his boss. "The country had never really stopped sliding since the end of the Second World War, in spite of an occasional dramatic event that seemed to be staying the tide, and not all the impulsive pyrotechnics of Truman, the placid drifting of Eisenhower, the sometimes erratic empirics of Kennedy and Harley's predecessor, or the stubborn courage of Harley himself, had seemed to reverse the trend," explains Drury's narrator.[13]

Advise and Consent hit bookshelves three years before *A Shade of Differ-ence*. With details that could only come from an eyewitness to the pushing and pulling of the levers that make the federal government run, Drury cap-tures the romanticism, skepticism, and optimism of politics in the nation's capital with Georgetown parties, Capitol Hill hearing rooms, and the Oval Office, all of which made the novel a must-read for any political operative, aficionado, or scholar.

There is an aura surrounding the political infrastructure that can be seductive to politicos who may at first see the District of Columbia as a governmental entity fixed in transience; living, working, and socializing in the nation's capital are matters of the moment that could last until a politician's latest term is finished, but power's allure can ensnare officeholders in the House and the Senate without warning. It's like a pendant dangled in front of every worker drawing a federal-government paycheck, from congressional pages to the president of the United States.

There is no hope for an escape; they really don't want to pursue any avenue of exit once they taste the sweetness of influence. According to Drury's narrator in *Advise and Consent*,

> Washington takes them like a lover and they are lost. . . . Some are big names, some are spoiled for the Main Streets without which Washington could not live, knowing instinctively that this is the biggest Main Street of them all, the granddaddy and grandchild of Main Streets rolled into one. They come, they stay, they make their mark, writing big or little on their times, in the strange, fantastic, fascinating land in which there are few absolute wrongs or absolute rights, few all-blacks or all-whites, few dead-certain positives that won't be changed tomorrow; their wonderful, mixed-up, blundering, stumbling, hopeful land in which evil men do good things and good men do evil in a way of life and government so complex and delicately balanced that only Americans can understand it and often they are baffled.[14]

At the heart of Drury's story is Bob Munson, the Senate majority leader from Michigan. In a monologue halfway through *Advise and Consent*, Munson explains that the Senate's procedures prevent the implosion of freedom. Forces in each of the three branches of government jockey for position with a healthy friction between them. Each acts as a deterrent to the other gaining a disproportionate hold on the gears of government. Judges ought not act as legislators; the president ought not declare war without congressional fiat; legislators ought not create laws that they know will be overturned by a judiciary deeming them unconstitutional. The balance is a "never-decided contest between diffusion and concentration of power."[15]

Munson must contend with Fred Van Ackerman, the savvy Wyoming senator whose alignment with peaceniks is so apparent, one might think that he's designing a new American flag with a hammer and sickle to replace the stars. Van Ackerman is a member of the Committee on Making Further Offers for a Russian Truce (COMFORT); he endorses the president's nominee for secretary of state—Robert Leffingwell. "As for me, I had rather crawl on my knees to Moscow than die under an atom bomb!" exclaims Leffingwell at a COMFORT rally, as Van Ackerman introduces him.[16]

Drury captures the essence of Washington, both its beautiful side and its darker nuances. Using the editor of the *Washington Post* as his Mercury, Drury writes, "This is a cruel town, when you get on the wrong side of it. A great town and a good town, and a petty town and a cruel town. And nobody ever knows from day to day which face it is going to put on."[17]

The Leffingwell nomination causes a firestorm in the Senate that Munson must manage before it becomes a raging blaze engulfing the presidency of his close friend and former colleague. Unbeknown to Munson is the past of Utah senator Brigham Anderson, who had a homosexual experience in Hawaii after serving in the military during the Korean War; Anderson chairs the subcommittee in charge of vetting Leffingwell. Van Ackerman has discovered Anderson's secret and uses the information to blackmail the senator and his family. Embarrassed by the prospect of the experience becoming public knowledge, Anderson commits suicide by shooting himself in his office.

The president contemplates his role in the chain of events that led to the blackmail. Indeed, Anderson was a victim. So too is the president. But his dedication to a détente with the Soviet Union does not in any way justify in his mind the sacrifice of an officeholder who was a fundamentally decent man, one who succumbed to shame after the violation of a private sanctum entered long before he married and had a daughter and earmarked as a box never to be reopened, with contents never to be disclosed.

Ruminating about his predecessors, the president reminds himself of the danger that power can have when it is in the hands of an ignoramus or an egomaniac: "Every once in a while the electoral process tosses to the top someone smart and glib and evil, without basic principle, without basic character, and without restraints. Sometimes these are on the conservative side of the fence, sometimes on the liberal; but the essential personality pattern is the same, the gambler, the sharpie, the thug in the blue-serge suit. Such men can be used for certain purposes, but there is always the risk that they will get out of hand."[18]

A subplot of *Advise and Consent* is the launch of a Soviet project to send cosmonauts to the moon. In Drury's parallel universe, the Soviets are the first to land on the moon. Their initial statement contrasts the American view of space as an arena to explore without political division:

> "We wish to report that representatives of the Union of Soviet Socialist Republics have established a successful permanent base on the moon, which we claim for the Union of Soviet Socialist Republics and for all the peace-loving peoples associated with the USSR.
>
> "Everything went well on our journey. We are in good health and preparations are now under way for a return of part of our party to Earth.
>
> "A base party has been established and will remain, equipped to repel capitalist imperialist invaders should any be so foolhardy as to attempt a landing on the moon.
>
> "All hail the peoples' peace!"[19]

America responded with its own mission "to claim the moon for the United Nations and to plant thereon the flag of the United Nations."[20]

The film version of *Advise and Consent* reduces the book's details to focus on the Leffingwell nomination, so the moon project story line is eliminated, the presence of Senator Orrin Knox is reduced to a cameo, and the backstory of southern firebrand Seab Cooley is neither mentioned nor hinted. There is also no mention of the Supreme Court justice who has an impactful role in the novel, and the home state of DC lothario Lafe Smith is changed from Iowa to Rhode Island.

Otto Preminger directed *Advise and Consent* with performances that are seamless. Walter Pidgeon, a figure of paternal calm, plays Munson. Peter Lawford, the brother-in-law of President Kennedy, who once had a playboy image on Capitol Hill during his days as an unmarried member of Congress, portrays a bachelor of ease with women and a senator with respect for his older colleagues. Paul Ford, who also plays River City's mayor in *The Music Man*, plays Majority Whip Stan Danta. Franchot Tone has the role of the president, who weakens and dies before hearing the outcome of the Leffingwell vote. Lew Ayres is the gentlemanly vice president, Harley Hudson, who neither seeks nor wants the next rung on the ladder, though he changes his mind when news comes that the president is dead. A 50–50 vote requires him to break the tie, but he says to Munson that he'd rather pick his own secretary of state, so he refuses to vote. George Grizzard plays the dastardly Van Ackerman. Don Murray portrays Brigham Anderson, at first confident about leading a hearing with decorum, then panicky as he tracks down his long-ago liaison and discovers the true source of the information about the past. Charles Laughton, in his last film role, offers the terrific combination of slyness, cynicism, and political wisdom in his role as Seab Cooley. With four decades of senatorial experience, Cooley knows where the gears of government are located, who makes them turn, and how they can run faster. Henry Fonda is Leffingwell, a person who will not be swayed from his convictions.

Washington insiders absorbed Drury's words like a sponge, calculating the parallels of the *Advise and Consent* characters to real-life influences. They did the same as they entered a cinematic world with realistic overtones. Too real, perhaps. *Washington Post* film critic Richard L. Coe praised Preminger's version of Drury's story and the cast: a "dignity of loneliness" (Tone); "striking balance between courageous vigor and sensitive vacillation" (Murray); and "canny, edgy underplaying" (Grizzard).[21]

Leffingwell never shows concern about losing the nomination, only about the possible embarrassment if his tangential communist leanings from years past are unveiled. Cooley, having been proven a liar by Leffingwell in a previous hearing, maintains an attitude toward the nominee that Munson and Danta label as "heatedness." Coe highlights Laughton's performance as the slow-talking, all-knowing senator with a gravelly voice: "Here is the brilliant man disappointed he has not quite gotten to the top and determined, under a highly personalized veneer, to stop anyone else."[22]

New York Times film critic Bosley Crowther, in an otherwise negative review, highlighted Pidgeon's portrayal of Munson: "This fellow, done by Mr. Pidgeon with consummate elegance and grace, is a model of party loyalty, patience and professional skill in politics. He is a beautiful, artful trimmer, but a fair respecter of our system of government."[23]

Drury's title *A Shade of Difference* has racial subtext, noted in a passage recounting the college days of Senator Cullee Hamilton, a Black lawmaker from California: "How self-conscious, he did not realize at first, but it was not long before he began to be aware that for all their outward camaraderie there was a subtle shade of difference, invisible but unmistakable, tenuous as fog but hurtful as acid, that separated him from his newly found white friends."[24]

A Shade of Difference uses the United Nations as its focal point, with an African leader challenging the United States on its policies and actions toward Black citizens. After all, if a country preaches liberty, it must concern itself with highly significant behavior to match its principles. "Terrible Terry," the prince of a British-run colony, goes to the South to accompany a Black girl to school. It entrances the press and enhances Terry's stature among the UN representatives and liberal Americans.

Several characters from *Advise and Consent* appear in *A Shade of Difference*, albeit with reduced roles. In a passage outlining Munson's dismay at America's stature being threatened, distorted, or modified, Drury identifies Prince Terry's brilliant act as an example of the most powerful country in the world being assailed for being the most powerful country in the world. America's goodness gets obscured by the magnification of its imperfections and ignorance of other countries' citizens regarding their own, sometimes dictatorial, leadership:

> Thus it did not matter that British rioted against their Negro immigrants, that French preached *liberté* and practiced *inégalité*, that in India the Pious the most vicious forms of racial discrimination were practiced, or that in Africa itself black murdered black. These peoples did not wish to look in their own mirrors, and so they were only too willing to ease their consciences by following eagerly when the Soviet Union pointed the finger at the United States.
>
> It was much nicer to forget all about what you were doing to the colored races yourselves and run happily off to thumb your nose at America. America was fair game. And America, he could not deny, at times deserved it.[25]

Advise and Consent reveals the pressure points of the nation's political machinery behind the scenes at poker games, in Capitol cloakrooms, and during debate on the floor of the U.S. Senate, where revelations are made, alliances are formed, and consequences are weighed. The sordid and the saccharine seem to be known to all who need to know. Drury's journalism experience offers realism for readers, helping them to understand the political, human, and reputational costs associated with public service in the august body and among those who govern from within it. The American system of government, in the end, is to be lauded, though the actions of its leaders can sometimes descend into despicableness.

In his alternate-history, post–World War II novel *The Man in the High Castle*, Philip K. Dick wondered what would happen if Germany and Japan had won World War II, if the United States didn't exist as a republic, and if the only sliver of a free society known to the public is depicted in the banned novel called *The Grasshopper Lies Heavy*. The plot of *The Man in the High Castle* is set in 1962, with the Axis powers controlling the land that was once the home of the brave and the land of the free—Japan rules the West Coast, Germany rules the East Coast, and a buffer zone exists in the Rocky Mountain region. Interpretations vary. Does Dick's heroine Juliana discover that she and her world are fictional and *The Grasshopper Lies Heavy* is the real world? Are there two separate universes, one where the United States and its allies won the war and one where they lost it? Does the characters' resistance to the oppressive governments indicate another revolution to come?

In 2015 Amazon premiered a television version of *The Man in the High Castle*. It lasted four seasons.

Whereas shoppers had once hurried to complete the chore of buying groceries, they now had reason to stop and examine every piece of fruit they handled with the attention of a forensic doctor—but without knowing what to look for. Rachel Carson's 1962 book *Silent Spring* blared warnings about the impact of pesticides and other chemicals on the forests, oceans, fields, and crops. There was nothing that shoppers could do about it, though, except worry; the food industry was committed to using pesticides to protect crops, and that stance was as unlikely to change as Coca-Cola changing its signature packaging from red to green. And the human body, though resilient, was ill-equipped to handle the burden of the pesticides in food, according to Carson: "The chemicals to which life is asked to make its adjustment are no longer merely the calcium and silica and copper and all the rest of the minerals washed out of the rocks and carried in rivers to the sea; they are the synthetic creations of man's inventive mind, brewed in his laboratories, and having no counterparts in nature."[26]

Carson's warnings, while perhaps initially classified as belonging to a Chicken Little type of outlook, captured the public's attention as more information about food safety came to light. Lawmakers took note too, and in 1970 President Nixon signed the National Environmental Policy Act and the Clean Air Extension Act. The Environmental Protection Agency was formed that year as well.

Women seeking solace or salvation in their pursuit of love, sex, and relationships in 1962 found a guide in Helen Gurley Brown's *Sex and the Single Girl*. Scripting a paradigm for the early 1960s woman, Brown highlights her personal experience while offering tips on cooking (including recipes), makeup, places to meet eligible men, decorating, wardrobe, and other areas that the single "girl," presumably in a metropolitan area, needs in order to survive the dating world. There is—surprisingly, given the title—very little discussion of sex.

Brown kicks off her thesis with a roster of assets in the second paragraph. At best it's a statement that she lives a life of comfort. At worst it's a declaration that things bought equal achievement realized: "We have two Mercedes-Benzes, one hundred acres of virgin forest near San Francisco, a Mediterranean house overlooking the Pacific, a full-time maid and a good life," writes Brown.[27]

Those are wonderful things to have if one possesses the significant amount of discretionary income necessary to complete the transactions. But to begin a guide for women by highlighting exuberance for luxury over enthusiasm for love raises the question of the value that she is placing on the burdens and benefits of marriage. The longest-lasting unions often expand with children and grandchildren. Family bonds often, one hopes, grow stronger by overcoming challenges—sickness, financial strain, physical infirmity. Brown posits, however, that a marriage's value protects the woman against her loss of appeal as she ages. It's a cavalier fiat underscoring the view of relationships with men as temporary. "I think marriage is insurance for the *worst* years of your life," writes Brown. "During your best years you don't need a husband.

You do need a man of course every step of the way, and they are often cheaper emotionally and a lot more fun by the dozen."[28]

Whether to have children or not is a decision reduced to one of economics rather than emotions, in Brown's view: once the children are grown, senior citizens have little, if anything, to offer. Death would be acceptable, perhaps preferred, in this view rather than remaining alive and dispensing maternal wisdom, affection, and enthusiasm.

It's enough to make Cupid hang up his bow and arrow.

"As for marrying to have children, you can have babies until you're forty or older," posits Brown. "And if you happen to die before *they* are forty, at least you haven't lingered into their middle age to be a doddering old bore. You also avoid those tiresome years as an unpaid baby sitter."[29]

For women having affairs with married men, Brown offers freedom from guilt. There is no reason to take, or even share, blame for a relationship: "A wife, if she is loving and smart, will get her husband back every time. He doesn't really want her *not* to. He's only playing. (She may have played herself on occasion.) If she *doesn't* get him back, it's probably because she's lazy, blind, or doesn't want him. If he's a hopeless chaser, like the Don Juan, he will chase regardless of who does or does not give him succor, so no need to feel guilty."[30]

Sex and the Single Girl classifies men as self-centered, sex-crazed, and stars-in-the-eyes beings conjuring images of women that could only be fulfilled in a *Playboy* spread: "When a man thinks of a single woman, he pictures her alone in her apartment, smooth legs sheathed in pink silk Capri pants, lying tantalizingly among dozens of satin cushions, trying to read but not very successfully, for *he* is in that room—filling her thoughts, her dreams, her life."[31]

It's quite a disservice to categorize all males in this two-dimensional manner while ignoring the other qualities that men find desirable in women: intelligence, a sense of humor, supportiveness.

Brown's conclusion offers no endorsement of women who followed the June Cleaver model of tending to the home: "Those who glom on to men so that they can collapse with relief, spend the rest of their days shining up their status symbol and figure they never have to reach, stretch, learn, grow, face dragons or make a living again are the ones to be pitied. They, in my opinion, are the unfilled ones."[32]

Although Brown embodies and presents herself as a liberated woman, her opinion is hurtful to a demographic that got tarred and feathered during the women's liberation movement of the 1960s: housewives.

First, women concerned with "shining up their status symbol" constitute a slim minority of wives. There are women with means, from Beverly Hills to Short Hills, who can afford luxury cars, five-star restaurants, and live-in maids. Most cannot.

Second, many of the women that Brown classifies as wanting to "glom on to men" are actually marrying out of tradition for the survival of their demographic. Until the mid-twentieth century, it was rare to see people marrying outside their ethnic tribes.

Third, a housewife's responsibilities to her family may not constitute a job in the traditional sense, but it's a job that most men wouldn't want for all the bourbon in Kentucky. The housewife is the CEO of the domicile. She is responsible for its upkeep and oftentimes the bookkeeping that keeps it from falling into disrepair. She is all things to all people at all times in the house. Chef. Janitor. Chauffeur. Plumber. Bookkeeper. Decorator. Therapist. Facilities manager. Seamstress. Social planner. Community organizer.

To pity a woman who chooses to stay at home rather than "making a living" snubs the superhuman efforts that come with being a housewife. In any given week she is called on to bake cookies for the PTA benefit, cook and host a dinner for her husband's new boss, soothe the fears of a teenage daughter whose heart is broken by her latest crush, hire a plumber to fix a long-standing problem with the downstairs bathroom, coordinate the carpool schedule for a group of parents to take the kids to school and pick them up, sew on the buttons that fell off her son's Boy Scout uniform, prepare bag lunches for the children, cook every dinner for the family, clean the house, do the laundry, make the beds, pay the bills, go grocery shopping, pick up the dry cleaning, and take the car to the mechanic for a tune-up, among other things.

Brown's pity is not only misplaced. It is arrogant.

There is a convenient though distorted notion that a housewife has an easy gig.

It's a slap in the face to the women of the 1960s and 1970s who stayed home either because they followed a traditional model or because they tired of the workforce once they decided to have children. While many a housewife is assumed to watch a favorite soap opera and engage in daily gossip with their network of like-minded females, these activities are temporary respites from a job that is a never-ending, back-breaking, soul-challenging vocation. It's not unusual to hear a husband tell a colleague over a couple of drinks that it's easier to negotiate a $10 million deal than run the household for a week.

Phyllis I. Rosenteur advocates for being unattached in *The Single Women*, which came out in November 1961 and became literary fodder for women considering marriage in the early 1960s. Her diatribes are filled with citations to works from decades past, including a book from 1835; condescension toward men not only drips from the pages—it pours. Her generalizations compound the insults. She cites researchers on the East Coast with a statistic that "a full two-thirds of males married well below their mental levels."[33]

But she doesn't mention the name of the study, the team, or the methodology used.

"To be stricken from the slate of likely mates, all a female has to do is manifest—*manifest*, not flaunt—a fairly high I.Q. The great majority of men will take a birdbrain over an egghead every time," wrote Rosenteur. "Though a college education ups the odds on any male's marrying, a woman's chances lessen in proportion to her learning."[34]

This view is undermined by the most famous couple in America at the time—the charismatic president and his wife, who reflected poise combined with knowledge and appreciation for art, culture, and history.

One of the pleasures of reading is plunging oneself into a series of stories revolving around a core group of characters. Fans of the cop genre could find this escape in Ed McBain's novels about the Eighty-Seventh Precinct detectives in Isola, a fictional borough in a five-borough metropolis patterned after New York City. Those novels were the basis for an NBC series starring Robert Lansing and Norman Fell that lasted just the 1961–62 television season. McBain—whose real name was Evan Hunter—produced his Eighty-Seventh Precinct novels from the days of peace and prosperity in the Eisenhower era to the post-9/11 funk of the 2000s.

McBain's descriptions capture the essence of civil servants battling chaos in a city teeming with violence. Steve Carella is the squad's leader. Although his precinct brothers may complain about everything, from the weather to the city's bureaucracy, they never lose sight of their mission of solving crimes.

In *The Empty Hours*, a 1962 anthology that has three stories, each focusing on a different detective, McBain projects the physical qualities of Carella into the beginning of the first story, which has the same title as the book: "Steve Carella had never been one of those weight-lifting goons, and the image he presented was hardly one of bulging muscular power. But there was a quiet strength about the man and the way he moved, a confidence in the way he casually accepted the capabilities and limitations of his body."[35]

NBC's one-season effort with the McBain material features a baseball-themed episode. "Idol in the Dust" shows Major League player Larry Brooks coming home to his Isola neighborhood. But his joy at being back home is countered by realizing that his ex-con brother consorts with the types of guys one might find in a 1930s Jimmy Cagney gangster movie.[36]

Starring Robert Lansing as Carella, *87th Precinct* had a teamwork atmosphere off the set, which was recognized in a *TV Guide* article published the week the series aired its last episode. Lansing's co-stars were Ron Harper (Bert Kling), Norman Fell (Meyer Meyer), and Gregory Walcott (Roger Havilland). "Although Harper and Fell get the most fan mail, their popularity does not seem to have caused Lansing and Walcott any particular anguish," wrote entertainment journalist Bob Johnson. "Lansing and Harper have become particularly close personal friends since last June and have taken it upon themselves to consult working Los Angeles policemen and read books on crime for tips on factual procedure which they pass along to Walcott and Fell. When Walcott decided to have *87th Precinct* calling cards printed with a badge and his name on them—to pass out at personal appearances—he had similar supplies of cards printed with his colleagues' names as a gift."[37]

The novel *One Flew over the Cuckoo's Nest*, by Ken Kesey, tackles the harshness of mental illness. This portrayal of a psychiatric ward sent shivers through fingers turning the pages to reveal the next set of antics orchestrated by Randall McMurphy against Nurse Ratched—a woman instilled with the qualities of Henry VIII, Attila the Hun, and a Marine drill instructor—in a battle for control of the patients' loyalty, behavior, and attitudes. McMurphy—a prisoner, a manipulator, and a self-described "gambling fool" with pride overflowing—prefers the confines of the hospital ward to the work at a prison farm; his transfer to the ward comes about because the court rules he's a psychopath.[38]

McMurphy claims that he arranged to get sent to the hospital.[39] That hospital has a detailed account of his violent, if not psychopathic, exploits: "McMurry [sic], Randle Patric. Committed by the state from the Pendleton Farm for Correction. For diagnosis and possible treatment. Thirty-five years old. Never married. Distinguished Service Cross for leading an escape from a Communist prison camp. A dishonorable discharge, afterward, for insubordination. Followed by a history of street brawls and barroom fights and a series of arrests for Drunkenness, Assault and Battery, Disturbing the Peace, repeated gambling, and one arrest—for Rape."[40]

The last charge was actually for statutory rape, though the alleged victim "refused to testify in spite of the doctor's findings. There seemed to be intimidation. Defendant left town shortly after the trial."[41] Fellow patient Harding advocates for McMurphy's self-interest, most evident in gambling: "He's a shrewd character with an eye out for a quick dollar. He doesn't make any pretense about his motives, does he? Why should we? He has a healthy and honest attitude about his chicanery, and I'm all for him, just as I'm for the dear old capitalistic system of free individual enterprise, comrades, for him and his downright bull-headed gall and the American flag, bless it, and the Lincoln Memorial and the whole bit."[42]

McMurphy physically attacks the iron-fisted Ratched, rendered speechless, injured, and mostly powerless without her stern voice. As a result he is given a lobotomy, which pushes him into mental limbo. Another patient, the Chief, kills McMurphy at the end of the story by smothering him with a pillow. It is in some way an act of mercy.

Kesey's work history as a night aide in a mental hospital gave him the background for writing *One Flew over the Cuckoo's Nest*. "Yes, McMurphy was fictional, inspired by the tragic longing of the real men I worked with on the ward, the sketches of whom, both visual and verbal, came more easily to my hand than anything before or since, and these sketches gradually enclosed for me the outline of the hero they wanted," divulged Kesey. "And yes, I did write the book both on the ward and on drugs, double-checking my material so to speak. After a few months I settled into a nice midnight-to-eight shift that gave me stretches of five or six hours, five days a week, where I had nothing to do but a little mopping and buffing, check the wards every forty-five minutes with a flashlight, be coherent to the night nurse stopping by on her hourly rounds, write my novel, and talk to the sleepless nuts."[43]

Kids fantasizing about growing up to be astronauts found a hero in Michael Alford Robert Samson, aka Mike Mars. Science fiction author Donald A. Wollheim zeroed in on the excitement about space exploration for middle-grades children and penned eight Mike Mars books between 1961 and 1964; two came out in 1962—*Mike Mars Flies the Dyna-Soar* and *Mike Mars, South Pole Spaceman*.

A controversy arose over the book *The Sex Cure*, which author Elaine Dorian set in the fictional town of Ridgefield Corners in upstate New York. It was based on Cooperstown, home of the National Baseball Hall of Fame and Museum. One passage describes the attitude of the main character, a doctor, who uses sex as a way of keeping score with his ego: "Without warmth, he was still trying to understand a man like Justin. But all he could grasp was that the more beds a man invaded, the less he had to bring to each of them. Emotions were a form of moral currency. If you went on spending more than you should, you became an emotional bankrupt, a person unable to care deeply any more [*sic*] about anything. The senator saw this emotional profligacy all about him, destroying this once-peaceful town as in time it might destroy the nation."[44]

Using the nom de plume Elaine Dorian, Isabel Moore chronicled a voyage into sexual cravings where musk and perfume collide in fits of carnal fury as a release from the quaint, sometimes straitjacketed life in an upstate New York village. Readers devoured the exploits of a sex-charged universe contrasting the quiet surroundings anchored by Otsego Lake. Cooperstown's population had an existential crisis; Moore's house was vandalized with red paint spelling nasty words and the admonition "Get Out." But the story was not entirely fictional. "Yes, but I didn't have to snoop for my facts," said Moore. "Some people here are so hungry for recognition they tell all about themselves."[45]

Regarding the vandalism, she said, "The people here like to hate."[46]

The novel led to a $600,000 libel lawsuit filed by June Dieterle, who claimed mental and reputational damage, plus a drop in clientele for her babysitting business, because Moore had mentioned Dieterle's name in the book. The parties settled.[47]

Comic books got prime-time exposure in the *Naked City* episode "Hold for Gloria Christmas."[48] A Manhattan detective solves the murder of a beatnik poet on Fourth Street in Greenwich Village by retracing his last hours. A few scenes feature a newsstand in the background, with one of the comic-book offerings being issue number 15 of *Amazing Fantasy*—the debut of Spiderman.[49]

The U.S. Information Agency used a custom-made comic book to promote President Kennedy and America's values to Latin America. *Newsday* took an opposing view, however, saying that it was "propaganda" for the president.[50] The comic book, produced in forty-five languages for distribution in sixty countries—depicts the president's life, from his childhood through his presidency.[51]

Dell honored the exploits of Kennedy and his PT-109 crew in World War II's Pacific theater with issue number 4 of *Combat* (June 1962). The comic summarizes the events that led to Kennedy's boat being smashed by a Japanese destroyer and the eleven survivors (two men died in the collision) battling to stay alive under Kennedy's leadership. The survivors swam to an island named Plum Pudding Island—and nicknamed Bird Island—for safety; Kennedy towed a severely burned crew member with the life jacket strap in his mouth. They spent six days awaiting rescue. The island was later renamed Kennedy Island.

Little Leaguers pored through the pages of Richard Mullins's novel *Most Valuable Player*, which pits the privileged against the poor when two boys on the Lansing High School Falcons baseball team compete for the Most Valuable Player Award. What starts as a rivalry fueled by jealousy turns into a friendship bonded by teamwork. Each boy declares that he won't accept the award unless the other gets it as well. For preteen kids blinded by individual statistics, fame, and glory, it's a reminder that baseball is a team sport.

Major League Baseball's second ownership change for a team in 1962 happened in mid-November, when Lou Perini sold the Milwaukee Braves to a Chicago-based entity—its six members were former White Sox stockholders—and to team president John McHale for $5.5 million. Perini retained a 10 percent interest in the team.[52]

Milwaukee mayor Henry Maier and Milwaukee county executive John Doyne praised the new owners' geographic link to Wisconsin. "Ownership closer to home might be just the thing the Braves need," said Maier, and Doyne added that "with local people owning the club, the community will have a different attitude."[53]

The Braves left Milwaukee for Atlanta after the 1965 season.

12

Hollywood Is for Heroes

By 1962 movie audiences had become accustomed to sophisticated fare that not only entertained but also challenged them to think about mores—societal and personal—that were flawed, impractical, and in some cases antiquated. On Christmas Day *To Kill a Mockingbird* premiered in Los Angeles, with a wider release occurring in 1963.[1] Based on Harper Lee's best-selling novel, the film featured a down-home Alabama lawyer who defends a Black man accused of assault and rape in the 1930s. The charges are bogus; it is clear from the evidence that the accuser blames Tom Robinson instead of her true abuser—her father. She may have even made up the rape charge to further enflame prejudice among the jury members and the townspeople of Maycomb; the doctor did not examine her for signs of sexual assault. The story depicts racism in its ugliest form, with tentacles reaching into the justice system.

Atticus Finch is a hero who has inspired generations of lawyers to pursue justice, especially for the downtrodden. After the trial, which he loses, he gathers his papers as Maycomb's Black citizens in the courtroom gallery stand up as a sign of respect for his noble but failed efforts. A Black minister, Reverend Sykes, says to Finch's daughter, "Jean Louise, stand up. Your father's passing."[2] It is a scene that lasts a little more than ninety seconds, all silent except for the reverend's dialogue, and says more about Finch's character and the racial bridge that he crossed than any dialogue could even begin to convey.

Robinson, the falsely convicted prisoner, tries to escape while being taken to prison. A deputy shoots and kills him.

Gregory Peck won an Oscar for his portrayal of Atticus Finch.

To Kill a Mockingbird is one of many movies supporting an argument for 1962 being the best year ever for Hollywood. And Atticus Finch is one of a series of film and television heroes that made audiences think about their own lives, values, and philosophies.

Days of Wine and Roses, starring Jack Lemmon and Lee Remick, displays the deceptive benefits of alcohol through the descent of Kirsten Arnesen, a bright secretary who catches the eye of Joe Clay, a San Francisco public-relations executive.[3] He originally mistakes her for a woman that he's hired to be eye-candy—and maybe something more—for a client's party; to his surprise, she's the client's secretary. At first they can't stand each other, but things loosen when they go on a date. Because drinking is a part of his job in wooing clients over dinners and lunches, Joe believes that a drink or two won't hurt; if anything, it will have a medicinal effect. Although Kirsten doesn't drink alcohol, Joe persuades her to try a Brandy Alexander.

Kirsten begins to drink. Regularly. She and Joe marry. And she drinks, heavily. Her drunkenness causes a fire in their apartment when Joe is out of town on business. Although Kirsten and their daughter, Debbie, survive, Joe sees that alcohol has transformed the once-teetotaling Kirsten into an addict who either refuses to acknowledge or prefers to ignore her dependency. Joe tries to get sober twice and succeeds on the second attempt. Fueled by the addiction, Kirsten looks elsewhere for validation, companionship, and drinking partners. Although Joe fell victim to her alcoholic seduction after the first time he sobers up, he won't let his love for her infect his newfound sobriety the second time.

What began as a boy-meets-girl type of movie confronts the horror of alcoholism at the end, when Kirsten refuses to come home under Joe's mandate that her days of boozing are over. She ventures into the San Francisco night, leaving Joe and Debbie to wonder if she'll come back.

Days of Wine and Roses is a master class on acting given by Lemmon and Remick. His character goes from confident and carefree to brash and belligerent, exemplified in a meltdown while looking for a hidden bottle of booze. His emotional arc is on the one-day-at-a-time track heralded by Alcoholics Anonymous. Sobering up clarifies how alcohol devastated his career and his emotional well-being. Remick's Kirsten, on the other hand, gets seduced by alcohol's gaslighting ability to make everything seem brighter, though it's a temporary state. Boredom is assuaged with a glass in her hand. Beer. Bourbon. Brandy. It doesn't matter to her, as long it's available.

With the ability to play an everyman, Lemmon summed up his passion for acting when he accepted the American Film Institute's Lifetime Achievement Award in 1988:

> But there is something that I hope all actors will remember during the dark days, which are most of them. There's another side of that coin that makes it very, very worthwhile, I think. If once, twice in your life, an actor can get a part with some kind of depth, he can go beyond entertaining and he can touch people and he can move them and he can make them think. And he can thereby enlighten them. And I think that is one precious gift that is given to very, very few mortals even once in their life. It is a noble profession. And I am damn proud to be part of it.[4]

Chris Lemmon is an actor and Jack Lemmon's son. He recalls,

> My father cared about the art of acting. He was offered a really good part, but he chose not to accept it because he felt that another actor could play it better. He was so enamored that he chose to produce it with his production company, Jalem Productions. He knew the actor and reached out to him. Consequently, Paul Newman was nominated for an Academy Award for *Cool Hand Luke*.
>
> He was one of the luckiest actors and the first to admit it. He said that the greatest role of all was the one allowing him to realize his dream of performing a mix of comedy and drama, instead of being pigeonholed as

comedic or dramatic. That piece was *The Apartment*. It was the first time that Hollywood allowed him to do what he did best and what he wanted to do best. *Days of Wine and Roses* came right after that.

He was a selfless actor. What he was onscreen was what he was off screen, but twenty times greater. If I had to encapsulate him in one word, that word would be "honest."

He was an actor, a director, and a producer. He compartmentalized. The best lesson that he ever gave me was just go do it. That's really what it's all about. You can take classes, but you also need experience. George Cukor was his first mentor. One of the greatest acting lessons that he learned was to just keep it simple. And he always learned from every person he ever worked with.[5]

If Michelangelo had lived in twentieth-century Hollywood, it's quite likely that Remick would have topped his list for sculpture subjects. Remick had chiseled good looks that made men's hearts beat faster with desire. Women's, with envy. And admiration. Her talent matched her beauty, making for a powerful combination that lit up movie theater and television screens; Remick's characters ranged from posh to poverty-stricken, seductive to sensitive. She could be a well-meaning shiksa in *No Way to Treat a Lady*, using mirroring techniques to overcome the bias of her boyfriend's domineering Jewish mother; a lovesick teenager succumbing to Andy Griffith's character, the lusty cowboy entertainer Lonesome Rhodes, and cheating on him with his manager and without remorse in *A Face in the Crowd*; a cool-headed, icy-hearted piano teacher arguing that her prodigy must sacrifice love for craft in *The Competition*; and a sultry wife who cheats on her husband, then acts demurely on the witness stand in his murder trial by claiming that she was raped by the man her husband shot and killed, in *Anatomy of a Murder*.[6]

Remick starred in another 1962 movie set in San Francisco. *Experiment in Terror* is a thriller revolving around a bank teller, a psychotic forcing her to steal $100,000, and a climactic capture at a Dodgers-Giants night game at Candlestick Park.[7]

"Red" Lynch (played by Ross Martin) attacks Remick's character Kelly Sherwood in her garage and threatens violence if she doesn't steal the money from the bank. Glenn Ford's FBI agent character takes her call, leading to a pursuit that has Ford's team trailing Lynch through the city's most notable spots, including Fisherman's Wharf and Chinatown.

Blake Edwards directed both of Remick's 1962 movies. He could compete frame-for-frame with cinema's best helmsmen. The *Los Angeles Times* praised him: "Director Edwards employs camera and mike [*sic*] effectively in the suspense tradition of Hitchcock, Andrew Stone, et al.—not only in the big baseball stadium, emptied of all but the killer, but also in the surreptitious placing of a corpse in a storeroom filled with mannequins. And the sound of the heavy-breathing murderer automatically establishes his presence time and again."[8]

Ford's G-man hero portrayal was in the Joe Friday mold of a law enforcement hero—follow the clues, solve the case, leave emotions at the door. But *Experiment in Terror* was in clear contrast to his preference for westerns. "It never seems like work when you make a western, somehow," explained Ford, who had co-starred with Rita Hayworth in the film noir classic *Gilda*. "I love the outdoors, you know, and cattle and ranching are my business. Westerns give you more margin for error because you have a tremendous panorama to assist you and it's pretty hard to miss when you have a dozen horses galloping with the Grand Canyon as a background."[9]

Stefanie Powers played Sherwood's kid sister, also in danger from Lynch. An alumnus of Hollywood High School, a breeding ground for talent, Powers later found stardom on television with the iconic shows *The Girl from U.N.C.L.E.* and *Hart to Hart*. She recalls,

> I got the role in *Experiment in Terror* through Tom Laughlin, who did the Billy Jack movies. He was a working character actor who had also done some independent art movies. I met him in the commissary through his script supervisor, who was going to work on *Experiment in Terror*. Tom had a patron in Jerry Wald, the film's producer. Wald championed everything that Tom did. Tom showed him this movie *The Young Sinner* that I had done with him. It was the first time that anybody had a house with a screen that came down from the ceiling. Behind every potted palm was a recognizable face. Jerry was responsible for me going to the 20th Century

Fox studio classes with contract players and then for casting directors. I was invited to do the same thing for MGM and Columbia.

Blake [Edwards] was a fantastic director in the sense that he found ways in individuals to unlock a moment and get the end result that he wanted. The cameraman would show me what a close-up looks like. It was a great learning experience because so few directors today ever walk on to the set and stand next to the camera.[10]

Based on Meredith Willson's Broadway musical of the same name, *The Music Man* stars Robert Preston, who re-creates his role of Harold Hill, a con man trying to get the denizens of River City, Iowa, circa 1912 to give him money in exchange for band uniforms, instruments, and manuals.[11] Under the guise of being a music teacher, he plans to leave River City once the goods get there. The story ends with a fantasy sequence of the kids decked out in their uniforms, marching through the River City streets, playing the instruments as well as any orchestra or philharmonic could.

Shirley Jones co-stars as Hill's love interest, librarian Marian Paroo; Buddy Hackett plays Hill's pal Marcellus Washburn. Ronny Howard gives new meaning to the word "precocious" when he lisps his way through the song "Wells Fargo Wagon," the title alluding to the bank's delivery service at the turn of the twentieth century, as River City's hopeful future musicians anxiously await the instruments promised by Hill.

The Music Man was the biggest thing to hit Iowa since corn. Mason City, Willson's hometown, welcomed its favorite son at the local airport for the premiere, with a high school band playing the show's famous song, "Seventy-Six Trombones." Along with Willson, Mason City had galactic star power with Jones and Preston traveling there for the event. A competition for high school bands—thirty in all—was another highlight; the winner got "a 10 day national tour and $10,000 worth of musical instruments." And Willson led the high school band in a march down the street, like his protagonist, in another rendition of "Seventy-Six Trombones."[12]

Preston debunked a Hollywood myth about the beginning of his stardom, which allegedly happened when Cecil B. DeMille spotted him parking cars at the Santa Anita racetrack. "Don't you believe it," said Preston to legendary gossip columnist Hedda Hopper. "That story was a publicity man's dream, concocted after I earned my first big break from De Mille [*sic*] in 'Union Pacific.'"[13]

Taking on the role of Harold Hill was an extraordinary challenge, given that Hill is a villain at the beginning of the movie. River City is a mark vulnerable for Hill to strip of its pride, trust, and money. By the end the children look and sound like a band. Preston needed a dual-edged appeal to keep the audience curious to know if he can pull off the con and equally curious to see the consequences if he doesn't. It was a risk that Preston identified as a key to being an actor: "One thing my experience has taught me is that people get in a rut when they try to play life safe. My philosophy is, if something starts fraying your nerves, get away from it. Take a chance. If you fail, try again. Nobody has to do anything he dislikes—except die."[14]

Willson's masterpiece was a Broadway standard before Hollywood offered its version. Debuting in 1957, *The Music Man* became a go-to piece for schools, regional theater, and television, and it had a Broadway revival in 2000. But the road to icon status was not a smooth one for the kid from Iowa who found stardom penning music and lyrics. In *But He Doesn't Know the Territory*—Willson's memoir about the challenges of writing, producing, and financing the Broadway production—he reveals his journey with self-deprecation, honesty, and humor: "But handing somebody a big fat script loaded with goodies, like the trunk in the attic, is like handing them the dictionary, saying proudly, 'It's all in there—just pick it out.' A sculptor is a guy who throws away rock, no question, no doubt. But it took me a while to find that out."[15]

Timmy Everett played Tommy Djilas, one of the River City kids in the film. Tanya Bagot, his sister, recalls that

> Timmy started studying dance at the age of four because my mom wanted him to. I started at that age too. We moved into Manhattan from Wilmington, North Carolina, when I was in the fifth grade. My mom came from an immigrant family of tobacco farmers. She was one of thirteen children, so she had to make herself known. She went to college and she was determined to get to New York.
>
> Timmy was like a shark. Dance was his life. Everyone on Broadway knew that the gift he had was magical. He exuded energy and movement.

It resonated in *Damn Yankees*. He also taught dancing. The dance studio became our safe haven. We had alcoholism in the family, so Broadway, music, and dance became our parents and family. Hal Prince is an incredible member of that part of our lives.

Acting was a big deal in New York at that time because of the Actors Studio. Timmy was in the program. He became Lee Strasberg's protégé. But Timmy abused drugs. He said that he was going to kick it.[16]

The Manchurian Candidate, directed by John Frankenheimer and based on the novel by Richard Condon, terrified audiences with the proposition that a Korean War hero, Raymond Shaw, was brainwashed by communists to be a sleeper assassin. He was to shoot his target when prompted by the sight of the queen of diamonds while playing solitaire; his mother, with whom there's an incestuous relationship revealed before the film's climax, is the communist agent in the United States. Her cover is brilliant: wife of the McCarthyesque senator and vice-presidential candidate John Iselin, who declares a number—always varying—of communists in the federal government.

At the end of the film, instead of shooting the presidential candidate at the convention in Madison Square Garden to open the slot for Iselin, Raymond shoots Iselin and his mother before killing himself. Frank Sinatra plays the film's hero, Major Bennett Marco—a fellow veteran who served with Raymond—and peels away the layers of the conspiracy, finally realizing the horror of Raymond's situation. Although the story is fictional, it puts forth a terrifying prospect during the Cold War.

Frankenheimer, Sinatra, and screenwriter George Axelrod reunited in 1988 to discuss the production; Sinatra praised Axelrod for creating the brainwashing sequence, remarking on the "marvelous invention changing the ladies of the garden of New Jersey into the communist Chinese and Russians. And that knocked me out."[17]

The first James Bond film, *Dr. No*, set off a fascination with the suave sleuth that Ian Fleming had created for his novels.[18] Fleming's hero, identified as a former British naval commander, had first appeared in the 1953 novel *Casino Royale*, and the following year Barry Nelson played Bond in a live performance of the story in the television show *Climax!*[19]

Whereas the *Dr. No* novel had the title character interfering with American missile tests, in the film it was the Project Mercury rockets at risk. Both versions of the story use Jamaica as the setting.

The iconic *Dr. No* scene of Ursula Andress—who plays Honey Ryder—emerging from the ocean with a knife strapped to her bikini set the standard of sexuality for future Bond girls. Bond's prowess is confirmed in the final scene, a common storytelling device for the secret agent who beds women with suggestive names. After defeating Dr. No, the hero and Honey escape by boat. When they're rescued by a British naval ship, he has second thoughts—he lets the tow rope slip into the ocean, drops out of sight to the bottom of the boat with Honey, and leaves the audience with clarity on how they will celebrate the completion of the mission.

Joseph Wiseman played Dr. No. Martha Wiseman is his daughter, and she recalls,

> I was barely ten when *Dr. No* came out; I had kids asking me in school if my father was Chinese and had hands. I was not allowed to see the movie. Didn't see it until my twenties. My father was embarrassed that he was known for it. He was a stage actor, and later in life he claimed that he didn't like movies. He received tons and tons of requests for autographs with pictures of Dr. No. I kept a few of them. Some of the obituaries quoted him as saying that he thought *Dr. No* was another Charlie Chan picture. He felt that he was typecast; he felt constrained and upset by offers of villain roles.
>
> The theater was his home. He felt that was where true actors and artistry were. He appreciated great films, but his heart was in the theater. He never wanted to teach or direct. He didn't believe that acting could be taught.[20]

Anthony Quinn starred in two movies in 1962—*Lawrence of Arabia* and *Requiem for a Heavyweight*.[21]

Lawrence of Arabia won seven Oscars—Best Picture, Best Director, Best Original Music Score, Best Cinematography, Best Film Editing, Best Production Design, and Best Sound Mixing. It depicts the heroism of British officer T. E. Lawrence during World War I; Quinn plays Auda Abu Tayi, a leader in the Great Arab Revolt. *Requiem*, a Columbia film based on a Rod Serling teleplay starring Jack Palance as the punch-drunk, over-the-hill boxer

Mountain Rivera, hit theaters with the power of an uppercut thrown by Jack Dempsey, who had a cameo as himself in the movie.[22]

Mountain faces a dilemma. Possessing limited skills, he has bleak prospects after ending his career. One beam of light is job counselor Grace Miller, a possible love interest who sees Mountain for what he is—a decent man with a poor education looking to make a place for himself after his usefulness in the ring has expired. He prizes his friendship with Maish, who wants Mountain to get into the wrestling world. But Maish has a selfish reason—he needs money to cover a gambling debt and the bookies control the wrestling industry. Disregarding potential injury to Mountain, Maish presses him while Army, Mountain's corner man in the ring, suffers mostly in silence. His efforts to stop Maish amount to nil. Even with his trust betrayed, Mountain agrees to perform as the character Big Chief Mountain Rivera, complete with head-dress, to help Maish pay off the bookies. His heroism is one of sacrifice—in this case, it's his dignity that will suffer, along with his body. Jackie Gleason plays Maish and Mickey Rooney plays Army.

In a nice bit of branding crossover, one scene shows movie posters for Columbia's 1962 movies *The Interns* and *The Notorious Landlady*.[23]

Katherine Quinn is Anthony Quinn's widow. She recalls that

Tony loved *Requiem for a Heavyweight*. He was a huge fan of boxing and bullfighting. He was of the school that saw them as beauty and art. He played in close to two hundred movies. Many early roles were villains because when he started, he was working heavily through the World War II era, when heroes were All-American types like John Wayne and Van Johnson. Because he could play ethnic roles, he was mostly the bad guy. There were stereotypes. Mexicans, for example. He had to get inside them and find their humanity. He searched for it even when he played mobsters. Sometimes the role didn't allow for him to express that, but he had to find a way.

With *Requiem*, he struggled to find Mountain Rivera. Tony knew that he found the voice for Mountain through Abie Bane, a Jewish boxer from New Jersey who came to the set. His voice was very strained because he had been punched in the throat. And he found the softer side. You see it in the scene with Julie Harris, when she dismisses him and he says, "I'm somebody." That scene was wonderful. He had a handful of characters that he loved, even though some of his favorite movies never became big.

Tony was respectful of work if people worked with integrity. It didn't matter what the job was. If it was gardening, he could tell if it was done with respect. It was something so important to him. How you do anything is how you do everything.[24]

Advise and Consent has no heroes, only victims—depending on how one views politicians.[25] By the end of the movie, the political world is revealed to be rife with blackmail, gossip, and personal destruction.

If there is a hero, it's Senate majority leader Bob Munson, played by Walter Pidgeon. The veteran Michigan lawmaker is fundamentally decent, objecting more to being surprised at the nomination—which makes troubleshooting and strategizing more difficult—than to the president's political objectives. Victims are everywhere: a senator takes his own life after a rival senator's anonymous threat of publicizing a homosexual alliance; his best friend in the Senate loses faith in politics after learning of the suicide; the unhealthy president dies, a death presumably hastened by the stress of the nomination process; and the nominee loses his chance when the vice president assumes the presidency after a 50–50 vote, refuses to break the tie, and prefers to name his own candidate.

The Man Who Shot Liberty Valance shows the power of myth in hero worship.[26] The people of Shinbone, a town in a small western territory on the verge of becoming a state, elect attorney Ransom Stoddard and local publisher Dutton Peabody to represent them at the statehood convention. Prizing the law above brutality, Stoddard refuses to seek vengeance against Liberty Valance, who had assaulted Stoddard during a stagecoach robbery. Although Shinbone's informal enforcer, Tom Doniphon, gives Stoddard shooting lessons, the idealistic attorney refuses to engage in violence until he sees Valance assault Peabody. And so he shoots and kills Valance in a gunfight. Or so he thinks.

It is actually Doniphon, hiding in the shadows, who kills the villainous scourge.

The film is bracketed by scenes from twenty-five years after the events. A senator and vice-presidential candidate, Stoddard returns to Shinbone to pay his respects after Doniphon dies. When a newspaper reporter asks about the reason, Stoddard explains the truth—he never deserved the accolades for eliminating Valance. The guilt has weighed on him like a boulder, but the truth has zero import for the scribe: "This is the West, sir. When the legend becomes fact, print the legend." When the journalist explains this harsh reality to Stoddard, it reflects the truth about storytelling—there's a bit of myth in almost any tale. George Washington didn't chop down the cherry tree. Magellan was not the first sailor to navigate around the world. And Ransom Stoddard did not kill Liberty Valance.

Casting a movie is an art form within an art form, and *The Man Who Shot Liberty Valance* proves that art can sometimes be perfect: Jimmy Stewart plays Stoddard, John Wayne plays Doniphon, and Lee Marvin plays Valance. Gene Pitney recorded a song of the same name for the movie, but the producers did not use it.[27]

Hollywood's output in 1962 is staggering. While scholars often cite 1939 as the film industry's best year, 1962 had films of considerable importance, quality, and diversity. *The Longest Day* is a docudrama about the D-Day invasion of Normandy.[28] Audiences could learn more from this film about the turning point of World War II than from any college textbook. There were others: an epic western (*How the West Was Won*); a Tennessee Williams drama laden with a gigolo leeching off the insecurity of a faded actress to build his own acting career (*Sweet Bird of Youth*); thrillers (*Cape Fear, Whatever Happened to Baby Jane?*); a World War II movie with Steve McQueen (*Hell Is for Heroes*); Eugene O'Neill's tragic, autobiographical tale (*Long Day's Journey into Night*); and a romantic comedy with Cary Grant and Doris Day featuring cameos by Mickey Mantle, Roger Maris, and Yogi Berra (*That Touch of Mink*).[29]

While audiences found idealized courting in the Grant-Day pairing, there was another love story that dropped jaws from Burbank to Bangor: *Lolita*.[30] "It is, in my opinion, a moral love story," said the producer, James Harris. "Age is not the important thing when two people are in love."[31]

But this was no May-September romance—more like February-September. Starring James Mason as middle-aged professor Humbert Humbert and fourteen-year-old Sue Lyon as the title character brimming with girl-next-door looks and sexual maturity, *Lolita* provoked audiences with the might of an Atlas booster on the Mercury missions. They might have chuckled at Humbert's first encounter with Lolita, when her mother, his potential landlord, talks about cherry pies. But they squirmed with discomfort when Lolita plays gently with Humbert's hair, whispers in his ear, and then says, "Alrighty, then," as the screen fades to black. There is no question what happens between the end of that scene and the beginning of the next one.

Lolita differed from Vladimir Nabokov's 1955 novel of the same name; Nabokov's Lolita was a prepubescent girl rather than a teenager.

Television competed for attention with its older, more established big-screen entertainment sibling. Boris Karloff, best known for his work in "horror" films, brought his talents to the small screen as host of the anthology series *Thriller*, which ran on NBC from 1960 to 1962. As his daughter, Sara Karloff, recalls,

By the time television came around in the late 1940s, horror films had entered a slack period. My father moved to New York City in 1949, and my father embraced the new medium of television. A lot of Hollywood stars were worried about live television, but my father had done some live theater when he learned the craft in British Columbia's repertory theater. He also acted in five Broadway plays. So, he was anxious to try television. He realized that it was an opportunity to reinvent himself and broaden the scope of his career by not doing just monster roles. And he was correct.

He appeared as a guest star on all the prominent shows of the day, and he had an opportunity to spoof his own bogey man image with Carol Burnett's and Dinah Shore's shows. He did the *Hallmark Hall of Fame* and *Playhouse 90* and ended up having three television series of his own— *Thriller*, *Colonel March*, *The Veil*. It was a wonderful decision that he made to go into television. Hollywood had been very good to him, but he loved New York and he was able to travel back there whenever he worked. Being in New York also allowed him to be closer to England.

Frankenstein was his eighty-first film. He had been in the business for twenty years. He was one of the founding members of the Screen Actors Guild—his card number was 9. Being a founding member of SAG was so important because he had been one of those actors treated poorly. When my father started out, he was nothing but a day player suffering at the hands of the studio bosses and working nineteen to twenty hours a day. He lost twenty-five pounds during the making of *Frankenstein*.

His most favorite work was performing in *The Lark* opposite Julie Harris. He was nominated for a Tony. My father adored the theater. The one thing that he wished he could have done but never did was be on the London stage. He loved working with and for children. He did twenty children's albums and played Captain Hook on Broadway in *Peter Pan*. He never talked about his work. The only time that he mentioned it was when he did the narration and the voice of the Grinch in *How the Grinch Stole Christmas!* My father called me and said, "You might sit down tonight with the boys and watch something that's going to air tonight. I think you and the boys would enjoy it. I think it's pretty good."

The fans are wonderful. And because my father was one of the very few people in the business about whom nothing was written negatively, they're so respectful and polite. He thought that he was the luckiest man alive to be able to spend his life working at something he truly loved![32]

The Many Loves of Dobie Gillis, created by Max Shulman, broke ground by showcasing stories from teenagers' point of view. It ran for four seasons on CBS, with Dwayne Hickman as the title character and Bob Denver as his best friend—beatnik Maynard G. Krebs. Shulman was a well-established author when *Dobie Gillis* premiered in 1958. His short story "Love Is a Fallacy" is standard reading for first-year college English courses.[33]

Martha Rose Shulman is Max Shulman's daughter and offers these observations:

Dobie Gillis was innovative in breaking the fourth wall. I think that my father was much more subversive than people think about. He really used dramatic conventions in television and talked about the fact that writing was hard work. He loved creating the plot. He like to make himself laugh, so he dreamed up jokes. He loved his characters. And he liked the money, but that wasn't why he did it. Eventually, he moved to Hollywood.

I think Dobie really grabbed that teenage audience. My father was famous by then, among the parents of the teenagers, because of the early novels. He was in Hollywood a month or two at a time. When the cast people came East, they would visit him. *Dobie Gillis* had real substance. There was an episode where Thalia wants Dobie to be a doctor because of the money. The use of language was sophisticated. Zelda told Dobie that love is "a matter of propinquity."

He used the grocery store setting for Dobie's father because he worked in a grocery store as a teenager. What's interesting about the house is that there are no interior sets. He named the high school Central High after his own high school in St. Paul.[34]

"It was the first show where the teenagers were the stars and the first where a beatnik was a major character," explains the author's son, Max. "When Dobie broke the fourth wall, he spoke directly to the teenage viewers about his problems, usually not being able to get the girl that he wanted," he said. "It was a funny show that was well written with free-association humor—jokes deriving out of language that precedes it. By the end of the 1960s, humor had more edge. A great example is *The Feather Merchants*, which my father wrote as a parody of *For Whom the Bell Tolls*. I think his best work was *Rally Round the Flag, Boys!* It was a funny look at suburbia but today it would be considered dark."[35]

The Defenders showcased legal, societal, and personal conflicts encountered by defense attorneys. The defenders of the title are Lawrence Preston and his son, Kenneth Preston—played by E. G. Marshall and Robert Reed, respectively—and they take on clients who may have been repugnant to their values. In the episode "The Iron Man," they represent Jack Powers, a college student embracing the idea of a totalitarian state with a leader in the mold of Mussolini or Hitler; it harkens back to the *Route 66* episode "To Walk with the Serpent."[36] The defense arises from Lawrence's belief that Powers is being falsely prosecuted for what two of his goons did: assaulting a heckler at a rally. It is proven that the attack happened without Powers's consent, encouragement, or approval.

The Prestons represent an abortionist in "The Benefactor," which caused CBS to lose sponsors for the episode.[37] In that episode a jury finds Dr. Montgomery guilty but makes a request for leniency. The judge tells Lawrence and the prosecutor that he will impose the maximum, but suspended, sentence.

269

One of the witnesses for the doctor is a twenty-nine-year-old, $50,000 per year fashion model named Audrey Gunther, played by Dee Hartford. Looking like she could stop traffic at the Indianapolis 500, Audrey explains that the man she loved didn't want children, but the doctor persuaded her to have the baby and be a single mother.

Lucille Ball had perfected her comedy brand in *I Love Lucy*, leaving behind her initial show business career as a glamour queen in RKO B-movies. Gone was the blonde with Rockette-like legs, and in came a redhead who got herself into situations that put America into hysterics. Ball and husband Desi Arnaz played the lead roles—Lucy and Ricky Ricardo. A performer and band leader at the Tropicana, Ricky often warned Lucy against her schemes in a husband-knows-best approach that went unheeded by Lucy. When the Ricardos joined Fred and Ethel Mertz, their best friends and landlords, for a trip to Hollywood so Ricky can star in a movie, the season revolved around Lucy causing chaos with Hollywood stars, including John Wayne, William Holden, and Harpo Marx.[38]

After *I Love Lucy* ended in 1957 with Ricardos and the Mertzes having moved to Westport, Connecticut, the foursome appeared in a new show christened *The Lucy-Desi Comedy Hour*—thirteen one-hour specials. Ball and Arnaz divorced during the show's run, which ended in 1960. Ball debuted her second sitcom, *The Lucy Show*, on CBS in 1962. In this series she plays the widowed mother of a teenage girl and a prepubescent boy, with pal Vivian Vance playing her best friend and neighbor, following the Lucy-Ethel paradigm. Slapstick plot elements showcased Ball's adeptness at physical comedy in all of her series work, and although her beauty was downplayed on *I Love Lucy*, Ball had plenty of opportunities to show her natural attractiveness.

And she ran a studio.

Arnaz had plunked down $2.5 million to buy RKO; he had formed Desilu Productions so the couple could produce and own *I Love Lucy*, then bowed out of the company when America's most famous marriage broke down. Arnaz was a pioneer who had created, with cinematographer Karl Freund, the three-camera format for situation comedies; it became a staple for shooting sitcoms on soundstages. Under Ball's solo leadership, Desilu produced the iconic shows *Star Trek* and *Mission: Impossible*. Although she was a hands-off manager, she was far from a figurehead. Her instinct for the public's attitudes, particularly finicky in the area of comedy, came from years in B-movies of the 1930s and 1940s as an attractive woman often cast for comic dialogue: "I don't think I'm too versatile, but that's sort of beside the point. If millions like this, it would be pretty silly of me to go astray. I've learned a lot about my trade over the years. I have a knowledge of physical comedy, my timing is reliable and I'm believable. People laugh where they should and they don't think I'm unbelievable, because I believe it all the way. I do what I do with all my strength and heart."[39]

The Lucy Show ran from 1962 to 1968, followed by *Here's Lucy*, which aired from 1968 to 1974.

Television tested the optimism of the early 1960s with glimpses into a possible dystopian future, as several episodes of *The Twilight Zone* did. But creator Rod Serling was not alone in his projections—*Alcoa Premiere* also showed a glimpse of a computer-dominated culture forty years hence in the episode "The Jail." A man on trial is found guilty by a computer jury and sentenced by a computer judge. His punishment—a switch in souls and brains with a hapless older man.[40]

Elvis Presley appeared in three movies in 1962: *Kid Galahad, Follow That Dream*, and *Girls! Girls! Girls!*

Gavin Koon and Robin Koon play twin brothers of Elvis's character in *Follow That Dream*, a story about a hodgepodge family constructed by Pop Kwimper, played by Arthur O'Connell. He adopts the children and sets up a makeshift home on a Florida beach.

Gavin Koon recalls,

We viewed it as summer fun, and we had a blast! It was our first jet airplane ride. Elvis was like a big brother to us. He'd goof around and spend time with us. Very friendly and not standoffish at all. We shot the film in 1961 and the space age was everywhere in Florida. Everyone was getting buzz cuts to look like the astronauts. But the producers wanted us to be kind of shaggy. My brother likes to make jokes that we started the long-hair craze.

There was a casting call that my parents heard about for twins. Imagine fifty pairs of twins around the same age. Somehow, we got picked. We did a couple of things after that, including Richard Boone's show.[41]

Robin Koon has these recollections:

Eight-year-olds have no idea what fame is. We didn't know why the girls were screaming for Elvis. He was very down to earth with us. Doing the movie was fun. The set was pretty much closed, so there weren't a lot of outsiders. Plus, we had security to keep them away. There's a scene in the movie where we're clapping hands because we couldn't snap our fingers. They had to change the song because of that.

We were curious kids, so we asked the crew a lot of questions. They played practical jokes on us, like pouring yellow gasoline in a car and claiming that cars ran on orange juice.

This was Florida in the early 1960s. A drinking fountain in the courthouse said "colored." We had no idea about segregation so we thought it meant the color of the water. When we were invited back to the courthouse decades later for an event celebrating the movie, the drinking fountain had been removed.

The courthouse where we shot the movie is a historic landmark. They used shots from the movie to restore it to its original state.[42]

There was a change in the air for music in 1962. Teenagers beamed to the new sounds of a quartet from Liverpool, England, and a group of guys heralding the joys of living in Southern California. The Beatles and the Beach Boys both made their debut albums that year. Only they weren't exactly new. The Beatles, by their own admission, borrowed their style, harmony, and simple, love-infused lyrics in "Love Me Do" and their other early songs from Buddy Holly and the Crickets.[43] The riff at the beginning of "Surfin' U.S.A." sounds like a twin of Ritchie Valens's "Come On, Let's Go," while "Fun, Fun, Fun" mirrors Chuck Berry's "Johnny B. Goode."[44] These songs and others were homages to rock and roll, which needed leaders after the 1959 plane crash that killed Holly, Valens, and J. P. "Big Bopper" Richardson.

Dick Dale and His Del-Tones also unveiled their first album—*Surfer's Choice*.[45] Landlocked teenagers could dream of sunshine, beaches, and the Pacific Ocean while their transistor radios pulsed the guitar licks of Dale and the harmonies of the Beach Boys.

But an episode of *Route 66* shows an underside to the surfing lifestyle. "Ever Ride the Waves in Oklahoma?" portrays surfers at Huntington Beach as listless, with no cares about work or obligations, just sunshine and a good wave. When a surfer dies by wiping out when trying to "shoot the pier" to take down the surfing king, Hob, it ignites fury in Buz; he asks Tod for two weeks to train, shoot the pier, and take down Hob. The word is that Hob doesn't have to work because of a bequest from his late uncle. Buz finds out the true story—Hob doesn't have inherited wealth and actually works on Saturday nights at a posh restaurant—and then confronts the king of the surfers. To protect his image, Hob keeps quiet about his job. "Oh that's right. Surfers aren't supposed to do anything but surf and look down their noses at all the slobs that hold up the world from nine to five," says Buz. "And surfers don't fight either, do they? Might damage their hands. Hey, King, did you ever ride the waves in Oklahoma? They got surfers in Oklahoma, too. Getting tanned under the poolroom lights. Like they got guys that hang around the drugstores in Brooklyn. And guys that watch the trucks unload in Kansas City. And guys that hide all day in downtown movie houses. Surfers. Just like the bums on skid row. All surfers. Except they lie on asphalt instead of beach."[46]

Innovation is the goal of network programmers because they hope it attracts viewers, but at the same time it is the bane of their existence because they fear it scares advertisers. That tension is evident in NBC's *It's a Man's World*. Sprinkled with drama and comedy, the characters and story lines are not simply of the cookie-cutter variety.

The show revolves around four male characters—aspiring gas-station attendant Wes, his teenage brother Howie, carefree friend Tom-Tom, and quiet folksinger Vern. They live on a houseboat; Wes and Howie's parents are deceased. Irene, Wes's girlfriend, and other characters populate the young men's lives.

In the episode "The Beavers and the Otters," Wes and Irene struggle to find time alone for intimacy. The word "sex" is never uttered but heavily implied when Wes, out of frustration, says he'd settle for ten minutes. Finally, it seems that they can be alone at Irene's sister's house. But when the realization that they might have sex, presumably for the first time, hits Irene, she crumbles in Wes's arms and they both look at the pictures of Irene's sister and husband

and the nephews and nieces. After the tears, they get in the car to go home and a friendly banter ensues regarding the type of house they'll buy after they get married and have children.[47]

Television critic Cecil Smith called the episode "an intensely moving piece of work, an almost tortured study of young love."[48]

It seemed that *It's a Man's World* was getting a loyal audience. "I'm sure we're on the right track because the viewers from our mid-Western states are beginning to write letters, telling us how much they like the show because it reminds them of what's going on in their own town," said Peter Tewksbury, the show's co-creator with Jim Leighton, about six weeks after the premiere episode.[49]

The two men's vision broke a mold for a demographic populated by boy-crazed girls, gee-golly boys, statuesque sexpots, and muscle-bound men. "We want to do young people as they really are, avoiding all the TV clichés—the juvenile delinquents, the namby-pamby, the precocious," they told a reporter. "We wanted to show youth with its positive values, its confusions. Kids solving problems without family authority, working out where they're going in this civilization."[50]

Hal Humphrey, a *Los Angeles Times* television critic, hinted at the show's potential in a summary of the upcoming season, calling it "the first seen by this reporter which has anything looking even slightly different from the ordinary, highly polished product coming out of Hollywood now." He suggested that "Tewksbury has achieved this difference through the simple technique of writing about real characters and letting them tell their stories with half as much dialogue as one finds in most TV drama."[51]

It's a Man's World aired for one season on NBC.

Bob Greene, the best-selling author, nationally syndicated columnist, and unofficial spokesperson for baby boomers, has chronicled his popular-culture childhood in *Be True to Your School: A Diary of 1964* and other critically acclaimed books:

> There had been kind of a vacuum after Elvis Presley went into the Army in 1958. You had a lot of one-hit wonders and manufactured, purported idols, but no one had come along to replace him, and Elvis himself, once

he was back to civilian life, had stopped doing live performances and was mainly making bland movies. Everyone was waiting to see who the next guy would be—and it turned out that it was not one guy, it was four guys, from over in England. No one saw that coming, but then, that's how such things often work: the big changes in just about every field are the ones that no one anticipates.

The appeal of the Beach Boys was precisely because we could barely imagine what their lives were like. The ocean, surfing, bright sun and warmth all year 'round—that sounded like a dream to guys growing up in the landlocked Midwest. Which was exactly the point: the Beach Boys, Jan and Dean[,] and the other surf groups were selling a dream, and we were the perfect audience to buy that dream. What they had was what we wanted.[52]

Movie studios loosened the shackles of benignity in 1962. *Bachelor Flat* showcases Tuesday Weld shaking her shapely backside in a CinemaScope close-up that widens to reveal her prancing around a kitchen while she makes breakfast.[53] It uses the word *sex* freely and comedically, an unheard etymological strategy during the previous decade, when *I Love Lucy* couldn't even use the word *pregnant* to describe Lucy's condition. Film critic Murray Schumach noted that the film *Bachelor Flat* would appeal to "viewers with a tolerance for brash vulgarity and a fitful pace."[54]

Weld was part of a transition in sex symbols. "They all seemed to be in the same mold as Yvette Mimieux—there was Ursula Andress (although she was a movie star, not a TV star); there was Marianne Faithful (a singing star who made her name performing on television); all of them had a kind of anti–Marilyn Monroe image," Greene notes. "They were beautiful, but they weren't marketed as Monroe-style 'bombshells,' which was the point. They were marketed as women who, if not exactly approachable, were at least imaginable. Boys back then could not even conceive of being with Marilyn Monroe; the Yvette/Ursula/Marianne generation of female stars seemed one step closer to living in the actual world we did."[55]

Richard Crenna showed his comedy chops—first seen in the 1950s sitcom *Our Miss Brooks*—once again as Luke McCoy in *The Real McCoys*. "People would come up to me and say *The Real McCoys* was the only show that we could identify with," says Crenna's daughter, Seana. "It always had a good message, a family that struggled but loved each other. My father adored Walter Brennan and considered him a mentor. They shot most of it on MGM's back lot in Culver City. They'd sit on a pile of hay and have lunch. My father never asked for anything special on a set, just a chair and a bottle of water that wasn't chilled. He never asked for a costume designer or hair stylist. He just jumped out of bed in the morning and went to work. He loved what he did."[56]

Broadway got attention on prime-time television on December 9 with the *Car 54, Where Are You?* episode "142 Tickets on the Aisle."[57] It focused on the Fifty-Third Precinct's Brotherhood Club trying to get tickets for a hit Broadway play—142 tickets for officers and their wives. With every smash show sold out for months, *Little Miss Pioneer*, destined to be a flop, is the only offering with that many seats available. When the press thinks that the police are arresting the producer and the cast for obscenity, the show becomes a hit. Controversy sells.

The episode chronicles the exteriors of Broadway shows in 1962 as the officers trek from box office to box office: *How to Succeed in Business without Really Trying, No Strings, Camelot, Milk and Honey, Carnival!, A Funny Thing Happened on the Way to the Forum*, and *Mary, Mary.*[58]

A box-office clerk for one of the sold-out shows jokes that the Kennedys had attended a performance but that Jackie had to sit in the balcony.[59] The joke has a connection to reality—President and Mrs. Kennedy attended the Washington premiere of the Irving Berlin musical *Mr. President* at the National Theatre in September. It was a fundraiser for family charities commemorating the president's late brother, Lieutenant Joseph P. Kennedy Jr., and serving the needs of children with developmental disabilities.

President Kennedy got to the National Theatre a bit late, only able to catch the last act of Berlin's comedy about life in the White House. The play then went to Broadway and ran for less than a year. In the *New York Times* Howard Taubman called it "mechanical in an old-fashioned way" but noted, "Mr. Berlin, missed on Broadway in recent years, is not at the top of his bent, but his second-best is superior to the generality of machine-made songs."[60]

The space age continued its reach into popular culture with "Telstar," by the Tornadoes. It was a clavioline-backed instrumental that made it easy to imagine the song being transmitted from the satellite.[61] President Kennedy found that he had an alter ego in Vaughn Meader, a comedian with a dead-on impersonation in voice and gesture. Even hard-core Republicans found humor when Meader made guest appearances on prime-time comedy and variety shows with mimicry that was never nasty and always tongue-in-cheek. On his comedy album *The First Family*, Meader and a group of performers imitate Kennedy's inner circle. During a mock press conference, he's asked if there is a Kennedy dynasty in politics. Meader responds, "I don't believe it, nor does my brother Bobby, nor does my brother Ghengis."[62]

At a press conference on December 12, Kennedy got a question about whether the album and other popular-culture offerings, including comic books, produce "annoyment or enjoyment." Kennedy smiled through his response, receiving laughter from the press corps: "Annoyment. Yes, I have read them, and listened to them and actually I listened to Mr. Meader's record, but I thought it sounded more like Teddy than it did me, so he's annoyed."[63]

There was a serious issue to be addressed, though. The White House was concerned about Meader using his Kennedy-like voice for endorsements.[64]

Naomi Brossart played Jackie Kennedy on *The First Family*. She recalls,

> I was apprehensive about this job since I'd never done an album, and the recording was scheduled to take place in front of a live audience on the night President Kennedy was to give his Cuban missile crisis speech. On the day of the recording, I remember thinking, *Tonight the entire world is anxious about the possibility of nuclear war, and I'm worried about my performance!* It also occurred to me that with everyone focused on the Cuban Missile Crisis, the audience might not be receptive to our light-hearted portrayal of the first family. However, as I spoke my first lines in our "tour of the White House" segment and heard the audience respond with a roar of laughter, all was again well with the world.[65]

Kennedy's stature during the Cuban Missile Crisis had increased thanks to Cuban exiles looking to escape the dragon's breath of Fidel Castro's oppression. The president and Mrs. Kennedy welcomed thirty-five thousand people to Miami's Orange Bowl to celebrate freedom and the hope that the exiles' beloved land would be free from the shackles of communism. Among the crowd were Cubans from Brigade 2506, held prisoner by Castro after the Bay of Pigs invasion—more than a year and a half earlier.

The United States and Cuba worked out a deal, bolstered by the latter's need for medicine and baby food. Corporations stepped up and gave $53 million worth of products to get the prisoners sent to Florida.[66] Kennedy underscored the tyranny of Cuba's leadership as he praised the exiles for their courage: "For your small Brigade is a tangible reaffirmation that the human desire for freedom and independence is essentially unconquerable. Your conduct and valor are proof that although Castro and his fellow dictators may rule nations, they do not rule people; that they may imprison bodies, but they do not imprison spirits; that they may destroy the exercise of liberty, but they cannot eliminate the determination to be free."[67]

In this last month of 1962, which began with the Ranger 3 mission missing its lunar orbit and moon landing, NASA closed out the year with a victory when the spacecraft for the Mariner 2 project flew past Venus, becoming "the first successful mission to another planet."[68] The distance between Venus and Earth is 36 million miles, and the spacecraft got to within slightly more than 21,000 miles of the second planet from the sun. Its forty-two-minute encounter was the crowning moment of a trip that had begun with the launch in August. Schoolchildren marveled at this latest achievement in space while their grandparents engaged in the game of "When I was your age . . ." and talked about the Wright Brothers being the first human beings to go airborne in a plane.

Besides the scientific breakthroughs, including information on solar wind, it was another indicator of optimism in 1962 that America, however imperfect, has moments that ignite wonder, inspiration, and unity.

Anything was possible.

Notes

1. "TO WALK WITH THE SERPENT"

1. Emerson, *Concord Hymn*, line 4.
2. Caption, United Press International photo, *El Paso Herald-Post*, January 4, 1962, 22.
3. Quoted in Associated Press, "Jackie Surprised," *Christian Science Monitor*, January 24, 1962, 10.
4. Newton Minow, "Television and the Public Interest" (address, National Association of Broadcasters, Washington DC, May 9, 1961), reprinted in Minow, *Equal Time*, 52.
5. Richard K. Doan, "For the Millions and Few," *New York Herald Tribune*, September 3, 1961, C6.
6. Gilbert Seldes, "Television '62: 'We Might Still Create an Art of Television,'" *TV Guide*, April 7–13, 1962, 14.
7. Quoted in Aleene B. MacMinn, "A Star Answers Critics," *Los Angeles Times*, January 21, 1962, A2.
8. Jayne Barbera, telephone interview by author, January 19, 2017.
9. Hanna with Ito, *Cast of Friends*, 87–88.
10. Til Ferdenzi, "Achin' Back? Nope! Moose Trips Twist, Latest Dance Craze," *The Sporting News*, January 17, 1962, 9.

11. Dorian, *Sex Cure*, 70–71.

12. Waggner, *77 Sunset Strip*, season 4, episode 18. In the closing credits, Waggner's name is spelled in lowercase letters except for the Gs in his last name: george waGGner.

13. Byrnes with Terrill, *"Kookie" No More*, 90.

14. Rich, *Dick Van Dyke Show*, season 1, episode 23. The song "The Twizzle" was written by Mack David (lyrics) and Jerry Livingston (music).

15. Paris, *Dick Van Dyke Show*, season 4, episode 20.

16. Paris, *Dick Van Dyke Show*, season 2, episode 20; Paris, *Dick Van Dyke Show*, season 5, episode 27.

17. Rich, *Dick Van Dyke Show*, season 1, episode 24.

18. Gist, *Route 66*, season 3, episode 4.

19. Addiss, *Saints and Sinners*, season 1, episode 8.

20. Karlson, *Kid Galahad*. According to IMDb.com, the song "I Got Lucky" was written by Dolores Fuller, Fred Wise, and Ben Weisman.

21. *The Twist*, July–September 1962.

22. Hughes, "John Force, Magic Agent."

23. Hughes, "John Force, Magic Agent."

24. Robert C. Seamans Jr., "The Next Five Years," *Space World*, January 1962, 18; "Project Pilgrim," *Space World*, January 1962, 26; Gherman Titov, "I Rode the Vostok into Space," *Space World*, January 1962, 12.

25. Bare, *Twilight Zone*, season 3, episode 4.

26. Miner, *Twilight Zone*, season 3, episode 32.

27. De Caprio, *Car 54, Where Are You?*, season 1, episode 16. Nat Hiken created *Car 54*. His first show was the 1950s army-themed sitcom *The Phil Silvers Show*, starring Silvers as Sergeant Ernie Bilko, who excelled at small-time cons and schemes, though unforeseen obstacles always caused Bilko's elaborate plans to be poorly executed. Silvers called Hiken "the most fertile comedy mind in the business." Phil Silvers, interview by Dick Cavett, *The Dick Cavett Show*, season 5, episode 134, aired April 1, 1971, on ABC.

28. Quoted in Robert Goldborough, "This Cop Once Feared Police," *Chicago Daily Tribune*, April 1, 1962, N21.

29. Barbera and Hanna, *The Flintstones*, season 2, episode 30.

30. Koch, *Hawaiian Eye*, season 1, episode 1.

31. Gregory Orr, interview by author, New York NY, January 6, 2017.

32. Heyes, *77 Sunset Strip*, season 1, episode 2.

33. Heyes, *77 Sunset Strip*, season 1, episode 2.

34. Sheldon, *Route 66*, season 2, episode 14. The car the two men drive around in seems to change during the series. In this episode it's described as a "gray sports car" bearing New York license plate 2D-7876. In a later episode it has New York license plate IC-9150. Gist, *Route 66*, season 3, episode 6.

35. "Dispute Holds Up 'Route 66' Episode," *Boston Globe*, November 3, 1961, 18.

36. Percy Shain, "Night Watch: Route 66 Boston Show Distasteful Abomination," *Boston Globe*, January 8, 1962, 10.

37. Judith Milner, telephone interview by author, August 1, 2016.

38. George Maharis, telephone interview by author, March 30, 2019. People often believe that the *Route 66* car was red. This was probably because the box for the *Route 66* board game featured an artistic rendering of Buz and Tod in a red Corvette.

39. "Johnny Crawford . . . 'the Son of Rifleman,'" *Palm Beach Post*, May 24, 1959, 103.

40. "Chuck Connors Is Back on Target," *TV Guide*, January 20–26, 1962, 17.

41. Bruce Lambert, "Chuck Connors, Actor, 71, Dies; Starred as Television's 'Rifleman,'" *New York Times*, November 11, 1992, D21.

42. Heller, *What's My Line?*, season 11, episode 2.

43. Heller, *What's My Line?*, season 11, episode 2.

44. Heller, *What's My Line?*, season 11, episode 2.

45. Heller, *What's My Line?*, season 11, episode 2.

46. Heller, *What's My Line?*, season 11, episode 2.

47. "Text of Rusk's Speech Urging Inter-American Action to Punish Cuban Regime," *New York Times*, January 26, 1962, 4.

48. John W. Finney, "U.S. Moon Rocket Drifts Off Path; Will Miss Target," *New York Times*, January 27, 1962, 1.

2. "GO, BABY, GO!"

1. John Fitzgerald Kennedy, "Inaugural Address," January 20, 1961, John F. Kennedy Presidential Library and Museum, Boston MA (hereafter, JFK Library), https://www.jfklibrary.org/archives/other-resources/john-f-kennedy-speeches/inaugural-address-19610120.

2. "The Bay of Pigs," JFK Library, https://www.jfklibrary.org/jfk/jfk-in-History/The-Bay-of-Pigs.aspx.

3. "President Orders a Total Embargo on Cuban Imports," *New York Times*, February 4, 1962, 1.

4. "Statement by the President upon Signing Bill and Proclamation Relating to the Cuban Sugar Quota," July 7, 1960, The American Presidency Project, University of California, Santa Barbara, https://www.presidency.ucsb.edu/documents/statement-the-president-upon-signing-bill-and-proclamation-relating-the-cuban-sugar-quota.

5. Quoted in "U.S. Files Protest on Cuban Seizure of Oil Refineries," *New York Times*, July 6, 1960, 1.

6. Perry Wolff to Pamela Turnure, September 29, 1961, Series 1.1.2, Subject Files: CBS (1 of 5), Pamela Turnure Files, JFK Library.

7. Perry Wolff to Pamela Turnure, December 4, 1961, Series 1.1.2, Subject Files: CBS (1 of 5), Turnure Files, JFK Library.

8. Wolff to Turnure, December 4, 1961.

9. Edward R. Murrow to Pierre Salinger, December 19, 1961, Series 1.1.2, Subject Files: CBS (1 of 5), Turnure Files, JFK Library.

10. Roy Frisby to Mrs. John F. Kennedy, February 15, 1962, Series 1.1.1, Mary Gallagher Files, CBS: TV Show, February 14, 1962, Messages of Congratulations (1 of 2), JFK Library.

11. Margaret V. Knudsen to Mrs. Kennedy, February 15, 1962, Series 1.1.1, Mary Gallagher Files, CBS: TV Show, February 14, 1962, Messages of Congratulations (2 of 2).

12. Press Files: Coverage, Television and Film, CBS Show of the White House (1 of 2), JFK Library.

13. Press Files: Coverage, Television and Film, CBS Show of the White House (1 of 2).

14. Press Files: Coverage, Television and Film, CBS Show of the White House (1 of 2).

15. Lucy Billingsley, telephone interview by author, May 1, 2015.

16. Charlotte Jones Voiklis, telephone interview by author, August 10, 2016.

17. Wolfe, *Right Stuff*, 58.

18. "Briefing Eisenhower on Astronaut Selection," in Kaufman, *Right Stuff*.

19. Wolfe, *Right Stuff*, 58.

20. George M. Low, Director, Spacecraft & Flight Missions Office of Manned Space Flight, NASA, Statement to the Special Committee on Qualification of the Astronauts of the Committee on Science and Astronautics, U.S. House of Representatives, Box 69, Mercury Program—Subject Files—Speeches & Statements by NASA Administrations, 1961–62, John H. Glenn Archives, Ohio State University, Columbus OH (hereafter, Glenn Archives).

21. Glennan, *Birth of NASA*, 282.

22. Hugh L. Dryden, recorded interview by Walter D. Sohier, Arnold W. Frutkin, and Eugene M. Emme, March 26, 1964, John F. Kennedy Library Oral History Program, JFK Library, https://www.jfklibrary.org/asset-viewer/archives/JFKOH/Dryden%2C%20Hugh%20L/JFKOH-HLD-01/JFKOH-HLD-01.

23. Dryden, recorded interview.

24. Chaikin, *Man on the Moon*, 58.

25. President John F. Kennedy, Remarks at the Dedication of the Aerospace Medical Health Center, San Antonio, Texas, November 21, 1963, JFK Library, https://www.jfklibrary.org/Research/Research-Aids/jfk-Speeches/San-Antonio-tx_19631121.aspx.

26. G. Nelson, *I Dream of Jeannie*, season 1, episode 1.

27. Leonard, *My Favorite Martian*, season 1, episode 1.

28. Hopper, *Gilligan's Island*, season 3, episode 22.

29. Arnold, *Gilligan's Island*, season 2, episode 9.

30. Arnold, *Gilligan's Island*, season 2, episode 4.

31. Donohue, *Lucy Show*, season 1, episode 6.

32. Depew, *Beverly Hillbillies*, season 4, episode 26.

33. Carl Barks to Ed Shifres, November 2, 1991, reprinted in Shifres, *Space Family Robinson*, 230–31.

34. Shifres, *Space Family Robinson*, 112–13.

35. Quoted in Stuart H. Loory, "Glenn's Calm, but Seas Aren't—His Advice to Nation: Just Relax," *New York Herald Tribune*, February 19, 1962, 4.

36. John Glenn, personal note on capsule name selection, undated, Box 69, Mercury Program—Subject Files—Friendship 7 Space Flight, MA-6, Glenn Archives.

37. Glenn with Taylor, *John Glenn*, 186.

38. Gay Talese, "50,000 on Beach Strangely Calm as Rocket Streaks Out of Sight," *New York Times*, February 21, 1962, 20.

39. Transcript of communications between *Friendship 7* and Cape Canaveral, February 20, 1962, 62, Box 65, Mercury Program—Subject Files—Friendship 7, Space Flight, MA-6, Air/Ground Communications Transcript, released February 27, 1962, Glenn Archives.

40. Transcript of communications between *Friendship 7* and Cape Canaveral, February 20, 1962, 25.

41. Transcript of communications between *Friendship 7* and Cape Canaveral, February 20, 1962, 87.

42. Glenn with Taylor, *John Glenn*, 270.

43. Quoted in "Was Glenn Rescued from Dire Danger?," *New York Herald Tribune*, February 21, 1962, 6.

44. Transcript of communications between *Friendship 7* and Cape Canaveral, February 20, 1962, 102.

45. Note from Friendship 7 press pool, February 20, 1962, Box 66, Mercury Program—Subject Files—Friendship 7 Space Flight, MA-6, U.S. Information Agency Releases and Statements, 1962, Glenn Archives.

46. Memorandum for NASA's Administrator, Deputy Administrator, Associate Administrator regarding MA-6 Contingencies, January 16, 1962, with attached notes by JHG and his draft of letter to family in case of Friendship 7 Flight failure, Box 47.1, Mercury Program—Subject Files—Friendship 7 Space Flight, MA-6, Glenn Archives.

47. Memorandum for NASA's Administrator, January 16, 1962.

48. Memorandum for NASA's Administrator, January 16, 1962.

49. Memorandum for NASA's Administrator, January 16, 1962.

50. Carpenter et al., *We Seven*, 437.

51. Walter W. Powers to Col. John Glenn, July 4, 1963, Box 24, Fan Mail—Book Consideration—Investment, Endorsements, Other Proposals, 1962–64, Glenn Archives.

52. John H. Glenn Jr., Lt. Colonel, USMC, NASA Astronaut, to Walter W. Powers, January 15, 1964, Box 24, Fan Mail—Book Consideration—Investment, Endorsements, Other Proposals, 1962–64, Glenn Archives.

53. John H. Glenn Jr., Lt. Colonel, USMC, NASA Astronaut, to Harold Rosner, June 19, 1963, Box 24, Fan Mail—Book Consideration—Investment, Endorsements, Other Proposals, 1962–64, Glenn Archives.

54. Harold Rosner to John H. Glenn Jr., Lt. Colonel, USMC, NASA Astronaut, August 30, 1963, Box 24, Fan Mail—Book Consideration—Investment, Endorsements, Other Proposals, 1962–64, Glenn Archives.

55. Robert E. Engwer to Colonel John H. Glenn Jr., March 27, 1962, Box 25, Fan Mail—Book Consideration—Schools Named After John Glenn, Streets Named After John Glenn, 1962–63, Glenn Archives.

56. "Warrant of Arrest," Commonwealth of Virginia, Arlington County, Box 19, JHG Personal—Correspondence—Family, Friends, and VIPs, February 1962, Glenn Archives.

57. Tina Privitera, telephone interview by author, May 11, 2016.

58. Nancy Napier Cain, telephone interview by author, May 17, 2016.

59. Marj Bryan, telephone interview by author, February 18, 2019.

60. Richard Gordin, telephone interview by author, January 23, 2017.

3. SHOOTING 'EM DOWN

1. Fred Hofheinz, telephone interview by author, May 24, 2016.

2. "Joe Medwick," National Baseball Hall of Fame and Museum, https://baseballhall.org/hall-of-famers/medwick-joe.

3. B. Brown and Acosta, *Houston Astros*, 13.

4. Titchener, *George Kirksey Story*, 72.

5. Titchener, *George Kirksey Story*, 74.

6. Ray, *Grand Huckster*, 258.

7. Titchener, *George Kirksey Story*, 76.

8. Titchener, *George Kirksey Story*, 76.

9. Houston Sports Association press release, 1958 (no specific date), Folder 15, HSA-Continental League, 1959–62, Box 8, George Kirksey Papers, University of Houston Libraries, Houston TX.

10. Hofheinz, telephone interview.

11. Dinn Mann, email to author, March 9, 2019.

12. Hofheinz, telephone interview.

13. Bob Aspromonte, telephone interview by author, June 29, 2016.

14. Martin's persona as a happy-go-lucky boozer was largely fictional, however.

15. Mickey Herskowitz, "Colts' Bob Aspromonte Favorite of the Ladies," *Houston Post*, February 1, 1962, sec. 4, 1.

16. Al Thomy, "Most Eligible Bachelor . . . How about Aspro?," *The Sporting News*, July 12, 1969, 15.

17. Quoted in Thomy, "Most Eligible Bachelor," 15.

18. Quoted in Thomy, "Most Eligible Bachelor," 15.

19. John Wilson, "Aspro or Young Billy: Who's Helping Whom?," *Houston Chronicle*, July 27, 1963, sec. 1, 4.

20. Quoted in Oscar Larnce, "Mejias of Waco Batting .345 for Pirate Farm Club," *The Sporting News*, August 11, 1954, 35.

21. Quoted in Larnce, "Mejias of Waco."

22. Quoted in Mickey Herskowitz, ".45s Charge Puny Attack with Missile Man Mejias," *The Sporting News*, June 2, 1962, 23.

23. Quoted in Les Biederman, "Mejias Disappointed at Being Passed Up for All-Star Game," *Pittsburgh Press*, July 15, 1962, 63.

24. Quoted in Zarko Franks, "Mejias' Season of Milk, Honey?," *Houston Chronicle*, May 30, 1962, sec. 8, 1.

25. Hy Hurwitz, "Reunion of Mejias, Kin Due to Efforts of Sox," *Boston Globe*, March 17, 1963, 81.

26. Frank Finch, "Break for Dumbo: Norm Larker Looks Forward to Steady Employment in Houston," *Los Angeles Times*, January 7, 1962, L5.

27. Bob Hunter, "Ump Bump Costly: Larker Fined, 'Out' One Day," *Los Angeles Examiner*, August 5, 1960, sec. 4, 3; Mickey Herskowitz, "A Nieman Scholar Made Non-Catch That Cost Larker '60 Batting Title," *Houston Post*, May 14, 1962, sec. 4, 2; Cleon Walfoort, "Larker Sets Bat Throwing Record with Underhand Style from Dugout," *Milwaukee Journal*, August 2, 1962, 13.

28. "Larker Has Temper, Ulcer, 'Dumbo' for a Nickname," *Milwaukee Journal*, March 31, 1963, Sports sec., 3.

29. Dick Peebles, "Didn't Need Crystal Ball," *Houston Chronicle*, October 18, 1961, sec. 7, 1.

30. Quoted in Herskowitz, "Nieman Scholar Made Non-Catch," sec. 4, 2.

31. Walfoort, "Larker Sets Bat Throwing Record," 13.

32. Bob Hunter, "EXCLUSIVE: Dodger Stars Wills, Larker in 'Shushed' Fist Fight," *Los Angeles Examiner*, June 22, 1961, sec. 4, 1.

33. Quoted in Associated Press, "Unrecognized as Star, Complaint of Reds' Little Johnny Temple," *Cincinnati Enquirer*, March 17, 1957, 67.

34. Quoted in Associated Press, "Unrecognized as Star," 67.

35. Cincinnati Baseball Club press release, 1952, Johnny Temple File, A. Bartlett Giamatti Research Center, National Baseball Hall of Fame and Museum, Cooperstown NY (hereafter, Giamatti Center, Baseball Hall of Fame).

36. Quoted in Gayle Talbot, Associated Press, "Tebbetts Likes Reds' John Temple: 'Toughest Monkey,'" *Charlotte (NC) News*, March 26, 1954, 7B.

37. All quoted in "One Error Brings on Another—Temple Takes Sock at Scorer," *The Sporting News*, July 3, 1957, 6.

38. Quoted in Mickey Herskowitz, "Johnny Temple Instills Pride in Colt Rejects," *Houston Post*, September 2, 1962, sec. 4, 2.

39. Dick Forbes, "Johnny in Tears: Temple Sobs over Phone—'Never Understand Why It Was Me,'" *Cincinnati Enquirer*, December 17, 1959, 51.

40. Forbes, "Johnny in Tears," 51.

41. Johnny Temple, "Temple Traded for 3 Players: Johnny-on-the-Spot Says Farewell to Fans," *Cincinnati Post and Times-Star*, December 16, 1959, 1.

42. Clark Nealon, "Temple's Tip: 'Watch Colts Rise on Air-Tight Twirling,'" *The Sporting News*, March 23, 1963, 26.

43. Cook, *Johnny Temple*, 161.

44. Quoted in Earl Lawson, "Temple, Otero Fight in Reds Clubhouse," *Cincinnati Post and Times-Star*, August 29, 1964, 1.

45. Dan Hafner, "Farrell Dunks Larker in Pool—Wow!," *Los Angeles Examiner*, July 25, 1961, sec. 4, 1.

46. "Publications: A Frolic with Farrell," *The Sporting News*, June 8, 1963, 28.

47. Quoted in Mickey Herskowitz, "Dick Farrell: A Guy Has Got to Grow Up," *Sport*, October 1964, 108.

48. Larry Merchant, "Losing 20 Games Isn't Easy," *Saturday Evening Post*, June 8, 1963, 58.

49. Quoted in Herskowitz, "Dick Farrell," 107.

50. Wells Twombly, "Swinger after 30," *Houston Chronicle*, May 10, 1967, sec. 7, 4.

51. Quoted in Jack Agness, "Bonus Boy Looks So Good GM Richards Is Undecided," *Houston Post*, June 27, 1962, sec. 4, 2.

52. Quoted in "Craft Stays with Erring Bonus Boy," *Houston Post*, July 8, 1962, sec. 4, 5.

53. Zarko Franks, "Bob Lillis Most Aggressive Colt .45," *Houston Chronicle*, June 3, 1962, sec. 8, 3.

54. Quoted in Franks, "Bob Lillis Most Aggressive Colt .45," sec. 8, 3.

55. Quoted in Mickey Herskowitz, "Lillis Credits Swat Spurt to 'Good Deal,'" *The Sporting News*, February 9, 1963, 3.

56. Quoted in "Astros Tab Lillis Manager," Houston Astros press release, November 2, 1982, Bob Lillis File, Giamatti Center, Baseball Hall of Fame.

57. Quoted in Gary Ronberg, "Baseball: Houston's Boy Is Now a Man," *Sports Illustrated*, August 14, 1967, 54.

58. Bob Dellinger, "Return of Rusty: Staub Rides Hot Bat Back to .45s," *The Sporting News*, September 19, 1964, 27.

59. Quoted in Dellinger, "Return of Rusty," 27.

60. Quoted in Houston Colt .45s Baseball Club press release, January 20, 1962, Harry Craft File, Giamatti Center, Baseball Hall of Fame.

61. Quoted in Houston Colt .45s press release, January 20, 1962.

62. Quoted in Houston Colt .45s press release, January 20, 1962.

63. Mike Acosta, "Rain or Shine: How Houston Developed Space City Baseball," *Houston History Magazine*, Summer 2009, 22, https://houstonhistorymagazine.org/wp-content

/uploads/2011/01/acosta-astros2.pdf. Season ticket holders could pay for membership to the Fast Draw Club, a "Wild West–style saloon" (22–23).

64. Dinn Mann, interview by author, New York NY, March 4, 2019.

65. Thomas Schlamme, interview by author, New York NY, April 3, 2017.

66. Bill Ford, "Foundation Approves Sale of Reds," *Cincinnati Enquirer*, March 24, 1962, 1. The article points out that DeWitt and his brother owned more than half the stock in the Browns before selling to Bill Veeck in 1951.

4. CHAVEZ RAVINE

1. Shakespeare, *Troilus and Cressida*, 2.3.217. References are to act, scene, and line.

2. Associated Press, "O'Malley Tells Reasons for Moving," *Los Angeles Times*, October 9, 1957, C2.

3. Frank Finch, "Sale of Angels Spurs L.A. Big League Hopes," *Los Angeles Times*, February 22, 1957, 1.

4. Quoted in Finch, "Sale of Angels," 1.

5. H. C. McClellan, "McClellan Tells 'Full Truth' of Dodgers' Coming to L.A.," *Los Angeles Times*, August 25, 1963, J1.

6. McCue, *Mover and Shaker*, 199.

7. "Chavez Ravine Family Evicted; Melee Erupts," *Los Angeles Times*, May 9, 1959, 1.

8. Podair, *City of Dreams*, 224.

9. Jack McCurdy, "Half the Fun Is Going There," *Los Angeles Times*, April 8, 1962, SF12.

10. Al Wolf, "Tight Squeeze, but Dodger Stadium's Ready," *Los Angeles Times*, April 8, 1962, C1.

11. Jim Murray, "Norrie's Nest?," *Los Angeles Times*, April 9, 1962, B1.

12. Brian Sidney Parrott, telephone interview by author, July 24, 2016. Cookie Lavagetto's hit in that game doomed Bevens's no-hitter.

13. Parrott, telephone interview.

14. F. Thompson with Rice, *Every Diamond Doesn't Sparkle*, 210.

15. Parrott, telephone interview.

16. Bill Becker, "Wills: A Young Man in a Hurry," *New York Times*, September 9, 1962, 204.

17. Quoted in Jimmy Cannon, "Sports Today: Wills . . . the Good Thief," *New York Journal-American*, April 7, 1963, 48-I.

18. Maury Wills, telephone interview by author, August 26, 2016.

19. For a few years there were two All-Star Games each summer. In 1962 the first was held in Washington DC. Chicago hosted the second game, which the American League won 9–4.

20. Quoted in Jimmy Powers, "The Powerhouse" (column), *New York Daily News*, August 24, 1962, 17C.

21. Quoted in Powers, "The Powerhouse," 17C.

22. Quoted in Frank Finch, "Here's the Pitch: Stardom Seen for Tom Davis," *Los Angeles Times*, April 1, 1959, C2.

23. Bob Johnson, "Bragan Tabs Davis Future Dodger Dandy," *The Sporting News*, August 19, 1959, 29.

24. Powers, "The Powerhouse," 17C.

25. Quoted in Bob Hunter, "D Stands for Davis, Dodgers—and Dynamite," *The Sporting News*, December 22, 1962, 5.

26. Sid Ziff, "Fans Cool to Hero," *Los Angeles Times*, August 3, 1962, B3.

27. Quoted in Ziff, "Fans Cool to Hero," B3.

28. Quoted in Huston Horn, "Ex-Bad Boy's Big Year," *Sports Illustrated*, August 20, 1962, 26. Scott responded, "Nonsense. My mother is like all the rest, and by that I mean you can never trust them when they start talking about how good their boys are" (26).

29. Quoted in Vincent X. Flaherty, "Drysdale: He Makes Good," *Los Angeles Examiner*, January 23, 1958, sec. 4, 1. (This article was part of an *Examiner* series called "Here Are the Dodgers.")

30. Quoted in Al Stump, "Headhunter with a Horsehide," *True*, May 1960, 98.

31. Drysdale with Verdi, *Once a Bum, Always a Dodger*, 180.

32. Quoted in Stump, "Headhunter with a Horsehide," 98.

33. Flaherty, "Drysdale," sec. 4, 1.

34. Kelly Drysdale, telephone interview by author, August 27, 2016.

35. Pedro Gonzalez batted .371 with the Modesto Reds in seventy-eight games and 318 at bats, but that was not enough to qualify for the batting title because he did not have enough at bats. Chris R. Lampe, email to author, February 11, 2019.

36. The statistics are from the Baseball Reference website, https://www.baseball-reference.com/. A biographical sheet for Davis at the Hall of Fame indicates different numbers for the 1960 season: runs (125), batting average (.347), triples (25), stolen bases (29), and total bases (344). It also says that 7 of Davis's 12 home runs were inside-the-park-home runs. Willie Davis, Biographical Sheet, Giamatti Center, Baseball Hall of Fame.

37. Quoted in Joe Donnelly, "Ron Perranoski: A Study in Confidence," *Sport*, November 1963, 67.

38. Quoted in Donnelly, "Ron Perranoski," 67.

39. "Eye Witness Measures Off Howard's Homer at 550 Ft.," *Los Angeles Times*, May 26, 1960, C1.

40. Quoted in Roscoe McGowen, "Gilliam Shifts into Second—Jackie Pulls Up at Third," *The Sporting News*, March 25, 1953, 17.

41. Quoted in McGowen, "Gilliam Shifts into Second," 17. "Charley" refers to Charlie Dressen, the Dodgers' manager from 1951 to 1953.

42. Quoted in McGowen, "Gilliam Shifts into Second," 17.

43. Quoted in McGowen, "Gilliam Shifts into Second," 17.

44. Quoted in McGowen, "Gilliam Shifts into Second," 17.

45. Quoted in Sid Ziff, "Gilliam for MVP?," *Los Angeles Times*, September 8, 1963, J3.

46. Quoted in United Press International, "One Final Good-Bye to Jim Gilliam," *Santa Rosa (CA) Press-Democrat*, October 12, 1978, 51.

47. "Brooks Sign Koufax, Pitching Star at UC," *Cincinnati Enquirer*, December 15, 1954, 30.

48. Sandy Koufax as told to Milton Gross, "I'm Only Human," *Look*, December 1963, 52.

49. Koufax as told to Gross, "I'm Only Human," 52.

50. Quoted in Ross Newhan, "Koufax Makes Hall with Record Vote," *Los Angeles Times*, January 20, 1972, E1.

51. Quoted in Newhan, "Koufax Makes Hall with Record Vote," E1.

52. Snider with Gilbert, *Duke of Flatbush*, 198.

53. Alston with Tobin, *Year at a Time*, 168.

54. Quoted in Mal Mallette, "Boss Man of the Bums," *Saturday Evening Post*, August 17, 1957, 69.

55. Kim Ogle, telephone interview by author, August 4, 2016.

56. Quoted in "Reaching for the Stars: 1955–April 20, 1961," in Becker, Stein, and the HistoryLink Staff, *Future Remembered*, 13.

57. Robert S. Bird, "Fairest of Fairs at Seattle, but a Crash Darkens Day," *New York Herald Tribune*, April 22, 1962, 4.

58. "Special Coverage of the World's Fair," KING-TV, April 21, 1962, https://www.youtube.com/watch?v=lXqQejclKdI.

59. "Special Coverage of the World's Fair."

60. Remarks of Danny Kaye, in "Special Coverage of the World's Fair."

61. "Special Coverage of the World's Fair."

62. Joe Hyams, "Seattle: Plenty of Culture—and, Oh Yes, Girls," *New York Herald Tribune*, April 22, 1962, 4.

63. Vincent Price, "The Wonderful Life of the Eye," Souvenir Program, Seattle World's Fair 1962, Century 21 Exposition, 40, personal collection of the author.

64. Emmett Watson, "The Lively, Lovely Pacific Northwest," Souvenir Program, Seattle World's Fair, Century 21 Exposition, 74, personal collection of the author.

65. Associated Press, "2 Die as Plane Crashes in Aerial Salute to Fair," *Los Angeles Times*, April 22, 1962, 8.

66. National Security Action Memorandum No. 144, April 11, 1962, Box 307a—Space Activities General, April 1962–May 1962, National Security Files, JFK Library.

67. Lyon, *Perry Mason*, season 5, episode 25.

5. *AURORA 7*, WHERE ARE YOU?

1. Sweson, Grimwood, and Alexander, *This New Ocean*, 455–56.

2. Associated Press, "'Darned Near Cried,' Rescue Pilot Says," *Bridgeport (CT) Telegram*, May 25, 1962, 10.

3. *What's My Line?*, season 13, episode 37, aired May 27, 1962, on CBS. A little more than four months later, Carson debuted as the host of *The Tonight Show*, a post he held for thirty years.

4. Quoted in Carpenter and Stoever, *For Spacious Skies*, 303.

5. Kranz, *Failure Is Not an Option*, 91.

6. Marvin Miles, "Spaceman's Saga: Astronaut Saved from Atlantic after Missing Pickup Location," *Los Angeles Times*, May 25, 1962, 1.

7. Quoted in Lennick, *Rocket Science*, in the episode titled "Missiles to the Moon."

8. Carpenter et al., *We Seven*, 53. "Orders to O-05" meant the U.S. Navy's active duty personnel office at the Pentagon.

9. Carpenter and Stoever, *For Spacious Skies*, 164.

10. Carpenter et al., *We Seven*, 56.

11. Carpenter et al., *We Seven*, 57.

12. Kris Stoever, email to author, March 8, 2019.

13. Stoever, email.

14. Richard Witkin, "Carpenter Orbit Off to Thursday," *New York Times*, May 20, 1962, 41. There were four postponements of Carpenter's flight. "This gives me more time to bone up on the flight plan," said Carpenter about the latest delay. Quoted in Witkin, "Carpenter Orbit Off," 41.

15. Gay Talese, "'Space Comics' Cheer Astronauts," *New York Times*, May 24, 1962, 14.

16. Carpenter and Stoever, *For Spacious Skies*, 265.

17. Quoted in Associated Press, "Ex-hurler Bo Belinsky Dead at 64," *New York Post*, November 27, 2001, 42.

18. Quoted in Al Wolf, "Champagne Fails to Make Hit with Belinsky," *Los Angeles Times*, May 7, 1962, B1.

19. Quoted in Charles Maher, "'It Couldn't Happen to Nicer Team'—Bo," *Los Angeles Times*, May 6, 1962, G4.

20. "No-Hit Ball Worth $1,060 to Belinsky," *Los Angeles Times*, May 10, 1962, B2.

21. Satenstein, *Stage Show*, season 2, episode 18; Bleyer and Kiley, *Ed Sullivan Show*, season 17, episode 19. *Stage Show* was a comedy-variety show hosted by renowned bandleader brothers Jimmy and Tommy Dorsey.

22. Dick Cavett, "You Gave Away Your Babies?," *Opinionator—A Gathering of Opinion from around the Web* (blog), *New York Times*, June 8, 2012, https://opinionator.blogs.nytimes.com/2012/06/08/you-gave-away-your-babies/.

23. Quoted in Karen Abbott, "Bombshells Away," *Salon*, July 19, 2000, https://www.salong.com/2000/07/19/mamie/.

24. Quoted in Richard Goldstein, "Bo Belinsky, 64, the Playboy Pitcher, Dies," *New York Times*, November 27, 2001, D6.

25. Quoted in Myron Cope, "A Dialogue between Baseball's Bigmouths," *True*, August 1965, 56.

26. Quoted in Pat Jordan, "Once He Was an Angel," *Sports Illustrated*, March 6, 1972, 79.

27. Quoted in Maury Allen, "Bo Belinsky Reveals: How I Won and Lost Hollywood's Sexiest Stars," *Sports Today*, October 1973, 22.

28. Allen, "Bo Belinsky Reveals," 22.

29. Quoted in Allen, "Bo Belinsky Reveals," 22.

30. Allen, "Bo Belinsky Reveals," 22.

31. Quoted in Allen, "Bo Belinsky Reveals," 22.

32. Quoted in Cope, "Dialogue between Baseball's Bigmouths," 31.

33. Quoted in Cope, "Dialogue between Baseball's Bigmouths," 56.

34. Quoted in Allen, *Bo*, 92.

35. Quoted in Allen, *Bo*, 92.

36. Quoted in Harley Tinkham, "Belinsky Challenged by S.D. Sportscaster: Did Bo Run Away from Fight?," *Los Angeles Herald-Examiner*, September 9, 1966, D-1.

37. Quoted in Tinkham, "Belinsky Challenged by S.D. Sportscaster," D-1.

38. Quoted in Harley Tinkham, "Bo Just Laughs Off S.D. 'Fight,'" *Los Angeles Herald-Examiner*, September 10, 1966, C-1.

39. Quoted in "Angels Suspend Belinsky after Fight with Writer," *Washington Post*, August 15, 1964, D1.

40. Paul Zimmerman, "Belinsky May Get His Wish," *Los Angeles Times*, August 16, 1964, C2.

41. Braven Dyer, "Bo Hedges on Plan to Give Up Baseball," *Los Angeles Times*, August 14, 1964, B5, quoting Charles Maher, Associated Press, August 13, 1964.

42. Zimmerman, "Belinsky May Get His Wish."

43. Jim Murray, "Bo as in 'Bo,'" *Los Angeles Times*, August 18, 1964, B1.

44. "Autry Glad Nobody Hurt as Fire Razes Ranch," *Los Angeles Times*, August 29, 1962, 18.

45. Don Richardson, telephone interview by author, August 27, 2016.

46. Jo Ann Abajian, telephone interview by author, August 26, 2016.

47. Tyler Corder, telephone interview by author, August 17, 2016.

48. Quoted in Si Burick, "Si-ings: Bo Belinsky's Philosophy," *Dayton (OH) Daily News*, March 23, 1970, 10.

49. Quoted in Si Burick, "Si-ings: One-Time Playboy Belinsky Literally Hungry for Job," *Dayton (OH) Daily News*, April 9, 1970, 20.

50. Quoted in Bob Hertzel, "Relaxed Man in the Bullpen," *Cincinnati Enquirer*, April 9, 1970, 51.

51. Quoted in Ritter Collett, "Belinsky Shipped Out," *Dayton (OH) Journal Herald*, May 20, 1970, 19.

52. "Tourists Add Bo Belinsky to Hill Staff," *Asheville Citizen-Times*, August 19, 1970, 19.

53. Quoted in Chris Foster, "Bad Boy Bo Gets Better," *Los Angeles Times*, July 2, 1992, 224.

54. Richardson, telephone interview.

6. MEETING THE METS

1. David Dempsey, "Says Mrs. Payson of the Mets, 'You Can't Lose Them All,'" *New York Times Magazine*, June 23, 1968, 30–31.

2. Robert Shaplen, "How to Build a Ball Club," *Sports Illustrated*, March 5, 1962, 42.

3. Shaplen, "How to Build a Ball Club," 44.

4. Dan Daniel, "Over the Fence: New York and the National League," *The Sporting News*, October 23, 1957, 12.

5. Koppett, *New York Mets*, 73.

6. Thomas Constance, interview by author, New York NY, February 24, 2017.

7. Drysdale with Verdi, *Once a Bum, Always a Dodger*, 8.

8. Quoted in Frank Finch, "24 Losses? 'A Good Season,' Chirps Craig," *The Sporting News*, January 5, 1963, 3.

9. Quoted in Finch, "24 Losses?," 3.

10. Quoted in Scott Miller, "Winning with Jackie, Losing with Casey Part of Craig's Charmed Life," CBS Sports Digital, May 28, 2013 (no longer available).

11. Quoted in Phil Pepe, "For Little Al: No Tears at All," *New York World-Telegram and Sun*, August 15, 1962, 32.

12. Quoted in Rich Marazzi, "One of the Original Mets: Al Jackson," *Sports Collectors Digest*, September 1, 2000, 71.

13. Quoted in Jack Mann, "Kanehl's on Hill of Small Success," *New York Newsday*, June 2, 1962, 37.

14. Mann, "Kanehl's on Hill of Small Success," 37.

15. Richard Goldstein, "Rod Kanehl, 70, an Original Met, Is Dead," *New York Times*, December 31, 2004, A25.

16. Quoted in Golenbock, *Amazin'*, 132–33.

17. Quoted in Leonard Shecter, "Can't Anyone Here Use Kanehl?," *Sports Illustrated*, August 8, 1966, 61.

18. Stan Isaacs, "Out of Left Field: Manager Kanehl? It's Very Possible," *New York Newsday*, June 3, 1964, 50C.

19. Stan Isaacs, "Out of Left Field: Will Rod Kanehl Touch All Bases?," *New York Newsday*, August 22, 1962, 17C.

20. Cliff Cook, Biographical Sheet, Giamatti Center, Baseball Hall of Fame.

21. The 1962 Mets had two pitchers named Bob Miller. The one referenced here was Robert Gerald Miller.

22. Quoted in George Vecsey, "Maybe the New Cliff Cook Can Earn a Job," *New York Newsday*, March 15, 1963, 29C.

23. Quoted in Vecsey, "Maybe the New Cliff Cook Can Earn a Job," 29C.

24. Quoted in Rick Firfer, "'Lefty' Bob Miller: From Pitcher to Philanthropist," *Sports Collectors Digest*, December 31, 1999, 110.

25. Quoted in Walt Daley, "Softball to Majors Breeze for Thomas," *San Francisco Call*, May 6, 1958, 24.

26. Quoted in Joe Donnelly, "Inside the Frank Thomas Comeback," *Sport*, January 1962, 46.

27. Harry T. Paxton, "That House Where the Ballplayers Live," *Saturday Evening Post*, September 10, 1949, 36.

28. Joe King, "Ashburn's Glove Could Save Mets in Polo Grounds," *The Sporting News*, February 14, 1962, 26.

29. Howard M. Tuckner, "Show of Courage by Ashburn Marks Mets' Double Setback," *New York Times*, September 4, 1962, 40.

30. Quoted in Steve Jacobson, "Stengel Picks Chacon—but Takes Mantilla," *New York Newsday*, April 3, 1962, 17C.

31. Quoted in Associated Press, "Crestfallen Mantilla Says He Was Off Balance," *New York Herald Tribune*, September 30, 1959, B2.

32. Quoted in Associated Press, "Crestfallen Mantilla Says He Was Off Balance," B2.

33. Tom Meany, "Big Galoot from Vinegar Bend," *Collier's*, May 11, 1956, 70.

34. Stan Isaacs, "A Newsday Profile: Thinking Man's Pitcher," *New York Newsday*, April 24, 1962, 44.

35. Steve Jacobson, "Hook Just Can't Be This Awful," *New York Newsday*, June 18, 1963, 48C.

36. Jay Hook, telephone interview by author, July 26, 2016.

37. Cincinnati Reds Scouting Report, Hobart Neal Landrith, 1951, Hobie Landrith File, Giamatti Center, Baseball Hall of Fame.

38. Robert Lipsyte, "Mets Drop Jones, Buy Throneberry," *New York Times*, May 10, 1962, 45.

39. George Vecsey, "On Baseball: Marv Was Indeed Marvelous, His Own Way," *New York Times*, June 26, 1994, F11.

40. Quoted in Maury Allen, "Ed Kranepool: Mine Enemies Grow Older," *Jock*, May–June 1970, 94.

41. Michael Iachetta, "Diamonds Are a Boy's Best Friend," *New York Sunday News*, May 12, 1963, 76.

42. Quoted in Irene Janowicz, "Woman in the Family," *New York Mirror*, April 28, 1963, 72.

43. Quoted in Janowicz, "Woman in the Family," 72.

44. Quoted in Ross Forman, "Clem Labine: Former Hurler Recalls His Days in the Majors," *Sports Collectors Digest*, December 6, 1991, 54.

45. Quoted in Forman, "Clem Labine," 54.

46. Quoted in Maury Allen, "Roadblock Jones: Simply Amazin'," *New York Post*, April 13, 1982, 62.

47. Ken MacKenzie, "My Life as a Fringe Player," *Sport*, May 1965, 41.

48. MacKenzie, "My Life as a Fringe Player," 43.

49. Quoted in Roy McHugh, "The Press Box: On the Fringe as a Baseball Literary Lion," *Pittsburgh Press*, June 11, 1965, 34.

50. Quoted in Larry Fox, "Mets' Hunter Wins 2 in Day," *New York World-Telegram and Sun*, August 24, 1964, 13.

51. Quoted in Fluffy Saccucci, "Craig Anderson, an 'Original Met' Pitcher," *Sports Collectors Digest*, December 3, 1993, 150.

52. Quoted in Saccucci, "Craig Anderson, an 'Original Met' Pitcher," 150.

53. Bob Wolf, "Braves Go High for Badger Star—Bonus Estimates Hit 100 Grand," *The Sporting News*, June 5, 1957, 27.

54. Barney Kremenko, "Smith's Bat Lands Met Job," *New York Journal-American*, April 6, 1962, 33.

55. Quoted in Associated Press, "Top Rookie Bouchee Faces Morals Count," *Centralia (WA) Daily Chronicle*, January 18, 1958, 8.

56. Quoted in Associated Press, "Ed Bouchee Says Guilty to Charges," *Centralia (WA) Daily Chronicle*, February 21, 1958, 4.

57. Associated Press, "Ed Bouchee Is Committed," *Centralia (WA) Daily Chronicle*, March 7, 1958, 5.

58. Associated Press, "Phillies to Start Bouchee at First Base on Thursday," *Centralia (WA) Daily Chronicle*, July 2, 1958, 4.

59. Quoted in Arthur Daley, "Sports of the Times: For Whom the Bell Tolls," *New York Times*, March 29, 1955, 35.

60. "Taylor Says He'll Quit If Not Traded," *Chicago Daily Tribune*, April 25, 1962, C1.

61. Ed McAuley, "Three-Time Bat King in Minors, Woodling Sprouts as Tribe Prize," *The Sporting News*, March 21, 1946, 9.

62. Barney Kremenko, "Gene Blows Top; Explosion Knocks Him Out of Met Job," *The Sporting News*, March 16, 1963, 30.

63. Quoted in David Condon, "In the Wake of the News: Hickman's Roots Quite a Story, Too," *Chicago Tribune*, March 13, 1977, B4.

64. "The Old Mets? Only Hickman Qualifies," *New York Times*, April 16, 1966, 51.

65. Dan Daniel, "Weiss Has Cash, Can't Spend It," *New York World-Telegram and Sun*, December 18, 1961, 27.

66. Chris Cannizzaro, Biographical Sheet, Giamatti Center, Baseball Hall of Fame.

67. Quoted in Robert Markus, "Sports Trail: Who Is the First Met Who, and Who?," *Chicago Tribune*, July 4, 1968, G3.

68. George Vecsey, telephone interview by author, January 20, 2019.

69. L. Nelson, *Hello Everybody, I'm Lindsey Nelson*, 277.

70. Harold Rosenthal, "Koufax No-Hits Mets, 5–0, Fans 13," *New York Herald Tribune*, July 1, 1962, B1.

71. Graham, *Route 66*, season 2, episode 32.

7. THE BEST SECOND-PLACE TEAM

1. "Matt and John Talk about Sports, Politics, and Interracial Marriage," in Kramer, *Guess Who's Coming to Dinner*.

2. Quoted in Joe David Brown, "'The Onliest Way I Know,'" *Sports Illustrated*, April 13, 1959, 133.

3. "'Best Arm in Baseball,' That's Junior Mays at 19," *New York World-Telegram and Sun*, March 21, 1951, 44.

4. Quoted in Barney Kremenko, "The Willie Mays Story: It Was 'Love' at First Sight for Willie and Leo," *New York Journal-American*, June 29, 1954, 20. This article was the third in a series of six articles on Mays, described as the new "Wonder Boy."

5. Quoted in Kremenko, "Willie Mays Story," 20.

6. Quoted in Milton Gross, "Speaking Out," *New York Post*, July 3, 1951, 35.

7. Bill Corum, "Sports: Everybody Called Him Willie," *New York Journal-American*, May 22, 1952, 26.

8. Quoted in Milton Gross, "A Visit with Willie Mays," *Saturday Evening Post*, May 20, 1961, 68.

9. Jack McDonald, "Giant Ticket Rush Overshadows Small Draw by Mays in 'Frisco," *The Sporting News*, November 13, 1957, 7.

10. "Seals' Last-Out Ball Put in Shrine," *The Sporting News*, November 13, 1957, 7. The ball remains in the Hall of Fame's collection.

11. Bob Stevens, "'Gotta Learn to Play Center All Over at Seals' Park'—Willie," *The Sporting News*, November 13, 1957, 7.

12. Quoted in Dick Friendlich, "Did Mays Top 1954 Series Catch?," *San Francisco Chronicle*, May 18, 1961, 39.

13. Bob Hunter, "Mays Catch in Ravine Better Than '54 Series," *Los Angeles Herald-Examiner*, August 25, 1964, C-1.

14. Willie Mays, interview by Bob Costas, *Costas Now*, aired May 2, 2006, on HBO, available at https://www.youtube.com/watch?v=Rpkco2rHsKc.

15. John Drebinger, "Giants Beat Mets, 7–1, 6–5; Players, Coaches and Umpires Fight on Field," *New York Times*, May 28, 1962, 35.

16. Quoted in Sam Whiting, "Willie McCovey Recalls '62 Series—50 Years Ago," *SF Gate*, March 25, 2012, http://www.sfgate.com/giants/article/Willie-McCovey-recalls-62-Series-50-years-ago-3432936.php.

17. Quoted in Nick Peters, "From Mobile . . . to Cooperstown," *The Sporting News*, January 20, 1986, 42.

18. Quoted in Skip Myslenski, "Milwaukee Jelled When This Winner Came," *Chicago Tribune*, October 3, 1982, C1.

19. "Kuenn Gets Rookie of the Year Award," *New York Herald Tribune*, December 15, 1953, 38.

20. Quoted in Associated Press, "Traded 140 Singles for 42 Home Runs," *New York World-Telegram and Sun*, April 18, 1960, 22.

21. Quoted in Associated Press, "Traded 140 Singles for 42 Home Runs," 22.

22. Mrs. Ralph J. Dark, "My All-Star Son," *Guideposts*, May 1955, 11.

23. Quoted in Dick Young, "Players Pegging Dark as Peerless Pilot: Once Terrible Tempered, Skipper Al Speaks Softly Now; Mays Leads Cheering for Giant Leader," *The Sporting News*, May 24, 1961, 3.

24. Young, "Players Pegging Dark as Peerless Pilot," 3.

25. Quoted in Al Stump, "Alvin Dark: Missionary among Baseball's Heathens," *True*, August 1963, 81.

26. Quoted in Stump, "Alvin Dark," 82.

27. Quoted in Earl Lawson, "Baseball's Cockiest Star," *Saturday Evening Post*, May 24, 1958, 80.

28. Lawson, "Baseball's Cockiest Star," 79.

29. Cincinnati Reds Scouting Report on Ed Bailey, 1951, Ed Bailey File, Giamatti Center, Baseball Hall of Fame.

30. Quoted in Earl Lawson, "Baseball's Cockiest Star," 80.

31. "Haller Quits Illinois for Giants," *Chicago Daily Tribune*, February 27, 1958, D3.

32. Quoted in Bob Stevens, "Digger Big Gem in Giant Dark Age: O'Dell Found Winning Key in Al's Plan for Steady Work," *The Sporting News*, June 22, 1963, 3.

33. Cepeda fared less well for the Salem Rebels in the Appalachian League; he batted .247 in twenty-six games in 1955.

34. Willie McCovey as told to Bruce Lee, "Why Do They Underrate Cepeda?," *Sport*, July 1964, 43.

35. McCovey as told to Lee, "Why Do They Underrate Cepeda?," 43.

36. Quoted in Milton Gross, "The Press Box: Cepeda Grows Up; He's Starting to Act Like a Team Man," *Pittsburgh Press*, July 2, 1961, 55.

37. Quoted in Bob Stevens, "Collegian Garibaldi Nabs Record Giants' Bonus of 150 Gees," *The Sporting News*, July 14, 1962, 9.

38. Quoted in Art Spander, "Bob Garibaldi's New Career," *San Francisco Chronicle*, July 6, 1973, 47.

39. Quoted in Arthur Daley, "Sports of the Times: The Hard-Luck Kid," *New York Times*, March 15, 1956, 51.

40. Quoted in Bob Stevens, "Little-Guy Pagan King-Size Spoke in Giants' Wheel," *The Sporting News*, September 8, 1962, 9.

41. Felipe Alou with Arnold Hano, "Latin-American Ballplayers Need a Bill of Rights," *Sport*, November 1963, 77.

42. Alou with Hano, "Latin-American Ballplayers Need a Bill of Rights," 76.

43. Alou with Hano, "Latin-American Ballplayers Need a Bill of Rights," 77.

44. Mike McCormick, telephone interview by author, October 30, 2017.

45. Quoted in Bob Stevens, "Davenport's Rare DP Pulls Stuffing from Phil Rally," *The Sporting News*, July 14, 1962, 9.

46. Gary Davenport, telephone interview by author, November 3, 2017.

47. Quoted in Art Spander, "Game Was Stoneham's Passion and Blind Spot," *The Sporting News*, January 22, 1990, 6.

48. Joe King, "Now It's Certain Giants Will Move after This Year," *The Sporting News*, July 24, 1957, 14.

49. Jack Walsh, "Three's Crowd in New York, Says Stoneham: Horace Blunt about Desire of Giants to Move to Coast," *The Sporting News*, July 24, 1957, 13.

50. Dan Daniel, "Hail-Fellow Horace Pegged as Perfect Host: Cordial Stoneham Marking 25th Year as Chief of Giants," *The Sporting News*, July 12, 1961, 7.

51. Quoted in Robert Shaplen, "The Lonely, Loyal Mr. Stoneham," *Sports Illustrated*, May 5, 1958, 76.

52. Shaplen, "Lonely, Loyal Mr. Stoneham," 72.

53. Shaplen, "Lonely, Loyal Mr. Stoneham," 72.

54. Quoted in Carl Steward, "Entering Hall, Simmons Feels Like Tourist," *Oakland Tribune*, July 25, 2004, Sports sec., 6.

55. Quoted in Jeff Vella, "Frick Winner Steals Show—Again," *Oneonta (NY) Daily Star*, July 26, 2004, Sports sec., 17.

56. Larry Wolters, "Cubs Leap to Europe from Wrigley Field," *Chicago Daily Tribune*, July 24, 1962, 2.

57. "NASA's Kennedy Space Center Celebrates 50th Anniversary July 1," NASA press release, June 29, 2012, https://www.nasa.gov/centers/kennedy/news/releases/2012/release-20120629.html.

58. Associated Press, "First Venus Shot Fails; New Try Set," *Washington Post*, July 23, 1962, A1.

59. Richard L. Coe, "One on the Aisle: Preminger Mounts Hill," *Washington Post*, June 7, 1962, B20.

60. Kenneth Killiany, telephone interview by author, July 2, 2018.

8. MISS SHERRI, MARY, AND MARILYN

1. Sherri Chessen, telephone interview by author, February 25, 2018.

2. Chessen, telephone interview.

3. Dorothy Kilgallen, "Sherri Finkbine Says 'I Won't Be Crusader,'" *Miami News*, September 6, 1962, 13.

4. Quoted in Myra MacPherson, "Some States Loosen Abortion Laws," *Arizona Republic*, December 28, 1968, 91.

5. Chessen, telephone interview.

6. [Name withheld] to Mary Early, February 11, 1958, Folder 6, Box 1, Series I, Mary Frances Early Papers, Richard B. Russell Library for Political Research and Studies, University of Georgia Libraries, Athens (hereafter, Early Papers, Russell Library).

7. Students for Passive Resistance, *A Proclamation*, 1961, Folder 2, Segregation-Universities, Box 9, Sub-series A, Series I, Early Papers, Russell Library.

8. Billy Dilworth, "Ga. University Admits 2 Negroes under Pressure of Federal Courts: Classes Expected to Function Today," *Anderson (SC) Independent*, January 11, 1961, 1.

9. Holmes et al. v. Danner, Civil Action No. 450, U.S. District Court, Middle District of Georgia (January 6, 1961), 11–12.

10. Holmes et al. v. Danner, 21.

11. Holmes et al. v. Danner, 21.

12. Holmes et al. v. Danner, 23.

13. Holmes et al. v. Danner, 27.

14. Holmes et al. v. Danner, 27.

15. Danner v. Holmes et al., U.S. Court of Appeals, Fifth Circuit, January 9, 1961.

16. "Text of Statement by Gov. Vandiver," *Atlanta Constitution*, January 14, 1961, 6.

17. Quoted in "University Student Tells Aims of Demonstrations," *Macon Telegraph*, January 13, 1961, 1.

18. Quoted in "University Student Tells Aims of Demonstrations," 1.

19. Mary Frances Early, letter to author, December 31, 2018.

20. Mary Frances Early, telephone interview by author, June 20, 2016.

21. University of Georgia background investigation on Mary Frances Early, April 25, 1961, Folder 3: Investigative Report, Box 3, Series II, Early Papers, Russell Library.

22. University of Georgia background investigation on Mary Frances Early.

23. Early, letter to author.

24. Early, letter to author.

25. Dorothy D. Elder to Mary Frances Early, February 19, 1962, with Early's handwritten notation thereon, Folder 6: Housing Issues, Box 3, Series II, Early Papers, Russell Library.

26. Dorothy D. Elder to Mary Frances Early, March 9, 1962, Folder 6: Housing Issues, Box 3, Series II, Early Papers, Russell Library. Early's handwriting is in the margin of the letter.

27. Mary Early, speech delivered at Turner High National Alumni Association gathering, March 27, 2004, Folder 61, Box 1, Series I, Early Papers, Russell Library.

28. Acquanetta Riley to Mary Early, October 25, 2004, Folder 30, Box 1, Series I, Early Papers, Russell Library.

29. Mary Frances Early, "What's a Computer Doing in My Music Room?," presentation at the On-Line with Education Conference, Georgia State University, March 17, 1988, Folder 56, Box 1, Series I, Early Papers, Russell Library.

30. Mary Frances Early, president, Georgia Music Educators Association, to Dr. Warner Rogers, Associate Superintendent of Schools, Atlanta, April 11, 1983, Folder 84, Box 1, Series I, Early Papers, Russell Library.

31. Mary Frances Early, "MENC Adviser," *Teaching Music* 9, no. 2 (October 2001); 9, no. 4 (February 2002); 10, no. 2 (October 2002); 10, no. 5 (April 2003); 11, no. 3 (December 2003); 11, no. 4 (February 2004); 12, no. 3 (December 2004); 12, no. 5 (April 2005), all in Folder 107, Box 1, Series I, Early Papers, Russell Library.

32. "Guitar Babies," *Newsweek*, July 28, 1969, Folder 121, Box 1, Series I, Early Papers, Russell Library.

33. Winfred Harris, Acting President, Clark College, to Mary Frances Early, January 28, 1988, Folder 65, Box 1, Series I, Early Papers, Russell Library.

34. Mary Frances Early, "Music for the Blind," May 14, 1962, Folder 21: Term Paper, EDC 712 (University of Georgia), Box 3, Series II, Early Papers, Russell Library.

35. Ruth H. Satterfield, Director, Staff Personnel Services, Atlanta Public Schools, to Mary F. Early, August 14, 1962, Folder 7, Box 1, Series I, Early Papers, Russell Library.

36. Alonzo A. Crim, Superintendent, Atlanta Public Schools, to Mary Frances Early, September 3, 1981, Folder 28, Box 1, Series I, Early Papers, Russell Library; Early, letter to author.

37. Early, letter to author.

38. Early, letter to author.

39. Quoted in Kay Gardella, "Hollywood Mourns for 'a Warm Human Being,'" *New York Daily News*, August 6, 1962, 4.

40. Quoted in "Film World Stunned by Death of a Queen," *New York Journal-American*, August 6, 1962, 3.

41. Earl Wilson, "MM: Pills and Despair," *New York Post*, August 6, 1962, 3.

42. Susan Griffiths, telephone interview by author, March 19, 2018.

43. James Gill, telephone interview by author, March 21, 2018.

9. PINSTRIPES

1. Tommy Holmes, "Yankees Win A.L. Pennant, Rip Nats, 8–3," *New York Herald Tribune*, September 26, 1962, 29.

2. Quoted in Charles Dexter, "Born to the Majors," *Baseball Digest*, October–November 1962, 70.

3. Russ Herron, "Series Star Tresh Solid Hit on Campus," *The Sporting News*, December 8, 1962, 3.

4. Quoted in Herron, "Series Star Tresh Solid Hit on Campus," 3.

5. Edward Linn, "Is He the Next Great Yankee?," *Saturday Evening Post*, June 7, 1958, 111.

6. Stan Isaacs, "Out of Left Field: The Greasy-Kid-Stuff Guys Got to Kubek," *New York Newsday*, March 6, 1963, 14.

7. Quoted in Isaacs, "Out of Left Field," 14.

8. Quoted in Harold Rosenthal, "Dream Comes True for Kubek as Yankee: He Always Hoped to Be in Stadium," *The Sporting News*, August 7, 1957, 3.

9. Quoted in Larry Fox, "Tresh Ready for Yanks, but Kubek's in the Way," *New York World-Telegram and Sun*, July 22, 1961, 14.

10. Quoted in Dan Daniel, "Tresh Certain He's It," *New York World-Telegram and Sun*, February 7, 1962, 34.

11. Quoted in Steve Jacobson, "Tresh 'Star' at Short; Or, at Least, He Was," *New York Newsday*, July 17, 1962, 20C.

12. Quoted in Phil Pepe, "'Too Early to Judge Tresh as a Shortstop,'" *New York World-Telegram and Sun*, August 10, 1962, 10.

13. Joe King, "Can Tresh Hit Enough to Stick in Outfield? Tom's on Spot with Kubek at Shortstop Again," *New York World-Telegram and Sun*, August 17, 1962, 22.

14. Tommy Holmes, "Yanks Sign Maris for $70,000—Raise of $32,500," *New York Herald Tribune*, February 27, 1962, 24.

15. Sid Gray, "Meet Mr. Ford—Pitcher" (first of a series), *New York Post*, August 28, 1961, 60.

16. Quoted in Dan Daniel, "'He-Needs-a-Rescuer' Rap Rankles Ford: Top Item on Yank Ace's Agenda—More Complete Games," *The Sporting News*, January 17, 1962, 3.

17. Richardson with Thomas, *Impact Player*, 5.

18. Quoted in Leonard Shecter, "Bobby Richardson's Drive for Respect," *Sport*, October 1964, 74.

19. Quoted in Steve Jacobson, "Bobby Talks Softly, Carries Big Stick," *New York Newsday*, March 25, 1961, 74.

20. Quoted in Shecter, "Bobby Richardson's Drive for Respect," 74.

21. Quoted in Shecter, "Bobby Richardson's Drive for Respect," 74.

22. Richardson with Thomas, *Impact Player*, 209.

23. Bobby Richardson, "Athletics and Life," *Decision*, June 1971, 3.

24. Leonard Shecter, "A New Role for Richardson," *New York Post*, June 4, 1962, 60.

25. Quoted in Shecter, "New Role for Richardson," 60.

26. Shecter, "New Role for Richardson," 60.

27. Sam Lacy, "How Yanks Treat Howard: Vicious Campaign Being Conducted," *Baltimore Afro-American*, March 20, 1954, 1.

28. Quoted in Steve Jacobson, "Hector Lopez: From First to Jobless," *New York Newsday*, June 9, 1970, 37.

29. Quoted in George Vecsey, "Hector Never Forgot How to Swing," *New York Newsday*, July 9, 1962, 17C.

30. Pepitone with Stainback, *Joe, You Coulda Made Us Proud*, 41.

31. Pepitone with Stainback, *Joe, You Coulda Made Us Proud*, 32.

32. Pepitone with Stainback, *Joe, You Coulda Made Us Proud*, 35.

33. Pepitone with Stainback, *Joe, You Coulda Made Us Proud*, 45.

34. Pepitone with Stainback, *Joe, You Coulda Made Us Proud*, 48.

35. "Newest Yank," *New York Daily News*, August 14, 1958, 62.

36. Quoted in Dave Rosenbloom, "Globetrotters Vie in Geneva Tonight," *Rochester (NY) Democrat and Chronicle*, November 5, 1958, 28.

37. John Lake, "Our Joe P. in Joe D's Footsteps," *Binghamton (NY) Press and Sun-Bulletin*, April 10, 1960, 44.

38. Lake, "Our Joe P. in Joe D's Footsteps," 44.

39. Quoted in Harry Grayson, "Yankee Farm Director Got Job through Newspaper Ad," *Orlando Evening Star*, June 25, 1960, 10-A.

40. United Press International, "Seven Amarillo Players on TL's All-Star Club," *Odessa American*, July 9, 1961, 27.

41. Quoted in John Drebinger, "Brooklyn Talent at Yankee Camp," *New York Times*, February 8, 1962, 50.

42. Red Smith, "Age of Yogi," *New York Herald Tribune*, June 12, 1962, 24.

43. Marilyn Stasio, "Nobody Don't Like Yogi," *Variety*, October 26, 2003, https://variety.com/2003/legit/reviews/nobody-don-t-like-yogi-1200538373/.

44. Paul Linke, telephone interview by author, April 9, 2019.

45. J. Devine, "1951 Phoenix School Report: Wm Skowron," Moose Skowron File, Giamatti Center, Baseball Hall of Fame.

46. Quoted in Dan Daniel, "Moose Revives Yank First-Base Power," *The Sporting News*, August 1, 1956, 3.

47. Quoted in Til Ferdenzi, "Healthy and Happy Moose Set to Play Full Sked for Bombers," *The Sporting News*, February 7, 1962, 7.

48. Quoted in Til Ferdenzi, "Skowron Mulling Over Purdue Job; May Quit Game," *The Sporting News*, December 22, 1962, 6. Skowron had left his studies at Purdue to sign with the Yankees.

49. Quoted in Til Ferdenzi, "'Knew I Was Going . . . Wasn't Sure Where,'" *New York Journal-American*, November 27, 1962, 23.

50. Quoted in Bob Hunter, "Rampaging Moose—The Comeback King," *The Sporting News*, October 19, 1963, 3.

51. Quoted in Shirley Povich, "Skowron Conquers Nats—$42,000 in Pay for .203 Mark," *The Sporting News*, January 25, 1964, 21.

52. Quoted in Povich, "Skowron Conquers Nats," 21.

53. Quoted in Joe King, "Boyer's 'Oh-Boy' Plays Rate Yank Raves," *The Sporting News*, November 15, 1961, 7.

54. Quoted in Roger Birtwell, "Meet the Boyers, No. 1 Baseball Family," *The Sporting News*, November 14, 1964, 3.

55. Quoted in Andrew Marchand, "'I Hate Casey Stengel,'" *New York Post*, October 19, 1998, 87.

56. Quoted in Til Ferdenzi, "Twirler Terry Sees Tip-Top Year on Tap," *The Sporting News*, May 16, 1962, 3.

57. Houk, *Ballplayers Are Human, Too*, 93.

58. Kiersten "Kiki" Ebsen, telephone interview by author, April 2, 2018.

59. Carla Kirkeby, telephone interview by author, August, 8, 2016. Arnold Kirkeby had a partial-ownership interest in the Fountainbleu.

60. "Governor Releases Statement on Case," *Jackson (NY) Clarion-Ledger*, October 1, 1962, 1. Barnett's racism was on display at one of the trials that ended in a hung jury for Byron De La Beckwith, accused of killing civil rights leader Medgar Evers. The governor and the defendant shook hands before the jury deliberated. De La Beckwith was later found guilty of first-degree murder, in 1994, based on new evidence. His punishment was a life sentence in prison.

61. John F. Kennedy, Address at Rice University on the Nation's Space Effort, Houston, September 12, 1962, JFK Library, https://www.jfklibrary.org/learn/about-jfk/historic-speeches/address-at-rice-university-on-the-nations-space-effort.

62. Kennedy, Address at Rice University.

10. "WELL, HANG ON TIGHT"

1. Howard Simons, "Schirra Lands Safely in Pacific after Flawless 6-Orbit Flight," *Washington Post*, October 4, 1962, A1.

2. Howard Simons, "Recovery in Target Area Is Made without a Hitch; Way Set for 18 Circuits," *Washington Post*, October 4, 1962, A1.

3. Howard Simons, "First Orbit Could Have Been the Last If Schirra's Suit Hadn't Cooled Down," *Washington Post*, October 5, 1962, A1.

4. Schirra with Billings, *Schirra's Space*, 87.

5. "Mars Meteorites," Jet Propulsion Laboratory, accessed September 8, 2020, https://www2.jpl.nasa.gov/snc/.

6. Frank Finch, "Dodgers Throw Away Flag to Giants," *Los Angeles Times*, October 4, 1962, B1.

7. Scott Baillie, "Mays' Dramatic Homer Gives Giants New Life," *Eureka (CA) Humboldt Standard*, October 1, 1962, 17.

8. Roseboro with Libby, *Glory Days with the Dodgers*, 202.

9. Quoted in Frank Finch, "Mays Tired, but Keeps Wearing Out Pitchers," *Los Angeles Times*, October 2, 1962, C1.

10. Quoted in Finch, "Mays Tired, but Keeps Wearing Out Pitchers," C1.

11. Quoted in Leo H. Petersen, "Again Need 1951 Finish vs. Dodgers," *San Mateo (CA) Times*, October 2, 1962, 20.

12. Quoted in Petersen, "Again Need 1951 Finish vs. Dodgers," 20.

13. Quoted in Ron Reid, "Vets Don't Know Reason for Slump," *San Mateo (CA) Times*, October 2, 1962, 20.

14. Ford, *Alcoa Premiere*, season 2, episode 1.

15. Quoted in Braven Dyer, "'Sanford Was Worn Out,'" *Los Angeles Times*, October 3, 1962, B2.

16. Quoted in Associated Press, "Leo—Giants Had 'Perfect' Play, Then Didn't Make It," *San Francisco Examiner*, October 3, 1962, 54.

17. Finch, "Dodgers Throw Away Flag to Giants," B1.

18. Quoted in Leonard Shecter, "The Dodgers Can't Believe They Lost," *New York Post*, October 4, 1962, 69.

19. Quoted in "Giants, Dodgers Had a Word for It," *New York Post*, October 4, 1962, 68.

20. Peter Trimble, "Champs Home—A City Gone Wild: Shades of S.F's [sic] V-J Day," *San Francisco Examiner*, October 4, 1962, 1.

21. "Series Attracts All, Bar None," *New York Herald Tribune*, October 5, 1962, 24.

22. Quoted in "'Decisive' in Victory, Says Houk," *New York Herald Tribune*, October 5, 1962, 24.

23. Bill Becker, "'Wornout' Cepeda Benched by Dark," *New York Times*, October 5, 1962, 54.

24. Alou with Kerasotis, *Alou*, 115.

25. Quoted in Joe Trimble, "Dark Chants: We'll Win; Houk: Whitey's the Best," *New York Daily News*, October 5, 1962, 67.

26. Quoted in Ken Smith, "10th Ford Series Win Flips Frisco," *New York Mirror*, October 5, 1962, 42.

27. Quoted in Associated Press, "Maris Is Relaxed Despite the Boos," *New York Times*, October 5, 1962, 53.

28. Quoted in Associated Press, "Maris Is Relaxed Despite the Boos," 53.

29. Associated Press, "Maris Is Relaxed Despite the Boos," 53.

30. George Hower, "Today's Comment: Wrong Twice Already, 'Experts' Pick Yankees," *Santa Rosa (CA) Press-Democrat*, October 4, 1962, 18.

31. Red Smith, "Red Smith: Only the Brave," *New York Herald Tribune*, October 5, 1962, 24.

32. Associated Press, "Celebrator Gets Light Fine: Judge Is a Yankee Fan, Too," *New York Times*, October 6, 1962, 16.

33. Harold Rosenthal, "Sanford: Cold War," *New York Herald Tribune*, October 6, 1962, 13.

34. John Drebinger, "Giants Defeat Yanks, 2–0; Sanford Pitches a 3-Hitter," *New York Times*, October 6, 1962, 1.

35. Drebinger, "Giants Defeat Yanks, 2–0," 1.

36. Associated Press, "Jack Really Hit Spot; Gives Mates New Life," *New York Mirror*, October 6, 1962, 33.

37. John Drebinger, "Yanks Win, 3 to 2, and Lead Series; 71,434 at Game," *New York Times*, October 8, 1962, 1.

38. Quoted in Louis Effrat, "Maris Pits Two Legs against One Strong Arm and Wins Day's Key Gamble," *New York Times*, October 8, 1962, 26.

39. Quoted in Joseph M. Sheehan, "Dark Says Ball Deflected by Stafford Robbed Felipe Alou of a Crucial Hit," *New York Times*, October 8, 1962, 27.

40. Drebinger, "Yanks Win, 3 to 2, and Lead Series," 1.

41. Quoted in Sheehan, "Dark Says Ball Deflected by Stafford Robbed Felipe Alou of a Crucial Hit," 27.

42. Quoted in Jim McCulley, "'Didn't See Blood'—Houk; Giants Want Bat Screen," *New York Daily News*, October 8, 1962, 36.

43. Joseph M. Sheehan, "A Borrowed Bat Does Yankees In," *New York Times*, October 9, 1962, 48.

44. Quoted in "A Switch in 'Time' Didn't Save Houk Nine," *New York Post*, October 9, 1962, 81.

45. Quoted in Jim McCulley, "Hiller: 'Iron Hands' to Hero; Whitey: 'Lost My Good Stuff,'" *New York Daily News*, October 9, 1962, 69.

46. John Drebinger, "Giant Grand Slam Evens the Series; Yanks Lose, 7–3," *New York Times*, October 9, 1962, 1.

47. Quoted in "Mr. Hiller Got the Pitch He Wanted," *New York Post*, October 9, 1962, 83.

48. Quoted in "Hiller Hit Fast Ball and 'Ran Like Hell,'" *New York Mirror*, October 9, 1962, 38.

49. Arthur Daley, "Sports of the Times: A Slight Case of Rain," *New York Times*, October 10, 1962, 10; Ed Sinclair, "Dream Pitch . . . My Biggest Thrill, Says Tresh," *New York Herald Tribune*, October 11, 1962, 28.

50. Quoted in Red Foley, "Tom: Fastball Down Pipe; Jack Glad to Get 2 in 1st," *New York Daily News*, October 11, 1962, 103.

51. Quoted in Louis Effrat, "Tom Tresh Hits the Winning Homer, and in the Stands Another Tresh Weeps," *New York Times*, October 11, 1962, 66.

52. Quoted in Milton Gross, "Speaking Out: SF Once Soured on Sanford," *New York Post*, October 11, 1962, 98.

53. John Drebinger, "Giants Top Yanks on Coast, 5 to 2; Tie World Series," *New York Times*, October 16, 1962, 1.

54. Quoted in Joseph M. Sheehan, "Decision on Ford Defended by Houk," *New York Times*, October 16, 1962, 68.

55. Quoted in Milton Gross, "Speaking Out: The Giants Had Faith in Pierce," *New York Post*, October 16, 1962, 77.

56. Quoted in Gus Steiger, "'I Didn't Throw Hard,'" *New York Mirror*, October 16, 1962, 32.

57. Quoted in Dan Parker, "Yanks' Sure Thing Now Fades to Last Chance," *New York Mirror*, October 16, 1962, 33.

58. Quoted in Associated Press, "Tresh Catch in 7th 'Saved' It—Houk," *New York Herald Tribune*, October 17, 1962, 37.

59. Quoted in Associated Press, "Tresh Catch in 7th 'Saved' It—Houk," 37.

60. Quoted in "Tresh's Catch Saved the Day for Yankees," *New York Post*, October 17, 1962, 101.

61. Quoted in "'I'm Luckiest Guy in World'—Terry," *New York Herald Tribune*, October 17, 1962, 37.

62. Quoted in "'I'm Luckiest Guy in World'—Terry," 37.

63. Quoted in Joe Trimble, "'Luckiest Man in Country . . . by Inches,' Says Terry," *New York Daily News*, October 17, 1962, 77.

64. Quoted in Leonard Shecter, "Mickey's Teammates Took Him Off Hook," *New York Post*, October 17, 1962, 100.

65. Quoted in Milton Gross, "Speaking Out: Mickey Mantle—The Big Out," *New York Post*, October 17, 1962, 100.

66. Quoted in Shecter, "Mickey's Teammates Took Him Off Hook," 100.

67. Gus Steiger, "'I Wanted to Pitch to Him,'" *New York Mirror*, October 17, 1962, 42.

68. Dan Parker, "Terry Was Terrible Just Like McGovern," *New York Mirror*, October 17, 1962, 44.

69. Dick Young, "Moose Scores in 5th on Double Play; Giants Barely Miss in 9th-Inning Bid," *New York Daily News*, October 17, 1962, 75.

70. Marion A. Leonard, memorandum to Roy L. Morgan, Director, Office of Field Services, U.S. Department of Commerce, June 8, 1961, Box 35A, National Security Files, Cuba-General 6/61–12/61, Countries, Declassified by Executive Order 12958, sec. 3.5, July 26, 1996, JFK Library.

71. "Maria" to John F. Kennedy, President of the United States, May 27, 1961, Box 35A, National Security Files, Cuba-General 6/61–12/61, Countries, Declassified by Executive Order 12958, sec. 3.5, July 26, 1996, JFK Library.

72. Carmine Bellino, memorandum for P. Kenneth O'Donnell, Special Assistant to the President, June 28, 1961, Box 35A, National Security Files, Cuba-General 6/61–12/61, Countries, Declassified by Executive Order 12958, sec. 3.5, July 26, 1996, JFK Library.

73. "Curtis LeMay," Atomic Heritage Foundation, 2019, https://www.atomicheritage.org /profile/curtis-lemay.

74. "The Cuban Missile Crisis, October 1962," Office of the Historian, Department of State, https://history.state.gov/milestones/1961-1968/cuban-missile-crisis.

75. Edward R. Murrow, "Wires and Lights in a Box," speech presented at the Radio-Television News Directors Association convention, Chicago, October 15, 1958, https:// www.rtdna.org/content/edward_r_murrow_s_1958_wires_lights_in_a_box_speech.

Some sources label the organization without the hyphen: Radio and Television News Directors Association.

76. Telephone Recordings, Dictation Belt 30.2, Cuban Missile Crisis Update, October 22, 1962, Digital Identifier JFKPOF-TPH-30-2, JFK Library, https://www.jfklibrary.org /asset-viewer/archives/jfkpof/tph/jfkpof-tph-30-2/jfkpof-tph-30-2.

77. Telephone Recordings, Dictation Belt 30.2, Cuban Missile Crisis Update, October 22, 1962.

78. Telephone Recordings: Dictation Belt 41.2, End of Cuban Missile Crisis, October 28, 1962, Digital Identifier JFKPOF-TPH-41-2, JFK Library, https://www.jfklibrary.org /asset-viewer/archives/jfkpof/tph/jfkpof-tph-41-2/jfkpof-tph-41-2.

79. Telephone Recordings: Dictation Belt 41, Digital Identifier JFKPOF-TPH-41, JFK Library, https://www.jfklibrary.org/asset-viewer/archives/jfkpof/tph/jfkpof-tph-41 /jfkpof-tph-41.

80. Kenneth Jack, telephone interview by author, February 20, 2019.

81. John F. Kennedy, Radio and Television Report to the American People on the Soviet Arms Buildup in Cuba, October 22, 1962, JFK Library, https://www.jfklibrary.org /archives/other-resources/john-f-kennedy-speeches/cuba-radio-and-television-report -19621022.

82. Kennedy, Radio and Television Report to the American People on the Soviet Arms Buildup in Cuba, October 22, 1962.

83. Sorenson, *Kennedy*, 700, quoting Kennedy, Radio and Television Report to the American People on the Soviet Arms Buildup in Cuba, October 22, 1962.

84. Sorenson, *Kennedy*, 700.

85. Medford, *Eleventh Hour*, season 1, episode 4.

86. Michael Beschloss, "The Man Who Gave Air Force One a Lift," *New York Times*, August 9, 2015, Sunday Business sec., 3.

87. The story relies on Loewy's statements. But there is no concrete evidence at the JFK Library to support those statements. Abigail Malangone, Archivist, JFK Library, email to author, February 11, 2019.

11. SOMEWHERE, ERASMUS IS SMILING

1. Sweeney, *Andy Griffith Show*, season 3, episode 7.

2. David Browning, email to author, March 18, 2019.

3. Former Vice President Richard M. Nixon, news conference, Beverly Hilton, Beverly Hills CA, November 7, 1962, https://www.youtube.com/watch?v=JA1edgj1U5E. See also Jason Schwartz, "55 Years Ago: 'The Last Press Conference,'" Richard Nixon Foundation, November 14, 2017, https://www.nixonfoundation.org/2017/11/55-years -ago-last-press-conference.

4. Henry Cabot Lodge Jr., the candidate's father, had been a member of the U.S. House of Representatives, the Senate, U.S. ambassador to the United Nations, and Republican candidate for vice president in 1960. His brother, John Davis Lodge, had been governor of Connecticut and U.S. ambassador to Spain under President Eisenhower. His paternal great-grandfather, Henry Cabot Lodge, defeated Kennedy's maternal grandfather, John F. Fitzgerald, in Boston's 1916 mayoral race. Lodge's mother had politics in her bloodline as well; she was part of the venerable Frelinghuysen family of New Jersey. Great-great-grandfather George Cabot was a senator from Massachusetts. The Kennedy family's politicians included the father of the president (Joseph P. Kennedy had served as U.S. ambassador to the Court of St. James under Franklin Roosevelt), Attorney General Robert Kennedy, and the new senator, Ted Kennedy.

5. Laurence L. Winship, "Senator Kennedy—Easy; Governor Peabody—Close," *Boston Globe*, November 7, 1962, 1.

6. Medford, *Sam Benedict*, season 1, episode 8.

7. "The Case of O'Brien vs. O'Brien," *TV Guide*, October 27–November 2, 1962, 16.

8. Dwight David Eisenhower, "Farewell Address," press release, January 17, 1961, Final TV Talk (1), NAID #16972219, Box 38, Dwight D. Eisenhower Presidential Library, Museum and Boyhood Home, Abilene KS.

9. Knebel and Bailey, *Seven Days in May*, 6.

10. Knebel and Bailey, *Seven Days in May*, 325.

11. Burdick and Wheeler, *Fail-Safe*, 278.

12. Quoted in Jack Raymond, "Pentagon Backs 'Fail-Safe' Setup," *New York Times*, October 21, 1962, 69.

13. Drury, *Shade of Difference*, 282.

14. Drury, *Advise and Consent*, 21.

15. Drury, *Advise and Consent*, 267.

16. Drury, *Advise and Consent*, 435.

17. Drury, *Advise and Consent*, 439.

18. Drury, *Advise and Consent*, 452.

19. Drury, *Advise and Consent*, 579–80.

20. Drury, *Advise and Consent*, 590.

21. Richard L. Coe, "One on the Aisle: Preminger Mounts Hill," *Washington Post*, June 7, 1962, B20.

22. Coe, "One on the Aisle: Preminger Mounts Hill," B20.

23. Bosley Crowther, "Screen: 'Advise and Consent' Opens," *New York Times*, June 7, 1962, 31.

24. Drury, *Shade of Difference*, 327.

25. Drury, *Shade of Difference*, 407–8.

26. Carson, *Silent Spring*, 7.

27. H. G. Brown, *Sex and the Single Girl*, 3.
28. H. G. Brown, *Sex and the Single Girl*, 4.
29. H. G. Brown, *Sex and the Single Girl*, 5.
30. H. G. Brown, *Sex and the Single Girl*, 25.
31. H. G. Brown, *Sex and the Single Girl*, 6.
32. H. G. Brown, *Sex and the Single Girl*, 267.
33. Rosenteur, *Single Women*, 90.
34. Rosenteur, *Single Women*, 91.
35. "The Empty Hours," in McBain, *Empty Hours*, 3.
36. Taylor, *87th Precinct*, season 1, episode 26.
37. Bob Johnson, "The Workaday Cop Comes into His Own," *TV Guide*, April 28–May 4, 1962, 9.
38. Kesey, *One Flew over the Cuckoo's Nest*, 13.
39. Kesey, *One Flew over the Cuckoo's Nest*, 67.
40. Kesey, *One Flew over the Cuckoo's Nest*, 40.
41. Kesey, *One Flew over the Cuckoo's Nest*, 40.
42. Kesey, *One Flew over the Cuckoo's Nest*, 229.
43. Kesey, "Who Flew over What," 368. This essay by Kesey was originally published in his 1973 collection *Kesey's Garage Sale*. A copy of that book is in the Henry W. and Albert A. Berg Collection of English and American Literature at the New York Public Library, Astor, Lenox and Tilden Foundations, Stephen A. Schwarzman Building, 476 Fifth Avenue, New York NY.
44. Dorian, *Sex Cure*, 39.
45. Quoted in "Persecution Theme of 'Sex Cure' Sequel," *Binghamton (NY) Press and Sun-Bulletin*, November 5, 1962, 3.
46. Quoted in Associated Press, "Cooperstown Finds Itself in Sex Novel and Doesn't Like It," *New York Times*, November 3, 1962.
47. "Baby Sitter Sues 'Sex Cure' Book Publisher for $600,000," *Binghamton (NY) Press and Sun-Bulletin*, December 21, 1962, 4; Pete Dobinsky, "'Sex Cure' Libel Suit Is Reported Settled," *Binghamton (NY) Press and Sun-Bulletin*, November 28, 1964, 3.
48. Grauman, *Naked City*, season 4, episode 1.
49. Lee, *Amazing Fantasy*, no. 15 (August 1962). The character is called "Spider-Man" in this issue of the Marvel Comics offering. The hyphen was later dropped.
50. "A President in the Comics," *New York Newsday*, July 13, 1962, 33.
51. Joseph Albright and Robert Mayer, "Smilin' Jack: Hero of the USIA," *New York Newsday*, July 13, 1962, 35.
52. Dan Hanley, "Braves' Destiny in Hands of Young Owners," *Sheboygan Press*, November 17, 1962, 19.

53. Quoted in Bob Wolf, "Mayor Sees Sale Creating 'More Community Interest,'" *The Sporting News*, December 1, 1962, 11.

12. HOLLYWOOD IS FOR HEROES

1. Mulligan, *To Kill a Mockingbird.*
2. "Atticus Leaves Courtroom," in Mulligan, *To Kill a Mockingbird.*
3. Edwards, *Days of Wine and Roses.*
4. "Jack Lemmon Accepts the AFI Life Achievement Award in 1988," YouTube (quote begins at 4:15), posted April 10, 2009, https://www.youtube.com/watch?v=6UMOX7YYdJM&list=LLQrsHMZnszlWzc46sCV_jtQ&index=4843.
5. Chris Lemmon, telephone interview by author, September 3, 2016.
6. Smight, *No Way to Treat a Lady*; Kazan, *Face in the Crowd*; Oliansky, *The Competition*; Preminger, *Anatomy of a Murder.*
7. Edwards, *Experiment in Terror.*
8. Philip K. Scheuer, "Anyone for the Jitters? Here's a Double Dose," *Los Angeles Times*, March 25, 1962.
9. Quoted in Don Alpert, "Actor Is a Fool to Complain about His Job—Glenn Ford," *Los Angeles Times*, March 4, 1962.
10. Stefanie Powers, telephone interview by author, February 21, 2017.
11. DaCosta, *Music Man.*
12. Louise Hutchinson, "Hails Creator of 'Music Man,'" *Chicago Tribune*, June 19, 1962, 1.
13. Quoted in Hedda Hopper, "The 'Music Man' Sounds Off," *Chicago Tribune*, February 4, 1962, B14.
14. Quoted in Hopper, "'Music Man' Sounds Off," B14.
15. Willson, *But He Doesn't Know the Territory*, 99.
16. Tanya Bagot, telephone interview by author, November 7, 2016.
17. "Frank Sinatra / *Manchurian Candidate* interview, 1988, 26th anniversary," YouTube, https://www.youtube.com/watch?v=YXdEjSemo1w.
18. Young, *Dr. No.*
19. W. H. Brown, *Climax!*, season 1, episode 3.
20. Martha Wiseman, telephone interview by author, May 9, 2018.
21. Lean, *Lawrence of Arabia*; R. Nelson, *Requiem for a Heavyweight.*
22. The television version was also directed by Ralph Nelson: R. Nelson, *Playhouse 90*, season 1, episode 2.
23. Swift, *The Interns*; Quine, *Notorious Landlady.*
24. Katherine Quinn, telephone interview by author, May 10, 2018.
25. Preminger, *Advise and Consent.*
26. Ford, *Man Who Shot Liberty Valance.*

27. Gene Pitney, vocalist, "The Man Who Shot Liberty Valance," by Burt Bacharach and Hal David, Musicor, Master No. MU 7039, A side, 45 rpm, distributed by United Artists Records, discogs.com.

28. Annakin, *Longest Day*.

29. Ford, Hathaway, and Marshall, *How the West Was Won*; Brooks, *Sweet Bird of Youth*; J. Thompson, *Cape Fear*; Aldrich, *Whatever Happened to Baby Jane?*; Siegel, *Hell Is for Heroes*; Lumet, *Long Day's Journey into Night*; Mann, *That Touch of Mink*.

30. Kubrick, *Lolita*.

31. "Producer Cites Positive Side of His Movie Version of 'Lolita,'" *New York Newsday*, June 5, 1962, 2C.

32. Sara Karloff, telephone interview by author, February 23, 2017.

33. The story "Love Is a Fallacy" was first published in *Cosmopolitan* in June 1951. Inventory of the Max Shulman Collection #196, Howard Gotlieb Archival Research Center, Boston University, http://hgar-srv3.bu.edu/finding-aid/finding_aid_122771.pdf.

34. Martha Rose Shulman, telephone interview by author, May 5, 2018.

35. Max Shulman, telephone interview by author, April 11, 2019.

36. Kulik, *The Defenders*, season 1, episode 25; Sheldon, *Route 66*, season 2, episode 14.

37. Petrie, *The Defenders*, season 1, episode 30.

38. Kern, *I Love Lucy*, season 5, episode 2; Asher, *I Love Lucy*, season 4, episode 16; Asher, *I Love Lucy*, season 4, episode 28.

39. Quoted in Gilbert Millstein, "Lucy Becomes President," *New York Times*, December 9, 1962, 129.

40. Lloyd, *Alcoa Premiere*, season 1, episode 13.

41. Gavin Koon, telephone interview by author, February 10, 2019.

42. Robin Koon, telephone interview by author, February 25, 2019.

43. The Beatles, vocalists, "Love Me Do," by John Lennon and Paul McCartney, released October 5, 1962, Parlophone, R4949, A side, 45 rpm, discogs.com.

44. The Beach Boys, vocalists, "Surfin' U.S.A.," by Brian Wilson, released March 1963, Capitol Records, 4932, A side, 45 rpm, discogs.com; Ritchie Valens, vocalist, "Come On, Let's Go," by Ritchie Valens, released 1958, Apex Records, 9-76369, A side, 45 rpm, discogs.com; The Beach Boys, vocalists, "Fun, Fun, Fun," by Brian Wilson, Capitol Records, released February 1964, 5118, A side, 45 rpm, discogs.com; Chuck Berry, vocalist, "Johnny B. Goode," by Chuck Berry, released August 1958, London Records, FL 1748, A side, 45 rpm, discogs.com.

45. Dale and His Del-Tones, vocalists, *Surfer's Choice*, November 1962, LMP-1001, Deltone Records, 33⅓ rpm, reissue Deltone T-1886, Capitol Records, March 1963, 33⅓ rpm, discogs.com.

46. Gist, *Route 66*, season 3, episode 4.

47. Tewksbury, *It's a Man's World*, season 1, episode 6.

48. Cecil Smith, "The TV Scene: Teahouse—Pause That Refreshes, Man's World Seg above Average," *Los Angeles Times*, October 30, 1962, C10.

49. Quoted in Hal Humphrey, "Man's World Too Good to Qualify as Press Agent's," *Los Angeles Times*, November 6, 1962, D14.

50. Quoted in Cecil Smith, "Houseboat Saga to Ride Airwaves," *Los Angeles Times*, September 17, 1962, D14.

51. Hal Humphrey, "Except for the Names, What Else Is New in TV for Fall?," *Los Angeles Times*, September 9, 1962, A20.

52. Bob Greene, email to author, January 24, 2019.

53. "Libby Makes Breakfast," in Tashlin, *Bachelor Flat*.

54. Murray Schumach, "Hollywood Slate: New Year Is Marked by Bustling Pace and Variety of Major Productions," *New York Times*, January 21, 1962, 101.

55. Greene, email.

56. Seana Crenna, email to author, March 28, 2019.

57. Prager, *Car 54, Where Are You?*, season 2, episode 13.

58. *How to Succeed in Business without Really Trying*, directed by Abe Burrows, 46th Street Theatre, October 14, 1961–March 6, 1965; *No Strings*, directed by Joe Layton, 54th Street Theatre, March 15, 1962–September 29, 1962, Broadhurst Theatre, October 1, 1962–August 3, 1962; *Camelot*, staged by Moss Hart, Majestic Theatre, December 3, 1960–January 5, 1963; *Milk and Honey*, staged by Albert Marre, Martin Beck Theatre, October 10, 1961–January 26, 1963; *Carnival!*, directed by Gower Champion, Imperial Theatre, April 13, 1961–December 15, 1962, Winter Garden Theatre, December 20, 1962–January 5, 1963; *A Funny Thing Happened on the Way to the Forum*, directed by George Abbott, Alvin Theatre, May 8, 1962–March 7, 1964, Mark Hellinger Theatre, March 9, 1964–May 9, 1964, Majestic Theatre, May 11, 1964–August 29, 1964; *Mary, Mary*, directed by Joseph Anthony, Helen Hayes Theatre, March 8, 1961–November 28, 1964, Morosco Theatre November 30, 1964–December 12, 1964. All information sourced at IBDb.com.

59. Prager, *Car 54, Where Are You?*, season 2, episode 13.

60. Howard Taubman, "Theater: Irving Berlin's 'President,'" *New York Times*, October 22, 1962, 32.

61. The Tornadoes, vocalists, "Telstar," by Joe Meek, Decca Records, released August 17, 1962, 11494, A side, 45 rpm, discogs.com.

62. *The First Family*, recorded October 22, 1962, Cadence CLP 3060, vinyl album, originally released in 1962. The cast recorded the album the same night that President Kennedy addressed the nation about the Cuban Missile Crisis. Meader's success sparked imitators: *The Other Family* (Nikita Khrushchev), *The Last Family* (Fidel Castro), *My Son, the President* (a Jewish president), and *Funniest Dream on Record* and *The Next Family* (a Black president). *Sing Along with JFK* imagined the Kennedys'

musical talents. *The President Strikes Back!* shows a fictional response from Kennedy to Meader's portrayal. A sequel to *The First Family* debuted in the spring of 1963. In 2013 the Library of Congress added *The First Family* to the National Recording Registry. Ronald L. Smith, "The First Family," Library of Congress, http://www.loc.gov/static /programs/national-recording-preservation-board/documents/first%20family.pdf.

63. President John F. Kennedy, news conference, State Department Auditorium, 4:00 p.m. EDT, December 12, 1962, Washington DC, JFK Library, https://www.jfklibrary.org /archives/other-resources/john-f-kennedy-press-conferences/news-conference-46.

64. Meader, Vaughn, Presidential White House Central Name File, Digital Identifier JFKWHCNF-1842-015-p0001, JFK Library. This folder has letters, telegrams, and a memorandum indicating the administration's concern that Meader's audio portrayal had the potential to deceive the public into thinking it was the president if Meader endorsed products or services as Kennedy. Kennedy's assassination on November 22, 1963, ended Meader's career. Show-business lore has comedian Lenny Bruce performing on the night of November 22, 1963, and opening with the line, "Well, Vaughn Meader's fucked." In a 1997 interview Meader said, "In a way, I'm better off than I've ever been. When I had the album, all those lowlifes around me who said they were friends, what I didn't realize was they were in it for the business. Now the funny thing is I'm a bum and I find people who really care. I have a wife who cares, friends who care." Quoted in David Lamb, "A Long Way from Camelot," *Los Angeles Times*, April 20, 1997, http://articles.latimes.com/1997-04-20/news/ls-50483_1_abbott -vaughn-meader.

65. Naomi Brossart (Bergman), email to author, April 23, 2019.

66. "The Bay of Pigs: The Aftermath," JFK Library, https://www.jfklibrary.org/learn/about -jfk/jfk-in-history/the-bay-of-pigs.

67. Quoted in "Text of the President's Speech to Exiles," *Miami Herald*, December 30, 1962, 11-A.

68. "Mission to Venus: Mariner 2," Jet Propulsion Laboratory, California Institute of Technology, https://www.jpl.nasa.gov/missions/mariner-2/.

Bibliography

Addiss, Justus (Jus), dir. *Saints and Sinners*. Season 1, episode 8, "Daddy's Girl," written by Gabrielle Upton. Aired November 12, 1962, on NBC.

Aldrich, Robert, dir. *Whatever Happened to Baby Jane?* Warner Bros., 1962.

Allen, Maury. *Bo: Pitching and Wooing*. New York: Dial, 1973.

Alou, Felipe, with Peter Kerasotis. *Alou: My Baseball Journey*. Lincoln: University of Nebraska Press, 2018.

Alston, Walter, with Jack Tobin. *A Year at a Time*. Waco TX: Word Books, 1976.

Annakin, Ken, dir. *The Longest Day*. 20th Century Fox, 1962.

Arnold, Jack, dir. *Gilligan's Island*. Season 2, episode 4, "Smile, You're on Mars Camera," written by Al Schwartz and Bruce Howard. Aired October 7, 1965, on CBS.

———. *Gilligan's Island*. Season 2, episode 9, "Nyet, Nyet, Not Yet," written by Adele T. Strassfield and Robert Riordan. Aired November 18, 1965, on CBS.

Asher, William, dir. *I Love Lucy*. Season 4, episode 16, "Hollywood at Last," written by Jess Oppenheimer, Madelyn Davis, and Bob Carroll Jr. Aired February 7, 1955, on CBS.

———. *I Love Lucy*. Season 4, episode 28, "Lucy and Harpo Marx," written by Jess Oppenheimer, Madelyn Pugh, and Bob Carroll Jr. Aired May 9, 1955, on CBS.

Barbera, Joseph, and Hanna, William, dirs. *The Flintstones*. Season 2, episode 30, "Kleptomaniac Caper," written by Warren Foster, Michael Maltese, and Arthur Phillips. Aired April 13, 1962, on ABC.

Bare, Richard L., dir. *The Twilight Zone*. Season 3, episode 24, "To Serve Man," written by Rod Serling. Aired March 2, 1962, on CBS.

Becker, Paula, Alan J. Stein, and the HistoryLink Staff. *The Future Remembered: The 1962 Seattle World's Fair and Its Legacy*. Seattle: Seattle Center Foundation, 2011.

Bleyer, Robert, and Tim Kiley, dirs. *The Ed Sullivan Show*. Season 17, episode 19, "Meet the Beatles." Aired February 9, 1964, on CBS.

Brooks, Richard, dir. *Sweet Bird of Youth*. Metro-Goldwyn-Mayer, 1962.

Brown, Bill, and Mike Acosta. *The Houston Astros: Deep in the Heart—Blazing a Trail from Expansion to World Series*. Houston TX: Bright Sky Press, 2013.

Brown, Helen Gurley. *Sex and the Single Girl*. New York: Bernard Geis, 1962.

Brown, William H., dir. *Climax!* Season 1, episode 3, "Casino Royale," written by Antony Ellis. Aired October 21, 1954, on CBS.

Burdick, Eugene, and Harvey Wheeler. *Fail-Safe*. 1962. New York: Ecco Press, 1999.

Byrnes, Edd, with Marshall Terrill. *"Kookie" No More*. New York: Barricade, 1996.

Carpenter, M. Scott, L. Gordon Cooper Jr., John H. Glenn Jr., Virgil I. Grissom, Walter M. Schirra Jr., Alan B. Shepard Jr., and Donald K. Slayton. *We Seven*. New York: Simon and Schuster, 1962.

Carpenter, Scott, and Kris Stoever. *For Spacious Skies: The Uncommon Journey of a Mercury Astronaut*. New York: Harcourt, 2002.

Carson, Rachel. *Silent Spring*. 1962. New York: First Mariner Books, 2002.

Chaikin, Andrew. *A Man on the Moon: The Voyages of the Apollo Astronauts*. 1994. New York: Penguin Books, 2007.

Combat, no. 4. Art by Sam Glanzman. New York: Dell Comics/Western Publishing, June 1962.

Cook, William A. *Johnny Temple: All-Star Second Baseman*. Jefferson NC: McFarland, 2016.

DaCosta, Morton, dir. *The Music Man*. Warner Bros., 1962.

De Caprio, Al, dir. *Car 54, Where Are You?* Season 1, episode 16, "The Sacrifice," written by Tony Webster and Nat Hiken. Aired January 7, 1962, on CBS.

Depew, Joseph, dir. *The Beverly Hillbillies*. Season 4, episode 26, "The Folk Singers," written by Paul Henning and Mark Tuttle. Aired March 23, 1966, on CBS.

Dick, Philip K. *The Man in the High Castle*. New York: G. P. Putnam's Sons, 1962.

Donohue, Jack, dir. *The Lucy Show*. Season 1, episode 6, "Lucy Becomes an Astronaut," written by Bob Carroll Jr., Madelyn Martin, Bob Weiskopf, and Bob Schiller. Aired November 5, 1962, on CBS.

Dorian, Elaine. *The Sex Cure*. New York: Beacon, 1962.

Douglas, Gordon, dir. *Follow That Dream*. United Artists, 1962.

Drury, Allen. *Advise and Consent*. Garden City NY: Doubleday, 1959.

——. *A Shade of Difference*. Garden City NY: Doubleday, 1962.

Drysdale, Don, with Bob Verdi. *Once a Bum, Always a Dodger: My Life in Baseball from Brooklyn to Los Angeles*. New York: St. Martin's Press, 1990.

Edwards, Blake, dir. *Days of Wine and Roses*. Warner Bros., 1962.

——. *Experiment in Terror*. Columbia, 1962.

Emerson, Ralph Waldo. *Concord Hymn*. 1837. Poetry Foundation. https://www.poetryfoundation.org/poems/45870/concord-hymn.

Fleming, Ian. *Casino Royale*. London: Jonathan Cape, 1953.

——. *Dr. No*. London: Jonathan Cape, 1958.

Ford, John, dir. *Alcoa Premiere*. Season 2, episode 1, "Flashing Spikes," written by Jameson Brewer. Aired October 4, 1962, on ABC.

——. *The Man Who Shot Liberty Valance*. Paramount, 1962.

Ford, John, Henry Hathaway, and George Marshall, dirs. *How the West Was Won*. Metro-Goldwyn-Mayer, 1962.

Frankenheimer, John, dir. *The Manchurian Candidate*. Metro-Goldwyn-Mayer, 1962.

Gist, Robert, dir. *Route 66*. Season 3, episode 4, "Ever Ride the Waves in Oklahoma?," written by Stirling Siliphant. Aired October 12, 1962, on CBS.

——. *Route 66*. Season 3, episode 6, "Lizard's Leg and Owlet's Wing," written by Stirling Siliphant. Aired October 26, 1962, on CBS.

Glenn, John, with Nick Taylor. *John Glenn: A Memoir*. New York: Bantam Books, 1999.

Glennan, Thomas Keith. *The Birth of NASA: The Diary of T. Keith Glennan*. Edited by J. D. Hunley. Washington DC: National Aeronautics and Space Administration History Office, 1993.

Golenbock, Peter. *Amazin': The Miraculous History of New York's Most Beloved Baseball Team*. New York: St. Martin's Press, 2002.

Graham, William A., dir. *Route 66*. Season 2, episode 32, "From an Enchantress Fleeing," written by Stirling Siliphant. Aired June 1, 1962, on CBS.

Grauman, Walter E., dir. *Naked City*. Season 4, episode 1, "Hold for Gloria Christmas," written by Arnold Manoff (as Joel Carpenter). Aired September 19, 1962, on ABC.

Greene, Bob. *Be True to Your School: A Diary of 1964*. New York: Atheneum, 1987.

Hanna, Bill, with Tom Ito. *A Cast of Friends*. Dallas: Taylor, 1996.

Heller, Franklin, dir. *What's My Line?* Season 11, episode 2, "Branch Rickey and June Allyson." Aired September 13, 1959, on CBS.

Hemingway, Ernest. *For Whom the Bell Tolls*. New York: Scribner, 1940.

Heyes, Douglas, dir. *77 Sunset Strip*. Season 1, episode 2, "Lovely Lady, Pity Me," written by James O'Hanlon and Douglas Heyes. Aired October 17, 1958, on ABC.

Hopper, Jerry, dir. *Gilligan's Island*. Season 3, episode 22, "Splashdown," written by John Fenton Murray. Aired February 20, 1967, on CBS.

Houk, Ralph. *Ballplayers Are Human, Too*. New York: G. P. Putnam's Sons, 1962.

Hughes, Richard E. "John Force, Magic Agent." *Calling John Force . . . Magic Agent*, no. 1. Art by Paul Reinman and Pete Costanza. New York: Best Syndicated Features, January–February 1962.

Irving, Robert. *Electronics*. New York: Knopf, 1961.

Jones, Chuck, and Ben Washam, dirs. *How the Grinch Stole Christmas*. Aired December 18, 1966, on CBS.

Karlson, Phil, dir. *Kid Galahad*. Metro-Goldwyn-Mayer, 1962.

Kaufman, Philip, dir. *The Right Stuff*. Ladd Company, 1983.

Kazan, Elia, dir. *A Face in the Crowd*. Warner Bros., 1957.

Kern, James V., dir. *I Love Lucy*. Season 5, episode 2, "Lucy and John Wayne," written by Jess Oppenheimer, Madelyn Pugh, Bob Carroll Jr., Bob Schiller, and Bob Weiskopf. Aired October 10, 1955, on CBS.

Kesey, Ken. *Kesey's Garage Sale*. New York: Viking, 1973.

———. *One Flew over the Cuckoo's Nest*. 1962. New York: Penguin Books, 2003.

———. *One Flew over the Cuckoo's Nest: Text and Criticism*. Edited by John Clark Pratt. Rev. and exp. ed. New York: Penguin Books, 1996.

Knebel, Fletcher, and Charles W. Bailey II. *Seven Days in May*. New York: Harper & Row, 1962.

Koch, Howard W. *Hawaiian Eye*. Season 1, episode 1, "Malihini Holiday," written by Robert J. Shaw and Juanita Sheridan. Aired October 7, 1959, on ABC.

Koppett, Leonard. *The New York Mets: The Whole Story*. New York: Macmillan, 1970.

Kramer, Stanley, dir. *Guess Who's Coming to Dinner*. Columbia Pictures, 1962.

Kranz, Gene. *Failure Is Not an Option: Mission Control from Mercury to Apollo 13 and Beyond*. 2000. New York: Simon and Schuster Paperbacks, 2009.

Kubrick, Stanley, dir. *Lolita*. Metro-Goldwyn-Mayer, 1962.

Kulik, Buzz, dir. *The Defenders*. Season 1, episode 25, "The Iron Man," written by David Davidson. Aired March 10, 1962, on CBS.

Laughlin, Tom, dir. *The Young Sinner*. T. C. Frank, 1965.

Lean, David, dir. *Lawrence of Arabia*. Columbia, 1962.

Lee, Stan. *Amazing Fantasy*, no. 15. Art by Steve Ditko. New York: Marvel Comics, August 1962.

Lennick, Michael, dir. *Rocket Science*. Episode "Missiles to the Moon." Casablanca Media TV, 2004.

Leonard, Sheldon, dir. *My Favorite Martian*. Season 1, episode 1, "My Favorite Martin," written by John L. Greene. Aired September 29, 1963, on CBS.

Lewis, Sinclair. *It Can't Happen Here*. Garden City NY: Doubleday, Doran, 1935.

Lloyd, Norman, dir. *Alcoa Premiere*. Season 1, episode 13, "The Jail," written by Ray Bradbury. Aired February 6, 1962, on ABC.

Lumet, Sidney, dir. *Long Day's Journey into Night*. Embassy Pictures, 1962.

Lyon, Frank, dir. *Perry Mason*. Season 5, episode 25, "The Case of the Angry Astronaut," written by Samuel Newman. Aired April 7, 1962, on CBS.

Mann, Delbert, dir. *That Touch of Mink*. Universal-International, 1962.

McBain, Ed. *The Empty Hours*. 1962. Las Vegas: Thomas & Mercer, 2011.

McCue, Andy. *Mover and Shaker: Walter O'Malley, the Dodgers, and Baseball's Westward Expansion*. Lincoln: University of Nebraska Press, 2014.

Medford, Don, dir. *The Eleventh Hour*. Season 1, episode 4, "I Don't Belong in a White-Painted House," written by Mark Rodgers. Aired October 24, 1962, on NBC.

———. *Sam Benedict*. Season 1, episode 8, "Hear the Mellow Wedding Bells," written by Joseph Petracca. Aired November 3, 1962, on CBS.

Miner, Allen H., dir. *The Twilight Zone*. Season 3, episode 32, "The Gift," written by Rod Serling. Aired April 27, 1962, on CBS.

Minow, Newton N. *Equal Time: The Private Broadcaster and the Public Interest*. New York: Atheneum, 1964.

Mulligan, Robert, dir. *To Kill a Mockingbird*. Universal-International, 1962.

Mullins, Richard. *Most Valuable Player*. New York: Funk & Wagnalls, 1962.

Nabokov, Vladimir. *Lolita*. Paris: Olympia Press, 1955.

Nelson, Gene, dir. *I Dream of Jeannie*. Season 1, episode 1, "The Lady in the Bottle," written by Sidney Sheldon. Aired September 18, 1965 on NBC.

Nelson, Lindsey. *Hello Everybody, I'm Lindsey Nelson*. New York: Beech Tree, 1985.

Nelson, Ralph, dir. *Playhouse 90*. Season 1, episode 2, "Requiem for a Heavyweight," written by Rod Serling. Aired October 11, 1956, on CBS.

———. *Requiem for a Heavyweight*. Columbia, 1962.

Oliansky, Joel, dir. *The Competition*. Columbia, 1980.

Paris, Jerry, dir. *The Dick Van Dyke Show*. Season 2, episode 20, "It May Look Like a Walnut," written by Carl Reiner. Aired February 6, 1963, on CBS.

———. *The Dick Van Dyke Show*. Season 4, episode 20, "The Redcoats Are Coming," written by Bill Persky and Sam Denoff. Aired February 10, 1965, on CBS.

———. *The Dick Van Dyke Show*. Season 5, episode 27, "The Man from My Uncle," written by Jerry Belson. Aired April 20, 1966, on CBS.

Pepitone, Joe, with Berry Stainback. *Joe, You Coulda Made Us Proud*. Chicago: Playboy Press, 1975.

Petrie, Daniel, dir. *The Defenders*. Season 1, episode 30, "The Benefactor," written by Peter Stone. Aired April 28, 1962, on CBS.

Podair, Jerald. *City of Dreams: Dodger Stadium and the Birth of Modern Los Angeles*. Princeton NJ: Princeton University Press, 2017.

Prager, Stanley, dir. *Car 54, Where Are You?* Season 2, episode 13, "142 Tickets on the Aisle," written by Tony Webster. Aired December 9, 1962, on NBC.

Preminger, Otto, dir. *Advise and Consent*. Columbia, 1962.

———. *Anatomy of a Murder*. Columbia, 1959.

Quine, Richard, dir. *The Notorious Landlady*. Columbia, 1962.

Ray, Edgar W. *The Grand Huckster: Houston's Judge Roy Hofheinz—Genius of the Astrodome*. Memphis TN: Memphis State University Press, 1980.

Rich, John, dir. *The Dick Van Dyke Show*. Season 1, episode 23, "The Twizzle," written by Carl Reiner. Aired February 28, 1962, on CBS.

———. *The Dick Van Dyke Show*. Season 1, episode 24, "One Angry Man," written by Leo Solomon and Ben Gershman. Aired March 7, 1962, on CBS.

Richardson, Bobby, with David Thomas. *Impact Player: Leaving a Lasting Legacy on and off the Field*. Carol Stream IL: Tyndale House, 2014.

Roseboro, John, with Bill Libby. *Glory Days with the Dodgers and Other Days with Others*. New York: Atheneum, 1978.

Rosenberg, Stuart, dir. *Cool Hand Luke*. Warner Bros.–Seven Arts, 1967.

Rosenteur, Phyllis I. *The Single Women*. New York: Bobbs-Merrill, 1961.

Satenstein, Frank, dir. *Stage Show*. Season 2, episode 18, "Elvis Presley." Aired January 28, 1956, on CBS.

Schirra, Walter M., Jr., with Richard N. Billings. *Schirra's Space*. Boston: Quinlan's Press, 1988.

Shakespeare, William. *Troilus and Cressida*. Folger Shakespeare Library, New Folger edition, edited by Barbara A. Mowat and Paul Werstine. New York: Simon and Schuster, 2007.

Sheldon, James, dir. *Route 66*. Season 2, episode 14, "To Walk with the Serpent," written by Bill Lorin. Aired January 5, 1962, on CBS.

Shifres, Ed. *Space Family Robinson: The True Story*. Salt Lake City: Windsor House, 1996.

Shulman, Max. *The Feather Merchants*. Garden City NY: Doubleday, Doran, 1944.

———. *Rally Round the Flag, Boys!* New York: Doubleday, 1957.

Siegel, Donald, dir. *Hell Is for Heroes*. Paramount, 1962.

Smight, Jack, dir. *No Way to Treat a Lady*. Paramount, 1968.

Snider, Duke, with Bill Gilbert. *The Duke of Flatbush*. New York: Zebra Books, 1988.

Sorenson, Theodore C. *Kennedy*. New York: Harper & Row, 1965.

Sweeney, Bob, dir. *The Andy Griffith Show*. Season 3, episode 7, "Lawman Barney," written by Aaron Ruben. Aired November 12, 1962, on CBS.

Sweson, Loyd S., Jr., James M. Grimwood, and Charles C. Alexander. *This New Ocean: A History of Project Mercury*. Washington DC: NASA Office of Technology Utilization, Scientific and Technical Information Division, 1966.

Swift, David, dir. *The Interns*. Columbia, 1962.

Tashlin, Frank, dir. *Bachelor Flat*. 20th Century Fox, 1962.

Taurog, Norman, dir. *Girls! Girls! Girls!* Paramount, 1962.

Taylor, Don. *87th Precinct*. Season 1, episode 26, "Idol in the Dust," written by Donn Mullally. Aired April 2, 1962, on NBC.

Tewksbury, Peter, dir. *It's a Man's World*. Season 1, episode 6, "The Beavers and the Otters," written by James Leighton and Benjamin Masselink. Aired October 29, 1962, on NBC.

Thompson, Fresco, with Cy Rice. *Every Diamond Doesn't Sparkle: Behind the Scenes with the Dodgers*. New York: David McKay, 1964.

Thompson, J. Lee, dir. *Cape Fear*. Universal-International, 1962.

Titchener, Campbell B. *The George Kirksey Story: Bringing Major League Baseball to Houston*. Austin TX: Eakin, 1989.

Waggner, George, dir. *77 Sunset Strip*. Season 4, episode 18, "Penthouse on Skid Row," written by Warren Douglas. Aired January 19, 1962, on ABC.

Whale, James, dir. *Frankenstein*. Universal Pictures, 1931.

Willson, Meredith. *But He Doesn't Know the Territory*. 1959. Minneapolis: University of Minnesota Press, 2009.

Wolfe, Tom. *The Right Stuff*. 1979. New York: Picador, 2008.

Wollheim, Donald A. *Mike Mars Flies the Dyna-Soar*. Garden City NY: Doubleday, 1962.

——. *Mike Mars: South Pole Spaceman*. Garden City NY: Doubleday, 1962.

Young, Terence, dir. *Dr. No*. United Artists, 1962.

Index